HOW TO SELL

YOUR SCREENPLAY

LYDIA WILEN   JOAN WILEN

SQUAREONE
WRITERS GUIDES

Cover Designer: Phaedra Mastrocola
In-House Editor: Marie Caratozzolo
Typesetter: Gary A. Rosenberg
Printer: Paragon Press, Honesdale, PA

Square One Publishers
Garden City Park, NY 11040
(516) 535–2010
www.squareonepublishers.com

Library of Congress Cataloging-in-Publication Data

Wilen, Lydia.
    How to sell your screenplay : a realistic guide to getting a television or
film deal / Lydia Wilen & Joan Wilen.
       p. cm. — (A Square One writers guide)
    Includes index.
    ISBN 0-7570-0002-9 (pbk.)
    1. Motion picture authorship.   2. Television authorship. I. Wilen, Joan.
II. Title.
    PN1996.W397 2001
    808.2′3—dc21

                                                        2001001642

Printed in the United States of America

10 9 8 7 6 5 4 3 2 1

CONTENTS

Acknowledgments, vii

Credits, ix

A Note on Gender, x

Introduction, 1

1. You, the Writer, 3
2. The Screenplay, 37
3. The Industry and Its Players, 89
4. Choosing Contacts, 125
5. The Pitch, 161
6. Using the Square One System, 203
7. The Deal, 235
8. If It Doesn't Happen, 261

Conclusion, 279

Resource List, 281

About the Authors, 299

Index, 301

PROSE FROM A PRO

The Nature of the Business, 6
by Phillip M. Goldfarb

What It's Like to Be a
Screenwriter, 8
by Jane Anderson

Advice to the Writer Who Just
Finished a First Spec Script, 10
by Josann McGibbon &
Sara Parriott

So Many Changes; So Many
Reasons, 16
by Richard Styles

Screenwriting at Its Best and
Worst, 25
by Barry Strugatz

Somewhere Between Drafts, 38
by Richard Styles

Learn to Take Criticism, 40
by Barry Strugatz

Show Gratitude, 41
by Barry Strugatz

Make It Easy on the Eye, 52
by Barry Strugatz

Plenty of White Space, 64
by Dov S-S Simens

How to Get an Agent, 96
by Dov S-S Simens

Do Everything, 103
by Terry Rossio

When Asking a Favor, 111
by Barry Strugatz

It May Cost, But It May Pay, 117
by Dale Launer

Differences Between Motion
Pictures and Television
Films, 130
by Phillip M. Goldfarb

The Importance of the Genre, 144
by Phillip M. Goldfarb

Do What It Takes, 148
by David Newman

Hook the Reader, 166
by Dov S-S Simens

Screenplay versus Query
Letter, 169
by Charlie Purpura

Pitch Meetings, 180
by David Newman

Timing, 185
by Charlie Purpura

Getting an Actor Attached, 207
by Phillip M. Goldfarb

Screenplay Writing and the
Movie Business, 208
by Dale Launer

Negotiating, 238
by Dale Launer

Step Deal Steps, 242
by David Newman

Rewriting, 243
by Josann McGibbon &
Sara Parriott

What Hollywood Buys, 263
by Charlie Purpura

Putting the Odds in Your
Favor, 264
by Richard Styles

The Key to Writing a Standout
Script, 267
by Gary Lennon

If It Doesn't Work, at Least It
Makes for a Good Story, 271
by David Mack

Passion Pays Off, 273
by Phillip M. Goldfarb

From script to Screen

Sleepless in Seattle, 29
by Jeff Arch

Caught, 33
by Edward Pomerantz

Anguish, 82
by Michael Berlin

Event Horizon, 85
by Philip Eisner

Summer of '42, 87
by Herman Raucher

Runaway Bride, 121
by Josann McGibbon &
Sara Parriott

A Soldier's Story, 123
by Charles Fuller

Friday the 13th, 152
by Victor Miller

The Whole Nine Yards, 154
by Mitchell Kapner

Hoosiers, 156
by Angelo Pizzo

Heaven Help Us, 195
by Charlie Purpura

Love 30, 99
by Susan Rice

Drunks, 201
by Gary Lennon

Loving Jezebel, 230
by Kwyn Bader

Detroit Rock City, 252
by Carl V. Dupré

Men of Honor, 255
by Scott Marshall Smith

White Water Rebels, 276
by Jim Kouf

Married to the Mob, 278
by Barry Strugatz

*We dedicate this book to the
Writers Guild of America, East and West
for protecting and defending the rights of writers.*

ACKNOWLEDGMENTS

The very first word Joany learned to spell, even before she knew how to spell her own name, was *movies*. That was because our mom, Lilly, would say to our dad, "Jack, do you want to take the girls to the m-o-v-i-e-s?" It didn't take long for Joany to catch on and start asking, "Mom, can we go to the m-o-v-i-e-s?" Going to the movies was always a special event in our young lives. It still is, and we thank our parents for instilling our love for and happy association with the m-o-v-i-e-s.

We also thank publisher Rudy Shur who asked us to write this book, assuring us that we would meet wonderful people in the process. Rudy, you were absolutely right about that, as attested to by the names below.

To editor Marie Caratozzolo, we appreciate your hard work, patience, and attention to detail.

To the following elite group of produced writers who generously shared their incredible stories and priceless insight, we thank you more than words can say—

Jane Anderson	Larry Gelbart	James Orr
Jeff Arch	Pete Hamill	Angelo Pizzo
Kwyn Bader	Mitchell Kapner	Edward Pomerantz
Ron Bass	William Katz	Charlie Purpura
Michael Berlin	Jim Kouf	Herman Raucher
Michael Colleary	Dale Launer	Susan Rice
Debra Dean Davis	Gary Lennon	Scott Marshall Smith
Carl V. Dupré	Gigi Levangie	Barry Strugatz
Philip Eisner	Josann McGibbon &	Richard Styles
Dennis Foley	Sara Parriott	James Toback
Charles Fuller	Victor Miller	Don Vasicek
Lowell Ganz &	David Newman	Daniel Waters
Babaloo Mandel	Steve Oedekerk	Mike Werb

Our admiration and deep appreciation to you industry professionals for your wonderful words—

Randee Mia Berman	Andrea McCall	Dov S-S Simens
David Brown	Wendi Niad	Larry "Ratso" Sloman
Phillip M. Goldfarb	Robert Pardi	Gary Stein
Marilyn Horowitz	Terry Rossio	Steve Weiss
David Mack	Marty Shapiro	

Many blessings to you magnificent networkers and facilitators with whom we've been blessed—

Lawrence P. Ashmead	Don Hauptman	Ben Peters
Erik Bauer	Rosemary "Maddie" Henri	Kia Portafekas
Patricia Burke	Erika Holzer	Lisa Ramshaw
Jeff Burton	James Igel	Reggie Resino
Myles P. Burton	Margo Katz	Arden R. Ryshpan
Morrie A. Buttnick	Charles C. Koones	Anna Salter
Lisa Calamaro	Lee and Jena Levinson	Claudia Salter
Caroline Carminati	Howard Meibach	Amy Savitsky
Tracy Clark	Linda Miller	Dorothy Senerchia
Brian Edwards	Robert Pardi	Judy Twersky
Adam Gale	Scooter Pietsch	Marilyn Wilson
D.B. Gilles	Richard A. Perozzi	Doris Wood

For your willingness to help in every way possible, our gratitude to the Writers Guild of America, East—

Mona Mangan, Executive Director	Giselle Miller, Manager, Events & Programs	Walter Bianco, Purchasing & Mail Coordinator
Alexis DiVincenti, Contracts Administrator	Lawrence Chance, Credits & Residuals Administrator	Kelly O'Brien, Signatories Administrator
James Kaye, Assistant Executive Director		

and to the Writers Guild of America, West—

Grace Reiner, Director of Contract Administration	Lewis Moore, Agency Administrator

CREDITS

The listing from *HCD Agents & Managers* on page 136 is reprinted with permission of Hollywood Creative Directory, © 2001. All rights reserved.

The "Irresistible Query Letter and Analysis" beginning on page 176 is reprinted with permission of Don Vasicek.

The Schedule of Minimums on page 241 is reprinted with permission of Writers Guild of America, East.

The excerpt on page 280 from "The Word's the Thing" by David Brown is reprinted with permission of Variety, Inc., © 2000.

A Note on Gender

To avoid long and awkward phrasing within sentences, the publisher has chosen to alternate the use of male and female pronouns according to chapter. Therefore, when referring to the third-person screenwriter or others who work in the film industry, odd-numbered chapters use female pronouns, while even-numbered chapters employ male pronouns. Please realize that no offense or slight is intended.

ℐNTRODUCTION

This book may be one of the best investments in your writing career. Why? Because it will teach you so much. We know how much we've learned while gathering the information for it . . . and we've been in the film business for years.

Yes, this book has the all-important basics like how to properly format your script according to industry standards, how to protect your work and minimize your chances of being ripped off, how to write an irresistible query letter, as well as how to set up an efficient distribution system for sending out those letters. You'll also learn who the industry players are and how to reach them, how to prepare for pitch meetings, and what you might expect when you get a deal.

As if all of that isn't enough, we've gone beyond the basics. Throughout the book you'll find interviews with industry professionals, from agents and managers to studio executives. As an added bonus, at the end of each chapter, you'll discover an exceptional collection of personal stories told by produced screenwriters. Their stories will amaze, impress, and enlighten you. They will give you advice, ideas, and even leads. And don't be surprised if you find yourself exhausted after reading what some of these writers went through to sell their scripts. Above all, these success stories will inspire and motivate you. Without a doubt, they will heighten your appreciation for every "Written by" credit you see on screen. And because they are true accounts, they will leave you with the feeling that if these writers did it, you can too. And you can! Let this book be your guide.

Read everything in this book, even if you think it doesn't apply to you. Trust us, if you're a writer, it applies (or will at some point). There is useable, valuable information on every page. Even those of you who are currently working in the business will read these pages and find yourselves thinking, "I didn't know that." If you don't believe us, just glance through "Show Biz Speak," our extensive glossary found in Chapter 1, and see how quickly you learn something about the industry that you didn't already know.

There are no hard-and-fast rules in the movie business. For every successful person who believes one thing, there is another successful person who believes the opposite. We present all of the possibilities in such a way as to help you decide what is right for you and your spec script. Important points are hammered home, many times in many ways. When you have finished reading this book, don't be surprised at how savvy you are about the industry.

Think of this book as a treasure hunt. You never know which line, which approach, which tip, which name that's mentioned, or which piece of advice may be the turning point in your career. So let the games begin. And let *How to Sell Your Screenplay* help you become a "player."

CHAPTER 1

$\mathscr{Y}$OU, THE WRITER

Congratulations on completing a spec script. In your case, "spec" may be short for "special" or "spectacular," as well as what it really stands for—"speculation." A *spec script* is written on speculation, without a contract, and is owned completely by the writer. Hey, that's you.

Writing a spec script is the fun part. Now the work *really* begins—selling it. So here goes.

Picture this . . .

You've written a spec script that's going to dazzle the film world. Now that you've rewritten one of the scenes three times on the advice of your film teacher, and your cousin proofed it and said it's perfect, you can't wait to get it into the right hands. You're really psyched. **Get Ready Hollywood!**

Next, you write a sensational query letter that's going to hook everyone who reads it, and you mail copies to five major film studios. **Hello Hollywood!**

A few days later, your phone rings. A studio development executive who received your query letter is calling. She wants to take a look at your spec script. She gives you her company's FedEx number and asks you to send your script immediately. The next day, there's another call. Another studio. Another FedEx number. Later that day when you go online, you find an e-mail from a studio producer. Why waste time FedExing? He wants you to upload your script so he can download it. He gives you his not-to-go-any-

further e-mail address. By then there are two more script requests hanging out of your fax machine. It's a good thing you sent out only five query letters. You've run out of copies of your script. **Make Way Hollywood!**

The buzz has started on you—probably due to ringers at FedEx—and the Trades have picked up on it. Agents start calling. You select the one who sent your mother flowers, congratulating her on giving birth to you.

Your hot-shot agent starts a bidding situation for your spec script, and you end up with a high six-figure deal, plus a percentage of the gross, cast-approval, and a hefty development deal for your next script, which you will direct. **Hooray for Hollywood . . . and You!**

Way to go! Selling a screenplay is a piece of cake, a walk in the park, a snap. Yeah, right. Get real! (And get rid of those clichés.) Although selling a script has never been as easy as the fantasy scenario above, there was a time when it wasn't so tough—but once talking pictures were invented . . . *fuhgedaboudit!* And as you will see, it keeps getting tougher.

THE WAY IT IS

The film industry—once composed of only a few studios and networks—has burgeoned into a world that includes an ever-growing number of major and minor film studios, independent production companies, countless cable networks, and we can't leave out the Internet, which is fast becoming an outlet for writing talent. So while the need for product is increasing, the number of writers is also increasing, but disproportionately. And unless you are an established screenwriter with a successful track record, realizing your dream of selling your spec script is going to be easier "dreamed" than done. It's important that you are aware of this up front, right at the beginning. For starters, here are some facts that you should know about the film industry. Brace yourself.

■ It is estimated that there are about 500 feature films produced annually in the United States and Canada. Most are independent movies that do not get theatrical distribution (which means they never make it into the theaters), and it's anyone's guess as to how or if the screenwriters of these films are paid or properly credited. With any luck, the films have some kind of life by going directly to videotape, and are distributed to video stores across North America. Otherwise, they sit in a can on a shelf in a storage facility, never to be seen, unless one of the actors in the film becomes a superstar, and a distributor tries to cash in on the actor's popularity. Depending on the film's quality and rating, the distributor may be able to sell it to television, release it in theaters, or distribute it to video stores.

■ In the year 2000, only 185 films of the nearly 500 produced were written by members of the Writers Guild of America (WGA)—a labor union that represents some 12,000 professional writers of the entertainment industry—film, television, and radio. If only this small number of scripts were produced, think of the thousands of others that were rejected. If professional writers can't get their scripts into production, what are the odds of first-time writers with spec scripts seeing their work on the silver screen? You do the math.

■ Most of the work for screenwriters is in Los Angeles. Of course, industry insiders agree that once a writer is established, he or she can be anywhere. The hard part, of course, is getting established.

■ Competition is fierce. Increasing numbers of colleges and universities throughout the country now have film schools or film programs from which countless numbers of hopeful screenwriters graduate each year, each with at least one spec script.

Are we painting a bleak picture? I guess we are, but only because we're being realistic. If you are discouraged by these industry facts, maybe screenwriting isn't the optimum career choice for you (and it's better to realize this early on rather than later). On the other hand, if you truly understand that stamina and determination are prerequisites for making it in this business; if you believe that you can stand up to rejection and criticism and continue forward in spite of it; if you are not afraid of competition and can maintain the belief that spec scripts are bought and turned into movies all the time, and yours has as good a chance as any others, then you might have what it takes to succeed. But don't give up your day job just yet.

Do You Have What It Takes?

Okay, so you believe in yourself and your talent, and feel that you can take a few punches and still keep your feet firmly planted on the ground. What exactly do you expect to achieve in this business? What

Writing is the hardest work in the world not involving heavy lifting.

—Pete Hamill
Journalist, Author, Screenwriter

The Nature of the Business
by Phillip M. Goldfarb

Unit Production Manager, Associate Producer, Line Producer, Co-Producer, and Executive Producer.
Film credits: *All The Right Moves, Taps, Taxi Driver.*
Episodic TV credits: *L.A. Law, Doogie Howser, NYPD Blue, Casey's Shadow.*

There are movies that have been made that shouldn't have been made; movies that weren't made and should have been. What I've come to believe is that, in a sense, it's astrological. I can't scientifically measure it that way, but when everything is in alignment—the money is available, the right actor is available, the director is available, someone in marketing and distribution says the magic words, "I know how to sell this picture."—the movie is made.

It's my feeling that every project for film or television that actually gets made is a miracle. It seems that all of the energy is devoted to resisting, rather than toward accommodating, mainly because it is so much easier to say *no* than it is to say *yes*. If you say *no*, you don't have to take on much responsibility. Whereas, if you say *yes*, obviously, you then have the responsibility to see that something hap-

pens. People are constantly looking for reasons to say *no*, primarily in scripts.

If one is writing for film or TV, the more fool-proof the material is, the less it can be held up to a kind of ambivalent criticism. That sounds like a vague term, but where the script is indecisive, where it's not clear cut, where either the storyline or the plot points are not clearly illustrated, all of that contributes to making it harder for it to get made.

Then again, it doesn't matter how good the script is, if someone in distribution says, "I don't know how to sell this picture," that's all she wrote. There's nothing left to talk about. The studio will not proceed by telling them to figure out how to sell the picture. They don't work that way. So it takes a series of *yeses*. Anywhere in that line, if a *no* comes, that's the end of the series. That is the nature of the business.

are your goals? What spells success to you? If you haven't given this much thought, it's time to do so now. Your goals and expectations should be clearly thought out before venturing forward.

Think about the following questions and considerations, which are designed to help you through this soul-searching process. They may also show you that success can be spelled in a variety of ways for a screenwriter.

Is your heart set on seeing your work produced? Or can you be happy just selling your script even if it doesn't make it to the silver screen? Have you given thought to the life of a freelance writer, as compared to having a job with a steady paycheck?

Are you a one-script wonder? In other words, do you have only one script and believe that it is all that you need to get your foot in the door? Consider that it isn't uncommon for agents and managers to love a spec script, and expect more where that came from. This means that as a writer, you should always be perfecting your craft. Do you have more than one spec script right now? If you were stuck in an elevator and the only other person with you was producer/director Sydney Pollack, how many film ideas could you pitch to him while waiting for the repairmen? (Do you even know how to present a pitch?) Are you working on your next screenplay now? Do you set aside time each day to write?

Do you really understand what it means to be a screenwriter? If you think it is a job that involves writing a script, selling it for hundreds of thousands of dollars, and then getting an invitation to the premiere, you've seen too many movies . . . or too few. A major part of being a working screenwriter is rewriting, rewriting, rewriting the script that everyone loved, loved, loved. Do you have the patience and stick-to-itiveness to rewrite a scene over and over again? Do you also have the flexible creativity that is needed to come up with fresh approaches to those scenes each time? Are you self-motivated? Are you disciplined? Do you learn from constructive criticism, and can you let go of destructive rejection?

If you can honestly say "yes" to all of these questions, you just may understand what being a screenwriter is all about. And if success to you means selling your spec script or getting paid as a working writer in films and/or television, then this book is for you.

So It's Going to Take Some Work

Now then, what are you willing to do to succeed? Did you say, "Whatever it takes?" Is that your final answer? Good. You have the right attitude and are ready to get to work. Using this book as your guide, let each chapter help you focus on a different and vital aspect of the script-selling process.

By following the steps and advice we present in this book, you will maximize your chances of success. You'll learn the components of a professional-looking screenplay, and how to properly format your script according to industry standards. You'll also discover the importance of registering your work, and learn how easy it is to do so. We'll

Industry Humor...

INTERVIEWER
How many writers does it take to change a light bulb?

WRITER
Change the light bulb? That's the best part!

PROSE FROM A PRO

What It's Like to Be a Screenwriter
by Screenwriter Jane Anderson

How to Make an American Quilt; It Could Happen to You; The Positively True Adventures of the Alleged Texas-Cheerleader Murdering Mom.

Being a screenwriter is like being a mother. You give birth, and you get to raise the child through age three—through the most wretched, vomitous, diaperish, nasty years of the child's life, where you clean him and teach him how to walk and help him to talk, and all of a sudden you have this child who's just about to communicate with you . . . and you're just about to see him really become a person, and then the adoption agency comes in and takes this kid away from you and someone else raises it.

Now that I'm a director, I understand more about the process of getting something from page to screen. The script is indeed the blueprint. It's the beginning of the vision. But it's not the end. The director, the cinematographer, the art director, the editor, the composer—not to mention the actors—all contribute to the art and shape of a film. It's a visual medium and a sound medium more than it's a word medium, which is a hard thing to accept when you're the writer. Give your vision willingly to the process. And just as willingly, you must let it go. Otherwise, become a playwright or a novelist. Theater and literature are the two mediums where the writer has the final word.

show you how to write an effective query letter that really hooks its readers, as well as how to set up an efficient distribution system for sending out those letters. Furthermore, you'll learn the best, most efficient way to prepare a wish list of producers, directors, and/or actors to attach to your script. You'll read about agents and pitch meetings and record-keeping and . . . Wait. Maybe this is too much to throw at you on the opening pages of the first chapter. Let's pause for a moment and start with some words of encouragement from James Orr (co-writer of *Three Men and a Baby, Sister Act 2, Mr. Destiny*). "All the doors in Hollywood are hard to open, but the easiest of the hard doors to open is writing." And, lucky you, you're a writer!

Okay, so far we've given you a realistic glimpse into the film industry in order to help you assess your goals as a screenwriter, and to discover if you have what it takes to become one. Now that you have determined you are willing and able to go forward with your efforts, it's important that you familiarize yourself with industry terminology, which is presented in the following section. Show Biz Speak is not just another glossary; it's an industry education. We urge you to read every word. Once you do, you will have a better understanding of the business, and should be able to "talk the talk." ("Walking the walk" will come a little later.)

In the next chapter, we'll be presenting information about your script itself, making sure that it conforms to those picky-picky-picky industry standards. We'll also show you how to protect your work by registering it. But for now, let's take a look at the lingo.

SHOW BIZ SPEAK

You're a screenwriter. You deal in words. It's important to familiarize yourself with the industry's terminology for two reasons: to get the most out of this book from the industry people who share valuable advice and information; and, to understand what's being said to you, especially when discussing your work. When you *take* a meeting, you don't want to have to fake it when a *D-girl* says, "I agree with my assistant's *coverage* on your script. I like the *hook,* but it needs *more event.*"

The carefully chosen industry words and expressions that are included in the following pages relate to writers and their work. They also provide insight into the way business is done in the film industry. We recommend that you read each entry to learn things you didn't know that you didn't know.

Above-the-line. The film's production budget that is allotted for its creative costs, including those of the writer, producer, director, and principal actors.

Academy of Motion Picture Arts and Sciences (AMPAS). The film industry organization, headquartered in Beverly Hills, California, that is devoted to supporting technical research and education in filmmaking. AMPAS has over 5,000 active members who represent all aspects of filmmaking. Its members nominate and vote for the annual Academy Awards. Membership to AMPAS is by invitation only.

Act breaks. The breaks at the end of each act during a teleplay on *free TV* (as opposed to the premium cable channels like HBO and Showtime). Two-hour *teleplays* have seven acts, and at the end of each there is a commercial break. In an effort to keep the audience from channel surfing, act breaks typically have somewhat of a cliffhanger—something dramatic or provocative—that will encourage the audience to stay tuned.

Action points. *See* Plot points.

Adaptation. A transformation of a fiction or nonfiction story from one form—stage play, novel, short story, newspaper article—into a treatment or screenplay for a television or theatrical motion picture.

AFI. *See* American Film Institute.

AFMA. *See* American Film Marketing Association.

AFTRA. *See* American Federation of Television and Radio Artists.

Agency meeting. A meeting that is sometimes held between an agency and a prospective client. Typically, during this meeting, the client's career goals, as well as the agency's plan of action to help achieve those goals, are discussed.

A-List. The ever-changing handful of bankable actors and actresses, directors, and writers who command huge salaries and help get projects *green lighted* because their names are attached.

Alliance of Motion Picture and Television Producers (AMPTP). Film industry organization that negotiates with unions and guilds on behalf of its members. It also advises members on compliance with labor laws, and monitors governmental activities affecting the industry on local, state, and federal levels.

PROSE FROM A PRO

Advice to the Writer Who Just Finished a First Spec Script

by Screenwriters Josann McGibbon & Sara Parriott

Exactly 3:30, Runaway Bride, The Favor.

Many people we meet, from dentists to grips, give us scripts. Although it's masked as, "What do you think of it," they're hoping we'll pass it on to our agent. Our advice to the writer who just finished a first spec script? Rewrite it. Do not fall in love with your first or second draft, especially if you're new at screenwriting. It usually needs many drafts and much thought and a lot of rewriting before it's good enough to use up a contact that may be able to help you.

American Federation of Television and Radio Artists (AFTRA). The craft union for actors who work on television, videotape, and radio.

American Film Institute (AFI). A nonprofit organization that is dedicated to advancing and preserving the art of the moving image. The AFI has headquarters in Beverly Hills, California, and Washington DC. It offers classes, work-shops, and seminars, and provides grants and industry internships.

American Film Marketing Association (AFMA). The trade association for the independent film and television industry. AFMA's global membership distributes (and often produces) the films and programs made outside the major U.S. studios.

AMPAS. *See* Academy of Motion Picture Arts and Sciences.

AMPTP. *See* Alliance of Motion Picture and Television Producers.

Ampersand. The character or sign (&) that represents the word "and." According to the Writers Guild of America, an ampersand between two or more writers' names on film credits, denotes *collaborators* or a writing team. When the word "and" is used between names, it means another writer (or writers) has been brought in to make changes in the script.

Ancillary rights. Rights agreed upon in a contract that guarantee additional revenue for anything derived from the screenplay's story and/or characters. This can include, for example, comic books, posters, action figures, toys, games, T-shirts, lunch boxes, and the novelization of the screenplay—anything that is a spin-off of the script. All of these rights must be named in the contract.

Anime. Animated movies that are produced in Japan.

Annotated script. A script that is based on fact, and to which notes identifying the source of each fact portrayed—events, characters, locations, dialogue—have been added.

Antagonist. The principal character (or force)

who opposes the protagonist or hero. In *The Perfect Storm,* the storm is the perfect *antagonist.*

Anticlimax. A scene that appears after a film's *climax,* and dissipates the impact of the climax. An anticlimax leaves the audience disappointed and dissatisfied.

Antihero. The *protagonist*—male or female—characterized by a lack of traditional heroic qualities. The perfect example of an antihero is the character Melvin Udall, played by Jack Nicholson in *As Good as It Gets.*

Arbitration, Credit. *See* Credit arbitration.

Arc. The imaginary curved line that represents the development of *plotlines* as they wend their way through the script. *See also* Character arc.

Archetype. The prototype of a specific stereotypical person, place, or thing. Archetype examples include Dracula, Dr. Jekyll and Mr. Hyde, the whore with the heart of gold, the nerd, Podunk, and widgets.

Arena. The general setting or environment of a film, such as a circus, Wall Street, and outer space. This term is commonly used for sitcoms.

At the end of the day. An L.A. way of saying, "After all is said and done." ("At the end of the day, I'd rather have Richard Curtis do the rewrites, but if he's not available, I'll settle for your guy.")

Attachments. Actors, directors, and/or producers who have agreed to work on a project. A studio or network may ask, "Who's attached?" or "Are there any attachments?" A project becomes more attractive if a star or well-known director is part of the deal; however, it may become less attractive and more expensive if several producers or writers are attached.

Auction. The mode of selling a script to the highest bidder. When more than one studio is interested in buying a script, the writer's agent will submit copies of the script to the interested studios. The studios in turn, will make bids on it. *See also* Bidding war.

Backend. The total profits from a movie, including its theatrical release, sale to television and video, novelization, soundtrack, toys, and all other marketing revenue. Often, with low-budget films, the writer, director, and/or actors will defer part of their up-front money for a hefty backend deal. *See also* Deferred payment; Points.

Backdoor pilot. A two-hour television movie that serves as a pilot for a television series. Often, backdoor pilots come about after an idea for a television series is pitched and rejected. The series idea will be converted to movie length, and then sold, hoping that once it airs, it is well received. Then, it may have a chance of becoming a series.

Backstory. A character's history that explains and justifies his or her behavior and/or situation in the scripted story.

Baggage. *Attachments* to a project that are not necessarily desirable. Star baggage, for instance, refers to the star's personal attachments—perhaps an executive producer, or a spouse, who must be hired on the project in some capacity.

Bankable. A word describing an actor, director, producer, or writer, who has just been part of a major hit, or who has a super successful *track record.* Having a bankable person attached to a project is ideal. It can help get the film financed.

Beat. 1) Used as a script direction for an actor, (BEAT) indicates a pause in the dialogue or action. 2) For writers, a beat is a scene's *plot point*—a turning point in the action of a script.

Beat sheet. A list charting the story's major *plot points.*

Below-the-line. The film's production budget that is allotted for its technicians, material, and labor, including processing fees, equipment, stage space, editing costs, and other production and postproduction costs.

Between brads. Another way of saying "the script is finished." *See also* Brads.

Bidding war. The financial competition between two or more buyers who are vying for the same property. This is one war that's very desirable for screenwriters. *See also* Auction.

Bit. Small piece of business, usually funny, as in a comedy bit. Also referred to as schtick.

Blockbuster. A film that is a smash hit—one that's packing them in, selling out showings, playing at more than one theater at the multiplex. In keeping with today's standards, a blockbuster is a film that grosses at least $100 million.

Blue pages. The pages of a shooting script that contain the first set of changes, which are dated and printed on blue paper. The original shooting script is always printed on white paper. After the blue pages, subsequent script changes traditionally are printed on pink-, yellow-, green-, and goldenrod-colored paper.

Box office. 1) Gross income from a film's ticket sales. 2) A term describing an actor's or a director's potential to sell tickets to the movie he's in or directs. For example, actor Mel Gibson is considered good box office, as is director Ang Lee.

Brads. Metal fasteners used to hold a completed script together.

Brass. Also called *top brass* or *suits,* this term refers to studio, production company, or television network executives, who wield some decision-making and plug-pulling power.

Breaking the fourth wall. A film technique in which the actor talks directly to the camera. The *fourth wall*—a term that is commonly used in live theater—refers to the invisible wall between the action on stage and the audience. Woody Allen used this technique effectively in *Annie Hall*; Bob Hope used it in the *Road* series.

'bu. Short for Malibu, the star-studded Southern California beach community.

Buck. This is show-biz shorthand for $100,000. So if you're offered "three bucks" for your spec script, don't take offense. Take the three bucks, but first make sure the buyer is talking "Show Biz Speak."

Budget. The above-the-line, below-the-line, preproduction, production, and postproduction expenses needed to produce a film.

Button. The term used for ending a scene with a figurative exclamation point, like a funny punch line or a dramatic action. ("The end of the scene needs a button," or "Button up the end of the scene.")

Buzz. The talk (always positive) within the industry about a script, an actor, a director, or a movie that hasn't been released yet. Often, this kind of buzz is started by the studio's public relations department.

Cameo. A small part played by a well-known actor. Typically, the bigger the star, the smaller the part, and the closer the friendship between that actor and the director, producer, or star of the film.

Cannes Film Festival. The world's most famous international film festival, which takes place each May in the South of France. *See also* Film festival.

Certificate of authorship. A form signed by an author of an original screenplay, stating that he or she is the sole creator of the work, and that the work itself does not defame, disparage, or libel another party, does not invade anyone's privacy, and will not cause the buyer of the work to be sued for any legal reason having to do with the integrity of the original work.

Character arc. The imaginary curved line that represents the metamorphosis of a character as he or she journeys through the screenplay.

Cliffhanger. Suspenseful teleplay *act break* ending that is designed to have the audience stay tuned. Cliffhangers are also associated with the end of each episode of a television series, miniseries, or soap opera.

Climax. The moment of greatest intensity— emotionally and/or physically—in a script, making it the turning point. The climax usually causes and ushers in the *resolution* of the story.

Collaborators. Two or more writers who work together on a project.

Concept. The basic premise of a film; its main idea.

Conflict. The dramatic opposition—ranging from disharmony and friction, to hostility and warfare—that motivates and shapes the action of the plot.

Contingent compensation. A stipulation in a writer's contract, stating that she is to be compensated monetarily in the event that something specific happens with the project in the future.

For example, a writer might be entitled to a predetermined bonus or, perhaps, a percentage of the film's profits if it grosses a certain amount on the opening weekend or is made into a television series. These and other compensation stipulations are negotiated into the contract, usually by the writer's agent or lawyer.

Co-producer. The *producer's* partner who is usually responsible for a major element, like finding the *property,* or *attaching* a star to it.

Courtesy read. The reading of a script as a favor.

Coverage. 1) Industry term for the in-depth written assessment of a *spec script.* This report, which is typically written by a *story analyst* or *reader,* is required by film studios, production companies, and agencies to help them determine whether or not to consider buying the script. In addition to a story analyst, coverage may be written by a person in *development,* or by an agent's assistant. 2) A term used to indicate any variety of camera shots—close-ups, reactions, etc.—in addition to the main or master shot.

Creative meeting. Typically, a bi- or tri-weekly meeting at which studio development departments meet to share information on new projects that are being considered, as well as material that is being sought. The status of projects currently in *development* is part of the agenda as well. Production companies and agencies have similar creative meetings.

Credit arbitration. An equitable system of determining credit(s) in dispute on a film or television program written by one or more WGA writers. The arbitration is conducted by the WGA; the arbiters responsible for the determination are WGA arbitration committee members.

Credits. Acknowledgments of the work done on a project. For film, writer credits include "Story by" and "Screenplay by," or "Written by." Television film credits include "Created by," "Story by," and/or "Teleplay by."

Crisis. The point (or points) in a story or drama when a *conflict* reaches its peak. Response to a crisis leads to a *climax*.

Cross between. A frame-of-reference method of describing a screenplay. For example, the story is about two women looking to find themselves, but find dead people instead. It is a "cross between" *Thelma and Louise* and *The Sixth Sense*. *See also* Meets.

Crossover. A motion picture that is targeted for a specific demographic audience, but draws an entirely different audience as well. For instance, many movies that are made for children are considered crossovers because adults enjoy them too. Examples of crossover films include *Babe, Blair Witch Project, The Lion King,* and *Toy Story*.

Dailies. *See* Rushes.

Deal memo. A brief letter-agreement documenting the contract terms that have been negotiated and agreed upon by all of the parties involved. A formal, detailed contract will follow.

Deferred payment.* A mode of payment for actors and other *above-the-line* talent in which less up-front money for work on a film is taken, opting instead for a deal based on the movie's profits. Considered *backend* deals, deferred payments are usually made on low-budget productions in an attempt to reduce a film's *negative costs*. It is a gamble, but it can also generate a big payoff if the movie is successful.

✳ Gene Hackman agreed to a deferred payment for the film *Hoosiers*. He took very little money up front, opting to take a piece of the film's backend instead. Hackman was taking a big chance because the screenplay was written by first-time screenwriter Angelo Pizzo, and it was David Anspaugh's first-time directing experience with a feature film. As it turned out, the film was a big hit and Hackman's risk-taking paid off in a big way.

Demographics. Human population segments that are used to define consumer markets; or, in the case of film, the potential target audience.

Denouement. The final clarification and resolution of the plot in which all of the loose ends are tied up.

Deus ex machina. An unexpected, artificial, or improbable character, device, or event that is introduced suddenly to resolve a situation or to untangle a plot. This technique was popular in Greek and Roman dramas, in which it was acceptable for a god to be lowered onto the stage to resolve a plot, or to extricate the *protagonist* from a difficult situation. This type of *resolve* would make today's audience feel cheated, and may be a real turnoff to producers.

Development. The start of a *property's* production process. After the script has been written and/or rewritten and polished, and the producer who put it into development is ready to go forward with it, development ends and *pre-production* begins.

Development deal. The contract or agreement between the scriptwriter and the studio, television network, or production company that is negotiated before a *property* is put into development. This deal spells out exactly what is expected of the writer during development—such as two sets of revisions and a polish.

Development girl (or guy). Most often referred to as *D-girl* (or guy), this is the person at the studio or production company whose job is to find screenplays or other forms of material—unpublished manuscripts, books, plays, magazine articles, or pitched concepts—that have the potential to be money-making movies.

Development hell. A common phrase used by those who put projects into *development* and who are frustrated at the negligible percentage of developed scripts that actually make it to the screen. It is also used by writers whose projects are in development for what seems like forever.

DGA. *See* Directors Guild of America.

D-girl (or guy). *See* Development girl (or guy).

Direct-to-video (DTV) films. Low-budget films that are made specifically for video, or films that were originally intended for release in theaters, but didn't turn out good enough for the investment of distribution and advertising expenses.

Directors Guild of America (DGA). The trade union for film, television, and radio that represents directors, assistant directors, unit production managers, production associates, and stage managers, among others.

Distributors. Companies that market, advertise, and promote motion pictures that they distribute or book into movie theaters. Many major studios do their own distributing.

Dovetail. To combine, link, or interweave one scene of a movie with another.

Downer. A depressing, bleak, downbeat film. Even a film that starts out cheerful and hopeful is considered a downer if it has an unhappy ending.

Dramatic rights. Legal permission to adapt a *property*—novel, newspaper, magazine article, song—for stage or screen.

DTV. *See* Direct-to-video (DTV) films.

El Paso. California-cutesy for, "We're going to pass on this script. ("It's El Paso.")

Episodic TV. Television series with recurring principal characters for which hour or half-hour weekly episodes are written.

Exclusivity. With regard to screenwriters, this is a contract stipulation, stating that no other writer will work on the screenplay.

Executive producer. Generally, the person who secures a film's financing. Sometimes this title goes to the star who gets the film *green lighted.*

Exhibitors. These are the owners and operators of movie theaters who rent motion pictures from *distributors.*

Exploitation films. Also known as sexploitation films, these films are made on a next-to-nothing budget, and typically are filled with any combination of sex, violence, gore, hostility, horror, and female degradation. (Find a better way to break into the business!)

Exposition. Information worked into the dialogue that tells the audience about the character's *backstory,* or something that occurs offscreen.

Fast track. A project that is slated to be made quickly. It's a good thing. It means the money man—often the studio boss—wants that motion picture *in the can* and fast! Why? Any number of reasons. For example, if an actor with *heat* agrees to a project, the studio may fast track it before the star agrees to another studio's project. Also, when two similar films are in production at two different studios, one may be put on the fast track to get it into theaters before the other.

Feature film. *See* Motion picture.

Film festival. A gathering of film industry professionals from around the world to screen new films, to network, to party, and to see and be seen. The screened films are eligible for awards in various categories. The Cannes, Sundance, and Toronto film festivals are considered the top three, followed by those held in Telluride, Berlin, Venice, and Seattle.

Film noir. French for "black film," this is a film genre that is characterized by its dark, downbeat themes and brooding characters. *Film noir* films are often shot in grays, blacks, and whites, and typically involve detectives or private eyes, prostitutes, petty criminals, and murderers—characters from the seamy side of life. The *protagonists* are usually flawed; they struggle, but ultimately lose. *Film noir* evolved in the 1940s, and its heyday lasted through the 1950s. Early black-and-white classics include *The Maltese Falcon, Double Indemnity, Sorry, Wrong Number,* and *Touch of Evil.* Later additions to this genre include movies like *Chinatown, The Usual Suspects,* and *L.A. Confidential.*

First-draft screenplay. A completed script that is ready for submission. When a writer is paid to revise the first draft for a producer, the rewritten script is considered the second draft.

First-look deal. An agreement whereby a film studio, production company, or television network has the opportunity to look at the screenplay before anyone else.

First run. The first public showing of a film in any market or area. Also called a *premium run.*

PROSE FROM A PRO

So Many Changes; So Many Reasons
by Richard Styles

Writer-producer-director: *Cease Fire, Shallow Grave, Escape, Sorceress II, Picture Perfect Murders.*

Everybody always wants changes. That's the nature of making a movie. Not only do changes start with a screenplay, they actually never stop until the film is in the theater. You're constantly re-editing that screenplay, that story, those characters, those scenes, until you have your final cut. And then after that, there may be changes that the distributor wants to make. The distributor may need a few different scenes that will make the film more saleable, maybe for the trailer that he sells the picture on, maybe for the artwork, the posters, maybe for the type of film that it is. He knows what formula works best in Germany or Italy or Spain.

These are considerations that most screenwriters don't think of when writing a film. Compromise has to happen along the way, starting with the screenwriter. I've had to live by those words. The people that put up the money and are making the film have the power. That is why many screenwriters become producers and/or directors . . . to keep their original vision in tact.

Fix it in the pinks. To make changes or "repairs" in a later draft of the script. *See* Blue pages.

Fluff. Derogatory reference to a work that is light and lacking substance. ("That screenplay is a piece of fluff.")

Foreshadowing. An indication or suggestion of an event that will occur later on. Also referred to as *planting*, this technique is generally used to build suspense.

Fourth wall. *See* Breaking the fourth wall.

Franchise. A series of films that includes a popular character or group of characters. Examples of franchised films include the *James Bond, Dirty Harry, Abbott and Costello, Planet of the Apes*, and *Star Trek* series. *See also* Tentpole movie.

Free TV. Television programming for which there is no charge.

Futuristic film. A film that takes place in the future.

Genre. A category of film that is marked by a distinctive style, form, or other classifiable element. Popular film genres include comedy, romantic-comedy, action-adventure, science fiction, thriller, and horror.

Get inside the script. A term directing the screenwriter to fill out a particular area of the script further, such as delving deeper into a character's motives or emotions, or fully exploring the possibilities that are inherent in a situation—you know, getting inside the script.

Give me more event. A directive that is given to the scriptwriter, usually by a studio executive, to make something that is happening in the script bigger and more important in terms of the plot.

Gofer. An industry intern or apprentice whose job description includes running errands ("gofer" this and "gofer" that) and performing small jobs. This person is paid poorly, but has the opportunity to learn a lot about the industry, and to meet people who may be able to help further her career somewhere down the road.

Golden retrievers. Savvy studio executives who know how to cut down on "golden time"—overtime with extra pay.

Green light. A term signifying that a project has the approval to go into production. A flashing green light means the project's green light is imminent.

Gross player. An industry player who is important enough to demand a percentage of a film's gross income.

Gross points. *See* Points.

Hang a lantern on it. A directive to revise an area of the script, usually a plot point, that is unclear.

Heat.* A term describing an industry player who has box office draw.

✳ Generally, superstar actors have heat. Occasionally, a director will have heat. Writers? They have prickly heat.

Heavy. 1) Term for a major player who has a great track record and lots of clout. This is a good person to know. The opposite of a heavy is a *lightweight* or *junior*. 2) Characters in films who are referred to as heavies are bad guys or villains.

Helm. A trade paper expression meaning to direct a film. ("Ron Howard will *helm* the film for Universal.")

High concept. A commercially viable, irresistible story idea that can be pitched in a sentence or two, and will knock the socks off the pitchee. According to one studio executive, a high-concept movie cannot have a *sequel*.

Hip-pocketing. A term signifying that an agent or agency is representing a writer or another talent for one specific project, with no agreement to continue representing that individual once that project is completed.

Hook. The plotline or incident that grabs or

hooks the reader, producer, director, actor, and ultimately, the audience.

Hostage. A bargaining ploy that may be used by a screenwriter who has a hot script that a studio or network really wants. If that writer wants something out of the ordinary in return—maybe to direct the film—the potential buyer will have to cater to the demand. If the exec cannot get the script without meeting the writer's demand, the writer is said to be holding the script hostage.

Housekeeping deal. An arrangement in which a studio "houses" producers and other creative people—writers, actors, directors—giving them office space and paying their overhead. In return, the studio receives first crack at the projects that are found and/or developed by these people.

Hyphenate. Industry term referring to someone in the business who wears more than one hat (and we don't mean writer-waiter). For example, after a screenwriter's first successful teleplay credit, she may produce her next project as well. This would make her a producer-writer—a hyphenate.

Idiot page. *See* Synopsis.

Inciting scene. The scene that launches the main action of the story. It is almost always in the beginning of the script, as part of the *setup*.

Independent producer. A producer who develops projects and gets financing from sources other than a major studio. There are times when an independent producer will get such financing from a studio or network, but will retain creative control over the film.

Independent production company. A production company that makes films independ-

ently, rather than under the control of a major Hollywood film studio. Majors have bought independent film companies, for instance: Disney owns Miramax, Time Warner owns New Line.

Indie. Term for a film that is made by an independent production company. Indies may or may not be distributed by major studios.

In-house producer. A producer with a *housekeeping deal.*

Ink. To sign a contract.

Internal story. A story in which there is a lot of thinking going on in the script. This is most effective in novels, not in movies, which are a more visual medium.

Iowa. Hopelessly amateurish. A producer may refer to a script as being "strictly Iowa." As a state, Iowa is a lovely place, but when referring to a script, it is not a good thing.

It's in the can. Another term for "The film is finished. Completed." Those big metal canisters that hold motion picture films are the cans from which this expression was derived.

Junior. *See* Lightweight.

Knowers telling knowers. An expression that refers to a character in the script who tells something to another character who already knows that information. This is considered a script boo-boo.

Leave-behind. A written account of a writer's story idea that was pitched during a meeting. This is requested when the person to whom the story was pitched likes it, and wants to pitch the idea to her boss. A leave-behind will help in retelling the story accurately. (Registering your work with the WGA before pitching it will allow you to feel comfortable if you are asked for a leave-behind.)

Legs. A term describing a *property* that is believed to have staying power, or potential for longevity.

Library shot. *See* Stock shot.

Life rights. The legal term for the rights given to a writer or producer for permission to make a movie of a living person's life story.

Lightweight. A person in the film industry who has very little, if any, clout.

Line producer. The film-production supervisor who deals with daily dilemmas. This person is responsible for seeing that the production sticks to the shooting schedule and stays on budget.

Live action. The use of real people and/or animals in a scene or film, rather than animation, computer animation, or claymation.

Logline. The very essence of a screenplay, told in one or two sentences.

Long-form TV. Made-for-television movies and miniseries, as opposed to sitcoms or episodic TV.

Majors. Term for major movie studios—Paramount Pictures, Twentieth Century-Fox, Warner Bros., Columbia Pictures, Universal Studios, The Walt Disney Co., Sony Pictures Entertainment, MGM/UA, and DreamWorks SKG.

Make it muscular. A directive that is given to the scriptwriter, usually by a studio executive, to give a scene more of an edge, or to make a character gutsier.

Master script. The shooting script that has all of the changes. The director, cast, and crew have copies of this script.

MBA. *See* Minimum Basic Agreement.

Meet-and-greet. A type of meeting that is set up by an agent or manager for the purpose of introducing a writer-client to a producer, development person, or anyone else involved in the industry who can buy a script or offer a writing assignment.

Meets. A frame-of-reference way of describing a screenplay. For example, if the story is about a monster who gets a job as a nanny, it might be described as *Godzilla* meets *Mrs. Doubtfire*. The movie *The Cell* is advertised as *The Matrix* meets *Silence of the Lambs*. *See also* Cross between.

Minimum Basic Agreement (MBA). The Writer's Guild of America's MBA is the contract between the Guild and industry management that governs the conditions, compensations, and rights and responsibilities under which members of the Guild work. The MBA is a collective bargaining agreement, renegotiated approximately every three to four years with the Alliance of Motion Picture and Television Producers (AMPTP), and ABC, CBS, and NBC.

Mise en scène. French for "What is put into the scene." In terms of a film or any one scene in the film, it refers to the physical environment or surroundings of a film or a particular scene; the look and feel of a place.

Mission. In screenplays, it is the description of the *protagonist's* pursuit—the hero's journey.

Motion picture. A film that is made for distribution to movie theaters. It may contain dialogue that is dubbed, or shots that are filmed for its eventual release to television, but the initial distribution of a motion picture is to movie theaters.

Motion Picture Association of America (MPAA). The organization of movie distributors. One of its prime functions is to determine ratings for films that are released in the United States.

Motivation. The incentive that compels a character to take action.

Movie studio. A major production company or corporation that is in the business of producing movies. It has its own movie-making facilities—a studio complex with buildings, stages, and lots. The movie studio uses its own producers as well as outside producers, who have their own production companies, to do the actual filmmaking.

MOW. Abbreviated term for a television movie-of-the-week.

MPAA. *See* Motion Picture Association of America.

Negative cost. A combination of a film's *above-the-line* and *below-the-line costs,* including the final edited and prepared negative of the film. Remaining costs include fees for prints, distribution, advertising, and promotion, which are often shared by the producer and distributor.

Net points. *See* Points.

Network, television. *See* Television network.

Nontheatrical distribution. Film distribution through markets other than motion picture theaters. This includes, for example, cable television, the Internet, home video, and educational markets.

Numbers. Box office receipts; the money taken in at the movie theaters.

On the nose. Term describing a lack of subtlety and originality in some part of the screenplay, most often in the dialogue, but it can also be in the story or character development.

One-sheet. Another term for the movie poster for a film. When the studio's marketing people are deciding whether or not to buy the script, they tend to think in terms of how it will translate on a one-sheet.

Open market. Term for a property that is unencumbered and for sale.

Open up. To develop or broaden the action of a plot, usually taking it beyond its central location. This expression often comes up when there's talk of adapting a stage play to film. A one-set, three-character play would need to be "opened up" for the big screen. Fill out the plot, add a subplot, give birth to more characters, take the action out of the living room and bring it into the rest of the world.

Option. An arrangement in which a producer, director, or star pays the writer for the exclusive right to develop or sell a property for a specified period of time.

Original screenplay. A script that is written directly for the screen, and not adapted from any other medium, including a novel, stage play, short story, article, or song.

Out on submission. Description of a script that has been sent out by agents to prospective buyers.

Outline. Generally three to ten pages long, the outline is a summary of a film's story. It's the step before the *treatment.*

Over the top. A story line, plot point, or performance that is unforgivably outrageous. Once an audience steps foot in a movie theater, they are prepared to suspend disbelief, but when you go *over the top,* you may be asking too much of the audience.

Over the transom. An old book-publishing

term that is sometimes used when referring to the way in which an *unsolicited script* arrives at an agency, studio, or production company.

Packaging. Arranging for an attractive combination of bankable creative elements for a film, such as a screenwriter with a script, a director, and a star or two. This is often done by producers to help finance the project. Also, big agencies like International Creative Management (ICM), Creative Artists Agency (CAA), and William Morris Agency, are great at packaging for studios because of their considerable and impressive client-talent pool from which to draw.

Page-oner. A phrase referring to a script that is so bad it needs rewriting from the first page on.

Pasadena. Film industry term for "We're going to pass on this script." ("It's Pasadena.")

Pass. A rejection. To pass on a project is to reject it.

Pay or play. A contract clause that guarantees payment whether or not the film is produced. If and when there is a pay-or-play deal, it's usually with a star, occasionally with a director, but rarely with a writer.

Payoff. Often the payoff is the punch line of a comedy bit or joke. With regard to a script, it refers to the realization of *foreshadowing*—something for the purpose of that eventual payoff.

Per diem. A daily allowance for meals, and sometimes lodging. Writers often get this when they're flown somewhere to do a rewrite, or while they are working on location.

Period piece. A film that takes place during an earlier time period. This typically means high *below-the-line* costs because of the necessary costumes, props, sets, and often the location itself.

Also, with a period piece, the production company misses out on *product placement*. Notice that none of the guys in *Braveheart* are drinking Bud Light?

Pickups. Completed motion pictures that major studios "pick up" for distribution, without having produced them.

Pipeline. A production company's or studio's list of projects in all stages—development, preproduction, production, and postproduction.

Pitch. To present an idea for a film or television project, hoping to get a deal on it. The pitch usually takes place at a *pitch meeting* also called a *pitch session*.

Pitch meeting. A meeting during which a screenwriter pitches story lines. She may pitch her spec script or ideas for films that are in other forms—outline, treatment, notes on a napkin—whatever is appropriate for the specific meeting. Also called a *pitch session*.

Pitch session. *See* Pitch meeting.

Planting. *See* Foreshadowing.

Players. Influential industry people, such as producers, studio executives, agents, and lawyers, who are well connected and able to make deals. It is advantageous to have players on your side.

Plot points. Turning points in the action of a script. Also called *action points* or *transition points*.

Plotline.* A script's main story—the plot. It is comprised of a chain of events within a situation.

✳ Writer Linda Palmer describes plot as "something that keeps the characters busy."

Points. The percentage of a film's profits, as negotiated in the deals that generally are made with the *above-the-line* talent.

Polish. To revise a screenplay more than a *tweaking* but less than a *rewrite*.

Post. *See* Postproduction.

Postproduction. The clean-up, clear-up, and completion work done after the film has been shot. This includes editing, looping, scoring, mixing, special effects, and printing—in other words, everything that needs to be done to finish the film. Within the industry, this is usually called "post," as in "That'll be done in post."

Preemptive bid. A bid on a script by a prospective buyer that allows the buyer a short period of time to attach a director or star. This type of bid prevents the script from being shopped elsewhere. Once the allotted time runs out, if the prospective buyer hasn't come through with a bankable element, the script is placed on the open market.

Premise. *See* Concept.

Premium run. *See* First run.

Preproduction. Preparations that are done before a film goes into *production*, starting with script development, and continuing with casting, production design, hiring the crew, building the sets, etc.

Prequel. A film that is part of a series in which the story takes place prior to the time of a pre-existing film in the series. Opposite of a *sequel*. The most famous proposed prequels are part of George Lucas's trilogy, and deal with life before the *Star Wars* trilogy.

Principal photography. The period of time during which a screenplay is filmed.

Producer. The person who finds the project, hires *above-the-line* and *below-the-line* personnel, and gets the script into *development* at a studio or network. The producer oversees the project during *preproduction, production,* and *postproduction.*

Producer's notes. A less literate form of a reader's report, or *coverage*, from studio development executives. The emphasis in this report is on the property's commercial potential.

Product placement. A brand-name product that is seen in a film. Product manufacturers pay production companies for this exposure.

Production. Putting the story on film after *preproduction* and before *postproduction*. Production includes construction of the set or sets, lighting, rehearsals, and shooting the film. When the film is actually being shot, it is referred to as being "in production."

Production bonus. Added income perk that is often built into the writer's contract, the amount of which is determined when the credits are established. If a sole writer gets *Written by* credit, she will get the entire bonus. The amount of the bonus decreases considerably with every additional writer that is credited.

Production company. A company helmed by one or more producers for the purpose of making films.

Property. Material in any form—treatment, outline, screenplay, novel, short story, article — that is the basis of a film.

Protagonist. The main character and driving force of the action of the story. The protagonist is not necessarily a hero or heroine, and each story can have more than one. *See also* Antagonist; Antihero.

Public domain. Intellectual property that is not protected under copyright, trademark, or other private claims like WGA registration. This type of material can be adapted, reprinted, produced, or used in any form without paying for it.

Punch up a script. The process of adding something to a script to enhance its genre. For instance, jokes might be added to punch up a comedy, or love scenes to a romance.

Query letter. A written pitch for a spec script that is sent to an industry player to elicit a request to read the script.

Quote. The most recent fee received by any of the *above-the-line* talent. ("We want Shane Black to write the script. Find out his quote.")

Ramp it up. A directive that is given to the scriptwriter, usually by a studio executive, to condense a scene that is too long. It's another way of saying "wrap it up."

Reader. *See* Story analyst.

Release form. *See* Submission agreement.

Residuals. Payments received by writers when their feature or TV films are rerun and/or sold to various markets, such as cable or pay TV. The rates are usually based on a percentage of the original salary. The owner of the film is responsible for paying residuals.

Resolution. The third-act conclusion of the story during which all of the loose ends are tied up, leaving the audience satisfied.

Re-up. To sign a contract or option agreement that is up for renewal.

Reveal. The moment that a secret within the story becomes known to the audience. (Surprise! She's really a he!)

Rewrite. Significant changes that are made to a completed screenplay by a writer. WGA members should be paid for each rewrite.

Rhyme. To link something from an early scene in the story to something in a later scene. For instance, early in the film, the child loved riding on the merry-go-round horses during the summer he stayed with his dad. We can rhyme this to the racehorse he saves from the glue factory later in the story.

Running gag. A comic *bit* or joke that is established early in the script and repeated occasionally. At the end of the script, that running gag or joke should have a *payoff*.

Rushes.* Also called *dailies*, this is the film footage that is shot during the day, then "rushed" to a lab and "rush-processed" so that it can be screened the following day. The director, producer, cinematographer, and editor usually view the rushes. It's the director's failsafe way of knowing that he got what he needs on film, before it's too late to reshoot.

✳ It is said that Moses was born in the House of Levi, and to prevent him from meeting an untimely demise by an order from Pharaoh, this sweet, innocent infant was put in a basket and set adrift in marshy water. As fate would have it, Pharaoh's daughter happened upon the babe in the basket, liked what she saw, and had him brought to her quarters in the palace. When he was handed to her, she took one look at the baby and winced. "Feh! What happened to him?" she asked. "He looked so good in the rushes."

SAG. *See* Screen Actors Guild.

Scale. For a screenwriter, it's the minimum payment that is set by the Writers Guild of America's *Minimum Basic Agreement.*

Scene. In terms of the *shooting script,* a scene is a unit of action and/or dialogue that takes place in the same location at the same time with the camera in the same position. Each scene is numbered.

Whenever any of these three elements (camera, location, time) change, it is considered a new scene and given the next scene number.

Scene cards. Index cards on which the scenes from a script are described—one scene per card—to help structure the script. These cards are laid out in full view, and then the writer arranges them in the order she thinks works best.

Schmooze. To mix and mingle with the hope of ingratiating yourself with someone who can help further your career.

Schtick. *See* Bit.

Screen Actors Guild (SAG). The craft union governing actors who work on film for television as well as for theatrical release.

Screenplay. The script for a motion picture. This includes all of the dialogue, locations, descriptions of actions, and a minimum of character and camera directions.

Script assignment. A writing job—usually for a script that is either based on someone else's idea, or an adaptation of an existing work, such as a novel, short story, magazine article, or song.

Script doctor. A person who may be called in just prior to the *principal photography* stage of a project to make the script "better." Script doctors who make a major contribution to the script may share screen credit with the original writer.

Script notes. A set of notes for a script in development that includes guidelines for the next draft.

Second-act curtain. The story's *climax*, as presented in a script's traditional *three-act structure*.

Secondary action line. *See* Subplot.

Self-promoting. A well-known project that has

a built-in audience. Prime examples include *Star Trek, Batman, Mission: Impossible,* and *Planet of the Apes* movies.

Sequel. A complete film that is a continuation of an already existing popular film. Opposite of a *prequel. Hannibal* is the sequel to *Silence of the Lambs.*

Sequence. A series of shots or connected scenes with a beginning, middle, and end, such as a chase sequence in an action film.

Setup. 1) The first act of a screenplay in which the situation(s) that needs resolving is established. 2) The positioning of the camera and other equipment, actors, set, props, and whatever else is required to get a shot.

Seven-act structure. The standard format for two-hour *teleplays* which are broadcast on *free television.*

Shelved. A script that is taken out of development and no longer in production. Completed films can also be shelved. However, in today's market, these films generally go directly to video stores instead of languishing on a shelf. *See also* Direct-to-video film.

Shoot. The actual filming of the movie. ("The shoot is scheduled for next week.")

Shooting script. The final revised, polished screenplay in which each shot or setup is numbered and all camera directions are included.

Shop. To send a *property* out to potential buyers. Agents usually shop properties to production companies.

Signatory. A studio, television network, production company, or producer who signs a contract agreeing to abide by the terms of the Writer's Guild's *Minimum Basic Agreement* when dealing with writers.

Sleeper. A film—produced either by a major studio or independent production company— that becomes a hit, much to everyone's surprise. Famous sleeper films include *National Lampoons' Animal House, Ghost, Pretty Woman,* and *The Crying Game.*

Soft. A script that is too bland, not edgy enough.

Spec script. A script that is written on speculation—without a contract—and owned completely by the writer. Having a great spec script is one way in which screenwriters establish themselves in the film and television industry. A spec script can be purchased by a movie studio, television network, or production company and made into a movie. It can also serve as a writing sample to help land an assignment.

Spine. The backbone or main *plotline* of a screenplay that is driven by visual actions rather than heartfelt emotions. Also called a *through line.*

Stakes. The *protagonist's* risk. The greater the risk (the higher the stakes), the more heightened the drama.

Standards and Practices. Department found in every major television network that monitors programming, making sure that scripts are politically correct, inoffensive, and in compliance with federal regulations.

Start date. The day on which *principal photography* on a project begins. Screenwriters often get a portion of the money that is due them on this date.

Step deal. A get-paid-as-you-go agreement between a screenwriter and producer, whereby the screenwriter is (or should be) paid for each "step" of the project's progress. This often starts with a *treatment,* followed by the *screenplay,*

PROSE FROM A PRO

Screenwriting at Its Best and Worst

by Screenwriter Barry Strugatz

Co-writer: *Married to the Mob* and *She Devil.*

Screenwriting at Its Best

❏ When you're writing and the story and characters just flow and veer off into new, unexpected places, better than what you've previously envisioned.

❏ Sometimes when you're writing and it's going well, the characters take on a life of their own and seem to effortlessly come up with great lines.

❏ When you're stuck or having a problem with a scene and an idea strikes that turns the weakness into a strength. For example, if you feel that there is too much confusing exposition in a scene—have a character acknowledge the confusing information.

❏ If you're lucky enough to have your screenplay produced, the supreme joy is seeing actors take your scenes and bring them to life. The great actors will add dimensions to your characters that you never imagined.

Screenwriting at Its Worst

❏ The heartbreak of the film not getting made. Scared producers second-guessing studio executives who are second-guessing their bosses. There are even some producers who seem to enjoy torturing writers.

❏ It's a very tough business. Perseverance and the ability to take huge amounts of rejection are as important as talent.

rewrites, a *polish,* and, if your luck holds out, "Lights, camera, action!" In a step deal, the writer can be cut off at any time, which means there is no advancement to the next step, and no pot of gold at the end of *principal photography.*

Stock footage. *See* Stock shot.

Stock shot. A film clip from a film library. When a film requires a shot of something that already exists on film, a production company will often buy a stock shot instead of going through the time and expense to recreate the scene. Also called *stock footage* or *library shot.*

Story. The basis of your original screenplay. Additionally, when you write an original screenplay, you own that story. After you've sold it, even if a dozen writers are called in to revise your script, and there's not one word of your original dialogue left, but your basic story stays intact, you should still get a "story by" credit.

Story analyst. Also called a *reader,* this is the person at a studio, production company, television network, actor's office, agency, or director's office who logs in and assesses submitted scripts. These written assessments, called *coverage,* help company executives determine if the scripts are right for their company. *See also* Coverage.

Storyboard. A sketched-out version of each scene or camera setup of a script. When directors storyboard a *shooting script,* generally each scene or camera setup is sketched out. It's like having a comic book version of the film. When writers storyboard their *spec scripts,* generally each scene is described in a few words on index cards that are tacked up in order on a corkboard.

Structure. The script's skeleton—its form, which has a beginning, a middle, and an end.

Studio, movie. *See* Movie studio.

Submission agreement. A release form that is signed by a writer when submitting an unsolicited manuscript to a production company.

Subplot. A story line that usually weaves in and out of the main story, generally involving characters that are not the leads. Also known as a *secondary action line.*

Subtext. A message within a script that is conveyed, in a sense, by reading between the lines. The words may say one thing, but the actor's reading of those words may convey an entirely different message to the audience. "It's not what you say, it's the way that you say it."

Suggested by. Credit for a fictionalized script that stems from a true happening.

Suit. *See* Brass.

Sundance Film Festival. Considered one of the top three film festivals in the world, Sundance is held every January in Park City, Utah. *See also* Film festival.

Synopsis. A short (one or two page) summary of a screenplay that may be requested by producers and agents, along with the screenplay. The synopsis, sometimes referred to as an *idiot page,* is less detailed than an *outline,* which is less detailed than a *treatment.*

T & A. Abbreviation for "tits and ass." This slang term is used to describe films that capitalize on voluptuous female figures.

Take. 1) An angle, slant, viewpoint. When a producer asks you your take on a subject, she wants your interpretation of it. 2) Film footage in which the camera is rolling for a single, continuous shot.

Teleplay. Script written for television usually in a seven-act structure.

Television network. A major television company that is responsible for the creation and development of programming, which is transmitted to stations that it owns as well as to its affiliates. Networks make a major portion of their money by selling air time and programming to advertisers, also called *sponsors*. The major neworks are ABC, CBS, NBC, PBS, FOX, WB, and UPN.

Tentpole movie. Usually a long-awaited movie that is expected to at least break even during its *first run*. Typically, tentpole movies are released during the summer or the Christmas season, and are often the start of a *franchise* or an installment of one. Movies like *Indiana Jones, Lethal Weapon,* and *Star Wars* are examples of tentpole movies. *See also* First run.

Theatrical film. *See* Motion picture.

Theme. The message, implication, or significance of a story.

Thin. A script with a weak, insufficient story that lacks substance.

Three-act structure. The traditional organization of a script. The three "acts" typically include a beginning or *setup* in which the situation is introduced and established; a middle, which includes complications and *conflicts* that build to the *crisis* and *climax*; and an ending, which has the *resolution* and *payoff*.

Through line. *See* Spine.

Tie-in. A money-generating commercial effort that is linked to a movie, such as a tape or CD of the movie's soundtrack, or a novelization of the story. A fast-food restaurant that offers miniature action figures from those in a children's blockbuster movie is another example of a tie-in.

Top brass. *See* Brass.

Toronto International Film Festival. This is considered the premiere film festival in North America, which takes place each September. *See also* Film festival.

Track record. A list of *credits*. Having no track record can be better than having a bad track record—you know, one flop after another. Those with excellent track records are *bankable*.

Trackers. Production company employees who "track down" news stories and anything else that has the potential to be successfully translated to film, before they've been published.

Trade papers. Industry periodicals, of which *The Hollywood Reporter, Daily Variety, Daily Variety Gotham* (New York), and *Weekly Variety* are the trade bibles.

Trades. *See* Trade Papers.

Transition points. *See* Plot points.

Treatment. The detailed story of a film, usually told scene by scene from start to finish. It is generally the first step of a development deal. Some writers include snippets of funny dialogue in treatments to show a sense of humor; some use dialogue to show a particular writing style; others may use it simply to give the producer an idea of how the characters talk. Treatments range in length, with the average being about fifty double-spaced pages.

Turnaround. A script that is no longer in *development* at a studio or production company, but, according to the contract, is able to be sold elsewhere by the writer.

Tweaking. A minor writing adjustment that is made to a script.

Twist. An unpredictable turn-of-events in a script. Producers love 'em; audiences love 'em.

Unsolicited script. A script that is submitted without the recommendation of an agent, lawyer, or other industry professional. *See* Submission agreement.

Vanity deal. A production deal given by a studio to a *bankable* actor, often to keep the star happy.

Vehicle. A script that has a star-making role, or a part that will help an actor make a comeback. *Rocky* was the vehicle that made Sylvester Stallone a star, while *Boogie Nights* was the perfect comeback vehicle for actor Burt Reynolds.

WGA. *See* Writers Guild of America.

Wide. A term referring to the expansive distribution of a movie, as in, "The film is opening wide—in about 3,000 theaters."

Work for hire. A legal copyright term that is used when a screenwriter is hired to write a specific script for which the employer holds the copyright. Consider the implications. If the script is produced and a sequel is made, legally, the writer doesn't have claim to payment for the sequel.

Writers Guild of America (WGA). A labor union representing writers in all areas of the entertainment industry—motion picture, television, and radio. The Guild has over 12,000 members and offices on both the East and West Coasts. Although the Writers Guild East (WGAE) and Writers Guild West (WGAw) are affiliates, each has its own officers, which form the Guild's National Council. (For more information on the WGA, see the inset below.)

Written by. A coveted on-screen credit signifying that the story and script is the original work of the writer or writing team.

Written By. The name of the monthly journal of the WGAw.

Writers Guild of America

The Writers Guild of America (WGA) is made up of two unions—the New York-based Writers Guild East, and the Los Angeles-based Writers Guild West. Members of the WGA (of which there are over 12,000) are the primary creators of what is heard and seen on radio, television, and film in the United States. East and West are united for the common purpose of promoting and protecting the professional and artistic interests of the creative community.

Guild members may work on either coast or in between. They share the same benefits and work under the same rules and contracts. Members are obligated to work for *signatories*—producing entities who have contractually agreed to abide by the terms of the Guild's Minimum Basic Agreement (MBA). The MBA governs the conditions, compensation, rights, and responsibilities under which members of the Guild work. In addition to the Guild's contract with companies, they have a contract with agents. Members are obliged to be represented by only those agents who are signatory to the Guild's agreement.

Sleepless in Seattle

Screenplay by Nora Ephron and David S. Ward and Jeff Arch
Story by Jeff Arch

The following story is by Jeff Arch

Awake in Virginia

When you do a love story, you have to know what's going to keep the two people apart before you start the story. A love story is about the obstacles. I got very frustrated thinking of obstacles because they've all been taken—age: he's older, she's younger; she's older, he's younger, or different races, or political differences. None of them moved me. I wanted to come up with a love story that hadn't been done over and over again.

I was living in Virginia at the time, and I went into a room and started to think about it. And I got so frustrated that I actually got mad at these characters, and said, "The hell with it—what if they don't even meet?" And then I thought, what about two people who don't even know each other, but they meet on the very last page, on top of the Empire State Building on Valentine's Day.

Then I had to think about where I got those ideas. The two people that don't meet came from a French film called, *And Now, My Love*, written by Pierre Uytterhoeven and Claude Lelouch who also directed it. It tells two parallel stories that are not linked at all. You're watching this guy and you're watching this woman. Then at the very end, these two people who you've been tracking throughout the whole movie, sit down next to each other on an airplane. One thing Lelouch did that was kind of cool and I definitely stole it, is that throughout the movie, he connected them in these tiny subtle ways—like when each of them has coffee, they take three lumps of sugar in it. So they sit down in the airplane, both take coffee from the stewardess, both get three lumps of sugar. They look at each other and it

cuts to a shot of their bags going up on the conveyor belt together. This was the most romantic thing in the world, even though it was really only 30 seconds of the movie. The rest of the movie wasn't romantic at all. It had a lot to say. It was very political, and covered a whole century of turmoil in Europe, from the First World War on. But the ending was so powerful that everybody remembered, G_d, what a romantic movie. I never forgot that—two people who were living completely separate lives, sort of randomly destined, hooking up at the very end of the movie.

That gave me the courage to keep thinking of *Sleepless* in those terms—two romantic leads, destined for each other, who don't meet until the very end.

As for the Empire State Building, I remembered seeing *An Affair to Remember* when I was in college. Somehow the characters in my story had to decide, separately, to be there at the same time, so I had to figure out how that would happen. I thought about having the girl and her best friend watch the movie and the girlfriend says, "That's it! Send him a letter and say you're going to meet him there."

So that's pretty much the two big elements: a man and a woman meeting on top of the Empire State Building on Valentine's Day, and being linked by the best friend who gets her ideas by watching a classic tearjerker on TV.

Underneath all of this, there really is a boy-meets-girl, boy-loses-girl, boy-gets-girl story. It is a conventional three-act picture. It's just that they don't meet on camera. They meet when she hears him on the radio and that's the end of the first act. That's when her life and the story changes. Up until then, we're watching two separate people. They become linked when she hears him on the radio show.

Hear Ye! Hear Ye!

People always say, "Listen to that little voice inside you." Unless you're psychopathic, that little voice is always right. We always call it the *little* voice. I thought, how come we always listen to all of the big voices that are wrong and why don't we pay more attention to the *little* one that is right. So when she turns up the radio, to me that was a giant metaphor for what I was going through in my life at that point, which was turning up the voice I wanted to hear and tuning out all of the voices of discouragement and forget about it—all of the negative things that writers hear when we're trying to do what we're trying to do. I thought if this *little* voice is right, how come it's so little? And why don't we listen to it all of the time? It wasn't like I did this scientifically, but that was the thought process going on in my mind. I was listening to that *little* voice and coming up with this idea.

They All Laughed at Christopher Columbus...

I pitched the story to producers and studios and was told, "It's a really nice pitch, but you're out of your mind." Everybody said I was crazy. Everybody said that this movie will never get made. When I asked why not, I was told, "You couldn't write this." I wasn't taking that personally. They were saying that no one could write a 120-page romance between two people who don't meet till the very end. "And even if you could write it, no one will buy it. And if someone buys it, they won't be able to cast it because what two stars will want to be in it if they can't be in scenes together? And who's going to distribute a movie where the two stars don't get together until the last frame?" It was just too weird for everybody.

Don't Take "No" for an Answer

There wasn't a big bidding war for the script. A lot of places passed, but my agent had sent it to producer Gary Foster and he loved it. He sent it to TriStar and they passed. Gary suspected that they passed because they read the coverage on it, which wasn't good. He said, "You guys didn't read the script." He staked his reputation on it, saying, "Don't only read the coverage, you gotta read the script." When everybody at TriStar read the script, there was a four-four tie whether to buy it and make it or to pass on it again. Mike Medavoy, who was running the show at the time, had to be the tiebreaker. He read the script over the Memorial Day weekend and said, "Let's make the kid an offer."

Gary Foster, a producer whose passion to get up higher in the world was as strong as mine, had turned a "no" into a "yes." He wasn't doing it for me; he was doing it for himself, but he brought me along when he didn't have to. For that he's got eternal loyalty from me. I go to him first with every idea I get. He might have eventually made it bigger than he did; I might have eventually made it bigger than I did, but that's the one we made each other on.

Meanwhile, Back at the Studio...

As soon as Mike Medavoy said "yes," it was on a fast track. It was my first experience this far inside. In my mind, I wrote it for Kevin Costner and Meg Ryan. They both saw it very soon after TriStar bought it, and they both wanted to do it.

They sent the script to writer Gary Ross *(Pleasantville, Dave, Mr. Baseball, Big)*. Gary did a wonderful thing. He read my original first draft and sent it back saying, "What do you guys want to change about this? It's great. Don't change a word. Just shoot it." It was the best review I ever got, coming from a writer like Gary Ross. TriStar didn't want to hear that because they were nervous. I couldn't figure out why everyone was so nervous about this. It was what they wanted and they had two stars attached. They said it just puts more pressure on them to come up with a good rewrite. I said, "That's your problem? I'll do a good rewrite." I did a good rewrite.

They hired director Nick Castle. Nick decided to go with another writer, who will remain nameless, and who killed it. Emptied all the life out of it. Nick and Gary brought me back to resurrect it and I did, but what happened in the meantime is that the studio got more nervous and decided they wanted a rewrite where the two leads do meet. They said, "Let's have them meet under the same circumstances–the radio show, a widower–just have them meet earlier, then break them up for some reason, and have them get back together on top of the Empire State Building.

I was totally against that, but I could see why they wanted it. It was getting time to spend money. They were scared and wanted something more conventional. I wrote what they wanted and they were going to go ahead with it, but they still felt nervous, so they sent out the script to a lot of big writers.

There Are No Accidents

Eventually, they sent it to David Ward. Here's where the fluke came in. They meant to send David my rewrite where I had them meeting much earlier in the film, but somebody in the mail room at CAA, sent him the wrong one. They sent him my first draft.

David took the meeting and started off by saying, "Why do you want to change this?" During the course of their conversation, it came out that David and the studio were talking about two different versions of the script. When they finally realized that David was talking about my original one, and TriStar was talking about the draft where the two meet long before the end, David said, "You guys, this (my original script) is the one to do." And since he won an Oscar (*The Sting*, 1973), they said, "Okay." They didn't believe it from me, but they believed it from him.

Then they said, "Let's just make it funnier." David's brought them back to their senses, and for that I'll share credit with him forever.

Punch It Up

His draft still wasn't deemed funny enough. Gary Foster had this idea that Nora Ephron was the one. When he got her to take a look at it, she said, "Yes." Picture a slot machine where the wheels are spinning and one of them finally stops. That's what it was like when Nora came on. Something locked in and in an industry that worships stars, she was a star writer, and the fact that she wanted to do it meant something.

Nora's draft was funnier. The director didn't like it, so they played "creative differences," and hired Nora to direct. Nora brought on her sister Delia, and she and Nora did another rewrite.

In the meantime, the regime at TriStar changed. Everyone who had been in development with it and who knew me was gone. The new people that came in inherited a project that was just about a go picture, but they only knew Nora and the new team, so I got lost at the studio. Gary was smart and shrewd and nice and kept me involved the whole time, or I would have been gone from that point on.

Lights, Camera, Reaction

They shot it in 1992 and it premiered in '93. Everything that everybody said was wrong. We did get somebody to buy the script; and they got two people to be in it. Kevin Costner fell out along the way, but Tom Hanks and Meg Ryan were perfect. It wouldn't have occurred to me to cast Tom because my drafts had the character being a lot more reflective and sort of wistful. But Tom made it amazing–he was perfect–and like the rest of the world, now I can't see it any other way.

Often, reviews will pick on how *sentimental* a film is, as though it's a bad thing. I know what they mean by too *sentimental,* but to a lot of people *sentimental* is already *too* sentimental.

Nora was hired to throw some battery acid on it and keep it hip and cynical–the stuff that she does so well. Tom did a lot of his own stuff on it. Bringing Rob Reiner in, improvising a lot of that stuff, made it really funny. Rita Wilson's improv made it really funny. There are big belly laughs that I can't take credit for except for the fact that I set the foundation for them. I think that if you were laughing, you probably weren't laughing at anything I directly wrote, but if you were thinking about the movie a month later, that's probably something I did. I've been told that all the glibness and the belly laughs couldn't cover up the real human thing going on in the film.

Make Someone Happy. . .

How to sell your screenplay? The answer sounds like a Disney movie poster: Believe in yourself, and it's going to happen. Look at all of the screenwriters' stories and you'll see that the common denominator is that belief in themselves. Sometimes in life, not every time, but sometimes, you can be the only one who is right.

It all started one night, in that room in Virginia, and as soon as I heard those words in my head, *Sleepless in Seattle,* I knew that it was going to go all the way. I knew it was going to attract all the right people and also going to attract some wrong people, but it was going to be big enough and strong enough to shake them off, and every good thing that could come was going to come from doing this.

For like fifteen or twenty years before that, I kept thinking, I want to be successful. I want to be interviewed on television, in newspapers and magazines and have everyone think I'm wonderful. The question I was asking was, "What can I do to get famous?" Nothing happened. I got better as a writer, but nothing hap-

pened. Somewhere along the way, about two or three months before I thought of *Sleepless,* I started asking a different question. It was, "How could I get people to walk out of a movie in Finland holding hands?" Why Finland? If they've heard of you in Finland, they've heard of you everywhere. I just kept asking myself, "How can I get people in Finland to walk out of a movie holding hands?" That was the challenge.

What I noticed was that I switched to thinking about the audience rather than thinking about me. And as soon as I started thinking about what I'm going to *give* instead of what I'm going to *get,* I started getting everything I wanted. And it wasn't like a sneaky way to do it because I really was thinking of what can I give. I was reading books at that time that talked about seeing your work, not as a job, but as a service, and I bought into it because I didn't like what I'd been taught all of my life. Everything that my family would have laughed at or shaken their heads over, started making more sense than the stuff that they were telling me to do. It meant loving them, but throwing off all of the attitudes and taking on new attitudes that actually worked for me. Believing this Dale Carnegie kind of stuff worked. When I started thinking that I was given this ability and it's not for me, it's for the audience–how can I use it to please an audience–gradually I got everything I ever wanted, including the TV, newspaper and magazine interviews. Weirdly enough, one of the first places I was invited to speak was at an event in Helsinki–and there were the Finnish people holding hands.

When I was a twenty-two-year-old screenwriter trying to hit it overnight and I would see a screenwriting book, I would say, "Dammit, I want to be in one of those." Now I've been in a few, and I still think the whole thing is way more fascinating than I'll ever be. And as much as I hated that it took this long, I'm glad it did. I had too much to learn along the way.

Caught

by Edward Pomerantz
Based on his novel *Into It*

Getting a movie made is a miracle; getting it made well is a victory. *Caught* was *both*. Okay, so it took twenty-three years.

Establishing a Relationship

A bunch of us, including Sam Shepard and John Guare, were given grants to be playwrights-in-residence at the Yale Drama School. One of the requirements of the grant was to attend a film course that was given by directors Michael Roemer and Robert (Bob) M.Young. That's how I met and eventually became friends, collaborators and partners with Bob.

About seven years after my stint at Yale, in the early seventies, Dial Press was publishing my novel, *Into It*. Even then, I could feel it as a movie, so I gave Bob Young the galleys. He fell in love with it and instantly optioned it.

I wrote the first draft, and it was awful. I knew nothing about screenwriting then and just went CUT TO: CUT TO: CUT TO: In other words, I was faithful to the book, without turning it into a movie.

Bob and I weren't able to get the film made. The option expired and we each went on with our respective careers. Bob directed at least a dozen movies including, *Dominick and Eugene, Short Eyes, The Ballad of Gregorio Cortez, Triumph of the Spirit,* and *Extremities;* I went on to have a very comfortable career as a writer of television movies, miniseries, episodes, sitcoms, etc., for twenty years.

Actually, I got my first television writing job through Bob. I wrote an Afterschool Special called *Snowbound,* and Bob directed it. The day the Special aired, there was a national blizzard and all of America stayed home and watched it. My first television movie and it had one of the highest ratings in the history of daytime TV.

Over the years, even though Bob and I went on with our separate careers, we always kept in touch and would occasionally partner up on some project because we just love working together.

Staying *Into It*

Throughout the '80s, even though I was very busy writing four television movies a year, between assignments I would always go back to the adaptation of my novel, just simply out of a stubbornness on my part, to get it right. One of the problems with it is that it's an ensemble piece, telling the story of four people. But it was like trying to get five fingers into a four-fingered glove, there was always one story left dangling. It wasn't fully integrated. It wasn't the script it had to be yet.

The novel, *Into It,* on which the eventual film, *Caught* was based, was always a great writing sample for me to get film assignments. It's very tight, economical and dialogue-driven. If people wanted to see how I handled dialogue, they wouldn't just read a script of mine, they would read this particular book. When I had a meeting with someone who was intelligent and sensitive to language and to literature, I would say, "You know, you really ought to read my book as well as my latest screenplay." Every once in awhile, someone would read this book and just get knocked out by it. Around 1990, somebody working for a television production company, read the book and called up a friend of hers who was a hot young director and told him about it. The director read it and called me and said, "This is a great book. I want it to be my next movie." He was in Los Angeles and wanted to meet me. At the start of my career, I was told that in order to make my career as a screenwriter, I would have to move to L.A. I never did that. But I have and do spend a lot of time in L.A., and I was there then, and we met.

Caught in the Middle

The next draft came out of the relationship with this director. His interest gave me incentive to go on working on it. One of the reasons I don't want to be a director is I welcome and need to bounce off another person's intelligence and sensibility and point of view. I find that very stimulating. I need to be challenged. It also makes writing a much less lonely experience.

This director and I got along very well and the script really advanced. Then this director got a chance to make another movie and it turned out to be a huge hit. He said, "Eddie, now that I have the blockbuster and I've got my dolly and my crane, I can't go back to making low budget independent films."

That's what *Caught* clearly was, a low-budget, independent film. In the twenty-year period of trying to get it made, there were attempts to sell it to a studio. It was a waste of time.

This is a dark ambiguous piece—in other words, it's not *Rocky,* which put an end to the *Chinatowns* and *Shampoos*—you are not being asked to root for the character, or sympathize with him. What you're asked to identify with is the character's situation. It's a there-but-for-the-grace-of-God-go-I story, a story in which the character makes moves that make you cry, "No. No. Don't do it." And he does it. It's a movie that ends tragically, not happily for any of the characters. So if you're selling a dark, low-budget tragedy, I don't think you should try to convince MGM to make it. You'd be wasting your time. You

have to realistically assess your script, and you have to realistically assess the marketplace.

The Solution

When the other director said that he could no longer be involved with *Caught* because he was on another track, I introduced that director to Bob Young, with whom I had stayed in constant touch. They had lunch and basically, the other director passed the torch back to Bob. It was all very friendly and terrific. Bob read the new version and still had trouble with the last third of the script. That put me and Bob back into that creative partnership again . . . asking questions . . . talking. All of a sudden, something clicked and I knew how to solve the problem. That next draft gave Bob the confidence in the script that he needed to go out into his world to try to make it happen.

So now we're up to about 1993. After two years of the game we all play, thinking we have the money, then we don't, then we have it again, then not, Bob took another movie that, ultimately, paid off for us. The movie was with Maria Conchita Alonso, who Bob's wife Lili remembered two years later, when we had decided to make the family in our movie Latino. The reason for that change came about when I went back to the old neighborhood where my original novel took place, and I saw that the neighborhood was now completely Hispanic. That gave me an idea. Bob had worked with Edward James Olmos on many movies and was friendly with him, so I called Bob and said, "What if we do it with Eddie Olmos?" Bob said, "Fantastic." He went over to Eddie Olmos' house and he read the script to him. Eddie said, "Okay. I'm in." And then later Maria came onboard.

If this was a studio picture, the last thing you would do is change it to a Latino family. For all of the studios' talk about diversity, nobody's looking to make a movie about Latinos, with the exception of *La Bamba.* And this was no *La Bamba.*

Once we had Eddie and Maria, and Bob saw what a contribution they would make, it became very real. So now, it wasn't just me fighting for my baby's life, it was also Bob, Eddie and Maria. The package was slowly evolving because people wanted to work with each other; people loved the material; people saw this as an opportunity to do something deeper and richer than anything they had done before. This was a political statement for us—an opportunity to cast Latinos in parts that would ordinarily go to North American white people. We were involved in doing a crossover film. This became very exciting to us. It was also a handle on getting the movie made. Yeah, you may not be able to make it in the Hollywood world with that cast, but you can get it made in another kind of world. And once all the right elements were in place, that's all that mattered to us—getting it made.

Let's Hear It for Bob

Bob disappeared for eight months to do two Showtime movies. As soon as he finished them, he called and said, "Eddie, I made a lot of money doing my Showtime movies and, at this stage of my life and career, I'm committed to making the kind of movies I want to make. I don't want to be a director for hire. We are going to make this movie come hell or high water." It takes *that* kind of commitment to get a movie made.

So after three years, Bob went out and got the money. He called in favors. He got on a plane to Washington. He went to people who loved and respected his work. He was totally committed to raising the money, and within four months, he had it. We were in business. We also had total and complete artistic freedom and control. Bob believes in creating a climate of inclusion on all of his films. That means that the DP (director of photography), the editor, the costumer, the set designer—everybody—is encouraged to express themselves, come up with ideas.

After twenty-five years as a freelancer, after having written every kind of movie you can for television and features, I can tell you that *Caught* was the model for the way things should be for the writer. The film is absolutely faithful and true to what I wrote. What was on the page is on the screen and even more so. I was totally included in the filmmaking process. I was on the set. I was at the dailies. I was in the editing room.

It was an extraordinary experience . . . a very, very rare one.

The Way It Was

The first draft of *Caught* was written for Bob Young in 1972. The project came around again to Bob in 1993. We made the movie in '95. We were the centerpiece Sundance premiere in '96. That's when Sony Pictures Classics picked it up for theatrical distribution. We were in the theaters in the fall of '96. Bob and I did Q & A sessions across the country. The theaters were glutted at that time with independent films. We got raves from Rex Reed and the New York Press, and a mixed review from Janet Maslin in the New York Times. We were out of the theaters in about a month. Then we were given a great gift. On the last day of December in 1996, when the movie was already dumped, Margo Jefferson in the New York Times, wrote an article referring to *Caught* as "unjustly neglected." She went on to describe it as a "masterly little film that keeps generating tension and psychological force, placing the seamy sexual desperation of film noir alongside the rigorous proprieties of classical tragedy." It was a major review and as a result *Caught* was re-released in '97.

The Way It Is

My story is not, "How to Sell Your Screenplay and Get Rich." My story is about how to get your movie made, if you're lucky. Getting a movie made buys you other important things. It buys you an eternal life. This movie is constantly being discovered and rediscovered through video and through cable. It's on Bravo or IFC or the Sundance Channel every few months. When it's on, it generates more video sales because people may come in the middle of it and want to see it from the beginning, or it creates word of mouth. It has this regenerative life. It has also bought me the world, in the sense that I've been invited and gone to conferences all over the world with the movie, and still do. *Caught* has also given new life to the novel on which it was based. *Into It* is now available through: www.iUniverse.com.

The studios are there to hire you and fire you. You can get work, and if you're on an A-list or a B-list you get good bucks, but if you want to get your movie made, that's a whole different story. Get it made yourself.

If you realize that your script is a hard sell for any number of reasons—there's currently nothing out there like it; it doesn't follow a comfortable formula; there's something unique about it that makes them want to point to that something, and then say "no" because of it—whatever the reason, you've got to find someone who will legitimize your script. You must get a champion for it. That someone can be an agent, producer, star, or director. If the script is a hard sell, I go for a director that has some clout. I go to people I know. *Caught* bought me a lot of friends. I'm also very much out there in the world because of all of the conferences I attend. I'm a creative advisor at the International Sundance Lab every year in Mexico. I'm a visiting writer in Cuba. But there are times when I exhaust all of my connections. Then I do exactly what every twenty-year-old should do. I see a movie that I fall in love with, and I get in touch with the director or the producer. I figure out how to get to that person. Again, I do have the extra benefit of knowing people in the business, and of being able to say that I'm the guy who wrote *Caught*. But even without a track record, it's still possible to get to people.

The most important thing is that I don't contact anyone randomly. I very selectively choose those people whose work I make a deep connection with. I think there's a common sensibility here. If this person reads my material, I think he'll get it.

The champion of your movie—any of the four people to go after: agent, producer, director, actor—has to get as excited about making this movie as you are. That person has to locate what it is about this movie that makes them have as much of an investment in getting it made as you do. I'm not talking about money; I'm talking about some psychological or emotional investment. *Caught* was a major breakthrough for Maria Conchita Alonso. If the actor sees the script as an opportunity to do something different, something that the studio system doesn't allow him to do, you stand a chance of getting that actor attached. That's how you get a Bruce Willis and a Kevin Spacey.

You've got to write a great cover letter saying why that person (director, producer or star) is the one for your script. Of course there's no guarantee that the script, or even the letter, is going to get read, but you at least stand a chance.

A lot of people think writing a movie is easy. When you go to a play, you have to lean forward and listen. When you pick up a book, you have to read it. But when you go to a movie, you just sit there and the movie happens to you. You don't have to do any work. Well get this: The novel *Into It* was published after one draft; the screenplay *Caught* took twenty drafts over twenty years. So you can't tell me that writing a screenplay doesn't take the same commitment, sweat, talent and imagination that a novel or play does. The real miracle and victory is not just getting a movie made, it's writing a good one.

CHAPTER 2

THE SCREENPLAY

It's "all systems go." You are determined to get your screenplay read by the right people with the hopes of getting a foothold in the film industry. As you saw in Chapter 1, as long as you have faith in your talent and are persistent in your efforts, there is a good chance that you will be successful. To further stack the odds in your favor, it's important to be focused and to set a solid foundation for your plan.

This chapter is all about your screenplay. We're not going to tell you *how* to write it—you've already done that, right?—but we *are* going to give you pointers that can make your screenplay as saleable as possible. We'll begin by covering who should read your spec script for the purposes of gaining valuable feedback *before* you attempt to sell it. We'll even tell you how to instruct your family and friends to give you honest and helpful criticism. Then we'll provide you with the industry's standard submission guidelines for your script. Without the proper formatting and acceptable industry "look," your work may never be read. Finally, to help protect all of your hard work, we'll end this chapter with guidelines on how to have it registered and/or copyrighted.

BEFORE TRYING TO SELL YOUR WORK

Before trying to sell your screenplay, it is recommended that you have the script read and critiqued. Why? Because your screenplay represents you and your capabilities as a writer. Wouldn't you rather face some criticism early in the process when you can still do something about it, rather than experience the same criticism by way of a rejection from an agent, development exec, or producer? It's good common sense. The question is: Who should you ask to read your work? Your mother? Your next door neighbor? Your film teacher? The answer may be, "All (or none) of the above."

Initially, our personal feeling was that you should show your work only to people who could either buy it or help you sell it—in other words, those who are in some way connected to the film industry. However, after talking with many successfully produced screenwriters, we have come to change our tune. The majority agrees that if you know and trust the opinion of someone in the industry, have him read your script; but if you don't know anyone, and most people don't, it is important to get input from nonprofessionals.

We even suggest you continue letting carefully selected nonprofessionals read your spec script *after* it has been rewritten and polished and is ready to be sold. When you read the *From Script to Screen* stories at the end of each chapter, you'll see how important it is to get your work out there—and not only to industry people. You never know who is going to be the one who gets it to the one who gives you a deal. Still, there are major considerations in letting just anyone read your material, especially right after you've completed the first draft.

Getting Feedback

Everyone's a critic, and criticism can be harmful if it's not given properly. It can destroy confidence. Even worse, it can destroy a perfectly good script by causing you to change things that shouldn't necessarily be changed. It can also dampen your enthusiasm for the script. But by

---

PROSE FROM A PRO

Somewhere Between Drafts...
by Richard Styles
Writer-producer-director: *Cease Fire, Shallow Grave, Escape, Sorceress II, Picture Perfect Murders.*

Very few people write a first draft and sell it. Usually it's the twentieth draft of your screenplay that you sell. When I get to my fourth or fifth draft, I have a few people whose taste level I trust read it. They are people in the business who have made a few films. They understand the process. They understand what sells. I give them my script and tell them to be brutally honest with me. There comes a time when all screenwriters get too close to their material and lose objectivity. You need to have that third eye from several people who have taste and talent and who can tell you if there's something wrong with a character, or if certain questions weren't answered, or if certain things don't make sense.

Another technique I use is having a group of actors read my screenplay aloud. I'm always amazed at the inconsistencies I find when other people are reading it and all I'm doing is listening to it.

facing constructive criticism from people whose opinions you respect, and by assessing it appropriately, you can get your screenplay into the best shape possible before sending it out to be sold.

Professional *readers* or *story analysts,* whose role in the industry is detailed in Chapter 3, work for film studios, production companies, and agencies. They are the ones who read through scores of submitted screenplays, and then prepare detailed written assessments—called *coverage*—of each. Coverage helps company executives decide on whether or not to accept the projects. These readers advise that when choosing people to read your script, select those whose opinions you trust and who are savvy when it comes to television, the movies, and pop culture in general. Completing the *TV Guide* crossword puzzle doesn't necessarily mean that they qualify.

If you are like most starting-out screenwriters, you probably don't know any industry professionals who would be willing to critique your work. So where should you turn? The following list offers some suggestions.

■ Screenwriting classes at a college or film school are the perfect arenas to find help. A film teacher may be the most constructive critic of your work.

■ Fellow film students, who have some knowledge and interest in the film industry, can be good sounding boards. A give-and-take spec script exchange with classmates can provide helpful criticism for your work, as well as help sharpen your skills in analyzing the work of others.

■ A number of online websites provide services for analyzing screenplays—often by professional screenwriters. However, before you agree to pay for this type of service, be sure to check the credits of the story analyst. Ask for references and a sample coverage report. (See the Resource List for script consultants.)

In addition to sharing your work with people who are somewhat involved in the industry, you should also consider handing your script to any willing friends or family members. Invariably, you will hand them the script and say, "I want you to be honest and tell me what you really think." Just be aware that if your nearest and dearest do not absolutely love your work, you are likely to feel

There are many writers who begin the process of scriptwriting with a treatment—a detailed scene-by-scene account of the story. Then they tell the story to family and friends *before* writing the actual script. Judging by the reactions they get from the treatment, the writers are able to rework the story and its structure until it holds everyone's attention from start to finish. *Then* they write the story in script form. This way, the script may need fewer, if any, rewrites before it's ready to be submitted.

PROSE FROM A PRO

Learn to Take Criticism
by Screenwriter Barry Strugatz
Co-writer: *Married to the Mob* and *She Devil.*

When you finish a screenplay, it's hard to look at it objectively. You're too close to it. That's why it's a good idea to hear others' opinions. It may feel like a punch to the stomach, but it's all part of the process.

When first starting out, many writers have difficulty listening to criticism—they get defensive or they may think their ideas are obvious. But if several people are having the same problem, don't dismiss it. They're seeing something that you're missing. Figure out what's bothering them.

wounded. You may even harbor hidden anger toward the members of your family or circle of friends who tell you that your baby is ugly. But hey, get a grip. Remember way back in Chapter 1 when you told yourself that you have what it takes to be a screenwriter? That you can stand up to criticism and benefit by it? Don't forget this. If you can't handle anything but praise at this early stage of the game, maybe you ought to rethink your career and give this book to a writer who will put it to good use.

If you really want your family and friends to read your script, and they really want to read it, fine, but instruct them on how to give constructive criticism. Tell them to read your script with a pen and pad close by. (You may want to give them these items along with your script.) Ask them to jot down the page and line numbers of any spelling, punctuation, or unintentional grammatical errors they find. Also, instruct them to note any pages on which they have a question about a specific scene or character, or if something is unclear, or unjustified, or just doesn't sit right. Also tell them to make note of the pages with scenes that they absolutely love. Providing specific criteria will help structure their criticism so that it is most helpful and least damaging.

Keep in mind that just because advice is given, you don't have to follow it, unless, of course, you fully agree with whatever seems to need fixing. If you keep hearing the same criticism over and over, chances are you should rework that troublesome area. This is another reason why it is wise to get feedback for your work from a number of people, not just one or two.

While you're deciding on exactly who should read your screenplay, we suggest that you read Jeff Arch's *Sleepless in Seattle* story beginning on page 29. Jeff talks about one's "inner voice." Although he talks about it in a different context than script analysis, the point is to *always* trust your inner voice. Let it guide you in determining who should read your screenplay and which advice to heed.

A Gentle Warning

Many screenwriters take writing classes for discipline, to hone their craft, to commiserate with other writers, and to come away with inspiring and encouraging input from their teachers and fellow classmates. As mentioned earlier, this can be a great forum for gaining constructive criticism. However, we would be remiss if we didn't make you aware of a potential negative aspect of sharing your story with classmates.

Expose your script to other screenwriters and there's a chance you may find a poignant line of yours, or one of your sight gags, or even that clever plot twist you invented in one of the writer's next scripts. It can and does occasionally happen. With writers, these are not necessarily vicious acts of thievery, but rather subconscious acts of plagiarism.

Writing classes can be extremely helpful in many ways, and we certainly aren't advising against them, but forewarned is forearmed. To help curb any tendency that your fellow students may have to inadvertently use your ideas, offer to read your work in front of the entire class whenever the opportunity arises. This will establish the writing as yours in everyone's mind, and other members of the class may make a conscious effort not to *borrow* any dialogue or plot lines.

Another Thought

Reading and critiquing a script is a task that requires a lot of time. It's not always easy to find people who are willing to do it. And it's almost impossible to get people to read a script a *second* time. So, before you give your work to anyone—from your movie-loving best friend to someone who may know someone in the industry—make sure it's the best that it can be in terms of story, character development, dialogue, and entertainment value.

Also, out of respect to whomever reads your script, be sure to hand them a clean proofread copy. More about that later in this chapter.

PROSE FROM A PRO

Show Gratitude

by Screenwriter Barry Strugatz

Co-writer: *Married to the Mob* and *She Devil.*

When you ask someone to read a screenplay you've written, realize that you are asking that person to do two to three hours of solid work as a favor. So if someone agrees to look at your stuff, be appreciative.

GENRE

Screenwriter Daniel Waters (*Demolition Man, Batman Returns, Heathers, Hudson Hawk, The Adventures of Ford Fairlane*) presents an argument for giving your script to anyone who wants to read it. He showed his script to his roommates, who in turn gave it to their friends. A couple of those friends gave the script to their agents. One of those agents loved the script and, as Daniel Waters put it, "The rest is quasi-history."

While this book does not tell you how to write a screenplay, we would be remiss if we didn't start this chapter with the importance of genre, especially in relation to your script's first few decisively significant pages.

A film *genre* is a type, category, or style of film that has instantly recognizable elements, mainly the theme of the story, the setting, the structure, and its effect on the audience. Way back when films were churned out by a handful of major studios, there were a few plain-and-simple genres—action, adventure, comedy, gangster, horror, musical, science fiction, romance, and western. Now there are more genres and endless sub-genres, also called *crossbreeds* or *hybrids*. Why, you may be asking, is categorizing your script important?

Tell someone in the business that you've written a screenplay, and one of the first questions asked will be, "What genre is it?" The genre puts the listener into the frame of mind for the story that will follow.

Don't *you* think in terms of film genres? When you need a laugh, you watch a screwball comedy. When you feel like having a good cry, you get a box of tissues and rent a tragic love story. When you want to be frightened, you choose a thriller. The marketing of most movies emphasizes genre to help attract the audience that's partial to that specific movie type. There was even a genre-inspired panel discussion at a Writer's Guild of America West event that was billed as "Chick Flick versus Dick Flick."

The first few pages of your screenplay are crucial, and usually determine whether or not the entire script will be read. One of the deciding factors is whether or not your pages live up to the genre promised in your query and cover letters. Establish the genre as soon as possible. If you've written a comedy, give the reader something to laugh at within the first page or two—the sooner, the better. If it's a spy-thriller, find a way to intrigue the reader within the first few pages, even if it's not integral to your main story. Whatever the genre, set the appropriate tone almost immediately. Once the script sells, you may be able to change the beginning to one that doesn't introduce the genre loud-and-clear during the first minute or two of the movie. Then again, you may not. For now, help get the script read by delivering the genre the reader is expecting.

Identifying the Genre

Most films can be described by more than one genre, usually by three or more. For getting your foot in the door, and for pitching purposes, keep it simple by selecting the one or two genres that best describe the main theme of your script. What follows is an extensive list of film genres and sub-genres, along with brief descriptions of each. These categorizations are not an exact science. They don't follow any industry guidelines that are set in stone, and many overlap. To help you zoom in on the most appropriate genre (or genres) of your screenplay, Robert Pardi, video reviewer for *TV Guide Online,* has helped us provide examples of some quintessential films for each.

ACTION. Film that is characterized by exciting physical acts—daring feats, fights, and chases, usually with violence. And the hero wins.
> *Die Hard* (1988)
> *Speed* (1994)

ACTION-ADVENTURE. *See* Action; Adventure.
> *Romancing the Stone* (1984)
> *The Perfect Storm* (2000)

ACTION-SUSPENSE. *See* Action; Suspense.
> *Deliverance* (1972)
> *Ransom* (1996)
> *Double Jeopardy* (1999)

ADVENTURE. Exciting stories, often with elements of action, that commonly involve travel and exploration in exotic locales.
> *The African Queen* (1951)
> *Raiders of the Lost Ark* (1981)

ANIMATION. Considered by some to be more of a film technique than an actual genre, animated films—cartoons—are often geared toward children.
> *Fantasia* (1940)
> *Beauty and the Beast* (1991)

BIBLICAL EPIC. Classical story from the Bible.
> *The Ten Commandments* (1923, 1956)
> *Ben-Hur* (1926, 1959)

BIG HEIST / CAPER. Film with a major robbery as the pivotal theme.
> *Topkapi* (1964)
> *How to Steal a Million* (1966)
> *The Thomas Crown Affair* (1968, 1999)
> *Charley Varrick* (1973)

BIOGRAPHY. Film depicting the life of a real person.
> *Gods and Monsters* (1998)
> *Hurricane* (1999)

BUDDY. Film featuring two people of the same sex as the principal relationship.
> *Butch Cassidy and the Sundance Kid* (1969)
> *Thelma & Louise* (1991)

CAPER. *See* Big Heist/Caper.

COMEDY. A film that's funny.
> *The Full Monty* (1997)
> *Analyze This* (1999)

COMEDY, DARK / BLACK. Film that treats a serious subject with a cynical and mocking sense of humor.

Prizzi's Honor (1985)

Dr. Strangelove or: How I Learned to Stop Worrying and Love the Bomb (1964)

COMEDY, ROMANTIC. Film in which anything can happen and usually does (nothing too serious, just laughable to the audience) to keep the man and woman from becoming a couple . . . until it all works out at the end.

Runaway Bride (1999)

What Women Want (2000)

COMEDY, SCREWBALL. Zany and chaotic, these sophisticated lighthearted films, which were prominent in the 1930s, often featured a romance between a wealthy liberated woman and a middle-class man. Their political incorrectness provided a real escape for moviegoers during the dark days of the Depression.

Bringing Up Baby (1938)

Flirting With Disaster (1996)

COMEDY, SLAPSTICK. Film that is funny in a physical, pie-in-the-face way.

It's a Mad, Mad, Mad, Mad World (1963)

Ace Ventura, Pet Detective (1993)

COMING-OF-AGE. Film in which the lead goes through an event—perhaps a rite of passage—that results in a transformation from adolescence to adulthood.

Stand by Me (1986)

Circle of Friends (1995)

COURTROOM DRAMA. Film involving a legal case and a trial. Often a challenging and excellent showcase for powerful, intelligent writing.

Witness for the Prosecution (1957)

Inherit the Wind (1960)

CRIME. Film that depicts the rise and fall of a real or fictitious criminal(s)—bank robber, mur-derer, extortionist, kidnapper, or any other lawbreaker. Typically combined with other genres, such as detective, mystery, gangster, suspense/thriller, and film noir.

In Cold Blood (1967)

Dillinger (1973)

DATE. Usually a romantic comedy.

When Harry Met Sally (1989)

Sleepless in Seattle (1993)

DETECTIVE / MYSTERY. Film in which the detective—who may be an actual detective, or a lawyer, medical examiner, journalist, insurance investigator, determined mother, or rape victim—looks for clues to a crime and eventually solves it.

Murder on the Orient Express (1974)

Basic Instinct (1993)

DISASTER. Usually a big-budget film depicting a natural or manmade catastrophe or series of horrific events. Typically includes special effects.

Twister (1996)

Titanic (1997)

DOCUMENTARY. A film that presents a political, social, or historical subject in a factual manner. Often includes interviews that are accompanied by voice-over narration.

Nanook of the North (1922)

Hoop Dreams (1994)

DRAMA. A film with great conflict and strong emotions.

Casablanca (1942)

Castaway (2000)

You Can Count on Me (2000)

EPIC, HISTORICAL. Generally a full-blown depiction of an historic period of time, featuring a somewhat fictionalized version of the era's dramatic events and the characters involved. This genre dates back to the days of silent movies.

Braveheart (1995)

Elizabeth (1998)

EROTIC DRAMA. Sexually arousing film.

The Pillow Book (1996)

Eyes Wide Shut (1999)

FAMILY. Film that is geared for children, although adults may enjoy it as well. (Typically, adults don't attend family films unless they are accompanying children.)

The Parent Trap (1961), (1998)

Home Alone (1990)

FANTASY. Film that creates a world and/or characters and/or situations that defy the laws of nature, physics, and other earthly realities.

Big (1988)

Being John Malkovich (1999)

FANTASY MUSICAL. *See* Fantasy; Musical.

The Wizard of Oz (1939)

Brigadoon (1954)

FARCE. Film featuring exaggerated characters in exaggerated situations, often played for laughs.

La Cage aux Folles (1978)

FEEL GOOD. Film that is particularly satisfying because good triumphs over evil, the underdog wins, and everyone lives happily ever after.

Rocky (1976)

Music From the Heart (1999)

FILM NOIR. French for "black/dark film," movies in this genre are characterized by dark, bleak pessimistic moods, and cynical, disillusioned heroes and villains, usually set in a violent, seedy world of crime and corruption.

The Maltese Falcon (1941)

Sunset Boulevard (1950)

Touch of Evil (1958)

FISH-OUT-OF-WATER. Film in which the lead character is placed in an unfamiliar environment, making for fun and adventurous situations.

"Crocodile" Dundee (1986)

City Slickers (1991)

GANGSTER. Film that depicts the rise and fall of a real or fictional criminal or criminals.

The Godfather (1972)

Goodfellas (1990)

HOLOCAUST. Film involving any aspect of the genocide of European Jews and others by the Nazis before and during World War II.

Schindler's List (1993)

Life Is Beautiful (1998)

HORROR. Film in which the monstrous leading character terrorizes his victims, while appealing to the audience's fear of violence and death.

Psycho (1960)

Nightmare on Elm Street (1985)

JUNGLE. If it isn't a Tarzan adventure, this type of film is usually about a hunter or anthropologist who is in search of a lost artifact or other treasure that is hidden in the jungle.

Tarzan the Ape Man (1932)

Jungle Heat (1974)

MARTIAL ARTS. Action film in which most of the action is in a form of martial arts.

Rush Hour (1998)

The Crow (1994)

MELODRAMA. *See* Woman's film.

MILITARY. Film involving military personnel and most often linked with another genre, such as courtroom drama, action-adventure, and biography.

The Caine Mutiny (1954)

Dirty Dozen (1967)

A Few Good Men (1992)

MUSICAL. Real American-born film genre, featuring singing and dancing. Today, these films are mostly animation, while real people are cast in Musical Biographies.

Singin' in the Rain (1952)
The Sound of Music (1965)
Grease (1978)
Moulin Rouge (2000)

MUSICAL BIOGRAPHY. A film that depicts the life of a real person and includes song and dance numbers. In most modern musicals, the songs are an integral part of the story, unlike the traditional musicals in which an orchestra appears out of nowhere as the star bursts into song to emphasize a feeling.

Yankee Doodle Dandy (1942)
Funny Girl (1968)
Topsy Turvy (1999)

MYSTERY. *See* Detective/Mystery.

MYTH. Traditional, usually ancient story or legend, explaining a culture's basic beliefs about the universe.

Jason and the Argonauts (1963)
Highlander (1986)
First Knight (1995)

PRISON. Film that deals with some aspect of incarceration, often a prisoner who is unjustly jailed, or one who is planning an escape.

Escape from Alcatraz (1979)
The Shawshank Redemption (1994)
Dead Man Walking (1995)
The Green Mile (1999)

ROAD. Starting with the Bing Crosby/Bob Hope series of pictures in the 1940s and 1950s, these films, usually comedies, involve characters who travel from one place to another, experiencing mishaps along the way.

Road to Bali (1952)

Midnight Run (1988)
Boys on the Side (1995)

ROMANCE. Love relationship between two people, in which emotions, sentimentality, and sacrifice add to the story's romance. Often classified as a "woman's film."

Three Coins in the Fountain (1954)
An Affair to Remember (1957)
Sabrina (1954, 1995)
Notting Hill (1999)

ROMANCE, NERVOUS (OR NEUROTIC). Not-too-common sub-genre in which the romantic lead is a nervous or neurotic wreck.

Annie Hall (1977)
Modern Romance (1981)
As Good as It Gets (1997)

SATIRE. Film in which human vice or folly is attacked with irony, derision, or wit.

Network (1976)
Cold Comfort Farm (1995)
Wag the Dog (1997)
Bullworth (1998)

SCIENCE FICTION (SCI-FI). Type of fantasy film featuring persons, places, and/or things that are unknown or inexplicable, and often not of this planet. Typically, films in this genre involve futuristic technology, unknown forces, and fantastical feats such as time travel and interplanetary communication.

The Time Machine (1960, 2001)
E.T. The Extra-Terrestrial (1982)
Aliens (1986)
Independence Day (1996)

SENIOR CITIZEN. A film featuring people who are old enough to collect social security.

Cocoon (1985)
Grumpy Old Men (1993)
The Crew (2000)

SPOOF. Film with a funny or amusing spin on a noncomedic genre or subject.
> *Airplane!* (1980)
> *Austin Powers: The Spy Who Shagged Me*
> (1999)

SPORTS. Film that features the team, coach, and/or players of a specific sport.
> *North Dallas Forty* (1979)
> *Hoosiers* (1986)
> *A League of Their Own* (1992)

SPY / ESPIONAGE. Film that involves foreign agents whose mission typically is world dominance.
> *Notorious* (1946)
> *The Spy Who Came in From the Cold* (1965)
> *The World Is Not Enough* (1999)

SUPERNATURAL. Film that involves ghosts, spirits, miracles, or any other type of extraordinary phenomena, and is often combined with other genres, such as horror or comedy.
> *Ghost* (1990)
> *The Sixth Sense* (1999)
> *What Lies Beneath* (2000)

SUSPENSE / THRILLER. Anxiety-filled, suspenseful nailbiter in which the audience constantly fears for the life of the leading character or characters.
> *Cape Fear* (1961, 1991)
> *Wait Until Dark* (1967)
> *Fatal Attraction* (1987)

SWASHBUCKLER. Film that features the exploits of a swaggering swordsman or adventurer. The classic leading sword-wielding swashbuckler actor was Errol Flynn.
> *Captain Blood* (1935)
> *Robin Hood: Prince of Thieves* (1991)
> *Mask of Zorro* (1998)

THRILLER.*See* Suspense/Thriller.

VIGILANTE. Film in which the hero takes the law into his own hands.
> *Magnum Force* (1973)
> *Death Wish* (1974)
> *Eye for an Eye* (1995)

WAR / ANTI-WAR. Film acknowledging the horrors of war and often paired with other genres, such as romance, satire, and suspense. It can be an epic film with a cast of thousands, or a low-budget movie about an underground movement.
> *From Here to Eternity* (1953)
> *Paths of Glory* (1957)
> *Saving Private Ryan* (1998)

WESTERN. Film that takes place in the Western part of the United States, usually during the late 1800s, and features cowboys, Native Americans, and a good guys-versus-bad guys theme. Westerns are one of the earliest motion picture genres.
> *Silverado* (1985)
> *The Unforgiven* (1992)
> *Maverick* (1994)

WOMAN, GUTSY. Film in which a woman triumphs over a situation in which the odds are against her. This sub-genre of "Woman's Film" gets the *Norma Rae* Award for having a meaty part for an actress.
> *Silkwood* (1983)
> *Working Girl* (1988)
> *Erin Brockovich* (2000)

WOMAN'S FILM. Usually an emotional tearjerker. Sometimes dubbed "Chick Flick."
> *Mildred Pierce* (1945)
> *Terms of Endearment* (1983)
> *Steel Magnolias* (1989)

Making Genre Work for You

Some producers and
directors are partial to and
specialize in certain genres,
while others don't want to
be genre typecast—they
want to try something
new each time out.

When you want to submit your screenplay to a producer, director, or actor, take into consideration the genres of the films they tend to make. Be sure that your screenplay is the type of project they are likely to take on. On the contrary, if you come across a been-there/done-that producer, who wants to try something new each time out, make sure the genre of your script is one that he hasn't produced yet, and use it as a selling point.

In 1962, Frank Perry produced and directed *David and Lisa,* a low-budget, independent film about the relationship between two mentally disturbed teenagers. Much to the surprise of everyone who had anything to do with the film, including and especially Frank Perry, the film turned out to be a real sleeper. It grossed tons of money, and put independent filmmaking on the commercially viable map.

Years later, Lydia became Frank Perry's assistant. One of her responsibilities was to read the scripts that were sent to him. Almost every script that crossed her desk was about the relationship between two troubled teenagers. This film genre, however, was the only kind Frank did *not* want to do. He had done it already, and was interested in exploring other genres.

Just as there are producers and directors who don't want to be genre typecast, there are those who are partial to and specialize in specific genres. If you know that your screenplay fulfills the promise of the genre—your thriller will have 'em on the edge of their seats, your buddy-sports story will have them cheering out loud, your horror story will have them horrified—you may want to contact the development people who work for the appropriate genre producers or directors and use it as a selling point.

To help you find those producers and directors, make a list of films that fall into the same category as yours, then go online to the Internet Movie Database (www.IMDb.com) and type in the name of the films on your list, one at a time. Each film provides a complete list of cast and crew members. Click on the name of anyone—director, producers, writers, actors—and you will get a complete listing of the projects with which that person is affiliated. Looking at the director's (or producer's) complete body of work will help you determine whether or not he specializes in your specific genre. (More about preparing a list of prospective industry players is found in Chapter 4.)

Genre Plus Opportunity Equals a Sale

In some instances, your script's genre can help you get your foot in the door. If a development person is looking for a romantic-comedy for a particular actor, and you happen to have a romantic-comedy, your script has a good chance of being read and considered. Here's a perfect example of how the genre of a property was responsible for initiating a sale for our friend, novelist Erika Holzer.

Erika's first book, *Double Crossing*, had been published, and she thought it would make a good film. When she and her husband went to Los Angeles on "nonbook" business, she decided that while she was there, she would interview theatrical agents in the hopes of finding one who might be able to sell the film rights to her book. She asked writer-friends for contacts, and by the time she got to the West Coast, she had several appointments with prospective agents. Although she connected with an excellent agent, he wasn't able to get a film deal for her novel.

Erika wrote a second novel, *Inferno*, and thought that it, too, would make a good film. We agreed with its film potential, and were able to get the manuscript to Paramount Pictures' literary department in New York. This unpublished manuscript was returned with a "Thank you, but it's not for us at this time" rejection letter. We were told by our contact at Paramount that the reader saw the book's potential, but at the time, the studio was not looking for that kind of story.

Fast forward about a year later. *Inferno* was published in hardcover with a different title. Erika went back to the California theatrical agent, hoping that he would be able to sell the film rights to this book. According to Erika's experience, "Once a book comes out, there's a flurry of activity. If an agent doesn't get bites that result in an offer, the agent starts to doubt his opinion of the book; he loses confidence in it." That's what happened with the agent, and Erika's second novel was retired to the agent's bookcase.

At one point, a producer got in touch with Erika directly, and wanted to option the book for television. Erika had the agent negotiate the deal. Even though Erika and the agent weren't thrilled about a television deal, they both felt it was better than nothing. Before long, the option expired and Erika was back to nothing. And that seemed to be the end of it.

One day, months later, producer Michael I. Levy happened to

drop by Erika's agent's office. While he was schmoozing, he casually asked, "Do you, by any chance, have a 'female vigilante' story? Sherry Lansing (Chairman of Paramount Pictures) wants something like *Star Chamber*, the film about Supreme Court judges who take the law into their own hands, only with a *woman* as the vigilante." The agent plucked a copy of Erika's book from the shelf and handed it to Mike. Mike read it over the weekend. Monday morning, he took the book to Sherry Lansing and told her that this was the female vigilante story she had been looking for. Paramount didn't even bother with an option. They bought the book outright for six figures. About a year and a half later, *Eye for an Eye* premiered. The film, starring Sally Field, was produced by Michael I. Levy, directed by John Schlesinger, screenplay by Amanda Silver, and based on the book of the same name by Erika Holzer.

This story teaches us so much about the business. Think of all the lessons to be learned here, starting with the importance of your screenplay's genre, and ending with the truly great thing about the movie business: The next phone call or e-mail you receive—during the week or on the weekend, day or night—can be a life-changing, career-making opportunity.

Of course, no matter what the genre of your work, no matter how fantastic your story is, or how well you have told it, if your physical script doesn't conform to industry standards, it may not be read. Proper script formatting is a must if you, the writer, want to be regarded as a contender. The following section has all you need to know to get your script in professional shape for submission.

STANDARD SCREENPLAY FORMAT

When someone picks up your script and takes a first glance, the script should announce, "Professional writer here." If the script is too fat—Amateur! If the title page has fancy fonts—Amateur! If the script is expensively bound—Amateur! There are a lot more *ifs* to consider, and we cover them all. Read every one, even *if* you think you don't have to. Better safe than, "Sorry, we're not interested in your screenplay. Good luck placing it elsewhere."

If your script complies with all of the industry standards, you will be starting with an advantage. When a script is clean, the right size, bound with the acceptable brads, formatted properly, and free from

typos, whoever reads it, from story analyst to studio suit, has a subconscious, if not conscious, respect for the writer. They want to like
the script.

In our search for the definitive *standard script format*, we learned
that, although there are a few minor points that may vary among professionals, there is a "basic" acceptable industry standard. Marilyn
Horowitz, writer, producer, and NYU professor, compiled script format pages for her students, and graciously agreed to let us use her
work as the basis for ours. The mission of Marilyn's "Manual of Style"
is to provide a coherent breakdown of the rules that are acceptable as
industry standard, and to provide writers with the best tools to communicate their vision. As Marilyn so aptly puts it, "Don't rebel—Sell!"

Before going on, it's important to understand that the following
formatting guidelines are for spec scripts, not shooting scripts. A *spec
script* should be easy to read and free of technical directions. A *shooting script* is a tool used for the actual filming of the movie—getting it
from script to screen. In a shooting script, the camera angles, and
other technical information are included. Every scene is numbered.
And when a scene isn't completed on a page, the word CONTINUED
(or an abbreviation of this word) is added to the very bottom of that
page, and to the very top of the following page.

A spec script is a sample of your work that may result in a sale
and/or a writing assignment. Your spec script should be a pleasure
to read. Let it tell your story without bogging down the reader with
unnecessary technical instructions. When preparing a spec script,
stick to the following basic rules:

- Leave out the camera angles and directions. This includes terms
  such as DISSOLVE TO and CUT TO.

- Do not number the scenes.

- Do not use the term (CONTINUED) or (CON'T) at the bottom of a
  page and at the top of the following page to denote the continuation of the same scene.

- Including the term (CONTINUED) or (CON'T) at the end of a page,
  when a block of dialogue will be continued on the following page
  is optional.

- Including the term (CONTINUED) or (CON'T) at the top of a page,
  next to the character's name (sometimes referred to as a character

> If your script complies
> with all of the industry
> standards—it is clean, the
> right size, bound with
> acceptable brads, formatted
> properly, and free from
> typos—whoever reads it,
> from story analyst to studio
> suit, has a subconscious, if
> not conscious, respect
> for the writer. They want
> to like it.

PROSE FROM A PRO

Make It Easy on the Eye
by Screenwriter Barry Strugatz

Co-writer: *Married to the Mob* and *She Devil.*

Reading a screenplay is usually a chore. It's not the most reader-friendly form. It's hard to write a good, readable script. I think screenplays should read like prose . . . as lean and succinct as possible. At least we should strive for this. Leave out details such as angles and POVs—they are usually up to the director. But if these directions are crucial to the story, I think that they can artfully be hidden in your descriptive prose. For example a CLOSE-UP is mandatory if you describe a reflection in someone's eye.

cue), when that character's dialogue continues from the previous page is optional.

■ Including the term (CONTINUED) or (CON'T) after a character speaks when there is a break for directions, and then the same character is re-cued and speaks again is optional.

■ Denoting where the opening and closing CREDITS appear is optional. However, unless the credits play a part in the opening scene, we suggest that you don't include them. Why risk stopping the flow of the opening scenes with something over which the director has final say?

In addition to these general rules, there are other screenplay elements that you must follow. These range from the type of paper to use, to the proper tabs and margins to set, to the correct binding method to follow. All of these elements are presented in this section. Each one has been numbered and explained in detail.

Many of these screenplay components are included on the Sample Spec Script Pages, found on pages 56 and 57. As you will see, each example found on the sample pages has been given a number, which corresponds to the numbered component in this section.

I. SCREENPLAY LENGTH

A feature film script should be 90 to 120 pages in length. In the mind of a producer, one page of a script is equal to a minute of film, and no one wants more than 120 pages, or a two-hour movie. We've been told that the first thing most professional script readers do is look at the number on the last page. If it's higher than 120, the script may not be read. Made-for-TV movie scripts should be no more than 90 pages in length. Keep in mind that a two-hour television movie is actually a 90-minute movie with a half-hour of commercials. If your script is longer than the required length, don't even think about using narrow margins or a smaller font than the required 12-point Courier or Courier New. The people you want to have read your screenplay are wise to all the tricks. Don't start off on the wrong foot by trying to fool them.

When a screenplay needs trimming, start with the descriptive passages. Big blocks of text are off-putting. Remember, it's a screenplay you've written, not a novel. Give the readers enough description to get the picture, and then let their imaginations work for you.

PAPER AND COVERS 2.

For the script pages, always use white, 8.5-x-11-inch, 20-pound stock, three-hole punched paper. For the front and back covers of your script, use card stock that is at least 60 pounds. Office supply stores, copy shops, and a number of online stores (found in the Resource List), carry card stock in a variety of colors, although white or black is preferred. Keep the covers blank. No titles, names, designs, illustrations, or drawings. No nothing.

TYPEFACE 3.

Starting with the title page, then continuing with FADE IN: on page one, and all the way through to FADE OUT:, use 12-point Courier or Courier New. This is equivalent to 12-point pica on manual typewriters and 10-cpi Courier on electric models. This typeface has a look that is etched into the mind's eye of everyone in the industry who reads scripts. Not only does this typeface make the script easy to read, it also complies with the industry formula that one page equals one minute of screen time. And yes, as you might have guessed, this paragraph has been set in 12-point Courier New.

Spec Script Terms

FADE IN: Denotes the beginning of the first scene.

EXT. Signifies that the scene takes place in an "exterior" location. Used in a scene slug.

INT. Signifies that the scene takes place in an "interior" location. Used in a scene slug.

FADE OUT: Denotes the end of the last scene.

THE END. Optional term; denotes end of screenplay. Placed after **FADE OUT**.

4.   TITLE PAGE

The title of the screenplay should be placed about 3.5 to 4 inches from the top of the page, and centered, of course. Use all caps. It's okay to underline the title, or to put quotes around it. Remember to use 12-point Courier or Courier New. After the title, add one line of space, then type the word "by" (and yes, use a lower case "b"). Follow with another line of space and center your name. If you have a writing partner, separate your names with an ampersand (&) rather than the word "and." The ampersand means that you and the other writer (or writers) collaborated on the script; the word "and" usually indicates that another writer was hired by the producer to do a rewrite. It could also mean that the director made major changes, warranting a writing credit.

In the lower right-hand corner, about 3 inches from the bottom, place your street address. On the next line, add your city, state, and zip code. On the line below that, include your telephone number, starting with the area code. If you have a designated line for your fax, put that number on the next line. Finally, on the last line, place your e-mail address. Check out the sample title page on page 55.

If you have an agent, ask how the agency lists its name and contact information—it may use a special template—and place this on the title page instead of your information. If a lawyer will be submitting your script and has agreed to field calls for you, then put his contact information in the lower right-hand corner in place of yours.

Some writers want it known that their script has been registered with the Writers Guild of America (WGA) or with the United States Copyright Office. If you're one of these writers, and have registered your script with the WGA's West Coast office, add "Registered WGAw No.____" on the lower left side of the page opposite your address. If you have registered with the East Coast office, put "Registered WGAE No.____." Notice that the West Coast Writers Guild uses a small "w" for its abbreviation; while the East Coast "E" is capped. If you want to add copyright registration, simply put the copyright symbol (©) followed by the year of registration and your name. (Registration guidelines are presented later in this chapter.)

It's best not to put a date on the title page. Months fly by, and before too long your script will seem ancient. So think twice about putting that copyright registration year on your title page. Finally, never write "First Draft" (or any other draft number) on the title page or any other page of your script.

Sample Spec Script Title Page

When preparing a title page for a spec script, follow the formatting guidelines below. Refer to the facing page for details.

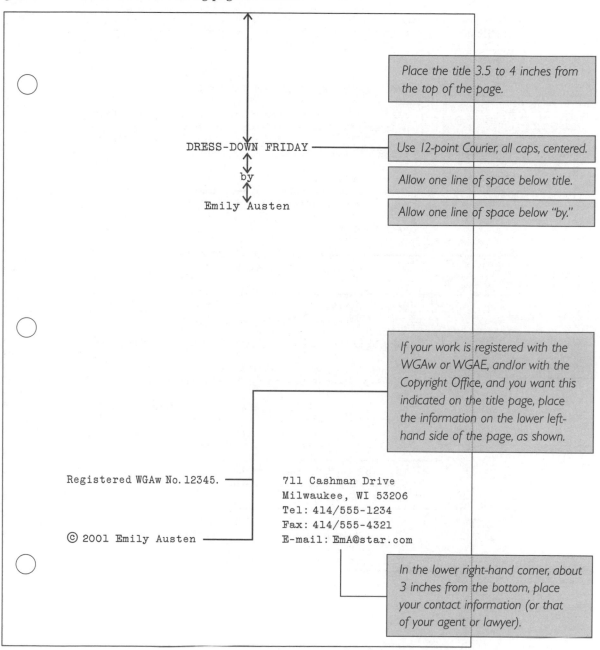

DRESS-DOWN FRIDAY

by

Emily Austen

Place the title 3.5 to 4 inches from the top of the page.

Use 12-point Courier, all caps, centered.

Allow one line of space below title.

Allow one line of space below "by."

If your work is registered with the WGAw or WGAE, and/or with the Copyright Office, and you want this indicated on the title page, place the information on the lower left-hand side of the page, as shown.

Registered WGAw No. 12345.

© 2001 Emily Austen

711 Cashman Drive
Milwaukee, WI 53206
Tel: 414/555-1234
Fax: 414/555-4321
E-mail: EmA@star.com

In the lower right-hand corner, about 3 inches from the bottom, place your contact information (or that of your agent or lawyer).

Sample Spec Script Pages

The numbers in the shaded boxes below and on the facing page refer
to the corresponding numbered elements detailed on pages 52–76.

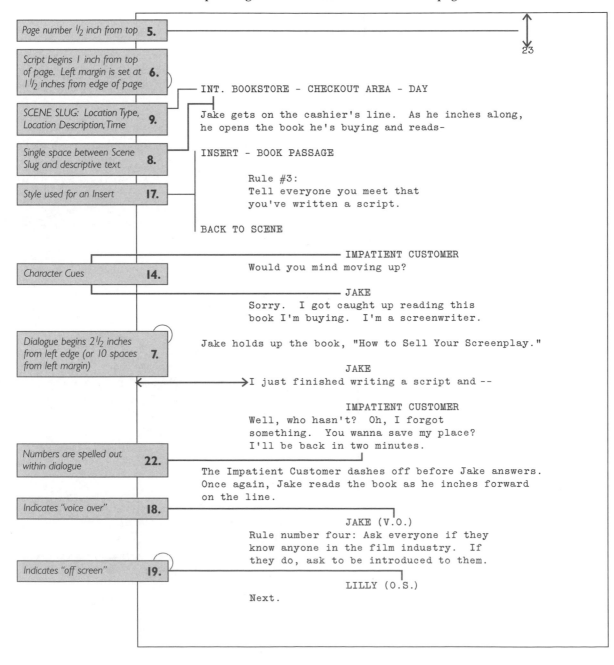

Page number ½ inch from top	**5.**
Script begins 1 inch from top of page. Left margin is set at 1½ inches from edge of page	**6.**
SCENE SLUG: Location Type, Location Description, Time	**9.**
Single space between Scene Slug and descriptive text	**8.**
Style used for an Insert	**17.**
Character Cues	**14.**
Dialogue begins 2½ inches from left edge (or 10 spaces from left margin)	**7.**
Numbers are spelled out within dialogue	**22.**
Indicates "voice over"	**18.**
Indicates "off screen"	**19.**

```
                                                                    23

INT. BOOKSTORE - CHECKOUT AREA - DAY

Jake gets on the cashier's line.  As he inches along,
he opens the book he's buying and reads-

INSERT - BOOK PASSAGE

          Rule #3:
          Tell everyone you meet that
          you've written a script.

BACK TO SCENE

                              IMPATIENT CUSTOMER
          Would you mind moving up?

                              JAKE
          Sorry.  I got caught up reading this
          book I'm buying.  I'm a screenwriter.

Jake holds up the book, "How to Sell Your Screenplay."

                         JAKE
          I just finished writing a script and --

                         IMPATIENT CUSTOMER
          Well, who hasn't?  Oh, I forgot
          something.  You wanna save my place?
          I'll be back in two minutes.

The Impatient Customer dashes off before Jake answers.
Once again, Jake reads the book as he inches forward
on the line.

                         JAKE (V.O.)
          Rule number four: Ask everyone if they
          know anyone in the film industry.  If
          they do, ask to be introduced to them.

                         LILLY (O.S.)
          Next.
```

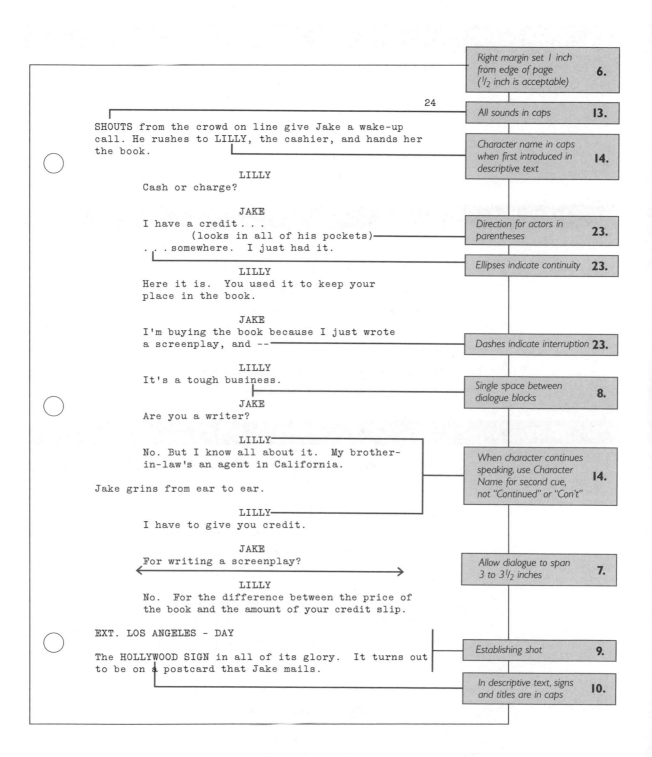

24

SHOUTS from the crowd on line give Jake a wake-up
call. He rushes to LILLY, the cashier, and hands her
the book.

                    LILLY
          Cash or charge?

                    JAKE
          I have a credit...
                    (looks in all of his pockets)
          ...somewhere. I just had it.

                    LILLY
          Here it is. You used it to keep your
          place in the book.

                    JAKE
          I'm buying the book because I just wrote
          a screenplay, and --

                    LILLY
          It's a tough business.

                    JAKE
          Are you a writer?

                    LILLY
          No. But I know all about it. My brother-
          in-law's an agent in California.

Jake grins from ear to ear.

                    LILLY
          I have to give you credit.

                    JAKE
          For writing a screenplay?

                    LILLY
          No. For the difference between the price of
          the book and the amount of your credit slip.

EXT. LOS ANGELES - DAY

The HOLLYWOOD SIGN in all of its glory. It turns out
to be on a postcard that Jake mails.

Callout labels (right margin):

- Right margin set 1 inch from edge of page (1/2 inch is acceptable) — **6.**
- All sounds in caps — **13.**
- Character name in caps when first introduced in descriptive text — **14.**
- Direction for actors in parentheses — **23.**
- Ellipses indicate continuity — **23.**
- Dashes indicate interruption **23.**
- Single space between dialogue blocks — **8.**
- When character continues speaking, use Character Name for second cue, not "Continued" or "Con't" — **14.**
- Allow dialogue to span 3 to 3 1/2 inches — **7.**
- Establishing shot — **9.**
- In descriptive text, signs and titles are in caps — **10.**

5. PAGE NUMBERS

The cover of a spec script and the title page are not counted as numbered pages. And although the first page of the script is considered "page 1," it should not be numbered. Actual pagination should begin on the second page of the script with the numeral 2 placed in the upper right-hand corner, about 0.5 inch from the top of the page. This number may or may not be followed by a period—your choice. Succeeding pages should be numbered the same way.

6. MARGINS

When preparing your script, use the following margin settings. Also note that the text should be ragged right, not justified.

Left margin: 1.5 inches (15 spaces from left edge of page)

Right margin: 1 inch preferred, although 0.5 inch is acceptable (about 8 spaces from right edge of page)

Top margin: 1 inch

Bottom margin: 1 inch (This is not rigid. You can add another line or two—at most—to complete a block of dialogue.)

7. TABS

The following tab settings are industry standards for the following components of a spec script.

■ CHARACTER CUE

- Set the character cue—another term for the character's name—24 spaces from the left margin (3.9 inches from left edge of page).

■ DIALOGUE

- Begin dialogue 10 spaces from the left margin (2.5 inches from left edge of page).
- Each line of dialogue should be between 3 and 3.5 inches wide.

■ PARENTHETICAL DIRECTIONS

- Begin actor's directions, which are in parentheses, 16 spaces from the left margin (3.1 inches from left edge of page).

- Parenthetical directions should not extend more than 45 spaces from left margin (not more than 6 inches from left edge of page).

■ CAMERA DIRECTIONS

For the most part, camera directions should be given only in shooting scripts. However, if a camera direction affects or plays a role in furthering the plot, it may be included in the spec script.

- Set camera directions flush against the right margin; use Courier or Courier New—all upper-cased:

```
                                      DISSOLVE TO:
                                           CUT TO:
```

SPACING   8.

When preparing a spec script, the following rules are industry standards for line spacing.

■ USE SINGLE SPACING:

- Within each block of dialogue.
- Within a direction or description paragraph.
- Between the character cue and the dialogue under it.

■ USE DOUBLE SPACING:

- Between FADE IN: and the first scene slug. (We'll get to scene slugs shortly.)
- From scene slug to description line (or lines).
- Between description lines and character cue.
- Between paragraphs of dialogue.
- Before and after camera directions.
- After the final directions (or final dialogue) to FADE OUT:.

■ USE SPECIAL SPACING:

- On the last page of the script, place THE END 4 to 6 lines below FADE OUT:, and center it.

Note: In addition to ending a spec script in the way just described, some writers choose to use only FADE OUT: while others use only THE END. All three styles are acceptable.

9. SCENE SLUGS

A scene slug defines the where and when of the scene. Scene slugs are ALWAYS IN CAPS and contain at least three pieces of information—location type, location description, and time of day. This info is always given in that order. Some scene slugs may also include establishing shots, as well as flashbacks, fantasies, dream sequences, and particular years, which are all explained in this section. All scene slugs should be followed by at least one line of description, as shown in the following example. This example is followed by explanations of the different parts of a scene slug.

```
INT. BILL'S BAR - NIGHT

A low-end dive filled with a seamy crowd.
```

■ LOCATION TYPE

Location type is the first bit of information included in a scene slug. It tells the reader if the scene takes place in an interior location or an exterior one. Use the abbreviation INT. for interior, and EXT. for exterior.

- If moving to a different part of an established interior location, you must reslug with INT., since this usually involves building another set.

- When moving to a different part of a single exterior location, don't repeat EXT., just note the type of setting. For example, the single exterior is A CARNIVAL, then note: COTTON CANDY STAND, or TICKET BOOTH, or SHOOTING GALLERY, or wherever the next exterior scene at the carnival takes place.

- If your scene is inside a train, plane, or big ship, it is considered INT. If your scene is on the deck, roof, or anywhere outside the vehicle, it is considered EXT.

- A car is an EXT. when it is on the road; that same car is an INT. when it's in a garage.

■ LOCATION DESCRIPTION

The second part of a scene slug is the location description. It tells where the scene takes place.

- When describing a scene's location, always go from the general to the specific:

Bad Example: INT. BEDROOM IN ALYCE'S APARTMENT - NIGHT

Good Example: INT. ALYCE'S APARTMENT - BEDROOM - NIGHT

- Avoid redundancies.

Bad Example: EXT. OUTSIDE ALYCE'S APARTMENT BUILDING - NIGHT

Since you've already slugged the location as an EXT., it's redundant to start your description with OUTSIDE.

Good Example: EXT. ALYCE'S APARTMENT BUILDING - NIGHT

- Cars don't exist in limbo. When a car is used in a scene, its description should include its location.

Bad Example: EXT. CAR - DAY

Good Example: EXT. CAR ON HIGHWAY - DAY

■ TIME OF DAY

Along with the location type and location description, the time of day is the third piece of standard information that is found in a scene slug. Simply put, it is the time of day—DAY or NIGHT—during which the scene takes place. Do not use terms like DAWN, DUSK, EARLY MORNING, or specific times, such as 4:00 PM or MIDNIGHT, unless it is relevant to a specific plot point.

- After the location type (INT. or EXT.) and location description (ALYCE'S BEDROOM), insert a space followed by a hyphen and then another space. Next add the time of day (DAY or NIGHT).

- If you've established the time of day for a location, and you return to the same location in the next scene, you can use LATER, as seen in the example below:

EXT. STREET CORNER - DAY

Bill hangs out drinking beer. He passes out.

LATER

Bill wakes up.

- If, however, the time of day changes—if Bill wakes up at NIGHT— you have to indicate the new time in the same way you indicated LATER in the example above. For instance:

```
EXT. STREET CORNER - DAY

Bill hangs out drinking beer. He passes out.

NIGHT

Bill wakes up.
```

- If a scene takes place right after the previous one, it is not necessary to time-slug it with CONTINUOUS or SAME TIME. The continuity is understood.

■ ESTABLISHING SHOTS

To let the reader and ultimately the audience know where they are at the beginning of the film or at any specific scene, you may want to have an establishing shot. It should be written in the scene text, not in the slug.

Bad Example: `EXT. NEW YORK CITY - DAY - ESTABLISHING`

Good Example: `EXT. NEW YORK CITY - DAY`

```
The sun's reflection adds polish to the Big Apple.
```

The line above is the scene text, which, when filmed, will be the establishing (or opening) shot of either the movie or a new location in the movie. It will tell the audience (initially, the reader) exactly where the scene they are about to see takes place.

■ FLASHBACK, FANTASY, DREAM SEQUENCE, OR YEAR

This is an optional part of a scene slug, and used only when appropriate. If the scene is a FLASHBACK, FANTASY, or DREAM SEQUENCE, or indicates a specific year, place this information in parentheses after the time of day, as seen in these examples:

```
INT. BILL'S APARTMENT - NIGHT (FLASHBACK)

EXT. CENTRAL PARK'S GREAT HILL - DAY (FANTASY)

INT. ALYCE'S APARTMENT - MORNING (DREAM SEQUENCE)

EXT. NEW YORK CITY - DAY (1953)
```

● Always add (REALITY) or (PRESENT DAY) to the slug that brings us back to the here-and-now:

```
EXT. CENTRAL PARK'S GREAT HILL - DAY (PRESENT DAY)
```

DESCRIPTIVE TEXT   10.

When it comes to descriptions, less is better. Pare everything down. Keep descriptive blocks to no more than four lines (that's *lines*, not *sentences*). Thick blocks of description will make readers want to skip ahead.

Bad Example: `INT. BAR - NIGHT`

```
A bar with dim lighting, a greasy atmosphere
and COUNTRY-WESTERN MUSIC WHINING from a seen-
better-days record player. ZEKE, in his 20s but
looks twice that, is a gaunt and ugly man. He
sits at the bar with an empty glass in front
of him into which he flicks the ashes from
his hand-rolled cigarette.
```

Good Example: `INT. BAR - NIGHT`

```
Dim, greasy. ZEKE, 20s, gaunt and ugly, sits
at the bar.
```

● Write descriptions in short, simple sentences. Avoid frequent use of the word "and."

● Don't include the reader in your descriptions. This means eliminating phrases like, "We realize that. . . " or "We see the. . . " Just state what's happening and leave "us" out of it.

● Always describe your setting before you describe characters or their actions.

● Don't duplicate information from your scene slugs:

Bad Example: `INT. DINER - DAY`

```
Amanda enters the diner.
```

Good Example: `INT. DINER - DAY`

```
Amanda enters.
```

- Don't describe the furniture unless it somehow interacts with a character, or is relevant to the story.

Bad Example: `INT. LIVING ROOM - DAY`

```
A tacky, messy, overcrowded living room with
a super-sized television, an opened sofa bed,
bridge chairs around a card table, and a wall
full of paintings on velvet. Gordon sits on
the open sofa bed, watching television.
```

Good Example: `INT. LIVING ROOM - DAY`

```
Tacky and cluttered. Gordon sits on the
opened sofa bed and watches television.
```

- Never begin your scene description with a pronoun. Always be specific and name names. You don't want the reader playing guessing games with your script's characters.
- Keep your verbs in the active, present tense. Avoid "ing" words. For example, instead of writing "Tom is flying solo," write "Tom flies solo."
- Avoid using terms like "starts" and "begins to." For example, instead of writing "Ellen starts to type a note," write "Ellen types a note."
- Make the words you use as descriptive as possible. Paint a picture.

Bad Example: `Larry starts eating the seafood.`

Good Example: `Larry devours the lobster.`

PROSE FROM A PRO

Plenty of White Space
by Dov S-S Simens
Founder, Hollywood Film Institute

If you have good, fast-paced dialogue, with little exposition and setting descriptions, there will be a lot of white space on the page. When there is a lot of white space, the reader's eye flows down the page. This is what script readers call "a good read."

- In descriptive text, spell out numbers zero through nine; use numerals for the number 10 and higher.
- Don't leave an abbreviated word that ends with a period, such as Dr., Mr., and Sgt., dangling at the end of a line. Move the abbreviated word down to the next line to link it with the word it modifies: Dr. Jekyll, Mr. Hyde, Sgt. Pepper.
- Don't hyphenate a word at the end of a line.

- Titles of movies, TV shows, or publications should always be underlined in dialogue. In descriptive text, titles and signs should be in CAPS.

- Avoid giving music cues. Just as the director will decide on the camera angles, so will the film composer decide on what music goes where. Jan Sardi who wrote the screenplay for *Shine*, a film about a troubled Australian piano prodigy, had good reason to include specific music cues, but most.screenwriters don't and shouldn't.

SPECIAL EFFECTS 11.

It used to be that effects (FX) or special effects (SPFX) in films were expensive and capable of scaring away potential producers. Although special effects are more sophisticated and even more expensive nowadays, they are desirable to some producers for some film genres. Many of today's special effects are created digitally via computer, and are labor-intensive and costly. The advantage is their versatility. You can place anyone anywhere and doing anything. When it comes to your spec script, however, describe a special effect without actually labeling it FX or SPFX.

MONTAGE 12.

Montage, the French term for *editing*, is the optical blending of a variety of quick shots, used most often to show the passage of time, and/or the progression of something important in the story, like a relationship. It may also be used for an artsy stream of consciousness. One way to properly format a montage is as follows:

```
MONTAGE - CURT AND ANGELA DO TOURISTY THINGS IN
NEW YORK CITY

-- They stand at the base of the Empire State
Building and point to the top, causing all the
passersby to look up.

-- Curt takes a picture of Angela with her arm
around the skeleton outside Jekyll & Hyde Restaurant.

-- Angela takes a picture of Curt in a bullfighting
pose in front of a painted street-cow sculpture.
```

```
-- They buy a strange-looking snack from a street
vendor in Chinatown.

-- Both sneak under the turnstile in the subway
and run into the waiting train.

BACK TO SCENE
```

Here is another acceptable montage format:

```
MONTAGE - CURT AND ANGELA DO TOURISTY THINGS IN
NEW YORK CITY

-- Empire State Building - They stand at the
base and point to the top, causing all the
passersby to look up.

-- Jekyll & Hyde Restaurant - Curt takes a
picture of Angela with her arm around the
skeleton at the door.
```

To end the Montage, use either:

```
BACK TO SCENE
```

or

```
END MONTAGE
```

or simply type the next scene slug.

13.   ACTIONS AND SOUNDS

When it comes to adding action instructions to your script, don't elaborate too much. Action screenplays are an exception, but even so, keep it short, crisp, and to the point.

- Use "bullet" sentences. You may want to *stack* them—put them on separate lines—as seen in the following example:

```
Agent Trent sees the fugitive running.
Chases him.
Pulls his gun.
SHOOTS him dead.
```

- Important actions and sounds should always be in CAPS, as seen in the examples below:

The phone RINGS.

The Doberman BARKS.

Lou CRASHES his Mercedes into the garage door.

Rayna PLUNGES the knife into the mugger's ear.

- Traditionally, the rule is to separate action from dialogue. There is now another school of thought. Some execs don't read descriptions, just dialogue; so you may want to keep some of the action in the dialogue blocks. Here are examples of both. You decide.

Example 1:
```
                Vince
    You know, Janey, you really steam me when
    you do that.
            (pulls out a gun)
    Maybe it's just cheaper to kill you.
```

Example 2:
```
                Vince
    You know, Janey, you really steam me when
    you do that.

Vince pulls out a gun.

                Vince
    Maybe it's just cheaper to kill you.
```

CHARACTER NAMES AND CUES   14.

Character cues refer to the name of the character on the line above the dialogue. In other words, it announces the character who is doing the talking.

- Keep character cues consistent. If a character is ROBERT SMITH the first time he speaks, his character cue must always be ROBERT SMITH. This rule includes characters who are identified by function. If Sergeant Robert Smith's character cue is SGT. SMITH the first time he talks, you have to keep cueing him as SGT. SMITH each time, even though he may be introduced in a later scene as Smithie, or Rob Smith, or The Sarge. It doesn't matter what names he's called within the dialogue, as long as his character cue is consistent.

- When introducing a character for the first time in descriptive text (not in a cue), the name should be in CAPS. If the name is followed by a possessive, use a small "s" after the apostrophe. For example:

```
INT. HOSPITAL ADMITTANCE AREA - DAY

As she awaits her turn, WILMA LANGE's body
language is that of a due-any-second pregnant
lady.
```

- When characters who do not have speaking parts first appear, it is not necessary to use all CAPS for their names. As a matter of fact, it may not be necessary to give them names at all. Unless a lead character refers to nonspeaking characters by actual names, it is generally more interesting and more effective to introduce them with good descriptions instead. For example, instead of referring to the character simply as Joe, it is better to identify him as a Scruffy Surgeon, a Hard-of-Hearing Piano Tuner, or a Frazzled Airline Passenger. Referring to a character as an Unkempt Gum-Chewing Receptionist paints a better picture in the mind of the reader than simply calling that same character Mary.

- Don't confuse the reader by giving two characters similar names, like ANDREAS and ELIAS. The only time to use names that are similar is when it is an important part of the story.

- Don't be too specific about a character's physical characteristics unless the elements are plot-critical. Use an age range, rather than a specific age. And describe the nature of the character, rather than the physical attributes—height, weight, complexion, and hair and eye color. This way, you're not limiting the casting possibilities. The following character description is from *On A Clear Day You Can See Forever*, screenplay by Alan Jay Lerner:

```
MRS. FROOD is the average, grey-plumed, plump-bellied,
mate-eating, predatory bird; half female and half
nothing.
```

Here's a character description from *Network,* written by Paddy
Chayefsky. It has a couple of no-nos, but is fun to read:

```
DIANA CHRISTENSON, dressed in slacks and blouse,
34, tall, willowy, and with the best ass ever seen
on a Vice President in charge of Programming.
```

- Character subtext should not be used. Only describe what is seen,
  and actions that characters perform. You may describe an emotional state, but keep it brief.

Bad Example: `Gloria is sad over her breakup with`
                    `     that loser boyfriend of hers.`

Good Example: `Gloria is sad.`

- Giving a character "business"—lighting a cigarette, fiddling with
  a wedding band—should be left up to the director unless it's relevant to the story.

TELEPHONE CONVERSATIONS 15.

When two people are speaking on the phone, slug both locations
for the first line or so of dialogue. Then add the INTERCUT line and
treat it as the same location. You save space by eliminating the back
and forth slugs, and it's a courtesy to the director, giving him the
choice of when to cut from one character to the other—a choice he
has anyway. Here's a good example of how to handle INTERCUTS
within a scene:

```
INT. BILL'S APARTMENT - NIGHT

The phone RINGS. Bill groggily awakens, picks up
the phone.

                    BILL
          What? Huh? Hello...

INT. PAULY'S APARTMENT - NIGHT

PAULY sits by the phone, sweating.

                    PAULY
          Bill, got a minute?
```

```
INTERCUT - BILL'S APARTMENT/PAULY'S APARTMENT

                    BILL
          What is your problem? I'm working on
          a hangover.


                    PAULY
          Sorry, Bill. I hate to ask, but I
          need some money. I really need it.
```

- If you can't get your characters to talk to each other face-to-face, and you must have a telephone conversation, consider handling it in the following way:

```
INT. PAULY'S APARTMENT - NIGHT

Pauly picks up the phone, dials.

                    PAULY
          Bill, got a minute?
                    (listens)
          You got a hangover? Bummer. I hate
          to ask, but I need some money.
```

16. TEXT ON A COMPUTER SCREEN

Keep this sort of scene to a minimum. If it goes on too long, the director will have to find an interesting way to intercut the computer screen with whatever is creatively appropriate.

- Skip a line after the directions that introduce the computer. On the next line, use either ON THE SCREEN or ON THE MONITOR. Skip another line, then write out the text in quotes in the dialogue block. For example:

```
Andrew tosses the empty bottle into the drawer, then
types on the keyboard.

ON THE SCREEN

                    "This may be the end of the world
                    as you know it, but it's just the
                    beginning of our life together."
```

- The following example shows how Nora Ephron & Delia Ephron

presented their computer text in the script for *You've Got Mail.*
(Please note that the complete dialogue is not included between the
directions.) The term (V.O.) indicates that the dialogue is a "voice
over," which is discussed beginning on page 72.

```
INT. JOE'S DEN - NIGHT

Joe writes on his computer. Brinkley on the floor
next to him. And cut between Joe and his computer
screen.

                    JOE (V.O.)
        Do you ever feel you become the worst
        version of yourself?

INT. KATHLEEN'S COMPUTER SCREEN - DAY

And cut between screen and

INT. KATHLEEN'S BEDROOM - DAY

As Kathleen reads the end of Joe's letter.

Kathleen hits the Reply key and starts to type:

                    KATHLEEN (V.O.)
        I know what you mean and I'm completely
        jealous.

INT. JOE'S COMPUTER SCREEN AND JOE'S DEN - NIGHT

As he replies:

                    JOE (V.O.)
        Wouldn't it be wonderful if --
```

INSERT   17.

The INSERT, often referred to as the CUTAWAY, allows the audience
to see a blowup of something—a photograph, newspaper headline,
letter, a will—that would ordinarily be too small to decipher. The way
it is inserted is similar to the way it was just done with the computer
screen example above. The following is an example of how to format
an INSERT:

Ted reaches into the safe and takes out a bundle of
papers. He shines the flashlight on them, pulls out
the one he wants and discards the others. He unfolds
the legal-looking document, and again, shines the
flashlight on it.

INSERT - THE WILL

> "I, Charlie Blake, am of sound mind - but
> I wouldn't give you two cents for the body.
> And that's why this will is probably being
> read out loud right now. Unless my jackass-
> son Ted broke into my safe. I wonder if he
> knows about the infra-red cameras I set up."

Ted drops the flashlight.

BACK TO SCENE

18. VOICE OVER

Voice Over (always abbreviated in scripts as VO or V.O. and placed within parentheses) is used for narration in the past or present tense. Surely you've seen a detective story in which the detective's Voice Over lets you in on his thoughts as he goes about his business.

Voice Over is also used to link two intercut scenes. Character A is talking in one scene. The dialogue continues and becomes a Voice Over as the camera cuts to Character B's scene. This use of Voice Over is not generally written in the script, but done in the editing room, after the film is shot.

The most common use of the Voice Over is during a telephone conversation. The dialogue belonging to the character who isn't seen, but whose voice is heard at the other end of the phone, gets a (V.O.) or (VO) next to his character cue, as seen below.

                    BILL (V.O.)
          I knew from that day forward that danger
          was my beer.

19. OFF SCREEN

When a character is in the location but not on camera—not seen but heard—use the abbreviation O.S. or OS within parentheses next to

the character cue. A good use of the Off-Screen direction is when a
character is in the next room of a house or apartment:

```
                    JOE (O.S.)
        I'm in the can.  Start without me.
```

POINT OF VIEW 20.

Use Point of View—P.O.V. or POV—and there you go, directing the film
again. Yes, P.O.V. is a camera direction and it's not a good idea to use
it in a spec script.

- Whenever you're tempted to write from a character's point of view,
  do so but without announcing it with P.O.V. or POV. The following
  is from the shooting script of the famous window scene from
  Network. It is followed by the way the same scene should read in a
  spec script.

```
MAX joins his daughter at the window.  RAIN sprays
against his face --

MAX'S P.O.V.

He sees occasional windows open, and, just across
from his apartment house, a MAN opens the front
door of a brownstone

                    MAN
              (shouts)
        I'm mad as hell and I'm not going
        to take this any more!

OTHER SHOUTS are heard. From his twenty-third
floor vantage point, Max sees the erratic landscape
of Manhattan buildings for some blocks, and,
silhouetted HEADS in window after window, here,
there, and then seemingly everywhere, SHOUTING out
into the slashing black RAIN of the streets --
```

- Now here is the way the same scene should read when written in
  a spec script:

```
MAX joins his daughter at the window. RAIN sprays
against his face.
```

```
He sees occasional windows open, and, just across
from his apartment house, a MAN opens the front
door of a brownstone --
```

The rest of the scene stays exactly the same. The scene is clearly from MAX'S POV, but it isn't necessary to write it as a camera direction.

21. DIALOGUE

Dialogue was discussed earlier under the section on Action. As mentioned, the traditional rule has been to separate action from dialogue. However, because some executives don't read descriptions, just dialogue, there is another option for screenwriters. In this option, some of the action is kept in the dialogue blocks. Examples are provided on page 67.

22. NUMBERS

- In descriptive lines, spell out numbers zero through nine. Use numerals for numbers 10 and higher.
- In dialogue lines, write out all numbers except years. Years are always in numerals. Both numbering styles for dialogue are shown in the following example:

```
                    DAN
        The two boys are five years apart.  One
        was born in 1972; the other in '77.
```

23. ELLIPSES, DASHES, AND PARENTHETICALS

- Ellipses (. . .) and dashes are generally used to make dialogue seem more like uh . . . like real people talking. And yet -- what was I going to say? Oh yes, if you use them too often, they can -- lose their impact. Dashes are used mostly when a character is interrupted, as in the following example:

```
                    NORAH
        I thought you were going to --


                    ELIZABETH
        I don't care what you thought.
```

Ellipses are used mostly for pauses within a block of dialogue. They are also used to indicate an interruption, which is then followed by continuing dialogue, as in the following:

```
                    NORAH
        Lizzy, I'm your sister...your flesh and blood.


                    ELIZABETH
        I don't even know you anymore.  Take your
        laptop...
                (opens the door)
        ...and leave.
```

- Parentheticals (words set within parentheses) are directions for actors. They are also known as *wrylies,* as in:

```
                    JOE
                (wryly)
        You see this here cue stick?  It's my ticket
        outta this burg.
```

Just as film directors don't want writers to put in camera angles, most actors prefer not to be given line readings. If the dialogue calls for some emotion or action that's necessary for the story, then include the direction. As a rule, keep directions to a minimum. Save space, and let the actors make their own choices. In the words of comedy writer Frank L. Visco, "Parenthetical remarks (however relevant) are unnecessary." Seriously, though, parentheticals can be used effectively when a character is talking to one person, then begins talking to another, as shown in the following:

```
                    JILL
        Gimme a break!
                (to Mary)
        He's always like that after a few beers.
```

- If a character pauses for a significant length of time, during which there's some sort of action, reslug the dialogue. For example:

```
                    JANE
        I don't know...

Jane reaches for the gun, replaces the clip and aims.

                    JANE
        Maybe I should just kill you.
```

24. OTHER FORMATTING RULES

There are other formatting rules that are important to follow when preparing your script.

- Jargon, accents, and dialects can be annoying to read. Just give the flavor of the accent or jargon. Be sure to read the dialogue aloud. If you stumble, then it needs to be simplified.

- If a word or phrase needs to be emphasized to have the reader (and ultimately, the actor playing the part) understand the <u>true</u> meaning of the line of dialogue, then underline the word(s). *Never* use italics. And <u>don't</u> make a habit of underlining.

- When a character spells out a word or a number, use hyphens, as shown in the following example:

```
                    SHARRON
        First name is Sharron. That's s-h-a-r-r-o-n.
        Apartment sixty - six-oh.
```

25. PAGE ENDINGS

When it comes to the end of a page, the following rules apply:

- Do not end the page with a scene slug.

- Always end each page with a complete sentence.

26. BINDING THE SCRIPT

When your script is finished, it is time to bind it, or get it "between brads." The brads of choice are 1.25-inch or 1.5-inch round-head brass fasteners. Use 1.25-inch brads for scripts that are under 110 pages long, and the 1.5-inch variety for scripts that are 110 pages or more. Bind your script between the appropriate front and back card-stock covers, and fasten with two brads—one through the top holes and the other through the bottom holes.

Screw posts are unacceptable because they're not easy to take apart if the reader wants to run the script pages through the copy machine. For the same reason, 2-inch brads that fold under are also unacceptable.

Proofread! Proofread! Oh Yeah, and Proofread!

It's very annoying and distracting to read a script with typos, grammatical errors, and misspelled words. It certainly won't score points with the readers, and, in fact, it's looked upon as being disrespectful to them. Don't expect anyone to take your work seriously if you haven't cared enough to take the time to make sure that your script is free of correctable mistakes. By now you must know that you cannot count on your spell checker to do the job for you. After you've gone over your script as many times as it takes for you to be sure it's word perfect, you may want to count on the kindness of someone capable to proofread it as well.

If you already knew the formatting principles we just reviewed, good for you. Be proud of yourself for preparing a script that will pass any reader's scrutiny in terms of form. If the information helped you improve the formatting of your script, good for you, too, and glad we could help. As shallow as this seems, the look of your script goes a long way in gaining a reader's receptiveness.

Now, are you ready for the next step? We have more vital information, and we hope it registers. Oh wait, we hope *you* register. . . your script, that is.

PROTECT YOUR WORK

Before setting out to sell your completed screenplay, we highly recommend that you register it with the Writers Guild of America (WGA) and/or register a copyright with the Library of Congress Copyright Office.

Registration proves priority of ownership. If you show your script to an agent or a producer before it's registered with the Writers Guild or Copyright Office, you will not be able to prove that the material is yours. Hopefully, you won't ever have reason to prove this, but you just never know. We are advocates of "better safe than sorry." Take steps to protect your work now, so you'll have no regrets later.

Register with Writers Guild of America

The Registration Service (or Intellectual Property Registry) of the Writers Guild of America registers over 30,000 pieces of literary material each year, and is available to members and nonmembers alike. Registration provides a dated record of the writer's claim to authorship of a particular literary property. If legal or official Guild action is initiated, the WGA will retrieve the material as evidence.

In addition to completed scripts, the Guild also accepts treatments, synopses, outlines, written ideas specifically intended for radio, television and theatrical motion pictures, video cassettes/discs, and interactive media. The WGA Registration Offices also accept stage plays, novels and other books, short stories, poems, commercials, song lyrics, and drawings. Although the WGA Registration protects work, be aware that it does not protect titles.

There are a number of ways to register your material. You can do so in person at either the East or West Coast office, or you can call or write for a registration packet. The WGA East also allows you to register online at its website. Fees vary for Guild members and nonmembers at each office. But everyone is allowed to register material on either coast, no matter where they live. For further details, please see page 294 in the Resource List.

Library of Congress Copyright

You wrote it; you own the copyright. *Copyright* is a form of protection that is provided by the laws of the United States for "original works of authorship." Proving authorship, however, is the hard part. Registering the copyright establishes a public record of the copyright claim. Before an infringement suit may be filed in court, registration is necessary for works of U.S. origin. Before showing you how to register for a copyright of your screenplay, we'd like you to be aware of some important information on the subject.

What Is and Isn't Protected by Copyright?

As mentioned above, copyright protects "original works of authorship." The original works must be "fixed in a tangible form of expression"—in your case, a screenplay. According to the copyright laws, "The fixation does not have to be directly perceptible, so long as it may be communicated with the aid of a machine or device." This would be applicable if your script is filmed and "in the can." Once in the can, the film can be copyrighted by the producer. Hopefully, this will concern you at some point down the road. Meanwhile, there are a number of areas that apply to you now.

First, let's talk about the subject of ideas or concepts. Basically, when it comes to this less-than-concrete area, there's both good news and bad. The bad news is that you cannot copyright an idea or a concept. This means, if you have a high-concept script, there's no way to protect that concept unless you never tell it or show it to anyone. And even then, great minds think alike. Chances are, at some point in time, another writer will come up with the same or a similar idea. Check out the lists of films that are in development (we show you how to do that in Chapter 4), and you'll be amazed at how many times you'll see two films—maybe more—based on the same exact subject or idea.

The good news is that your work encompasses more than just one idea—you have an entire screenplay, which *is* copyrightable. If a producer loves the idea or concept of your script, have faith. The reality is that he would rather buy your script than steal the idea and have to pay another writer to write it, and then run the risk of a lawsuit. If the producer isn't thrilled with your script, it's more likely that you will be asked to rewrite it. If your revision is still not what the producer wants, *then* another writer will be called in, after you've been compensated, of course.

Titles cannot be copyrighted either. This doesn't mean you can call your film *The Sixth Sense*. By doing so, you would be profiting by defrauding the public, which is against the law. And that's what you'd be doing by using a well-known title—causing confusion in the marketplace.

It is possible to find two films that have the same title and are not remakes. This can happen for a few reasons. Perhaps the earlier of the films was not much of a success or it was made so long ago that no one remembers it. Or maybe the genres of the two movies are totally different and the movies themselves have such diverse themes that having the same title doesn't matter. For instance, glance through a video movie guide, and you will find a listing for a 1980 romantic comedy called *Nothing Personal*. You'll also notice the listing for another movie titled *Nothing Personal*, which was produced in 1995. Only this one is about the terrorist factions in Belfast. Two entirely different films; same title. Had the 1980 film been a blockbuster, the 1995 film could not have used the same title.

Speaking of *Nothing*. . . Several years ago, we wrote a script for Ted Danson and his then-partner, Dan Fauci. It was called *Nothing*

Titles cannot be copyrighted. This doesn't mean you can call your film *The Sixth Sense*. By doing so, you would be profiting by defrauding the public, which is against the law. And that's what you'd be doing by using a well-known title— causing confusion in the marketplace.

to Lose. The title was so perfect for the concept of the film that Dan asked if there was any way we could copyright or register the title. Of course the answer was "no."

One day, while the film was in development hell, both of us were working in our office. The TV was on—some talk show—but neither of us was paying much attention to it. Martin Lawrence was the guest, and he began talking about his up-and-coming project—a film with Tim Robbins called *Nothing to Lose.* Nothing to Lose?! Well, he certainly got our attention. We immediately checked it out, and, sure enough, the film—which had the same title as our screenplay—was in production. We were devastated.

After we got the ranting and raving out of our systems, we started making a list of other possible titles. The Martin Lawrence film was released in 1997. It was painful seeing the movie posters plastered all over the city, but by then, our script had gone into turnaround and we had resigned ourselves to our new title. Since that Martin Lawrence film was no big whoop, we may be able to go back to our original title. It's worth a try. Hey, we have *nothing to lose.*

Length of Copyright Protection

When you copyright and/or register your screenplay, only the words—not its ideas or concepts—are protected. We all make ourselves crazy worrying that someone, somewhere will steal from us. Although this is possible, the reality is that most producers would rather buy your script than steal the idea and have to pay another writer to write it.

A work that is created on or after January 1, 1978, is automatically protected from the moment of its creation and throughout the author's life. This protection continues for an additional seventy years after the author's death.

Hopefully, you will not hold on to the copyright of your screenplay. Once you sell your script and it goes into production, you will have to transfer the copyright to the production company or studio that produces it. The screenwriter never owns the copyright of a motion picture or television movie.

Registration Procedure

To register for a copyright of your screenplay, you must complete a PA application form, which is for "published and unpublished dramatic works for the performing arts, including scripts." You can request a PA form by calling the Copyright Office's Forms and Publications Hotline, or by accessing one via its Fax-on-Demand service. You can also download a form from the Copyright Office website. For contacts and other registration information, see page 294 in the Resource List.

The Copyright Office receives more than 600,000 applications annually, and it can take up to eight months for the Office to process your application and mail you the certificate of registration. (It may take you less time to sell your script.) However, the copyright registration is effective on the date that all the required elements—form, fee, and script—are received in acceptable form in the Copyright Office. This means you don't have to wait for them to mail the registration in order to start submitting your script.

If you want to know when the Office receives your material, send your submission by registered or certified mail and request a return receipt from the Postal Service. Allow at least four to six weeks for the return of your receipt. Also, be sure to keep your dated canceled check, bank draft, or money order receipt.

Notice of Copyright or Registration

Once your screenplay is registered at the Writers Guild East or West, or at the U.S. Copyright Office, you may put the Notice of Copyright—you know, this one: © (which took me an hour to find on my WordPerfect program)—followed by the year it was registered, and your name. See the Sample Spec Script Title Page on page 55 to see how this is done.

Many people in the business feel that the copyright or registration notice on the title page is amateurish. It also dates your script, which is not a good thing. Think about it. Let's say that you registered your script in December of 2000. The following month, it will look as though it has been out there for a year. Take this into consideration when deciding whether or not to display these notices.

CONCLUSION

Before moving on to the next chapter, answer the following questions: Do the first few pages of your script set the tone for the genre? Does your script conform with standard industry formatting guidelines? Is it properly bound? Has an eagle-eyed friend checked your script for typos and other red flags? Have you registered your work and/or applied for a copyright?

If you have answered "yes" to all of the questions, you're ready to move on. Next stop? A closer look at the industry and the players who make it work—and who can give you work.

Anguish

by Michael Berlin

New York City—1970s

I was a working psychologist in the city, and I also taught a course called The Psychology of Humor. In the course, I used *Titters—The Woman's Book of Humor* by Ann Beatts, Deanne Stillman, and Judy Jacklin, who is John Belushi's widow. A lot of *Saturday Night Live* people wrote comedy bits for the book. Somewhere in it, there's a piece about graffiti on the men's room wall of a famous New York hotel. In the corner, as a throwaway, they put "John So-and-so is a pervert." Unbeknownst to Ann, Deanne and Judy, that John person was the vice president of that famous New York hotel. He didn't think it was very funny, and he sued them for a lot of money.

My friend, artist Miriam Wosk, had a party at her house. At the party, she introduced me to Ann Beatts who asked me if I would, if need be, testify on her behalf about the intentions of *Titters,* her book that I was using in my course. While I was ready to give a deposition, it never came to that, but I did become friendly with Ann.

Keeping In Touch

In about 1978, I decided to take a year's leave of absence to go to California to become a screenwriter. I made a slight detour and became the dean of a small college and graduate school here in Los Angeles. Then I did unemployment, I struggled, and I wrote some spec scripts.

A week before I moved out here, Miriam-the-artist moved out here, and Ann Beatts was staying at

her house. Ann threw a big party for all of the people on *Saturday Night Live,* and I was invited. I met Belushi, Ackroyd, Gilda Radner. It was a real wild Hollywood end-of-the-'70s party.

During the evening, I got into a conversation with Bigas Luna, a Spanish artist and director who had done movies in Spain and had somewhat of a cult following. We talked films and, after a while, he said to me and to another guy who was in on this conversation, "I want to do a movie with you," nodding at me, "and I want to do a movie with you," nodding at the other guy. If you've been in Hollywood for a while, you hear this line an awful lot. Bigas Luna left the party, and left the country, and I didn't hear from him.

Fast forward to about 1982 or '83. Bigas called me and said, "I'm living in Venice. (California, not Italy.) You know the idea that I told you about called *Anguish?*" At the party, Bigas, who had been learning English by watching televangelists, told me about an idea he had for a movie within a movie within a movie . . . somewhat voyeuristic . . . very scary . . . a statement about how people are transfixed. They don't like violence, but they'll always look at an-accident.

Bigas said, "I wrote the story. It's very rough. Would you read it? And if you're interested, would you do the words to it?" Those were his exact words, "Would you do the words to it?" I read the story. It was wild and wacky. I thought, I don't do this kind of stuff. I want to do serious writing and this is a horror film. Then I thought, it can really be interesting and different and I'd get a trip to Spain. So I started writing it on spec. He and I met every day to talk about the script. When I finished writing it, Bigas storyboarded every shot of the movie according to my script.

Going Where the Money Is

Okay, so I wrote this script and Bigas said, "Now we have to go out and sell it." We took a lot of meetings. Several people wanted to put up some money, so they talked about casting and where it would be shot. Bigas decided that the old woman should be Bette Davis. This was right before she died, when she looked gothic. Jennifer Jason Leigh and Elizabeth McGovern were available to play the parts of two young movie-goers. The prices for the three actresses were reasonable, but we couldn't get the cast approved.

Taking another approach Bigas said, "Let's go down to Miami and look at locations." So we got on a plane and went to Miami. Bigas, who had a production company in Barcelona, was fronting this travel money but didn't have enough to make the movie.

There we were in Miami Beach. Even though it was the beginning of 1984, it looked like old, broken-down Miami in the '50s, which was perfect for our movie. (A few months later, by the middle of '84, *Miami Vice,* which I eventually wrote for, changed everything in Miami for the better.)

After scouting Miami, we then flew to Orlando where Bigas had set up a meeting with two accountants who were representing some film company. We gave them the script and showed them the storyboards and told them that we had just come from Miami and it has the perfect look for our film. These two accountants wanted us to shoot the film in Tampa-St. Petersburg. Each time we brought up the possibility of different kinds of production challenges, for instance, union problems, they'd answer, "Union problems? You may get that in Miami, but you won't get that here." Whatever problem we raised, they assured us, in no uncertain terms, "Don't worry. You won't get that here." *Here*

to us, was the frequent-flyer first class lounge at the airport. We never got to see Orlando. We spent the whole day at the airport with those two accountants. It took awhile until we started to realize who we were actually sitting and talking to. They didn't look like Tony Soprano, but they had the same flavor.

We left Florida, went back to Los Angeles, and after trying but not succeeding in rounding up the money, Bigas said, "I'll call you again," and he left the country.

Something for Which to Be Thankful

In November 1985, I got a phone call from Bigas. He said, "We got the money. We can shoot the film. I'm coming to California for Thanksgiving." When he arrived in town, he took thirty-five rolls of color pictures of movie theaters, of the streets, of sign posts. If it didn't move, he took a picture of it. He was going to build Los Angeles in Barcelona. Bigas asked if I would go to Barcelona in January to rewrite the script. He said he would send me the ticket.

There is No Rain in Spain

Bigas signed Michael Lerner to be the killer, and Zelda Rubinstein as his mother. He hired Talia Paul and Clara Pastor as the young movie-goers. After we all met in Spain, the cast went into rehearsal while I sat in Bigas' studio-with-a-view, rewriting the script.

If you're writing a scary film, you want it to be scary. Zelda, the mad mother who's going blind, has created a killer in her own middle-age son. This son who works at an eye bank, kills his victims, then gouges out their eyes and brings them home to Mama. Eyes are very vulnerable. It's Bigas' thing about voyeurism. At one point, Mama gets a phone call that gets her angry. She has a letter opener in her hand and as she gets angrier and angrier, she carves something into the desk. Angry and talking and carving with the roar of thunder and flashes of lighting in the background, Mama hangs up the phone. We then see what she carved in the wooden desk–an eye–as she says the line, "Tonight, the eyes of the city are mine!" There I was, sitting in the studio, overlooking the mountains of Barcelona, on a clear, sunny, beautiful day, when I wrote that scene. I wanted to twirl my mustache.

In the movie, when Zelda says that ominous line, "Tonight, the eyes of the city are mine," you could palpably feel every body shift in their seats, and I'm thinking, so this is how it works. You write this stuff to scare the pants off people as you're sitting in some sunny room somewhere thinking, how do I make it scarier?

California Calls

I didn't have an agent for this film deal. I used a lawyer. It was my first deal. I wasn't a member of the Writers Guild at the time. I was just so happy to get a movie made and have my name on the screen.

The movie says, in effect, written and directed by Bigas Luna, screenplay dialogue by Michael Berlin. It's a credit I've never seen before and will probably never see again. I literally wrote every word of the screenplay.

Before I left for Spain, I was chasing around Los Angeles, like a chicken without a head, to sign with an agent. But it didn't happen. While I was in Spain, my wife phoned to tell me, "William Morris called and they want to sign you." It was like something out of a movie. I told my wife, "Tell them I'll call them when I get back."

A Once-in-a-Lifetime Experience

I've certainly made much more money doing a lot of other things, but when I was working in Barcelona, it was a dream come true. I thought this is what it means to be a writer. You write and they trust that you can do this and they believe in your words. Bigas never read anything I had written. He just liked me and we connected. He basically gave me his baby. . . his story. Then again, the price was right. I wrote it for him on spec.

Bigas was wonderful to work with. Since I had lived this with him for a long time, nobody knew the movie as well as we did. It was like a big inside joke between the two of us to finally see this thing happen. Then the topper was that *Anguish* won Best Picture at the Sitges Fantasy and Science Fiction Film Festival.

LUNAcy

Anguish was my introduction to being a produced screenwriter. It was everything it should and should not be. All the frustrations of hearing, "Yeah, let's make a movie together," and "I'm back and we're really going to do this," and then doing the work and it all dropped into a gigantic void for months and months. Then another phone call asking for my wish list of actors. Puff!–It all disappeared again. Six months later, a first class ticket to Barcelona.

One of the review lines on the video cassette cover describes *Anguish* as, "excruciatingly enjoyable terror." Come to think of it, that's kinda like being a screenwriter.

Tag

The other guy at the party to whom Bigas also said, "I want to do a movie with you," is Robert Dunn. Robert and Bigas did the film *Reborn* with Michael Moriarty and Dennis Hopper. So Bigas made good on his word to both of us. How often does that happen in Hollywood?

Event Horizon

Written by Philip Eisner

Script, Agent; Script, Deal

I'm from Fort Worth, Texas, went to Stanford University, then, in 1988, my first year out of college, I moved to New York where I wrote my first screenplay. It was about vampires.

My uncle knew Elaine Markson, a literary agent for authors. She met with me, then gave my script to Lisa Callamaro, the person in her office who handled scripts. Lisa read it, saw potential, and became my agent.

The second script I wrote was called *Wirehead,* and it got me a multi-picture deal with Largo Entertainment. It was a cyberpunk thriller, which is probably dead now that *The Matrix* came out.

Stunned

In February of '92, my father was killed in a skiing accident. Years before, my father had told me, "When someone tells you, 'This is going to cost you $1,000.' It hurts. When someone comes and says, 'This is going to cost you $500,000.' It doesn't hurt at all. It's stunning." He was referring to money, but it applies to his sudden passing. It's the difference between a paper cut and waking up and your arm isn't there. My father's dying was not painful, it was stunning. It changed who I was. I don't mean to downplay it, and I'm not being tough about it. It's that I went through this enormous transition and became a completely different person.

Pitch, Glitch and Ditch

A month after the accident, I felt it was time to get back to work. I thought I needed to get back to work. I still had this multi-picture deal with Largo. I went in with an original pitch called *Event Horizon.* It was an idea that I came up with while watching *The Shining.* I thought it would be so cool to take a haunted house and set it in space. I told them the idea, "Like *The Shining* in space." They said, "Good idea. Give us more details." I said, "I can't. I have to write it." We went around in circles for a while. They were being very gentle with me. I have the feeling that Larry Gordon, Largo's Chairman and CEO, said something like, "Hey, his dad just got killed. Let's let him do the script and see what happens."

I was already in a dark place and they sent me off to write a horror script. I had terrible writer's block. Writing, turned out perhaps not to be the best thing for me to be doing at that time. Even so, I dove into it and worked very hard. Luckily there was an executive at Largo named Marilee Wyman who was running Largo's New York office, and was the one who found my second script and brought it to Largo's attention. We struck up a friendship and even though, by then, I had moved to California, we maintained communication.

She stayed on me and kept me from wandering too far into the darkness. It took me about five or six months to write the first draft. When I turned it in, it was well received. They were very enthusiastic. They had one director who was immediately interested, but unfortunately his movie did terribly, so the fact that he was interested did not do it for Largo. At about that time, Larry Gordon and Largo parted ways and the script was held up for two or three years. I went off and was doing other work.

On Location

Once Largo sorted things out, we were back on track and got director Paul Anderson attached. I went through several drafts with Paul. All of that time, I kept asking Lloyd Levin, the producer, "Can I get excited yet?" "Nnnn—we're getting closer." But it was never, "Yes. Be excited." I've had films in preproduction that have folded, so I was trying to stay cool.

Finally, the director was in England, in preproduction, and they were building sets. They'd been faxing me some artwork, and I was changing the script to match the production design. About seven weeks before we were scheduled to start—I was still not letting myself think this is going to happen—they flew me out to do some work on the script.

There was a car waiting for me at the airport. It took me straight to the set. Everyone there was very respectful, which was a nice change from Hollywood. In England it's, "Oh he's the writer." It actually means something there, as opposed to Hollywood where it's, "Why is *he* on the set?"

I was told that Paul, the director, wanted to see me. They walked me around and into the James Bond stage, which is the largest stage in Europe, maybe even the world. It's a six-story building. I walked in and saw five stories worth of scaffolding, all the way to the ceiling. I was taken to the stairs on the outside of the scaffolding and told to go up. I climbed those stairs in this sort of amazing trellis of pipe. There at the top was Paul; his breath was steaming. It was cold and there were no heaters in there at all. He was standing on the edge of this scaffolding, looking down into this enormous set, which is easily the most dramatic set in the film—our evil heart of the ship. It was like this spherical steel nightmare. It was an absolutely gorgeous set. Everywhere there were workmen hammering and fixing and painting. Paul kind of looked over his shoulder and saw me coming. He didn't say "Hello. How was your flight?" Didn't say anything like that. He just grinned at me and said, "You did this."

That was one of the most satisfying moments of my life.

Writer at Work

The other thing that echoed was when I met the movie stars. I met Sam Neill. I got to meet Dr. Grant, *Jurassic Park's* dinosaur guy. Then there was Laurence Fishburne who walks into a room and fills it.

When I met these actors for the first time, we were at a script reading and I was making notes. I was there, literally, as a functionary. That was the first time I had been in a room with actors since I was in college theater. But this time, not only was I in a room with actors, but I was there with Oscar nominees Sam Neill, Laurence Fishburne, Kathleen Quinlan, and a fantastic supporting cast: Jack Noseworthy, Richard T. Jones, Jason Isaacs, Sean Pertwee, Joely Richardson. I was doing my job, listening and finding where things sounded klunky or didn't make sense, and I addressed questions.

I didn't hang out with the cast at all. A) I was busy, and B) I didn't know what to say to these people. So I was standoffish.

A couple of days after I had arrived, Paul wanted to talk to me. Meanwhile, they were doing lighting tests on all of the costumes, and they had Fishburne in this space suit. The space suit weighed about seventy pounds, and the weight of the backpacks where the oxygen tanks were, made them extremely uncomfortable because the weight wasn't evenly distributed over the shoulders and kind of pulled the wearer back. In between takes, they'd have a grip come out and support the back of the space suit so that the actor's back wouldn't get pulled out from just standing. Extremely uncomfortable. Okay, so they were doing these lighting tests. I didn't have any idea what was going on. I was just walking through to where Paul was, and as I did, I heard this enormous voice boom out really loudly,

"Eisner–" It was Fishburne in this space suit. He was pointing at me with this mean look on his face. "You! You Eisner! You did this to me!" That was so cool.

There were moments like those that gave me tremendous pleasure. Moments like that don't come often to writers. When they do, own them.

Summer of '42

Written by Herman Raucher

I can fill your book with tales of "how I sold my screenplays"–all of them different and all of them bizarre. All of them, I fear, unprintable, lest I endanger the lives of the guilty. I will, however, tell you one . . . But only because it's about the only time a screw-up worked out in my favor.

I wrote *Summer of '42* in the middle 1960s and received, along the way, something like forty-seven rejections: 'Too small, too dirty, too nostalgic–too bad.'

It found its way to Warner Bros. at a time when they had very little product and a lot of internal conflict. A young producer (Richard A. Roth) got it to Bob Mulligan (director of *To Kill A Mockingbird*). He took it to Warner Bros. who I don't believe ever read it. They just liked Bob Mulligan and "green-lighted" it. Also, it budgeted at about a million dollars. Also, they stayed away and let us do it however we wished.

Ah but how to pay the screenwriter of this dog-eared original? Warner Bros. didn't want to pay me much money up front–and didn't. My agents (nameless here) didn't much care and turned it over to a young agent as unknown as me. So, my agent and I worked out a deal where I'd get, I think, $30,000 and 15 percent of the net. Knowing that net meant zilch, Warner Bros. agreed.

Meantime, the film still in the can and not released, my agent said I should do a novelization of the film to help the film when it came out. I said, "I don't know *how* to write a book." He said, "Write anything." I did. The book came out ahead of the film and became a best-seller. So, when the film finally came out, the ad-line read: "Based upon Herman Raucher's national best-seller."

The rest, as they say, is history. The picture paid off in a half-hour and the net got to be rather 'over-the-moon.' I went from mortgaging Baltic Avenue to a hotel on Boardwalk. And really because no one was looking and fewer than no one cared. As a result, I suggest that all screenwriters write bizarre clauses into their contracts . . . collect forty-seven rejections along the way . . . and hang on for dear life.

Cheers.

CHAPTER 3

THE INDUSTRY
AND ITS PLAYERS

One of the reasons that navigating the film industry waters can be daunting is because the sea is so vast. And now that you have your spec script in hand, you don't want to waste any time floundering and thrashing around out there without a compass. It's time to start charting your course to help better steer you toward your goal. This chapter is designed to help by giving you an overview of the industry itself, and by introducing you to those all-important industry players. This awareness will help you better see how the entertainment industry operates and which players are best suited to help you move forward in the most appropriate direction.

We'd like to kick off this chapter with a brief overview of the film industry from its early days to the present. Then we'll be moving on to discuss the people who play an integral role in this world.

A BRIEF INDUSTRY OVERVIEW

In the early part of the twentieth century, 1908 to be exact, when New York City was the film center of the country and westerns were filmed in the wilds of New Jersey, a monopoly trust called the Motion Picture Patents Company (MPPC) was formed. It was made up of one distributor and nine leading film companies, including East Coast-based Edison, Biograph, and Vitagraph. Within a couple of years, this syndicate founded the General Film Company to control the distribution of films made by its members. Only MPPC members were allowed to use Edison's patented equipment and Eastman Kodak's film stock. Exhibitors, or movie theater owners, were permitted to show films provided they used the organization's licensed projectors, paid a royalty for each film as well as the machinery used to show them, and—this is the kicker—didn't show any films made by independent production companies.

Desperate to enforce its monopoly of the fast-growing film industry, the MPPC went so far as to hire thugs to disrupt filming at independent movie studios. It also had equipment and property destroyed at these studios, as well as at theaters that showed movies made by independents companies.

To get out from under the jurisdiction of the MPPC, the independents began moving west to Hollywood, which, at that time, was a sparsely populated suburb of Los Angeles. This area had a lot going for it in terms of filmmaking. The weather was good all year round, the scenery was picturesque with its mountains, ocean, and desert, and real estate was a bargain. By the time the MPPC trust was ruled illegal under the Sherman Antitrust Act in 1915, the film industry had a new home in Hollywood. Five years and fifty studios later, Hollywood was producing 90 percent of all American-made films.

By the 1930s, the "studio system" was in place. Hollywood's magnificent seven—Warner Bros., Columbia, Metro-Goldwyn-Mayer (MGM), Paramount, Twentieth Century-Fox, Radio-Keith-Orpheum Corporation (RKO), and Universal—were helmed by their own movie moguls. They were housed on huge lots with complete movie-making facilities, and staffed with their own under-contract writers, directors, cinematographers, musicians, actors, and technical crews—anyone necessary for the filmmaking process. The success of the studio system was due in large part to the cost effectiveness of shooting several films at the same time. Each major Hollywood studio produced anywhere from fifty to sixty films annually.

Another reason for the studios' success was due to their control of film distribution. Acquisition of theaters guaranteed ready markets for their movies, which were bringing in 80 million ticket buyers a week. The studios controlled the production, distribution, and exhibition of films. In other words, it had developed into an industry monopoly. "Déjà vu all over again."

The studio system started crumbling in the late 1940s when the government antitrust decision ordered studios to sell their movie theaters, divesting them of guaranteed outlets for their products. It continued to collapse with the blossoming of television and tax shelters that lured stars abroad with independent filmmakers.

By the early 1960s, independent film companies, called *indies*, were alive and thriving in the film industry. It was commonplace for the major studios, referred to simply as the *majors*, to rent out their facilities to these independent companies, as well as to television production companies.

The Industry's Changing Face

Most of the early major studios are still in existence. Today they are joined by new majors such as Disney and Sony Pictures Entertainment, and mini-majors like DreamWorks SKG. Each major studio produces about ten to fifteen films a year, and is also actively involved in film distribution, television production, and, ironically, in financing independently produced films.

The major studios are union signatories. This means that they agree to hire union talent and pay union wages, which is said to add at least 30 percent to a film's budget. It's one of the reasons that the cost to produce an average studio picture is conservatively estimated at about $30 million. Factor in promotion and distribution, and, in some cases, this price may double.

When a studio *options* or buys a story or a script, the property goes into *development*. While this is a great thing to have happen, it's still too early for any major celebrations. You see, a studio may have 100 projects in all stages of development at the same time, and of these, only a small percent will ever make it to production. Getting a film made usually depends on one studio executive—the president of production—saying, "Yes, let's do it!" Once your project is given the green light, you can up the celebration level a little, but keep in mind that it's still a long way from script to screen.

How do independent film companies differ from major studios? For starters, the independents may or may not be union signatories. Their project budgets are much lower than those allotted for features at the majors, and their financing may come from private sources. Today, with network, cable, and foreign outlets and territories, co-financing a film deal can be as creative as writing a film. Which brings us back to you, the writer. When the time comes to submit your

Write the script you want to write, not the script you think they're looking for. Who knows what they're looking for? They don't know what they're looking for, but they'll know when they see it. What's hot today is passé tomorrow and may be hot again next week. Timing is everything. If you put yourself and your work out there, your timing will be right at some point in time. Remember, even a clock that's broken is right twice a day.

screenplay, what is the best avenue to pursue? Are you better off sub-mitting your work to the major studios or independent production companies? What about independents that are backed by the majors? What are the pros and cons? Is one more advantageous than the other? Read on.

Majors, Indies, and the Novice Screenwriter

According to the American Film Marketing Association (AFMA), independent production companies are defined as "Companies engaged in the production and/or distribution worldwide in all media of all motion pictures and television programs that are not generated by the recognized major studios. It includes those independent productions, even though distributed by a major studio, in which the producer retains a significant ownership interest and is at risk for a significant portion of production costs."

The film and television industry has two principal production/dis-tribution trade groups. One is the Motion Picture Association of America (MPAA), which represents the major movie studios; the other is the American Film Marketing Association (AFMA), which represents the English language independent motion picture and television industry worldwide.

Since 1982, almost two-thirds of the films that have won the Academy Award for Best Picture were produced or licensed interna-tionally by AFMA members—independent companies. *The English Patient, Braveheart, Silence of the Lambs,* and *Dances With Wolves* are just a few of these winners.

Although there are no statistics available, the consensus in the industry is that new writers sell more spec scripts to indies than to the majors. It makes sense. Independent production companies are more likely to take on special little low-budget films starring unknown actors; majors are more involved in producing the big-budget block-busters starring superstars. Most spec scripts tend to fall into the smaller, more personal-type film category.

Another common belief is that independent production compa-nies accept unsolicited scripts more readily than the production com-panies that have deals with the majors. Again, no statistics and no substantiation, but this, too, makes sense. The production companies that have deals with the majors are less inclined to seek out spec scripts from first-time writers. They have studio backing and can afford to pay big bucks for spec scripts from writers with name value and a track record. However, experienced writers don't usually have to write on spec—they pitch their *ideas* to production companies. If a company sees potential in a writer's idea, it'll put the idea into devel-opment, and pay the writer to write the script. Small, independent production companies don't generally have the money for writers' development deals.

So new writers seem to stand a better chance of getting their spec

Writing the Greatest Film Ever

Amazon.co.uk—the United Kingdom's Amazon.com—analyzed the genre, plot, stars, and even the words in the titles of the 100 most popular films at its Internet Movie Database website (IMDb.com). To determine those 100 most popular films, close to 8 million votes were cast by IMDb users, from its catalogue of nearly 240,000 films.

The results will tell you something about the public's taste. Using these ingredients may help you structure a box office record breaker.

■ **Genre.** Dramas rate the highest, and include classics such as *The Godfather, The Shawshank Redemption,* and *Citizen Kane*.

■ **Plot.** The perfect plot combines boy-meets-girl and good-versus-evil, and is set in the future.

Think *Star Wars* and *Bladerunner,* with touches of *Casablanca* and the Japanese classic *The Seven Samurai (Schichinin No Samurai)*.

■ **Stars.** Harrison Ford, Robert De Niro, Humphrey Bogart, and James Stewart are the actors who appear most often in the 100 favorite films. Runners up include Tom Hanks, Kevin Spacey, Marlon Brando, Orson Welles, and Charlie Chaplin. The leading ladies include Jodie Foster, Diane Keaton, Marilyn Monroe, Carrie Fisher, and Sigourney Weaver.

■ **Titles.** Two-word movie titles are best and ideally should include a place, a person's name, or an animal. Examples include *Schindler's List, American Beauty, Citizen Kane, L.A. Confidential, Reservoir Dogs,* and *Raging Bull*.

scripts optioned or bought by independent production companies, rather than companies that have deals with major studios. When dealing with independents, writers have to guard against being exploited. Many indies are not Writers Guild of America signatories. A *signatory* is a company that signs a contract agreeing to abide by the terms of the Writers Guild's Minimum Basic Agreement (MBA) when dealing with writers. (More about this in Chapter 7, "The Deal.")

Getting a deal with a production company that has signatory status is a real plus for a new writer, who then becomes eligible to join the WGA. Furthermore, the production company must abide by the MBA, which significantly protects the writer's rights and substantially reduces her chances of being exploited.

Talk about exploiting the writer . . . There are times when a producer, particularly an indie with no seed money or startup money, loves a script, and wants to get behind it, with every intention of raising money and producing it. The producer may ask the writer for a free option on the script. That means the producer will be able to run

Producers want scripts rewritten for any number of reasons. The most common reasons are to make scripts more marketable, and to cut budget costs. Beware of the producer who starts flexing her creative muscles and asks for rewrite after rewrite, while slowly destroying the script's structure and everything else that attracted her to it in the first place, especially if there are no rewrite fees involved.

with the script for a specified amount of time—usually anywhere from six months to a year—without paying the writer any money. Remember, when your script is optioned, whether or not you get an option fee, no one else has the right to buy the script during the entire option period. If the script has already been shopped and no one else seems to want it, or if the writer has a great feeling about the producer and his ability to get the script on screen, the writer should seriously consider giving the producer a free option.

In addition to the free option, the producer may also ask for a free rewrite or two. The free option and rewrite may pay off, but first, the writer should invest in an entertainment lawyer to draw up an option agreement, spelling out the writer's financial participation if-and-when the film goes into production. The agreement should include additional compensation for the goodwill shown by the writer in the form of a free option and rewrites.

Lydia once had an acting teacher who repeatedly told the class, "You work for nothing; you're worth nothing." While we don't think this is always true, it is something to keep in mind when guarding against exploitive producers who keep asking for rewrites without pay.

Now it's time to learn all about the people who run the industry. As you read about these players in the next part of this chapter, you should get a clear picture of how the film industry game is played. And once you know that, you'll be able to plan your strategy, take the necessary steps, and, with any luck, become a player yourself.

THE PLAYERS

After writing a screenplay, you should focus your efforts on how to sell it to a studio, an independent film company, a television network, or a production company. There are people who can help you. They're called *players,* and they include agents, managers, lawyers, producers, development executives, readers, directors, actors, and writers. They come in all degrees of importance and power. The more important and powerful the players, the more people they have screening their calls, responding to query letters, and sifting through scripts.

If you have family connections, regardless of how remote—your cousin roomed with Susan Sarandon's children's nanny; your uncle is Ridley Scott's podiatrist; your sister-in-law's sister is married to the doorman of the apartment building where Nicolas Cage lives—*use them!* Use any connection you have. Talk about your ambitions to everyone who will listen. Ask people if they know anyone in the industry. You may be surprised to learn that a friend, neighbor, former classmate, or your dentist can introduce you to someone who may be able to help you realize your goals. You might even consider offering a finder's fee to anyone who introduces you to someone who helps you land a deal or get a writing assignment in the industry. You have nothing to lose. Wouldn't you rather have 95 percent of something (a finder's fee is usually 5 percent) than 100 percent of nothing?

If you are like the majority of hopeful screenwriters trying to break into this business, you probably won't have any contacts to help you get your foot in the door. This means simply that you'll have to forge the way for yourself. And you can. Start here by taking an in-depth look at the roles of the industry players from the writer's point of view. Learn how they can help you, and how you can reach them.

Agents

Agents represent talent. For the sake of this book, the talent we're referring to involves screenwriters. In California, *literary agents* represent screenwriters; in New York, those who represent screenwriters are called *theatrical agents.* (In New York, literary agents represent authors.) No matter what you call them, the literary or theatrical agent's job is to solicit work, negotiate, advise, and handle compensation for their screenwriter clients. In return for their services, agents normally receive 10 percent of their clients' gross earnings.

There are many advantages to having an agent. When an agent sends out your screenplay, it is no longer considered an *unsolicited* script. This is a major advantage because unsolicited scripts are often returned unread. Since it is an agent's job to know which studios, networks, and production companies are looking for what kinds of scripts, a good agent is able to target the most appropriate markets for your screenplay. Another major plus in having agent representation is that it gives you and your screenplay credibility. After all, the agent has read your work and believes in it strongly enough to send it out with her name.

During any kind of networking, whenever you're asked, "Who's your agent?" and you can respond with a name, you will instantly rise to professional status in the mind of the person to whom you're speaking, and the level of the conversation is likely to go up a notch.

So you want to be a part of this industry. Want to know who its power players are? *Premiere* magazine publishes "The 100 Most Powerful People in Hollywood" in its annual May or June issue. Also look for *Entertainment Weekly's* "101 Most Powerful People in Entertainment," which comes out each year in a late fall issue.

PROSE FROM A PRO

How to Get an Agent
by Dov S-S Simens
Founder, Hollywood Film Institute

Most Hollywood agents won't read a script from a first-timer. You'll always run into the phrase, "We don't accept unsolicited manuscripts." For the most part this is true, but don't let that stop you.

Most agents who handle writers also handle directors. If you call the agent and say you've written a script and need an agent, the agent's secretary will probably give you the "we-don't-accept" line. So, get the name of a director that the agent handles, and tell the secretary that you have written a script specifically for that director. No guarantee, but this approach will probably result in either the agent or the secretary telling you to send the script. Bottom line is it gets read. If the script is good enough, the agent will call you back. Voila! Remember, if you say you're just a writer looking for an agent, they'll probably hang up.

And that person may be more willing to help you in whatever way she can—after all, you're a writer with an agent.

There's also an advantage to being connected to an agent or agency that represents other industry talent, such as actors, directors, and producers. Through these other clients, an agent is in a good position to help package your project by, hopefully, getting a bankable name or two attached to it. This will make your project more appealing to a studio or network.

Furthermore, you don't have to pay an agent unless your material is sold. This means that you have a professional, experienced person working for you free of charge until your first sale. This makes the agent as eager for that sale as you are (well, almost as eager). When there's interest in your script, an agent will negotiate for you. She has everything to gain by getting you the best deal possible, since the agency's earnings are based on your earnings. The more you make, the more she makes for her agency. (Incidentally, the commission that you pay an agent is a tax-deductible expense.)

So, while you know that it is a good thing to have an agent, also know that it is extremely difficult to get one until you have interest from a producer for your spec script.

How Reputable Agencies Operate

Each state requires agencies to be licensed and bonded with the state. According to the California Labor Commission, this license must be posted in a conspicuous place in the agency. Always check out an agency *before* making contact. In addition to verifying that the agency is state licensed, find out if it is also a WGA signatory. Agencies associated with the WGA are most desirable. You may also want to find out the agency's commission. As mentioned earlier, most charge 10 percent. Every agency is required to file a fee schedule—the percentage it charges—with the Labor Commissioner. This, too, should be posted in a conspicuous place.

According to the Labor Commission, no talent agency is allowed to collect a registration fee from a client. If an agent asks for one, walk away. You don't want to be doing business with her. Also be aware that there are some shoddy agencies that ask writers to pay a fee for reading and critiquing their material. We suggest that you steer clear of these agencies as well.

Contracts between agents and writers are usually from one to three years, with two years being the most common. If the agent fails to make a sale or obtain employment for the writer for a period of at least four consecutive months, either party may terminate the contract. This is important. It may happen that a writer signs a two- or three-year contract with an agent who is all gung-ho initially and begins by sending out her client's work with great determination. Three or four rejections later, the agent may begin to lose confidence and interest in the writer and stop promoting the work. The agent may even stop returning the writer's calls. It's a bad situation. Although the writer signed a contract with this agent, the four-consecutive-month Labor Commission law is on the writer's side. At the end of four months, the writer can send a letter to the agent terminating the contract. (This must be done in writing.) Of course, the writer may not choose to terminate the contract unless and until she has other agent representation. Why? Even though the agent may not be doing much work, the writer can still say, "Yes, I have an agent."

For some insight on how to approach, win over, and work with agents, we strongly suggest that you read the interviews with talent agents Marty Shapiro (beginning on page 99) and Steve Weiss (beginning on page 100). Take their good advice. Both are very successful agents, and have been for many years. They are no-nonsense guys who tell it like it is.

Large Agencies or Small?

As a screenwriter, what type of agency will offer you the best representation? Is it better to set your sights on one of those big and powerful agencies like the William Morris Agency, International Creative

Agent Humor...

SCREENWRITER #1

My agent called, and while I was talking to him, my wife's lawyer served me with divorce papers. I put them on the stove. They caught fire and burned down the house.

SCREENWRITER #2

Your agent called you?

Management (ICM), Creative Artists Agency (CAA), or United Talent Agency (UTA), or would one of the mid-sized agencies such as Endeavor Talent Agency, The Gersh Agency, or Broder-Kurland-Webb-Uffner Agency be more appropriate? And what about the smaller agencies? Writers have debated over the agency issue for decades.

Those who are in favor of the big guys argue that your film can be packaged over a weekend—complete with producer, director, and stars. Another argument is that the agents who work for William Morris, ICM, CAA, or UTA have leverage, and are in a position to bargain, as in, "You buy this writer's screenplay, and I'll see if we can clear the schedule of the director you want for that other film."

The writers in favor of the smaller agencies argue that it is easy to get lost in the shuffle at the big agencies. The agent has to work hard to sell a writer who has no track record. And why should she, when she has a stable of experienced writers whose names are already known and who have acceptability? At a smaller agency, there seems to be more nurturing . . . more handholding. Agents at smaller agencies often spend more time bringing a new writer along, hoping to advance the writer's career as well as their own.

There was a time when writers were advised to shop around for an agency and agent. Interview more than one. Listen to that inner voice—your gut instinct—that tells you which agent is right for you. Unfortunately, those days are gone forever for a new writer. Now, with the popularity of film schools, there are gazillions of new writers out there, all with spec scripts, all looking for agents. So unless and until there's a buzz about your spec script or actual interest in it, it's very hard to get agent representation, especially without a personal recommendation. That being the case, initially, you may sign with any agent who is willing to represent you. Before you sign, just be sure to check that the agency is licensed by the state. If it is a WGA signatory, that's even better.

There is nothing like getting information from the source. This means if you want to know about agents and agencies, talk to agents at agencies, which is exactly what we did. Agents Marty Shapiro and Steve Weiss were gracious enough to take the time to answer our questions, and they have permitted us to share their input with you. Their Question and Answer sessions are found beginning on the next page.

Q & A with Agent Marty Shapiro

Marty Shapiro and Mark Lichtman started the Shapiro-Lichtman Talent Agency on July 4, 1969. It is a mid-sized agency that is located on Beverly Boulevard in Los Angeles. The agency represents writers, producers, directors, a very small group of actors, and a number of below-the-line people, including production designers, cameramen, and film editors.

What is the advantage of a screenwriter signing with your size agency?

Personalized attention rather than being part of a list at a big agency.

How should a new writer approach your agency for representation?

We consider new writers on a very selective basis. We follow up on recommendations from people we have relationships with, and we evaluate the query letters and backgrounds of those who have solicited us. The query letter and background of the writer has a lot to do with whether we'll look at the work. The person's background is important: Is the writer a novelist or a playwright? Has he or she worked at an ad agency, or completed studies at AFI or one of the top film schools like NYU, Columbia, USC, or UCLA? The writer's background, coupled with a clever query letter, and our present workload, influence our decision.

Does age matter?

I believe with new writers, it doesn't matter. If they have a piece of spec material, nobody knows if they're twenty years old or seventy. When I read a new writer's work, I'm evaluating the material. The work speaks for itself, whether it's written by a man or a woman, whatever minority, whatever age.

Once you decide to take it to the next step with a writer, what would be the next step? Would you meet with that writer?

Most of the time the writer isn't in California. We would ask for the script or the material on an exclu-sive basis, providing no other agent has seen it. We won't read in competition with other agents when it's a new writer. Once we ask for the material, we also ask for a commitment in advance, so that if we want to represent the writer, the writer will enter into a representation agreement with us.

What do you look for when you read a new writer's script?

A lot of things: dialogue, story originality, construction and overall development of the script. All of the above influence our decision. We know within the first twenty pages if the script is any good. The story can be great, but if the dialogue is weak, we'll know that within the first ten pages, and we probably won't continue reading the material.

Do you have creative input when it comes to a new writer's script?

I'm not going to represent material that has potential but is not well written. I don't tell writers how to rewrite their work. It's got to be pretty close to ready before I'll represent the writer. Of course, if we feel that a script is ready to market, but have a suggestion on how to improve it, we would expect the writer to take the suggestion. But the script should be marketable even without making any changes.

Do you plan down-the-road career goals for a new writer?

I think at some point you have to look down the road, but until that writer starts to sell, it's hard to plan ahead.

Do you prefer a new writer to come with a trunkful of scripts?

If somebody sends me a letter and says, 'I've written nine spec scripts and think now I've really honed my craft,' I wouldn't look at that writer. If that person has written nine spec scripts, shopped them, and they haven't sold, it's not a very good sign. It does not mean that the writer isn't talented, and sooner or later the scripts may sell; but we have limited time and take on very few new people, so we have to have some basis for narrowing down the field. We don't want someone who has been around and hasn't sold anything.

What's the formula for a good agent-writer relationship?

Trust.

Do you have any good, old-fashioned basic advice for writers?

If a writer approaches an agency, he or she should know who is at the agency. If I get a letter that says: To whom it may concern or Dear Agent, or I get a letter for an agent who hasn't been with us for years, I don't even read the letter. If a writer can't take the time to find out the name of the person to approach, why should the agency take the time to consider that writer? I look for reasons not to encourage someone to send me something. I have to. I get over 100 letters a week.

Of the 100 letters a week, how many receive responses?

We answer every letter, even if it's to say we're not accepting new clients. The biggest waste of time and money is when new writers skip the query letters and send us their scripts. We send them back and tell them we don't accept unsolicited material.

Aside from writing talent, what do you think is the secret of a screenwriter's success?

Luck! There are a lot of very talented people who can't put a career together. Then, there are some people who have less talent but get the right break. Luck plays a big part in success. Of course, there are a lot of other factors—hard work, coming up with the right project at the right time, and being in the right place at the right time, which is probably part of having luck.

Q & A with Agent Steve Weiss

In 1971, Steve Weiss entered the training program at the William Morris Agency—one of the top three international talent agencies in the world. His first job was in the mailroom. Now, a William Morris Agency Vice President, Steve represents writers and producers, and packages television movies and series.

How should new writers with one or more spec scripts approach the agency?

Any way they can!

Do you see new writers?

Yes, I'll see new writers. It will be because somebody has recommended them, or because I might have seen their work someplace, or because they have sent me a letter that intrigued me.

What do you look for in a new writer?

That innate ability to tell a story and be able to execute the story in the proper format.

Does that mean you would first meet with the writer?

Probably not. When I talk about the writer's ability to tell a story, I mean on paper. To meet with writers and have to listen to their histories and favorite colors and who they know isn't what I'm interested in. I'm interested in their work. I would want to read the material before I meet the writer, so that I have a point of view.

When you read a spec TV or film script, what is most important to you?

Something that captures my interest for that hour or two that I might be sitting with that screenplay. Obviously, a good story, in and of itself, is not the end all. It is the ability to take that good story and unite it with dialogue that rings true, and scene structure that keeps the story moving forward. Those are the first things that capture my interest... or not.

Once a new writer becomes a client, what is your job as agent?

First and foremost with a new writer, my job would be introducing that person's work to the marketplace, and making sure that the buyers who we depend on for writers' employment are aware of who this writer is.

Would you do that by sending out the writer's spec script?

We would talk about what material that writer has. If it is just one script, quite honestly, I would ask that writer to bring me something else. I wouldn't sign somebody based on just one piece of material. I want to be convinced that the writer is not just a one-shot wonder. I want to know that the writer has the ability to think creatively in other areas beyond that one spec script.

What do you expect of the writer?

When I have to do all the work of getting the marketplace familiar with a writer, I expect that writer to listen to the game plan and work with me to effectuate it. Sometimes this means asking them to write something specific. Right now, I'm dealing with a young writer who would like to break into television

writing in the drama area. This writer has a wonderful episode of *Law & Order,* but also wants to write for *Ally McBeal.* In order for me to get this writer considered for a show in another genre, I must have a sample script in that genre, or something else to show that is applicable. I cannot send a *Law & Order* script to the *Ally McBeal* people. They do not want to see it. It is not the same kind of writing. I need the right ammunition. The same applies to long-form writers who want assignments. And so, it is not unheard of for an agent to suggest to a writer, "Perhaps you should try writing one of these."

Would you suggest rewrites to a new writer for a spec script that has potential?

I don't know that I would encourage a writer that I wasn't already 100 percent excited and enthusiastic about to do additional work just to try and please me. There are too many new writers out there to keep telling somebody to come back when it's better. I'll do that with my clients who are writing something on assignment. They'll come to me with their first draft and I'll give them some notes and then they'll do what they want with it.

Would you deal with new writers who don't live in Los Angeles?

I wouldn't. Presently, I represent writers who live in New York, Boulder, and one in San Francisco. The difference is that these writers have already established themselves. They don't have to be here to take meetings with producers who are not familiar with them.

Doesn't that apply more to television episodic and movie-of-the-week writers than to feature film writers?

Feature film writers can and do live all over the world. But if we're talking about new writers, I, for one, would want them available to meet-and-greet. If they're not living here in L.A., then we have to be concerned with the time and cost of getting them here. We're talking about somebody who probably doesn't have a bank account and can't afford to breeze in and out of town at somebody's request. It's important to me that a new writer is here, within an hour's drive from any meeting that I set up. I wouldn't want to work any other way with someone new. I don't think you can.

In the motion picture area, if we're dealing with a writer who has a great spec script that we are going out to sell, then that writer doesn't have to be around. We send out the script and somebody will read it. It doesn't require a meeting. What often happens is that script may not be something a production company wants to produce, but if they like the writing, they may ask to meet the writer. It may result in a writing assignment. Or if that feature writer has an idea to pitch and not an existing script, he'd better be here to pitch to the person who has the money to pay for that idea to be developed into a script. If the writer is living in Iowa, a phone call isn't going to work. You have to be here. This is the center of the business.

I would think that a writer, actor, director, or producer—anyone serious about being in this business—would know that they have to be here and wouldn't even attempt to do it from afar because it would only put them that many steps behind everyone else who *is* here.

What is the formula for a good agent-writer relationship?

Open communication . . . honesty. I let my clients know what the realities of the marketplaces are, and keep them apprised of the cyclical fashion, or whatever it is that's influencing how the industry is moving. I don't give my clients false hope or make vacant promises. I have a policy of being honest. I learned a long time ago from a very wise man, my dad (Lou Weiss, Chairman Emeritus of William Morris), that lying only causes you to lie a second and third time to cover the first lie, so why do that to begin with? It's easier to tell the truth, and it makes for a happier and more productive agent-writer relationship.

Aside from writing talent, what do you think is the secret of a writer's success?

The ability to write *is* the secret. How exciting to pull something out of your mind that may or may not have a place in reality, and then be able expand it into something that other people want to see.

What advice can you give to new writers?

My advice to any writer or anyone involved in the creative arts is to practice your craft. Become as good as you can be. There are a lot of writers who have written a piece of material and believe it's the greatest thing in the world—and they live and die by that. Months or even years go by and they're still saying, 'I have this great script.' Yes, but what have you done lately? You don't get better at anything unless you practice. If writers aren't serious about their craft, then why should anyone else take them seriously? My advice to a writer: Write!

The words of advice from industry professionals Marty Shapiro and Steve Weiss give you a personal glimpse into the world of agents and agencies. If you decide to seek agent representation to help you sell your spec script, keep in mind that finding an agent can be a daunting task. As mentioned earlier, unless you have been recommended, are already established as a writer with credit as a play-wright, novelist, or journalist, or there is interest in your spec script, getting a good agent can be a real challenge. Difficult? Yes. Impossible? No.

When starting your agent search, there are a number of sources you can turn to for leads. For example, the Writers Guild of America offers a list of franchised agents, as do publications such as the *Hollywood Creative Directory—Agents & Managers*, and websites like www.hollywoodlitsales.com. Detailed information on these and other sources for finding reputable agents is presented in Chapter 4.

If you can get an agent to read your script, good. If that agent wants you as a client, great. If that agent is with a reputable, licensed agency, try to think of a reason not to sign with that agency. If you can't think of one, then sign! And congratulations on getting yourself an agent.

Managers

Managers are generally concerned with setting goals and guiding the long-term careers of their clients. They are not usually out there selling a writer's script, but they will do whatever is necessary to make that sale happen. For instance, a manager may help the writer find an agent and then keep after that agent to do right by the client. She may help the writer connect with a lawyer, a financial advisor, and other business-related people who may be able to advance or protect the writer's career. The manager may also use her contacts to get a star, director, or producer attached to a project.

> ### PROSE FROM A PRO
>
> ## Do Everything
> **by Screenwriter and Producer Terry Rossio**
> Co-writer: *Shrek, The Road to El Dorado, The Mask of Zorro, Aladdin.*
>
> Breaking into the film business is not a problem that resolves itself through a single answer or path. It's a problem that succumbs only to a process, a series of efforts taken over time. And the bitch of it is, you never know which is the right strategy until it pays off. So you do everything. Whether the odds are with you or not. You do everything.

Management firms, unlike agencies, are not licensed, bonded, franchised, or unionized. Anyone can hang out a shingle that says "Manager." State Labor Commissions do not govern managers and management firms. There are no industry standards with which to adhere, nor is there a ceiling on a manager's fee. If a manager asks for 20 percent of a client's earnings, and the client agrees, then 20 percent it is. This percentage of the writer's earnings is in addition to the agent's percentage. So, if a writer has a manager who charges 20 percent, and an agent who takes 10 percent, that writer will be giving up 30 percent. Of course, she will still wind up with 70 percent of "something." Without a manager, who got the agent, who sold the script, that writer may have 100 percent of "nothing." We're not pushing you, or even suggesting that you put your energy into finding a manager, we're simply presenting different angles for you to consider.

Large Companies or Small?

Just like agencies, there are large, medium, and small management companies. Does size count? Once again, just like agencies, there are positives and negatives for each.

Many industry pros agree that the novice writer may fare better at a smaller company or with a manager who has a limited clientele, and where there is a tendency to give more personal attention and interest to new writers. It is simply too easy to get lost and fall between the cracks at a large management firm. If you find a manager who cares about your career, forget about the size of the company. Take advantage of the opportunity by working hard to come up with more product for the manager to manage.

Getting a Manager

It is as difficult to get a manager as it is to get an agent. Needless to say, the best way to meet a manager is through personal recommendation. If you don't know anyone who knows a manager, you'll have to depend on getting names yourself (we tell you where to find them in Chapter 4).

Managers are not affiliated with the Writers Guild as signatories. This eliminates one way of checking on the legitimacy of a management firm. How do you know if a manager is legitimate? Unfortunately, there is no sure way. There are two organizations that managers can join and, chances are, those who are members, are on the up-and-up. These organizations are the National Conference of Personal Managers (NCOPM) and Talent Managers Association, Inc. (TMA). Of course, there are many wonderful, legitimate managers who are not members of these organizations.

The National Conference of Personal Managers was established in 1942. Its members abide by a code of ethics that includes having personal management as their primary occupation; dealing honestly and fairly with their clients; not deriving personal gains at the expense of clients; treating client relationships in a confidential manner; not encouraging artists to breach existing personal management contracts; being proud of the personal management profession; and exchanging information with other NCOPM members in the best interest of their clients. Most important, NCOPM members never accept a fee from a client on the promise of attempting to get work for the client.

Talent Managers Association, Inc. was founded in 1954. This non-profit mutual benefit corporation is an association of professional talent managers who have shown themselves to be ethical, knowledgeable and skilled as talent/artist/literary managers, and have thus been accepted as such by their peers. The Association exists for the benefit of its members, the talent represented by the members, and the profession of talent management. (Contact information for the National Conference of Personal Managers and for the Talent Managers Association is found in the Resource List.)

What to Look for in a Manager

Aside from the obvious—honesty, integrity, contacts, assertiveness, experience, and success—you want a manager who wants you, who believes in your talent, and who believes that she can help you make the most of that talent.

If a manager is interested in you, find out what she proposes to do for you. Listen to how she plans to advance your career. Before you sign any agreement, talk things over with her and make sure you understand exactly what she expects from you in return. Also, ask the manager about the clients she's presently representing. It's a good indication of how successful she's been. Many management companies have websites, which is an excellent way of learning a lot about them, including their client lists.

To get a better understanding of how a manager manages, we were fortunate enough to have an in-depth interview with Wendi Niad. Beginning on page 106, we present an eye-opening account of her role as an experienced manager in the film industry. It will help you to better understand whether or not a manager is right for you.

Before approaching a manager, find out about that manager, the management company and the kind of people they represent. Visit their websites. Check them out in the *HCD Agents & Managers Directory*. That way, you'll get a sense if yours is the kind of material they would be interested in. This is so basic, and most people don't do it. I get queries for things that my company doesn't handle. . . . Those people waste their time as well as mine.

—Wendi Niad
Manager

Q & A with Manager Wendi Niad

Before opening her own management company, Wendi Niad was an agent with International Creative Management (ICM), and then ran the literary department at another agency—Susan Smith & Associates.

Describe your company, Niad Management.

We're small and boutiquey, unlike an AMG or a Brillstein-Grey. We're more personal, more hands on, like the old-fashioned type management company. I sit down with my clients and ask them where they want to be five years from now. That's how we determine what it is that we want to accomplish, and then I structure a plan of action to get results.

Most of my clients have been with me for a number of years, and have become my friends as well. I love the people I work with. There's not one client who can't get me on the phone, and I never go home without returning a phone call. It's not a corporate environment. I have two people working with me and I also have interns. I handle all of the writers and directors represented by my company. Amy DeSouza, who is vice president of talent, handles all of the actor-clients.

For a screenwriter, what's the advantage of having a manager?

It's very easy to get lost in an agency when you're a screenwriter. Agents have lots of clients and usually more than one that writes in the same genre. In my case, I have one client per genre. None of my clients would ever compete for the same job. I will not take on a new writer who would be in direct competition with any of my clients. When I work for somebody, I work for that person alone in that genre, so I can either bug the agent, or I can do a lot of the legwork myself. An agent may do some of the legwork, but needs to do it for the other clients as well, and can't really show a preference.

Should a writer pursue an agent first, or a manager first?

An agent is the person who's supposed to sell a spec script and procure work for their clients; although, when my clients don't have agents, I have sold their spec scripts and procured work for them with the aid of an attorney. It may have to do with the commerciality of the writer—the type of material you have. If you can write scripts for Martin Lawrence or Jim Carrey, chances are you'll have an easier time getting an agent, and an agent will have an easier time selling your work. If you're into historical pieces or dramas—higher quality stuff—the line is much more blurred as to whether you need an agent or a manager. A lot of my clients have both and some only have me.

Is it legal for a manager to sell a script?

Yes, it is legal as long as I have a lawyer on the phone with me. Nowhere, to the best of my knowledge, does it say that it's illegal for a manager to sell a script.

What's the best way for a screenwriter to approach a manager for representation?

First, it's all about research. Before approaching a manager, find out about that manager, the management company and the kind of people they represent. Visit their websites. Check them out in the *HCD Agents & Managers Directory*. That way, you'll get a sense if yours is the kind of material they would be interested in. This is so basic, and most people don't do it. I get queries for things my company doesn't handle, like recently, on-camera hosting. Those people waste their time as well as mine.

Once you've established that the manager and management company are appropriate for you, send a query letter. The letter should tell how you found out about the management company. There should also be information that gives the manager a sense of who you are. Include a synopsis of your spec script. The synopsis in a query letter should be no more than a paragraph.

A query letter says a lot about the person who's sending it. If you take pride in your work, let the query letter reflect that. Don't have typos all over the page . . . and be sure to spell the manager's name correctly.

Do you and your company see new writers?

Absolutely. I love reading new writers. You never know where that next spec's going to come from or the next Joe Eszterhas or Steve Zaillian for that matter. After a writer does the research on my company, a query letter may be faxed, snail-mailed, or e-mailed to me.

What do you look for in a new writer?

Do you know what counts more than anything? The ability to take notes. My job is to know what makes a good script, what's wrong with a script, and how to fix it. I do a lot of script notes. When a new writer comes to me, his ability to take what I have to say and actually incorporate it in the next draft, says a lot about the kind of writer he is. They don't necessarily need to agree with me if it's something subjective, but many times I've given simple technical, structural notes to someone and they've argued with me as to why they're not going to do that. Usually it's only because they've rewritten it three times already and they don't want to do it again. If they do that with me, I'm certainly not going to put them in a room with an executive, because they're going to argue with that executive and that executive is going to call me and say, "Don't ever do that to me again."

Does a screenwriter's age make a difference to you?

I've got clients that are over forty and fifty—writers whose scripts are produced. I don't believe in ageism at all.

When a writer signs with your management company, how long is it for and what percentage do you get?

Our contract is for a year. I take a 15-percent commission. When I first started, I felt guilty about taking 15 percent, because, as an agent, I only took 10 percent. Everyone kept saying, as a manager, you can take as much as you want. The only reason I went up to 15 percent is because I spend so much time now doing notes and working closely with the writer.

Are you open to managing writers who don't live in L.A.?

I don't have a problem with it, but the writer needs to understand that he's limiting himself. I can't set up meetings and introduce him around town if he doesn't live in town.

What's the formula for a good manager-screenwriter relationship?

Every so often I have a client turn in a script and then not do anything for a year. That same writer will complain to me that *I'm* not doing anything. Well, if I've already sent out last year's script, and everyone has passed on it, I need something new to sell. I can't repitch the old script. You're only as good as the last thing you've done. Everyone is going to want to know, "Well, what has he written lately?" Getting back to the question, if I had to come up with a formula for a good manager-screenwriter relationship, it would be that the writer writes and the manager attempts to do something with it to build a career.

Aside from writing talent, what is the secret of a screenwriter's success?

A willingness to learn and grow. Not to have an ego. Every single writer gets rewritten by the studios, even the A-List writers. You have to be willing to deal with that . . . to deal with the fact that you can't please everybody. You have to know when to let go. Sometimes a writer has written all he can write; then he has to be willing to walk away from it. It's very difficult. It's incredibly personal. No matter who you are—Ron Bass* gets rewritten! You have to understand that that's the way it is.

---

* Screenwriter Ron Bass wrote *My Best Friend's Wedding, Passion of Mind, Waiting to Exhale, Dangerous Minds, Snow Falling on Cedars, Entrapment, Stepmom, When a Man Loves a Woman, What Dreams May Come, How Stella Got Her Groove Back, Sleeping With the Enemy, Joy Luck Club,* and *Rain Man,* to name a few.

Can you give an example of a manager's efforts paying off for a writer-client?

A writer I was working with back in 1990, when I was an agent at ICM, had a project set up with Bette Midler's company for Bette Midler to do as a feature. It languished and went into turnaround. It was then picked up by Paramount and Eddie Murphy's company. Never got made there. Three years ago, I started representing this writer when I started my management company. I researched all the stuff that we had done when I was with ICM, and I decided to get my hands back on this project. I sent it over to some of the cable networks, and, sure enough, TNT was interested in it and picked it up in turnaround. This writer just got paid *another* six-figure sum to adapt the story for TNT. She's now written this same "script" for three separate companies, getting paid three separate times. I love my job!

If you feel that having a manager is the way to go to help you get established as a writer, one of the best places to begin your search is with the *Hollywood Creative Directory—Agents & Managers.* This resource includes a country-wide listing of managers along with their contact information. Additional criteria on this directory and other resources for creating a list of managers, is presented in detail in Chapter 4.

Entertainment Lawyers

When you're an established screenwriter and have offers coming at you and assignments lined up for the next five years, you may opt for an entertainment lawyer instead of, or in addition to, an agent and/or manager. Lawyers negotiate their clients' contracts, and some even guide their clients' careers. There are high-powered entertainment lawyers whose law firms have star-studded clients. Much like agents at the big agencies, these lawyers can be matchmakers and package your script with any or all of the elements—producer, director, and a star or two.

Production companies, as a rule, do not want unsolicited material. All companies will accept a script that is submitted by a reputable agent; most will accept one that is submitted by an entertainment lawyer; but not many, especially in Los Angeles, will accept a script from a non-entertainment lawyer.

As a new writer, you may want to use an entertainment lawyer in place of an agent—not because you don't want an agent, but because you haven't been able to get one yet. One of the downsides is that lawyers are expensive—those with successful practices have fees that may start at $500 an hour. Also, as a writer with no track record, don't expect a lawyer to act as a packager or agent who's going to initiate submission of your script to a production company, director, or star. That's not in their job description. After *you* have done all of the legwork and have generated interest in your script, probably the most you can expect from the lawyer is to submit your script with a cover letter on her stationery. As a new screenwriter, unless you have a direct link to a hotshot entertainment lawyer who owes your family a big favor, it is more realistic to set your sights on one who is just breaking into entertainment law. He is more likely to charge a reasonable hourly rate.

If you don't have an agent and can't afford a reasonably priced entertainment lawyer, but happen to know a non-entertainment lawyer who is willing to lend a helping hand, fine. Just be sure that anyone, particularly a production company, who has responded positively to your query letter and wants to see your spec script, will accept your work from a non-entertainment lawyer. Be sure to bring up this matter only *after* the production company has expressed interest in seeing your work; don't mention it in your initial query letter. If the company won't accept the script from a non-entertainment lawyer, chances are, it will still want to see your script, and you will be asked to sign a Submission Release Form. This is a standard form that absolves the production company from a lawsuit if it produces a film that is similar to yours after reading your script. Detailed information on this form is presented in Chapter 7.

Getting back to the entertainment lawyer . . . Most seasoned screenwriters will tell you that as soon as you get an offer of any kind—from an agent, manager, or producer—it is advisable to sit down with an entertainment lawyer who can help protect you from being abused. Don't fool yourself by thinking that there is such a thing

Sometimes producers or studio executives come up with crazy ideas and suggestions that I don't agree with. But upon reflection I realize that these suggestions come from a valid problem they're having with the story. And if I can focus on the problem I can come up with a better solution.

—Barry Strugatz
Screenwriter

as a *standard* agreement or contract. There is room for negotiation in every legal document. Don't be sorry somewhere down the road that you didn't invest in a lawyer who could have explained and prevented costly ramifications of a contract you signed. Again, as soon as you get an offer, get an entertainment lawyer.

What to Look for in a Lawyer

If you want a lawyer to make submissions for you once you've made the contacts, ask everyone you know if they know a starting-out entertainment lawyer who would be willing to work with a screenwriter on a contingency basis. In other words, the lawyer gets paid only when you sell your script. The fee or percentage should be decided upon when the lawyer agrees to work with you, and before he makes the first submission.

If there's interest in your screenplay, and you begin searching for a lawyer to negotiate the deal, then it should be easy to get an entertainment lawyer. (At this point, however, you may want to take advantage of your desirable situation and get an agent. And you should also have an entertainment lawyer to review all contracts and agreements.)

If you're going to have a lawyer negotiate for you, choose one who has had contract experience in film and television. If you can't afford one, then go for a less-experienced lawyer who is willing to charge you an hourly rate once your contract is executed and you start earning money, or who is willing to accept an agreed-upon percentage of the earnings on that one property, just as you would pay an agent. Even if the lawyer isn't very experienced, chances are she will have the ear of an experienced industry lawyer who can guide her in doing a good job for you.

Be sure to settle the payment agreement up front and in writing. It will make for a good relationship. Also, the lawyer will respect you for getting and setting things straight right from the start.

Producers

A producer can champion your script. A producer can turn your script into an attractive package by attaching a director and/or star to it. A producer can get your script read at a studio or network. A producer can get you a pitch meeting at a studio or network. It's good to have a producer!

There are several kinds of producers. No, not classy or sleazy, generous or cheap, sweaty or cool. Well, that too, but for the purpose of knowing who to approach with your spec script, it is important to realize that there are different kinds of producers with varied job descriptions. At best, these descriptions are a bit sketchy, because in this industry, each film project is eked into existence with its own set of rules, deals, titles, and responsibilities. So, keep in mind that what follows is a "generally speaking" list of producer types.

- **Producer.** The finder, hirer, developer, arranger, and overseer. The producer finds the project; hires personnel, including a writer (if needed), director, cast, and crew; gets the project into development at a studio or network; arranges financing (that may be when an executive producer comes on board); and oversees the project during production. The producer is often the first person on a project and the last person off the project.

- **Executive Producer.** Most often, this title denotes power. Since money is power, the executive producer may have earned the title by financing or securing the financing for the film.

- **Co-Producer.** The producer's partner who is responsible for contributing a major element. A co-producer may be the one who brought the property to the producer, or who linked a star's name to it.

- **Line Producer.** The person responsible for supervising the entire production and making sue the shooting goes according to schedule and within budget. The line producer is also a troubleshooter, taking care of all of the crises that occur on a daily basis. You can be sure that *almost* every line producer has or is looking for a screenplay that she can set up at a studio, or for which she can get independent financing. This way she can be the producer, co-producer, or executive producer, and hire a line producer to do the day-to-day grunt work.

Now that you know the different types of movie producers, how can you find the ones who might be interested in your particular script? In many cases, production companies tend to make certain types of movies—ones that fall into a particular genre or genres. The trick is to figure out which companies would be most interested in your screenplay.

In addition to checking out resources, such as the *Hollywood Creative Directory—Producers,* which lists over 1,700 production companies, as well as the names of thousands of producers, studio and network executives, and development people, there are many other avenues for finding appropriate contacts, including a number of websites that offer valuable information. One such site is Hollywood Literary Sales (www.hollywoodlitsales.com), which provides an extraordinary online Spec Screenplay Sales Directory. This database of screenplay sales from 1990 to the present, allows you to see who's buying and selling your type of material. The list of resources goes on and on. In Chapter 4, detailed information on this and other sources will help you locate the best production companies for your work.

Development Executives—D-Girls and D-Guys

Studios, television networks, production companies, and many actors employ development executives, also known as *D-girls* and *D-guys,* and sometimes called *story editors.* These people are constantly on the lookout for properties to put into development. Once the D-girl finds what she considers a viable story—it can be in any form: spec script, treatment, pitch, novel, play, magazine article, song—and she does a selling job to the company's decision maker(s), she puts the property into development. *Development* is the nurturing stage of a project as it goes from script to screen (if it lives that long). It is estimated that one out of every forty projects in development makes it to the screen.

If you are interested in reaching a development person, the mentioned-earlier *Hollywood Creative Directory—Producers* offers a list of production companies and their staffs, including development personnel. If you know of a company that does your kind of films, and you don't have access to this directory, call the production company directly. Explain to the person who answers the phone why you're calling, and ask for the name of the person in charge of development. Get the correct spelling of the name and the person's title. Then send a query letter. As you will see in the following chapters, it's important to address your query letter to the appropriate person at the company. Do not send correspondence to the Development Department or the Director of Development. It is in your best interest to get a specific name. Always be prepared to pitch your script. (Chapter 5 will help you prepare.) Often, at small production companies, the person who answers the phone may also be the person in charge of development.

Specific guidelines for determining the most appropriate development executives to approach and how to do so are presented in Chapter 4. The best resources for finding these people are detailed as well.

Readers and Coverage

Production companies, agents, managers, actors, directors, and story or development departments at studios and networks are inundated with material. Since the execs and assistants can't possibly read everything that's sent to them, *readers*, also known as *story analysts*, are employed to do their initial reading for them. Most readers are recent college and/or film school graduates who are aspiring screenwriters or film executives. Generally, readers work freelance and are paid per script. Their job is to read a script and then write an in-depth assessment of it. This report is called *coverage* and is kept on record in a *coverage database*. Coverage helps company executives decide whether or not to consider buying the project.

If the reader gives your script favorable coverage and recommends it, you've passed the first line of resistance, and your script is ready to continue its climb to the head honcho. That's the good news. The not-so-good news is that if the reader, who is on the lowest rung of the industry's film-development ladder, says "pass," chances are your script is history at that company.

It would probably be worthwhile getting a copy of the coverage on your screenplay, but it doesn't work that way. Coverage is confidential. Of course if you have a friend at the company. . . . Meanwhile, take a look at a typical coverage form, which is found on pages 114 and 115. It presents the criteria that is assessed for each script. (Many of the terms used in a typical coverage form are further detailed in Chapter 5.) Assume the role of a reader and review your own screen-

When evaluating material, part of a reader's job is to know what the client is looking for—and every client is interested in something different. Often, mainstream producers and large studios look for high-concept scripts, while independent producers are inclined to look for more offbeat, innovative material.

Sample Coverage Form

This typical coverage sheet, which is filled out by readers, presents criteria that is assessed for each script.

TYPE OF MATERIAL: Screenplay, treatment, etc.

NUMBER OF PAGES: (Remember, no more than 120.)

SUBMITTED BY: Agent, lawyer, publisher, etc.

SUBMITTED TO: Producer or studio exec the material was meant to reach.

ANALYST: The reader's name.

COVERAGE DATE: When this form was completed.

TITLE: Name of the material.

AUTHOR: That would be you!

CIRCA: When the story takes place.

LOCALE: Where the story takes place.

GENRE: Category of the material.

ATTACHMENTS: Any talent that comes with the project.

LOGLINE / THEME: A few sentences that provide the essence of the story.

SYNOPSIS: A detailed summary of the screenplay, including the major and minor plotlines. A typical synopsis is anywhere from one to three single-spaced pages.

COMMENTS: The reader's assessment of the work, including the premise of the story and its potential as a viable property for the company. This may also include an evaluation of the writer's capabilities. Is the premise (idea) of the story a good one? Is the story well constructed? Does it constantly move along at a good pace? Are the characters interesting? Are they well-developed, believable, and appealing? Is the dialogue fresh? Is it appropriate? Is the work genre-true—does it deliver the genre prom-

---

Coverage Form

TYPE OF MATERIAL:	TITLE:
NUMBER OF PAGES:	AUTHOR:
SUBMITTED BY:	CIRCA:
SUBMITTED TO:	LOCALE:
ANALYST:	GENRE:
COVERAGE DATE:	ATTACHMENTS:

LOGLINE / THEME:

SYNOPSIS:

COMMENTS:

RATING CHECKLIST:

Area	Excellent	Good	Fair	Poor
Premise				
Story Line Construction				
Characterization				
Dialogue				
Pace / Flow				

PAGE 1

---

ised? Often, the topics in this comment area are included in the rating checklist. This comment section is usually one double-spaced page long.

RATING CHECKLIST: A rating box (or other form of quick reference, such as a 1 to 10 rating scale) is included in a coverage report. It provides an at-a-glance assessment of the material. This box, along with the reader's final recommendation (see page 2 of this form at right), is the first thing a studio, production company, or agency executive will look at.

Sample Coverage Form

Often, the last category—THE FINAL WORD—is the first (and only) item that most executives will look at.

BUDGET ASSESSMENT:

_____ High

_____ Medium

_____ Low

MARKET/ AUDIENCE:

_____ Adult (Mainstream)

_____ Youth

_____ Other

COMMERCIAL APPEAL:

_____ Strong

_____ Average

_____ Weak

THE FINAL WORD:

_____ READ / RECOMMEND

_____ CONSIDER

_____ PASS

PAGE 2

BUDGET ASSESSMENT:
High _____ Medium _____ Low_____

MARKET/ AUDIENCE:
Adult (Mainstream) _____ Youth _____ Other_____

COMMERCIAL APPEAL:
Strong _____ Average _____ Weak_____

THE FINAL WORD:
This section of a coverage report is the key to a script's destiny at a production company or agency. The reader will check one of the following three choices:

_____ READ / RECOMMEND
This recommendation is reserved for an outstanding script that the reader feels has great production potential. It is a "must read" for the development executives or agency bigwigs.

_____ CONSIDER
This recommendation is given to a script that still needs some work, but has definite potential and deserves to be read.

_____ PASS
Given to over 90 percent of scripts, this mark means the work has been rejected.

---

play by filling in the coverage form as objectively as possible. It may enable you to see your work in a new light, and possibly lead you to make constructive changes that will help sell your script. Or, it may give you more confidence than ever.

Keep in mind that only a very small number of scripts receive a CONSIDER rating, and even fewer get the coveted READ / RECOMMEND by story analysts. Most get the dreaded PASS. It's important to understand that although a script has been given a PASS, it does not necessarily mean the work is not good. There could be a number of reasons for the rejection, beginning with the possibility that the material is simply not the type of project the company is interested in producing—at least at that particular time. This is why it is so important to do your homework and determine which companies are best suited to accept your type of work. Of course, there are no guarantees, but at least you'll be maximizing your odds of success.

Now let's say that your script has been given a READ / RECOMMEND rating by a production company reader. Where does it go next? Most likely, someone in development—often the head of the department—will be next in line to read your script. She may decide against producing the work, but may keep it as a sample of your writing for future assignments with the company. Or, she may feel that your project should be slated for production. If this is the case, she is likely to pass your script on to other company execs to read. At the next development meeting, which is usually held once or twice a week, your script will be discussed along with other projects. If there is interest in your script, you (or your agent or lawyer) will be contacted to talk business and make a deal.

Directors

When a director comes on board for the making of a film, he usually takes over the creative part of the production. (When it comes to talking about directors, we use the pronoun "he" advisedly. In 1999, of the 263 feature films produced that year by members of the Directors Guild of America, only 17 were directed by women.) The director is responsible for translating the script from the written page to film, tape, or any other technological innovation that results in moving images.

Before shooting begins, the director works on the screenplay, sometimes (hopefully) with the screenwriter, but often not. It's more likely that the director will work on the screenplay with the stars of the film, tailoring their dialogue and making other changes to keep them happy. In some cases, the director makes enough changes to warrant a shared screen credit with the screenwriter. (Remember, the WGA determines screen credit. If the writer thinks the director is unworthy of a shared credit, she can put it into Writer's Guild arbi-

It May Cost, But It May Pay
by Screenwriter Dale Launer

My Cousin Vinny, Ruthless People, Dirty Rotten Scoundrels, Blind Date, Love Potion No. 9.

One thing you have to realize in the movie business is that producers often work like agents with scripts. They'll take them to a studio and will sell the idea to some executive. Their way of finding scripts is to either call agents directly, or hire somebody to call the agents and to sort of work the town to find and read scripts. They'll hire a development person, known as a D-girl or story editor. The D-girl will comb the agencies for scripts and they will read the scripts and then they will write story analysis or coverage of these screenplays. You can also call them reader reports, but in the business, it's just called coverage. The producers rely on their story editors to some degree. If the story editors find something that's good, they often have it in their deal that they will become associate producer on the project that they found. It's important for them to find something good.

If I had a script, and didn't know anybody in the business, I would get the *HCD—Producers* and look up the names of producers who do material similar to my script. If I had a *Die Hard*-type script, I'd probably look up Joel Silver. Then, I'd find that producer's D-girl, story editor, or his reader—they'll be listed in the *HCD*—and I'd call her. I'd probably have a good chance of getting her on the line. I would tell her that I don't know anybody in the movie business and I want to get a story editor or somebody to do coverage of my screenplay and I'm willing to pay $200 to $250. I would tell her that what I want from her is an objective opinion. I would say that I want a professional analysis from her, the way she would do any analysis for her boss. I would also say, 'Please don't be afraid of hurting my feelings.'

If she agrees to read the script and then really likes it, it's doubtful that she's going to charge the $200 to 250. What she'll do is give the script to her boss, the producer. In which case, I have just bought myself a conduit for $200, which I think is reasonable. In the big scheme of things, I think these people are somewhat underpaid, and it's fair to give them a little extra money, and give them a little extra work.

For the up-and-coming writer, I think it's an especially good idea, because you can direct the script to wherever you want it to go to get read. If the producer likes it, it's not a guarantee that it'll get sold, but it may. It stands a chance.

If the D-girl doesn't give your screenplay to the producer, and instead sends it back to you with her coverage, you may be able to benefit by her input. If what she says makes sense, and could improve your script, make the changes. Then you can always call and tell her you did a rewrite according to her analysis, and ask if she'd be interested in having you submit it to her. Or go on to the next D-girl.

Sometimes, a director will
make enough changes to
a script to warrant a
shared screen credit
with the writer.

tration for a fair evaluation.) The director also prepares the shooting script, which includes his choice of camera angles.

Once shooting begins, it's the director's show. He calls the shots, figuratively and literally. In recent years, a growing number of directors have become powerful enough to get a project into production. If you can get a director with some sort of track record interested in your script, you will have the start of an attractive package. That director's name attached to your script will get your script read. Actually, if a director wants to do your script, chances are he and his agent will help make it happen.

If you have a strong feeling about a specific director for your screenplay, and you want to get in touch with him, start by doing your homework. Learn as much about him as you can. See if you can find out about his upcoming projects to make sure they're not similar to your script. His bio may help you discover something in your script with which he will identify.

A good place to start your research is online, beginning with the Internet Movie Database (www.IMDb.com). Here you can find the genre and a synopsis of each film the director has worked on, plus cast and crew lists for these films as well. Bio info for some directors is also provided. This site offers another interesting feature—type in the director's name and another industry name, such as an actor you have in mind for the lead role, and it will tell you if there's a connection between the two (in other words, whether or not they've worked together). You can also research directors through the Director's Guild of America member directory. More detailed information on these and other sources for locating directors is presented in Chapter 4.

Actors

We've heard stories of scripts that were green lighted by a television network or movie studio before they were read, simply because they had bankable actors attached. Yes, that's one wonderful way to get a script into production. Actors are always looking for that Oscar- or Emmy-winning role.

Also, chances are a name actor will have an easier time getting a producer and/or director onboard than you will. The traditional, professional way to contact actors is through their agents or managers. Call Screen Actors Guild (SAG) or American Federation of Television and Radio Artists (AFTRA), and ask for the agency department. If the actor has been on stage, you can call Actor's Equity for a contact name and number.

Check the *Hollywood Creative Directory—Producers* to see if the actor on your wish list has a production company. We went through this index, and made a list of all the actors whose names we recognized and who have production companies. That list comes in handy whenever we are looking to attach a name to our screenplays. Generally, it's easier and more effective calling an actor's production company and talking to the development person than it is going through the actor's agent. More information on ways to contact actors is provided in Chapter 4.

Writers

Legendary MGM executive Irving Thalberg is credited with saying, "The writers are the most important single element in this business and we must never let them have any power." And so you may ask, "How can writers help other writers?" They can introduce you to agents, managers, and producers who are looking for product or writers-for-hire. The real question is, *"Why* would writers want to help other writers?" Judging from our experience, writers are extremely nice people. Successful writers—the kind that *can* help you—have work lined up and won't be threatened that you're going to take something away from them.

Several writers during the course of our interviews mentioned ways in which they were helped by other writers. Some talked about the new writers they have mentored in the past or are working with currently. Now, we are not suggesting that you seek out a successful writer and glom onto her, hoping that she'll help you in some way. We do suggest, however, that you mingle with writers. Join a writers' group in your area or on the Internet. Take classes. Attend seminars. Many local schools offer adult-education writing courses. Go to film festivals. Vacation at a writers' retreat. (Helpful information on finding film festivals and writers' retreats is presented in the Resource List.)

Networking is a big part of the business. As much as time and money will permit, place yourself in situations that are conducive to networking with writers as well as with other people in the business.

CONCLUSION

Now that you've met the players, you have some decisions to make. Will you go after an agent? Does the thought of a manager who can help you get an agent sound more appealing? Are you inclined to forget the middlemen and women—the managers and agents—and go directly to production companies? Or does it seem more appropriate for you to go after an actor that's perfect for the lead in your film, or for a director? Think about it. And think about it some more. Then turn to the following chapter, which is designed to help you find the people you want to contact, and take the next step in getting your screenplay sold—making a wish list.

Runaway Bride

by Josann McGibbon & Sara Parriott

I Do...Not

It all started when we met with two men—one was an executive at Paramount, the other was a producer at the production company, Interscope Communications. They told us that we should do a script called *Runaway Bride,* a classic movie idea about someone who runs away from the altar, and a reporter who does an article about her and becomes the romantic interest. That's what they came to us with.

We worked on it and went back to them with an approach that they loved. So we were paid by Paramount to do the script. We finished the first draft of *Runaway Bride* in March 1989. By the fall of '91, the second draft of the script attracted Geena Davis and Harrison Ford. Sara and I were running around saying, "We can't believe it." We were pinching ourselves. Then we had some bad luck with shifting ground. Much to our regret, the executive at Paramount who loved our script, left his job to become a producer with Sydney Pollack. We lost our champion. Then the head of the studio changed, and the new head of the studio thought our script was "Too TV."

Runaway Pride

Interscope stayed with our project, and with Geena Davis and Harrison Ford attached, they got Michael Hoffman to direct. As soon as he was attached, he said that he only uses his own writers. We were told we were going to be off the project that attracted these two huge talents. The ironic part is that Geena Davis and Harrison Ford didn't even want changes in the script. They were happy with it the way it was.

When director Michael Hoffman came in, as the saying goes, he turned a "go" movie into a development deal. Hoffman pulled Elaine May in to write a treatment for a whole new movie. Geena Davis and Harrison Ford got the treatment and said that it wasn't the movie they signed on to do. They lost confidence in the studio at that point and they dropped out and Michael Hoffman went away, and no one ever turned Elaine May's treatment into a script. Sara and I rejoiced, because we're idealistic idiots and because we were so upset that the whole thing was being turned into something else. So, even though we were going to have those incredible movie stars in our movie, it didn't feel as though it was going to be our movie. As Sara said when she summed up our perspective, "Looking at the *little* picture—"

Easy Come, Easy Go

Dave Madden was the fellow from Interscope who was in that original room tossing out the idea to us, and he was wonderful. He would joke, "You can't become a member of the DGA (Directors Guild of America) without being attached to *Runaway Bride* for a period." Through the years, it seemed as if every director was on and off this project. The directors for whom we wrote different drafts were David Ward and Martha Coolidge. We credit Martha Coolidge with getting the best draft out of us. While Martha was attached as director, Geena Davis, who was about to start the film *Angie* got interested in our script again. During preproduction of *Angie,* the director got fired. While we were off writing a new draft of *Runaway*

Bride, Geena got Martha to direct *Angie.* Before long, Geena decided that, while Martha is a great director, she didn't want to do two films in a row with her. So that was that for *Runaway Bride.*

Then it went fallow for a while. It's hard to remember what happened next. The years tripped by. Interscope changed hands, and Larry Gordon tried to become a producer on the project. Then Ellen Degeneres was almost signed to do it, but she opted for *Mr. Wrong* instead. Somewhere in there they got another writer who did a draft that kind of moved away from our story, and that draft got eliminated and they went back to our draft. We're looking at a bunch of horrible luck that had nothing to do with the writing, but if the film didn't get made, the writer would be blamed. For some reason, if it doesn't come together, everyone thinks that the problem must be with the script.

Somewhere along the line they got another writer to do it and made her go in a completely different direction. Many years later we found out that Julia Roberts had read that script and had rejected it. They had that other script out there for a long time–the one that wasn't working–trying to get people involved and we'd hear little burbles of what was going on.

Miss Congeniality

Sandra Bullock was interested and had her development person read all the drafts of the script. Her development person read our draft and gave it to Sandy. At that point, Sandy wanted to hire us back on, but Paramount still didn't want us. They hired someone else and that person worked from the draft we wrote for Martha Coolidge. So the script was brought back much closer to what it had always been. At least a year went by while this writer was working on a couple of drafts for Sandy, who wouldn't commit. Paramount finally told Sandy that she had to commit. Sandy said she wanted to go back to our draft and have us back

on. Paramount told her that if she committed to it, they'd talk about it, but if she wouldn't commit, they wouldn't talk. Sandy and Paramount went their separate ways. But during that time, we met with Sandy. All of us were sullied by the Paramount experience, and our meeting was like a healing process. We all agreed that while *Runaway Bride* was not going to happen for us with Sandy and Paramount, we could have something else that's good come out of it. We pitched a whole new original idea called *Exactly 3:30,* and sold it with Sandy to Disney. Since then, we did another script for Sandy that was sold to Warner Bros.

Here Comes the Bride

At that point, Paramount put Lakeshore Entertainment on it and was edging out Interscope. What was weird was that, by then, the producers from Interscope were working as producers for Paramount. They weren't at Interscope anymore. So Paramount gave it to Tom Rosenberg at Lakeshore and told them to see if they could make this with Téa Leoni. Téa Leoni wanted to do it with Ben Affleck. Paramount was ready to do it as a low budget, just to make it already.

Somewhere along the way, Tom Rosenberg showed it to Richard Gere. This is nine years after the first draft. Richard Gere read it over a weekend and the following Monday, said, "I'm in!–and I'm giving it to Julia Roberts." The following Monday, Julia said, "I'm in!" and they made a phone call to director Garry Marshall. Garry said, "I can't do it. I'm finishing *The Other Sister* and then I'm going to Europe with Barbara." Richard and Julia said, "Put Barbara on the phone." They then proceeded to convince Garry's wife to put the vacation on hold so that Garry could do our film. By the end of that conversation, we had the two stars and a director.

The thing about the script was that during those nine years it never disappeared for very long. Every meeting we ever went to within that time, the first thing people asked was, "What's happening with *Runaway Bride*?" Everyone knew about it and that it was a script that attracted talent—Tom Cruise and Nicole Kidman, John Travolta and Kelly Preston, and so many more actors were talked about for it—and everybody knew that one day it was going to get made.

Now people keep asking us if we wrote *Runaway Bride* as the sequel to *Pretty Woman*. We wrote our first draft a year before *Pretty Woman* was released. In Japan, their way of perhaps suggesting that our film was a sequel to *Pretty Woman,* or at least a way of reminding the public of the magic between Richard Gere and Julia Roberts, was to release *Runaway Bride* with the title *Pretty Bride*. Pretty crazy, huh?

A Soldier's Story

Academy Award nomination for Best Screenplay in 1985.
Adaptation of the 1982 Pulitzer Prize winning play "A Soldier's Play."
both by Charles Fuller

During the Off-Broadway run of *A Soldier's Play,* I learned that director Norman Jewison wanted to make it into a movie called *A Soldier's Story.* It excited everyone, especially the actors because most of them saw it as a chance to move from stage to screen. Luckily, a sizeable portion of the cast did get to be in the film version. Denzel Washington had already been in a film, but I believe Adolph Caesar and Larry Riley had not. Peter Friedman, Cotter Smith, James Pickens, Brent Jennings, Eugene Lee, Stephen Zettler, and Samuel L. Jackson would all go on to careers in film.

For myself, moving from script to screen was a challenge. Norman Jewison and I had discussed the play, and he had said there were plenty of scenes that were filmic, and ample room in the script for stretching things. My job would be to turn those *things* into a movie.

What I didn't want to do was write the same story twice. So I set about trying to separate myself from the play in as many ways as I could. I had written teleplays for a series that never made it to TV, so the form of things wasn't going to be difficult. What was difficult, however, was turning the corner from play to film script. I had always thought in words. It was a new experience to think in pictures, as well as "pictures in continuity" so that the story I was trying to tell made sense to the people in the seats.

I began by "running" the movie in my head. Scene by scene, discarding what didn't work—a lot of dialogue—and enhancing what did work—monologues that described action, but because of the limits of the stage, couldn't be visualized. And like all new writers to the screen, I thought I had it all done.

I took the First Draft of the screenplay to Norman and was horrified to learn I had not "done it all." There were a great number of things I hadn't considered. And here is the point, I believe, where one can separate the good Directors from the great Directors who are also great Teachers. For me, Norman Jewison proved to be both.

We talked about scene after scene, dialogue and structure, and as things progressed a film script began to emerge. Here's an example of the kind of help Norman provided to a novice: In the play, Davenport, the protagonist, arrives at the Fort on a train. And in the writing of the script, I made him arrive on a train—seemed simple to me. But in a conversation with Norman, he told me that renting a locomotive of the 1942–43 vintage would cost so much it would blow the budget (something I had never heard of before). I made a change—Davenport arrived on a bus—and it worked!

It was Norman who suggested that it would be a good idea to see the soldiers who belonged to a Smoke Generating Battalion, making smoke. And again, a scene I had written out in full—a moment when Sgt. Waters looking into a mirror sees something that happened during WWI—was translated by Norman into a beautiful monologue in which Sgt. Waters tells us what happened while looking at himself in a mirror.

What I realize now was that many things had to do with the constraints of a six-million-dollar budget, but everything fit, everything enhanced the vision of the film—a vision, I might add, that was always in line with what the play had to say. Norman helped at every turn, and without him it would not have been made.

What I learned from the experience was something I had encountered in the theater years before with Douglas Turner Ward, Director of the Negro Ensemble Company—a Director can help a writer expand his vision, and the right Director can make the writer's vision more complete. Unless you are working with a complete dope, and you can usually find that out in a few conversations, the Director's input can, in many ways, take you out of yourself and widen that eighty-foot screen into an entire world. And that's what a movie is about, bringing a world to the screen.

CHAPTER 4

CHOOSING CONTACTS

You have a well-written spec script that is formatted according to industry standards. You are aware of the people who make up this industry. Now it's time to go about getting your script read by the right people and getting it sold. Who are the right ones for you and your work? And how do you find them? In addition to all-important networking, there are a number of standard resources that can help you during your search. By the time you finish reading this chapter, you should have a good idea of the people you want to reach and how to go about reaching them.

KNOW WHO YOU WANT

Your script is ready, but who should you approach? You've got to select the *players* who can *play a part* in the sale of your spec script. Got any valuable connections? If you know someone who knows someone, and is willing to introduce you, that's where you should start. If you've asked everyone you know who they know, and no one knows anyone, then it's up to you to make your own contacts. Right now, decide which path or paths you want to take. Once you do, you will be ready to make your move, zooming in on specific people and companies.

Let's start with a quick recap of the key industry professionals you met in Chapter 3, and their relationship to writers:

■ **Agents** represent writers and their work. They introduce new writers by sending out their spec scripts to producers at production companies and development execs at studios, and by setting up meet-and-greet sessions with these people. They try to sell scripts and/or get assignments for writers. Typically, agents take 10 percent of a writer's earnings.

- **Managers** guide writers' careers and introduce them to agents, producers, directors, lawyers, accountants—people who can help them. Managers usually take at least 15 percent of a writer's earnings.

- **Producers and Production Companies with Deals at Major Studios or Networks** may option or buy your spec script, and get it financed by the studio or network. They usually look for high-concept, commercial properties. They also give assignments to writers and put pitched ideas into development.

- **Independent Producers and Production Companies that finance their own films** may be more open to off-beat, low-budget properties and first-time screenwriters.

- **Directors** with any kind of track record can move a project forward by attaching their names to it. A director may also be able to attract stars who want to work with him.

- **Actors** who are bankable can move a project forward and may use their own production companies to do so.

- **Entertainment lawyers** can submit scripts to production companies who do not accept unsolicited material. Those with clout may be in a position to help package a script by getting it to the right people, who may also be their clients. These lawyers are expensive. They charge hundreds of dollars an hour, and usually require a hefty retainer up front. Writers who don't have an agent and are in search of a lawyer, should look for an entertainment lawyer who is just starting out and may be willing to take them on for a reasonable fee, or on a contingency basis. Writers are often able to make financial per-project deals with these lawyers.

Now that we've reviewed the industry players and the parts they can play in helping you get your work from script to screen, you're ready for the next step—targeting specific players. This means creating a wish list.

CREATE A WISH LIST

Your goal is to sell your spec script. To realize your goal, the *right* people have to read that script. It's time to create a wish list of all those potentially *right* people. Take the time to do what it takes to build an appropriate wish list. You will be using it to send out your query letters, which we will be discussing in detail in the next chapter. Your wish list is groundwork that can eventually pay off in a wish-come-true way.

On lined loose-leaf paper, write down the names of any players who you believe can buy or help you sell your screenplay. You may want to have a separate page for each player category—Agents, Managers, Producers, Actors, Directors. You will be keeping these pages in a 3-ring loose-leaf binder, which will serve as your workbook. This workbook, as you will see in Chapter 6, will house all of your important clerical work—contact, submission, and follow-up information.

Consider this wish list an ongoing work to which you will constantly be adding and deleting names. Start with anyone your heart desires. Did you have actors in mind when you wrote your script? Put them on the list. Have you fantasized about a certain director directing the film? Add his or her name. Which producers and/or production companies do you think would package the film to perfection? Place them on the list, too. Do you know of any agents or agencies, managers or management firms that you'd be proud to say represent you? Get those names on the list. Why not? Just as you want them for your script, they just may want your script (and this is, after all, a "wish" list). The longer your list, the better.

Keep up with industry news on the Internet; read the trades, screenwriters' magazines, and daily newspaper gossip columns; and watch TV shows like *Entertainment Tonight, Inside Edition, Extra!, Access Hollywood*, and the E! Entertainment channel. By knowing who's doing what, you'll discover which players may be right for your spec script and how they may be reached.

Wish List Considerations

If you decide to pursue agents, you'll have to find agencies that will consider new writers. The same holds true for managers. If you're going to skip agents and managers, and go directly to producers, you'll want to consider the types of films they primarily produce—big-budget action adventures? low-budget character studies? a variety of genres and budgets? Think about whether or not your screenplay is in keeping with their specialty.

If you want to attach an actor or a director to your script, first find out everything you can about them and their bodies of work. Then put yourself in their place. Considering the films that they have either starred in or directed, how do you think they would answer the following questions with your script in mind:

■ Would playing this role or directing this film be a smart next-step career move for me?

■ Is it a stretch for me? Does it offer an artistic challenge?

■ Will it show a new aspect of my talent?

■ Does this role or film have Oscar or Emmy potential?

■ Is there an audience for this film?

This is the way most actors and directors think when assessing a script. And if they don't, you can be sure that their agents and managers think this way for them.

Refining the Wish List

Researching each name on the wish list will help refine the list as you determine if a particular actor, agent, director, development exec, or producer is, in fact, a good prospect for your project.

When you discover that someone is not open to reading unsolicited scripts, or is not available or approachable for one reason or another, simply cross out the name and go on to the next. When you check on someone and have every reason to believe that this person may be right for your script, put a little star next to his name, and fill out an index card for him with as much information as possible, including:

■ Name of the person and his company, studio, agency, or firm.

■ Street, e-mail, and website addresses.

■ Phone and fax numbers.

■ If it is a production company, what size and type of films (genres) it produces.

■ If it is a director or actor, list credits.

■ Any and all interesting or pertinent information.

Don't worry if anything is missing—you will be verifying all of the info, including correct spellings, before sending out any correspondence. For now, just concentrate on finding and reviewing the resources that will tell you what you should know about the people or companies on your wish list. You'll need this information when you get to Chapter 6.

Once you have refined your wish list, you can use the research sources to discover new prospects to add to the list. There are production companies you may never have heard of, and the same for agencies who may be perfect for you and your script. Once you learn about the resources described in this chapter, you will able to grow your wish list to as long as it takes for you to get a deal.

CONTACT SOURCES

To help you check out each name on your wish list, and to find new names to add to it, we're going to share some helpful entertainment industry resources with you. While we consider the following directories, trade magazines, industry newspapers, websites, and organizations most worthwhile, they are certainly not the only ones. Some of these industry resources involve minor investments, but they can result in major paybacks when it comes to helping you discover and check out the right people for your spec script. Any expenditures you incur while doing your research are also tax-deductible, so be sure to keep all receipts and canceled checks.

Trade Magazines and Newspapers

Trade magazines and newspapers will help you keep in touch with what's happening now, who's doing what, and who may be looking for something special, like your script. Always keep your eyes and ears open. Read entertainment gossip columns for industry information. Watch television shows that focus on the world of entertainment to keep abreast of what's happening—you just never know when you're going to read or hear something that might cause the spark that leads to the right connection for you and your script.

For starters, here is the list of newspapers and magazines that we feel offer the best information for screenwriters. They are always brimming with industry scoops. The newspapers *Daily Variety* and *The Hollywood Reporter* are standard reading material for anyone interested in show business, as are magazines like *Creative Screenwriting,*

PROSE FROM A PRO

Differences Between Motion Pictures and Television Films
by Phillip M. Goldfarb
Unit Production Manager, Associate Producer, Line Producer, Co-Producer, and Executive Producer.
Film credits: *All The Right Moves, Taps, Taxi Driver.*
Episodic TV credits: *L.A. Law, Doogie Howser, NYPD Blue, Casey's Shadow.*

Motion pictures stand on their own merit. The script is about itself. It's not about serving any other immediate master. You sell a motion picture script, it gets made, it's promoted, people will either come or not come, and the number of people who show up at the theater on those given days will determine your success.

With a TV film, you are selling to an entity that is using your script to sell something else to someone, so there is a one-degree removal from the audience. That means that people now have opinions over what will attract the demographic audience they are looking for. You will find that movies for television, mini-series, and episodic shows are more narrowly defined in certain respects, depending on what night it's on, depending on what hour it's on, depending on what network it's on; all that will determine the nature of the subject matter that's acceptable in those time frames.

Historically, for example, CBS has been skewed to a somewhat older audience. Certain projects that might sell at the Fox Network will not sell at CBS and vice versa. In each case, it would behoove a writer to do the research on what those companies like to put on. In the movie of the week area, it seems that *women in jeopardy* have been a constant over the past number of years, satisfying a large demographic audience of young to middle-age women. They're not looking to sell to teenage boys or to adult males, and so the projects that they may accept under those circumstances would be different.

NY Screenwriter, Scr(i)pt, and *Written By.* We recommend all of them. Further details for these and other well-respected industry publications, including contact and subscriber information, are provided in the Resource List beginning on page 283.

Daily Variety

Published since 1905, *Daily Variety* is considered the entertainment industry bible. If it's happening in show biz, it's reported in this daily newspaper, including deals that are made, scripts that are bought, companies being born, and cable TV expansions. The popular *Variety* columnists share all kinds of inside news about the industry and its players. These columns are good sources for information that may lead to names to include on your wish list.

With a motion picture, you have to look at the various genres that are currently in vogue. Action-adventure seems to be a major event in this day and age. Science fiction and other films brimming with special effects also seem to be extremely popular. There's a genre that's rather disparaging called *chick flicks*, which are those that have some romantic interest in them.

The other difference between a motion picture and a television film is that television films have *act breaks*. Television is designed around commercial interruptions. The storytelling has to arc itself to a greater degree of frequency so that it comes to a certain point at the commercial break, not necessarily a cliff-hanger, but leaving something undone so that the audience will stay tuned.

Television is not about the content. Television is about the commercials. We are the clothesline; the commercials are the clothes. They're hanging on us, but what the networks want and what the sponsors want are for people to pay attention to the sponsors. That's their *raison d'etre*. That's the justification for the form as it currently exists. (Obviously I'm absenting PBS, documentaries, public event television and that sort of thing.) As a result, there's almost an unstated agreement that you can't be too good. You can't be too powerful or too frightening or too emotionally overwhelming, because if you are, the audience will be stunned. They will not be paying attention to the commercials. And so projects get leveled a bit as a result of it.

I don't think the same script is interchangeable. I think you have to write for the medium. It happens on rare occasions that a film will start out as a film for television and someone will decide that it's strong enough—and they use those terms, *strong enough*—to be a motion picture script. But in most cases, writers will start off with the ambition of writing a motion picture and often it will end up as a movie for television because it is not as clearly differentiated; it is not as historically outlined. It's not the big idea for the big screen. Movies seem to generate more interest out of a large idea. Again, this is not a hard and fast rule. There are any number of exceptions to that rule and every other rule in the business.

In addition to the *Los Angeles Daily Variety*, there is the *Daily Variety Gotham Edition*, which targets industry happenings on the East Coast. There is also a weekly edition of this legendary trade publication that encompasses both coasts. All are available by subscription, as well as at major newsstands in select cities. Page through this newspaper in its printed form or view it online at www.variety.com. Again, it can result in names you may want to pursue—a producer who got a housekeeping deal at a network, a director who signed a three-picture deal with a major, a star who just happened to reveal an interest in the far-out subject of your script.

Most valuable to screenwriters is *Daily Variety's* once-a year issue that comes out at the end of June and includes a section called "'Facts on Pacts.'" This is a compilation of producers (including some stars) who have on-the-lot production deals at major studios—it's a great source for contacts. Additional information on *Daily Variety* is available in the Resource List.

The Hollywood Reporter

The Hollywood Reporter is a daily trade publication that is available by subscription. It is also found at major newsstands in select cities. If you don't subscribe to this paper, you can still keep up with industry headlines and see who has bought what, with a daily visit to *The Hollywood Reporter* website at www.hollywoodreporter.com. For complete articles and use of their archives, you must be an online subscriber.

In January or February of each year, *The Hollywood Reporter* publishes a special issue covering the American Film Market (AFM), which is the trade association for the independent film and television industry. This special issue lists the AFM's participating production company members, names of company principals, contact information, and debuting films along with their loglines, producers, directors, and casts. These are independent production companies that are active and have films in the can, ready for distribution.

The Hollywood Reporter East (THR East) is a full-color multi-page version of the print daily, which is sent electronically every business day to subscribers east of the Mississippi. Each day's issue contains more of the latest breaking news, reviews, and analysis of the film, TV, music, theater, advertising, media, and publishing industries, taking place in the eastern United States. You must subscribe to *The Hollywood Reporter* to receive *THR East,* which is available for a small fee. Check the Resource List for further details.

Creative Screenwriting

Creative Screenwriting can be a wonderful source for gathering wish-list contacts. Each issue of this bimonthly magazine includes a listing of spec script sales and pitch sales along with their loglines, and the agents, agencies, managers, producers, and studios involved in these deals. Among other features, it offers useful articles and pertinent interviews on the business of screenwriting; and informative columns that will assist you in marketing your finished script. For a closer look at this magazine's other valuable offerings check the Resource List.

You can also visit its website at www.creativescreenwriting.com. Available by subscription, *Creative Screenwriting* is also found at many large newsstands and major bookstore chains.

New York Screenwriter

This monthly publication bills itself as "Gotham City's Guide to Making It!" which may be a little misleading. Its informative editorials on getting read, represented, and produced, along with in-depth interviews with successful screenwriters, agents, producers, and studio executives, provide industry insight, no matter which coast you're on (or anywhere in between).

As an added bonus, subscribers to *New York Screenwriter* receive the annual *Screenwriters Guide,* which contains helpful information, including listings of Guild signatory agents and Guild signatory and non-signatory production companies. Although the information is not extensive, each listed agency and production company has expressed an interest in receiving query letters from screenwriters. This is most useful to readers who are looking for the right contacts. Nonsubscribers can also purchase the *Screenwriters Guide.* For further information about *New York Screenwriter,* check the Resource List, or visit its website at www.nyscreenwriter.com.

Scr(i)pt

A bimonthly publication, *Scr(i)pt* is dedicated to the art, craft, and business of writing for film. It is a great source for keeping writers in touch with what's happening now in the industry, who's doing what, and which player may be looking for something in particular. In addition to each issue's news, contest listings, market trend analyses, and interviews, there are helpful articles and tips from some of the industry's most successfully produced writers. This magazine serves as both a resource for the craft of screenwriting and a source of inspiration from professionals in the field. *Scr(i)pt* is available by subscription, and is also found at many large newsstands, and major bookstore chains. See the Resource List for contact information.

Written By

Written By is the monthly magazine from the Writers Guild of America West. It is written for and by film and television writers. Each issue

> Somewhere someone is looking for exactly what you have to offer.
>
> —Louise L. Hay
> *Spiritual healer*
> *and author*

contains interviews with writers and relevant in-depth articles about the craft and the business of writing. This journal is sent to WGAw members; nonmembers can pay for a subscription. It is also sold at many large newsstands, and major bookstore chains. Contact information is found in the Resource List.

Directories

Directories are handy references, memory joggers, and contact facilitators. There are a number of excellent directories that can help you when researching most professionals in the film industry, and we have listed the ones that we believe are the best.

Hollywood Creative Directory (HCD) Series

The Hollywood Creative Directory series from IFILM Publishing, the largest film-reference publishing company in the world, is devoted to tracking the comings and goings of companies and individuals in every aspect of the film, television, and new media industries. The series consists of the following directories: *HCD Producers, HCD Agents & Managers, HCD Distributors, HCD International Film Buyers, HCD Below-the-Line Talent, HCD Film Directors, HCD Film Actors, HCD Film Writers,* and *HCD New Media.*

The two directories that we find very helpful to writers with a spec script are *HCD Agents & Managers* and *HCD Producers.* Both are available in print form, and both are offered as one-year online subscriptions that are updated weekly. In addition to this comprehensive series of directories, the HCD website at www.hcdonline.com also offers a number of valuable services, including ScriptShark screenplay coverage and an entertainment industry Job Board. You'll find a visit to this site to be time well spent. For now, let's talk about those directories.

HCD Agents & Managers

When looking for representation by an agent and/or manager, this directory can be a great reference. It lists over 1,500 companies and nearly 5,000 names of agents and managers, along with their titles, phone and fax numbers, street and e-mail addresses, and websites where available. The entries also include union affiliations, the category of talent represented (literary, theatrical, etc.), and the specific talent within each category (screenwriters, television writers, producers, etc.).

The directory begins with a Resource Guide of Guilds, Unions, and Associations, and Libraries and Museums—most of which are in California and New York. Listings include addresses, phone and fax numbers, and website addresses. Following this Guide is the heart of the directory—an alphabetical listing of agencies, followed by another listing of management companies. There is also a dedicated section for film and TV casting directors. In the back section of the directory, these entries are also cross-referenced under the following categories:

- **By Type.** Listed according to the general types of talent each company represents, including commercial, theatrical, musical, and literary talent (literary talent is the California way of referring to screenwriters).

- **By Client.** Listed by the talent categories each company represents, including actors, below-the-line, book authors, children, comedians, composers, dancers, directors, extras, legitimate theater, lyricists, martial artists, models, music producers, musical artists, new media, newscasters, packaging, photographers, print, producers, screenwriters, songwriters, sports personalities, stunts/daredevils, television writers, variety artists, voice-over artists, writers, young adults/teens.

- **By Affiliation.** Listed by the unions to which the companies are signatories, including AAR (Association of Authors Representatives), AEA (Actors Equity Association), AFM (American Film Marketing), AFTRA (American Federation of Television and Radio Artists), AGVA (American Guild of Variety Artists), ATA (Association of Talent Agents), COPM (Conference of Personal Managers), CSA (Casting Society of America), DGA (Directors Guild of America), NCOPM (National Conference of Personal Managers), SAG (Screen Actors Guild), and WGA (Writers Guild of America).

- **By State.** Companies listed by the state in which they are located.

- **By Names.** Alphabetical listing of over 4,700 individual names of agents and managers, along with their affiliated companies.

In California, *literary agents* represent screenwriters; in New York, those who represent screenwriters are called *theatrical agents*. (In New York, literary agents represent authors.) No matter what you call them, the literary or theatrical agent's job is to solicit work, negotiate, advise, and handle compensation for their screenwriter clients.

HCD Agents & Managers is published biannually—the Fall/Winter issue comes out in February, and the Spring/Summer issue is available in August. You can order it online at the HCD website or by calling the toll-free number. HCD online offers one-year subscriptions to this database of agents and managers, which is updated weekly. You get all the same information that the print version provides, plus a powerful search engine that allows you to search by company, name, city, state, zip code, and phone number. (See the Resource List for contact information.)

Having representation by an agency that handles a variety of talent, such as screenwriters, directors, actors, and producers, can be a real asset. The agency can draw from its pool of clients to package a script.

The sample *HCD Agents & Managers* entry below is for Shapiro-Lichtman Talent Agency. As you can see, it is located on the West Coast and represents literary and theatrical talent. In California, "literary" means television and film writers (in New York, literary agencies are for book authors). The specific types of literary and theatrical talent—screenwriters, actors, directors, and producers—are also listed. The fact that this agency handles both types of talent can be a plus, especially if the agents are into packaging—putting a script together with a producer, actor, and/or a director. This is a good thing.

HCD SAMPLE ENTRY
AGENTS & MANAGERS

SHAPIRO-LICHTMAN TALENT AGENCY, INC.

8827 Beverly Blvd.
Los Angeles, CA 90048

PHONE	310–859–8877
FAX	310–859–7153
TYPES	Literary + Theatrical Talent
REPRESENTS	Actors + Below-the-Line + Directors + New Media + Producers + Screenwriters + Television Writers
AFFILIATIONS	AEA + AFTRA + DGA + SAG + WGA

Mark Lichtman	Principal (x123)
Marty Shapiro	Principal (x121)
Sarita Choy	Agent, New Media (x132)
Sean Davis	Agent (x145)
Budd Moss	Talent (x127)
Peggy Patrick	Agent (x125)
Laura Rhodes	Agent (x126)
Susan Salkow Shapiro	Agent (x128)
Yale Udoff	Agent (x134)

Take a look at this agency's affiliations. In addition to the actors' stage (AEA), television (AFTRA), and screen (SAG) unions, and the directors (DGA) union, the Shapiro-Lichtman Talent Agency is also a Writers Guild (WGA) signatory. It has signed a contract agreeing to abide by the Guild's standards for representing writers. This is a good indication that the agency is legitimate.

According to the staff listing, the agency has two principals and five agents. Principal players are usually the partners or CEOs of the company. In this entry, just by looking at their last names and the name of the agency, the principals are most likely to be the founding partners. If you, the writer, don't have a track record yet, we don't recommend putting a company's "principal" on your wish list. What you *could* do is add the agency name to the list along with its phone number. Then call and ask for the name of the agent who is ready to discover a great new writing talent. If you're given an agent's name, ask to speak to him. Chances are, you will be told either by the receptionist or by the agent's assistant to send a query letter, although you might be asked to pitch your script. So be prepared. We'll be helping you hone your pitching skills in the next chapter.

HCD PRODUCERS

In your search for a producer or production company, *HCD Producers* may prove to be a valuable reference and a wise investment. The directory lists over 8,100 individuals in over 1,700 companies, along with their titles, phone and fax numbers, street and e-mail addresses, and websites where available.

This directory starts with a Resource Guide of the names, addresses, phone numbers, and websites of Studios, Networks, and Majors; Guilds, Unions, and Associations; and Libraries and Museums—most of which are in California and New York. The Resource Guide is followed by a page of New Listings at a Glance—companies that were not listed in past editions. Then comes the major section of the directory, Production Companies and staff entries, alphabetically listed by company names. Each entry includes the types of projects the company produces, its credits, companies with whom it has deals, and titles of projects in development. Some entries include comments to explain more fully their wants or way of doing business. The list of staff members varies with each company and ranges from producer, president, and CEO to development executive, story editor, and assistant.

Following this main section is a listing of TV Shows and their staffs. The entries, listed alphabetically by the name of the TV show, include the production company that produces the series, the production office address, and phone and fax numbers. Most staff listings include the many kinds of producers (executive, co-executive, and co-producers, supervising, consulting, senior coordinating, associate producers, etc.), story editors, staff writers, and the person in charge of casting.

In the back section of the directory, production companies are cross-referenced under the following categories:

■ **By Deal.** Alphabetical listing of studios, majors, and networks, and the production companies with whom they have production or development deals. The list also includes the phone number of the production company that has the deal.

■ **By Type.** Listing of companies according to the types of projects they produce. Categories include animation, documentaries, features, direct to video, motion pictures, movies made for TV (MOW), new media, syndication, and television.

■ **By State.** Companies listed by the state in which they are located.

■ **Index by Name.** Alphabetical listing of over 8,100 production company staff members, along with their affiliated companies.

HCD Producers is published every March, July, and November, and can be ordered online at the HCD website or by calling the toll-free number. HCD online offers one-year subscriptions to this database of producers and production companies, which is updated weekly. You get all the same information that the print version provides, plus a powerful search engine that allows you to search by company, name, city, state, zip code, phone number, studio deals, and selected credits. (See the Resource List for contact information.)

A typical entry in *HCD Producers* is presented on page 139. When looking for a production company for your spec script, focus on those that produce films in the same category as your project. For instance, if you have a low-budget project that would appeal to the teen market, you may want to look for a company like the one in this example, which produces features that go directly to video.

HCD SAMPLE ENTRY
PRODUCERS

HALO PRODUCTIONS

3033 W. Olympic Blvd., Ste. 306
Santa Monica, CA 90404

PHONE 310–555–1000
FAX 310–555–1221
EMAIL . . . . filmmakers@halopro.com
TYPES   Motion Pictures + Television + Features Direct to Video
DEALS   Sony Pictures Entertainment
IN DEVELOPMENT   Lost and Profound – Everything and the Kitchen Sink –
                         Rainbow Love – C.J. and the Girls
CREDITS   Good to Go – Looking For Mr. Fright – Near Mrs.
COMMENTS   No unsolicited material. Fax all queries.

Herb Angel . . . . CEO/Exec. Producer
Tyler Larson . . . . Pres., Production
Lori Larson . . . . Producer
Angela Curt . . . . Producer
Virginia Sosa . . . . Development
John Turner . . . . Story Editor
Aidan Nicholas . . . . Exec. Asst.

According to this entry, Halo Productions has a deal with a major studio. Companies that have deals with networks, the majors, or as in this case, a studio, usually have money to option or buy properties, and may even have development money. This company *does* have development money, as you can see from the number of projects it has in development. If the company doesn't want your script, but likes your writing and ideas, it could pay you to develop one of your ideas (or one of theirs).

The entry also lists Halo's film credits, which provide insight into the kinds of projects this company may be partial to producing. If you are not familiar with the movies, simply check them out on a film database like the Internet Movie Database (see page 143), which provides information such as the film's genre, and even whether or not it made money for the company.

Another helpful bit of information provided by this entry is that Halo Productions is open to query letters (discussed in Chapter 5), which must be sent by fax. And it does not accept unsolicited scripts.

There are no hard-and-fast rules when it comes to determining the person with the title that's most appropriate for your wish list. If you have an unsolicited spec script, and want to send it to this company, first aim for the development person, then the story editor, but be willing to settle for the executive assistant. Even if you reach one of the producers who is willing to have you send your script to the company, chances are the executive assistant will read it first and give it coverage.

Some of the entries in the directory have only one or two producers listed. After looking at their credits, if you feel that the company is perfect for your script, call and ask to speak to the producer's assistant. Be prepared to pitch your story. (See Chapter 5 for pitching information.)

Director's Guild of America (DGA) Directory of Members

You have a director or two in mind for your work and you want to contact them. Where is the best place to turn? Along with *HCD Directors* (part of the series just discussed), another good source for contact information is the Director's Guild of America's *Directory of Members*. This sourcebook lists the name of every DGA member. Most listings include contact information—an office number, the name and number of an agent or business manager—and the director's credits. The *Directory* also includes a geographical listing of DGA members, as well as listings of ethnic minority members, women members, and agencies that are DGA signatories. The *Directory* is published every January or February and can be purchased through the DGA offices.

Check the DGA website at www.dga.org for a directory that lists member credits, but not contact numbers. This can be helpful when researching names for your wish list. It's worth visiting the website just for the insightful interviews with hot directors. If you need a contact name and number for a specific director, and you don't have access to the *Directory of Members*, call the Director's Guild and ask for it. The Resource List has DGA contact information.

A sample entry is found on page 141. If you wanted to get in touch with Myles Phillip Burton—the director in this entry—you would do so through his agent, Beverly Marcus. First, you must verify that she is still with the Rose International Talent Agency, and that she is still representing Burton. You can find this info easily enough with one

---

DGA SAMPLE ENTRY
DIRECTORY OF MEMBERS

BURTON, Myles Phillip   **DIRECTOR**

Agent: Beverly Marcus, Rose International Talent Agency (RITA) 12345 El Camino Dr., Suite 309, Beverly Hills, CA 90210; (310) 555–4321

Features: *Gust of Wind,* Icart Pictures; *Two Beauties,* Image Films; MOWs: *A House Named Louise,* Hallmark; *Sizzler,* USA Cable; *Hang A Louie,* Artist Productions.

---

phone call. If Burton is no longer with the agency, ask which agency is currently representing him. If Beverly Marcus *and* Burton are no longer with the agency, ask where Marcus can be reached.

The director's credits—in this case, feature films and television movies of the week (MOWs)— show his diversity or specialization in terms of genre, helping you gauge whether or not your script is appropriate for him. If these films are unfamiliar, check them out through a film database like the Internet Movie Database (see page 143). If you know that your script is in keeping with the type of projects with which the director has been involved, then it follows that the production companies that produced those films may be appropriate for your script. Add them to your wish list.

Writers Guild of America—Member Directory

The Writers Guild of America publishes a *Member Directory* every two years. The *Directory* contains listings of WGA members and their coast affiliation (East or West). The entries also include member credits and contact information—usually phone numbers of agents and/or managers.

The directory is arranged alphabetically by writers' names. Look up the names of those who write films in your genre and you will find the agencies that represent them. Keep in mind that some agencies welcome numbers of same-genre writers, while other don't—they don't want their clients competing against each other. When you call an agency to verify information for sending a query letter, mention the genre of your script and ask if it is a viable genre for the agency.

Another tip . . .
Before calling an actor's or director's agency, find out if it represents writers. If it does, and the opportunity presents itself (or if you can create the opportunity), ask for the name of the agent who is open to queries from writers. Any way to get your foot in the door . . .

WGA SAMPLE ENTRY
MEMBER DIRECTORY

PEROZZI, Richard A.   **WGAw**

Agency: Mimi Pinson, MPB Agency; 818/555–5555

MP: *August in Paris*, MGM/UA

TV: *Gossip*, Lifetime MOW; *Hiding Place*, USA MOW

Add'l Credits & Info: Unproduced: *Casanova and Conchita*, pilot, Fox sitcom.

As seen in the sample entry above, the writers listed in this directory have the option to list their credits and the production companies that have produced their work. In this entry for writer Richard Perozzi, his motion picture (MP) as well as television credits are listed. When you see an entry with films that are comparable to your script, you may want to add the production company to your wish list.

New writers with spec scripts may want the *Member Directory* to see which agents are representing screenwriters who are writing films in their particular genre. Also, many entries list production companies that produced the writers' scripts. They may be appropriate wish list additions.

You can purchase the *Member Directory* by visiting or calling the WGA office on either coast. See "Guilds and Organizations" in the Resource List for contact information.

Online Databases

In our opinion, the Internet Movie Database, Baseline, Inc., and Hollywood Literary Sales are among the finest online sources for entertainment industry information. One of the advantages of using any of these databases is that the information is current, well organized, and cross-referenced. Screenwriters, in particular, can use the information, which is updated daily, to figure out what Hollywood is buying, who is doing the buying, and which agents and producers deal with first-time writers.

As of this writing, most of the databases listed below charge subscription fees. Instead of asking, "How much does it cost," explore each website, get a feel for the comprehensive information each has to offer, and take advantage of any available free trials. Then ask, "How much is it worth?"

Internet Movie Database
www.IMDb.com

To help you find producers and directors who tend to work within a particular genre, make a list of films that fall into the same category as yours, then go online to the Internet Movie Database and type in the name of the films on your list, one at a time. Each film provides a complete list of cast and crew members. Click on the name of any-one—director, producer, writer, actor—and you will get a complete listing of the projects with which that person is affiliated. Looking at the director's (or producer's) complete body of work may help you determine whether or not he specializes in your specific genre. And here's the best news . . . use of the information on this website is free!

Baseline, Inc.
www.Baseline.Hollywood.com

Baseline.Hollywood.com is one of the entertainment industry's prime resources for film and television information, featuring over 1.5 million database records on projects tracked from development to release, cast and crew credits, box office grosses, celebrity biographies, talent contact information, company directories, and industry news. All are easily searchable online and updated daily.

After reviewing the tremendous amount of data on Baseline, we consider the following lists to be most relevant to writers who want to sell or produce their spec scripts:

■ **In Production.** Tracks approximately 7,000 films from development to post-production to domestic release, and nearly 2,000 TV projects from development to post-production to broadcast. All listings include contact phone numbers, key production credits, and, when available, synopses, production notes, and estimated budgets. This information can give writers a good idea of the kinds of TV and feature films that are in all stages of production, as well as those that are ready for release. If someone involved in a specific film is someone you want on your wish list, the current contact numbers (for a production office, for instance) can be very helpful.

PROSE FROM A PRO

The Importance of the Genre
by Phillip M. Goldfarb

Unit Production Manager, Associate Producer, Line Producer, Co-Producer, and Executive Producer. Film credits: *All The Right Moves, Taps, Taxi Driver.* Episodic TV credits: *L.A. Law, Doogie Howser, NYPD Blue, Casey's Shadow.*

I pitched a network story about 8 or 10 years ago. The premise was about a woman who needed a heart transplant. She got the call, got the heart, and then became obsessed with finding the heart donor's family. She meets and falls in love with the husband of the woman whose heart she got. We pitched it to ABC and they told me that they're doing another organ movie. They said they had a brain transplant story so they used up their quota for stories on organ transplants. This is the way the thinking works. From their point of view, this was the genre—organ movies—and because we were the second ones in, we couldn't sell our organ movie. Everybody is looking for justifications for their behavior and decisions, for reasons to say no. We couldn't place it anywhere on television. A feature film (*Return to Me*, screenplay by Bonnie Hunt & Don Lake) opened last year with an incredibly similar story.

■ **Cast and Crew Credits.** Includes resumés of over 700,000 film industry professionals, and over 400,000 TV industry professionals. These extensive credit listings are helpful when you want background information on the talent you wish to contact. For example, if you have an actor in mind for the lead in your TV film and want to know if he has ever appeared in TV films, this database will have the answer.

■ **Kagan's Film Revenue & Cost Estimates.** Presents the costs (budgets, ads, and prints) and revenues (worldwide theatrical and domestic video) of films made from 1985 to the present. These workups are for films in the following genres: action, adaptation, animation, biography, comedy, crime, documentary, drama, erotic, family, fantasy, foreign, horror, musical, mystery, performance, period, political, remake, rock'n roll, romance, sci-fi, sports, thriller, war, and western. If you're thinking of producing your own script, or if you want a ballpark idea of cost and profit for a same-genre film as yours, then this database may fill the bill.

■ **Biographies.** Has nearly 7,000 biographies of prominent actors and other entertainment industry professionals. Each entry or "document" includes, if available, date and place of birth, education, former occupations, career milestones, awards and nominations, a written bio, and family/companion information. There is always a chance of finding something in the bio information that may provide a key to connecting a producer, actor, or director to your script.

■ **Talent Contact Information.** Provides contact information for nearly 18,000 actors, writers, directors, and producers. A sample listing is provided on page 145.

■ **Entertainment Industry Directory.** This is a comprehensive directory of over 17,000 entertainment companies. Called the Directrex
Database, it includes media and entertainment companies—studios, networks, cable companies, film commissions, record companies, guilds, and unions. Each entry includes company name,
company type, location, phone, fax, website, e-mail address, personnel roster, and company description. The database is helpful
when researching and reaching production companies that are on
your wish list.

Check the website's sample documents to see if Baseline has the
kind of information you need, and then check their price list per category. Until recently, this online film and television information
resource was used primarily by production companies, television networks, and studios. Now, Baseline's subscription rates and à la carte
pay structure make its information affordable to the average consumer. There's a one-time subscription fee, plus a per-document fee.
For each Baseline document request, subscribers pay at least 50 percent less than nonsubscribers. This site also offers free film reviews a
calendar of film releases, interviews and profiles, box office rankings
and analyses, and a free monthly newsletter.

The sample entry below is from the Talent Contact Information
database. It is for actress Daisy Dane, and includes the names and
numbers of her agent and manager, as well as her public relations
(PR) contact. Entries with PR information are a plus, because if the
actor's or actress' agent and manager are not receptive to you and

---

BASELINE SAMPLE ENTRY
TALENT CONTACT INFORMATION

```
Daisy Dane
        OCCUPATION:  actor / producer
            AGENCY:  All Star Talent Agency
             PHONE:  (323) 555-9876
        MGR OFFICE:  McHugh Management
             PHONE:  (212) 555-7654
    PUB. RELATIONS:  Harris B.
         PR OFFICE:  Buttnick/Morris
             PHONE:  (323) 555-2121
```

your script, you can make a last-ditch effort by pitching your work to the PR person. If he is blown away by the idea and feels that it's perfect for his client, he'll mention it. It can mean brownie points for him. You just never know where that "break" is going to come from. If you have a contact like a PR person, use it. You have nothing to lose.

The information in this Talent Contact database entry is barebones. It gives only key contact names and phone numbers. This may be all the information you need to reach the actor or actress you want to attach to your spec script.

Hollywood Literary Sales
www.hollywoodlitsales.com

This site offers an online Spec Screenplay Directory that has a database of screenplay sales from 1990 to the present. With a click of the mouse, you can discover who is buying and selling your type of material. Each alphabetized script listing provides some or all of the following information: the title of the screenplay, a brief logline, the screenwriter, genre, agent, agency, buyer, company contact, lawyer, purchase price, and date of sale. Listings are cross-referenced by agent, agency, buyer, screenwriter, first-time sale by screenwriter, genre, lawyer, and keyword (such as the subject of the story or a main word in the title). The site is updated daily.

You will discover that this database is one of the best sources for getting the names of producers who are making deals with first-time screenwriters and the agents who are representing those writers. In addition to this sales directory, the website has good, usable information including interviews, articles, a forum to ask Hollywood pros questions, script coach consulting services, and a screenplay contest database.

A sample entry from this site's Spec Screenplay Directory is found on page 147. As you can see, it offers lots of information. With a little further investigatory work, you can learn even more about Rachelleah Productions, and determine if it's a good company for you to pursue.

By checking the credits of the screenwriters in this entry at the Internet Movie Database, you can determine if they have a track record. If their names are not listed there, and if they are not found in the WGA *Member Directory*, you will know that Rachelleah Productions buys spec scripts from unproduced writers. This is good news.

HOLLYWOOD LITERARY SALES **SAMPLE ENTRY**
SPEC SCREENPLAY DIRECTORY

Say Cheese

Type of Material:	Screenplay
Genre:	Comedy
Writer:	Radisch, Buddy Hartman, George
Buyer:	Rachelleah Productions
Purchase Price:	Low-six figures / mid-six
Producer:	Schreiber, Fred Schreiber, Ellen
Writer's Attorney:	Koster, Larry
Law Firm:	Kahn, Koster, Farin & O'Quinn
Exec. Who Found Project:	Jacobs, Eric Stephen
Date Logged:	05-29-2001
Agent:	Portafekas, Kia
Agency:	Phoenix Agency
Logline:	Photographer develops a seamless technique of picturing people together. When one of his more politically incorrect photos turns out to be "a lucky guess," it's not lucky for him when it falls into the wrong hands. Written in the same style as "Ace Ventura, Pet Detective."
Additional Information:	Rachelleah Productions, owned by dir/pro Fred Schreiber, and pres/pro Ellen Schreiber, plan on making 3 films a year.

According to the entry, you can also see that the writers have an attorney and an agent. Both are listed along with their law firm and agency names, and both may be prospects for your wish list. If you are interested in learning more about the Phoenix Agency—is it a Guild signatory? what is its status with regard to new writers?—check with the WGA at www.wga.org or www.wgaeast.org. These sites will also give you the agency's contact number and address.

You can also check out Eric Stephen Jacobs—the executive who found the property—by looking him up in the name index of *HCD Producers*. Chances are he works with or for Rachelleah Productions. If so, he is the person to query if you feel your spec script is appropriate for this company.

To familiarize yourself with the kinds of films this company has done, check them out on the Internet Movie Database. You can also check out the director's credits at this site. To learn more about the films that Rachelleah plans on doing, turn to *HCD Producers* for titles of films in development. This directory will also have the company's contact information.

As you can see, this entry provides lots of good information, and much of it can serve as a springboard for further investigation. A little research can help you zero in on the best production companies to pursue, as well as the names of agencies, law firms, and directors that may be appropriate for your project.

Organizations, Unions, and Guilds

Industry organizations have members you may want to contact. Generally, the mission of these organizations is to protect and support their members in every way possible. One of the support systems consists of acting as the intermediary between their members and the people who are trying to reach them. This means that you can send a query letter to an actor, director, producer, or writer in care of his union—be sure to print "PLEASE FORWARD" on the envelope—and your letter will be forwarded to the address designated by the union member. Most actors and directors request that their agents or managers receive mail that is addressed to them, while producers are likely to want their mail forwarded to their production company offices. You can also call each union and ask for the department that has members' agency information. The following organizations are among the most notable in the entertainment industry; their contact information is found under "Guilds and Organizations," beginning on page 286 of the Resource List.

Actors Equity Association (AEA)

If you want to reach a *legitimate* or *stage* actor, as opposed to a *television* or *film* actor, call Equity, the actors' union. Ask to be

---

PROSE FROM A PRO

Do What It Takes
by Screenwriter David Newman

Co-writer: *Bonnie and Clyde; There Was a Crooked Man; Bad Company; Superman I, II,* and *III.*

When Robert Benton and I started out as a team, we decided to use every industry connection we had, no matter how remote. Our first script was *Bonnie and Clyde.* It was a spec script, although that phrase *spec script* didn't exist then. We immediately got it optioned by some friends who were novice producers as we were novice screenwriters. We were lucky. It launched our careers.

If you know anybody—if you have a cousin whose brother-in-law is in the mail room at Paramount—use the connection. No matter how unlikely the connection seems, it may be a way in. If there's a crack in the door, push in the door. Don't be afraid of being pushy, or even obnoxious. If it's a way in, use it!

connected to the Membership department. Tell them who you want to reach, and you will be given a contact name and number, usually the actor's agent. If you're in New York City, you can also visit the Equity office, and use their *Agency Book* to find actors' representatives. That book is not for sale. As a matter of fact, it is not allowed to leave the reception area.

American Federation of Television and Radio Artists (AFTRA)

AFTRA, the television and radio actors' union, has offices in New York and California. If you are looking for the name and number of the agency or management firm of an AFTRA member, call the New York or California office and ask for "Agencies."

Directors Guild of America (DGA)

This organization represents directors. Information on its *Directory of Members* is presented on page 140 under "Directories."

National Conference of Personal Managers (NCOPM)

This association, in existence since 1942, is committed to the advancement of personal managers and their clients. Its website, at www. ncopm.com, lists the member-managers across the country and includes their contact information. The NCOPM takes calls from writers and may recommend managers who consider representing new talent.

Screen Actors Guild (SAG)

SAG, the screen actors' union, has dedicated telephone numbers on each coast for the purpose of supplying callers with the names and numbers of actors' agents and/or managers. In New York, contact the SAG "Talent Agency Department"; in California, contact the SAG "Actors to Locate." See the Resource List for further contact information.

Talent Managers Association, Inc. (TMA)

This association of professional talent managers, founded in 1954, is a Non-Profit Mutual Benefit Corporation. This means that it exists for the benefit of its members, the talent represented by its members, and the profession of Talent Management. Take a visit to its website at www.talentmanagers.org for a list of members and their business webcards, which include contact information. You can also call or write for member information.

Writers Guild of America (WGA)

In addition to contact information through the WGA's *Member Directory* (page 141), you can visit the WGAE website at www.wgaeast.org, or the WGAw website at www.wga.org for a list of agencies that represent screenwriters. You can also write or call either of the Guild offices for this list, which is updated bimonthly and available to non-members.

The agencies on this list are Guild signatories, and have promised not to charge fees to writers, other than the standard commission based on the writer's earnings through the agency. Some agencies on the list charge reading fees for other forms of literary material (e.g., novels or plays). If you find that any of these agencies charge fees for reading screenplays, film treatments, or film synopses, the Guild asks that you notify them immediately.

Each entry gives the name of the agency, its address, and its telephone number. It does not provide individual agent names. What makes this directory so valuable to writers is that each listing is coded to indicate the agency's policy on accepting new clients. When searching for an agent, it is great to be able to zero in on those who are open to new writers.

In addition to California and New York agencies, the WGA lists agencies in Arizona, Colorado, Connecticut, Washington, DC, Florida, Georgia, Idaho, Illinois, Indiana, Michigan, Minnesota, North Carolina, New Jersey, Nevada, Ohio, Oregon, Pennsylvania, Rhode Island, Tennessee, Texas, Utah, Virginia, Washington, Wisconsin, and Canada.

CONCLUSION

Every moment of every day, keep your eyes and ears open for new leads. Pay attention to entertainment news on television, in the trades, and on the Internet. Keep adding names to the list as you come across appropriate people and companies who may be open to reading spec scripts. Now that you know how to research and find contact numbers for the people who can either buy or help you sell your script, your wish list should be growing on a daily basis.

Once you have ten to twenty viable names on your list, and the same amount of corresponding index cards with contact information, you'll be ready to mount your query letter campaign. To get on the campaign trail, you'll have to prepare your pitch. The next chapter will help you do that.

Friday the 13th

Written by Victor Miller

To a Certain Degree

I just wanted to be famous. I didn't know at what. At first I wanted to be an actor, until a tech director at Yale was very kind to me. He took me aside after one of my performances and said, "Victor, you are the most self-conscious actor I have ever seen on stage." It could have been a really devastating thing, except I agreed with him. I was always sort of pretending to be an actor, but deep down, I think I knew I never was going to be one.

I was trained as an English major at Yale and a lit-crit theater major at Tulane where I got a Masters in literary criticism. That kind of training had to do with developing *critics* of drama more than *makers* of drama.

I had taken a lot of fiction courses at Yale, including a particularly good short-story writing class with Robert Penn Warren. I got into writing, but I never thought I'd make any money at it.

Who Loves Ya' Baby?

I was working in the education department at the Shakespeare Theatre in Stratford, Connecticut, teaching teachers how to teach Shakespeare. The director of development of the Theatre at that time was Milan Stitt, a trained playwright from Yale, who wrote the play and, subsequently, the screenplay for *The Runner Stumbles*. He said to me, "Why don't you write plays?" I said, "I don't know how to write plays." He volunteered to help me. I instantly wanted to write like Neil Simon, and so I wrote a couple of Neil Simon-like plays. Milan was very kind and helped me, and I also went to the Herbert Berghof Studio for a year.

One of my plays was produced Off-Broadway. It went in at 119 pages, and the actors kept throwing out scenes, "I can't play this." "I can't say this." It came out at 80 pages. I thought, I'll never write drama again. I can't deal with actors. So I became an author and wrote a detective novel. It was on the basis of the detective novel that I got my first paying job as a writer. The job was to turn nine hour-length *Kojak* episodes into nine novels. I may have had English degrees from Yale and Tulane, but I didn't know much in terms of craftsmanship. Somehow, through my pores, or osmosis, I learned to do this total structural rewrite, pulling the scripts apart and switching them into a whole other medium.

Thanks to the *Kojak* novelizations, I was able to quit my day job, and on the basis of those novels, I got a job turning Scott O'Dell's novel *The Black Pearl* into a screenplay. I had to borrow a screenplay from somebody to learn script format. After that I did some other novelizations. For a while there, I was this middle person. Anytime anyone had something that they wanted changed from one medium to another, I was a logical choice because I had learned this strange skill.

You Gotta Have Friends

In the course of adapting *The Black Pearl* into a screenplay, I met some people who wanted to be producers and directors, and who were at my level, which meant no level at all—the bottom. We did a lot of talking and coffee drinking and hanging out. They didn't have any money; I didn't have any money. This was before I was in the union, and we did a lot of things on spec.

I really encourage that kind of thing. Find a group of friends and work with them on projects. The first person I worked with that way was Sean Cunningham. He was a producer/director for no money and I was a writer for no money. We found this way of communicating that was a kind of shorthand that you get with somebody you work with for a while. We'd bat around ideas and do treatments. Even though we did a lot of failed projects, we worked well together, bringing out the best in each other.

What the World Needs Now...

Everybody kept saying, what this world needs is a good family film, so we did a couple of very low-budget family films. Sean found the minuscule amounts of money needed to produce them, and they played at drive-in theaters. All they did was earn their money back. No profit.

Right after the first *Halloween* film came out, we decided that maybe what this world really needs is more gore. I had not been a horror film junkie, so I had to figure out what the horror genre was all about. I saw *Halloween* and basically went to school on that movie. We set out to put together a wonderful roller coaster ride, and that's what we did when I wrote *Friday the 13th*. Sean found the funding for it, and the rest is history.

I don't think that could have happened for me by just sitting alone in my office, writing horror film after horror film and finally getting an agent to look at one. None of my jobs were gotten through agents. People think, "Gee, if I get an agent, I'll be able to sell a screenplay." By hanging out with people who were in the same situation as we were, we learned the business together. I think it was a great way to do it.

The Hot Shot

After *Friday the 13th,* I was hot for about a minute and forty-five seconds and sold some more screenplays. Then I switched over to daytime television.

I have a lot of screenplays in turnaround—screenplays that were bought and not made. You're in very good company when you're in turnaround. It just doesn't feel very good. It's sort of like being on hold on the phone.

As I look back on it, I realize that I still had the experience of getting that part of my life out on a piece of paper. I just didn't get the next part of seeing it on the screen. Well, it's better to have a film in turnaround than in your trunk.

As Long as It's Legal

The best piece of advice for any writer is not to become a Cyclops with the attitude: "I just want to write screenplays. That's all I want to do." I learned a lot more by messing around between plays, novels, and screenplays than I would have in any other way. I picked up a lot about each form in terms of what they can and can't do. If there's a message in here it's: Do anything! . . . Do everything!

I once listened to a lecture at Yale by John Knowles who wrote *A Separate Peace*. I think he wrote it in the mornings before he went to work, writing for a travel magazine. One of the audience members questioned the quality of his important writing, and whether it suffered because he was also writing travel articles. John said, "No. I think you should write anything you can. Write laundry lists if you can, but just keep writing."

That lecture had an impact on me. I never turned down a job. Well, I turned down one job. Someone asked me to write a snuff film. When you're at the bottom of the heap, you meet a lot of strange people and you get some strange offers. It's best to turn down the repulsive ones or your karma will come back and bite you.

No Shortcuts

When I look back, I see that I had to do whatever I did to get to where I am. Nobody could have cut out six years of *Sturm Und Drang* for me.

I had a wife and two children, and I didn't make any serious money until 1980, with *Friday the 13th.* Everything up to then was survival.

The year before, I read in the Bridgeport paper that this local drug research company would pay for blood from people who had had hepatitis and I had had it about five years prior to that. They were going to pay for the blood so that they could play with the antibodies. I went down, gave them a sample, they tested my blood and told me that I didn't have enough antibodies so they couldn't pay me the $30 I desperately needed. That was devastating. And the next year was *Friday the 13th.*

I was as surprised as anyone that *Friday the 13th,* a movie that cost something like $800,000 ended up making $78 million.

There's no way to know how any of this is going to turn out, which is why I guess my fate was good to me by just making me keep on keeping on.

The Whole Nine Yards

Written by Mitchell Kapner

Planting a Seed

Years ago, when I was still living in Brooklyn, Dave Martin, a friend of mine who was a reporter for the *New York Daily News,* called me and said, "John Gotti got busted last night. Do you want to go see his bail hearing?" The Brooklyn Federal Courthouse was practically down the street from where I lived, so I went.

I saw Gotti, and I also saw Sammy (The Bull) Gravano. I remember sitting there in the courtroom, looking at this guy and thinking, everyone knows John Gotti, but no one knows this killer Gravano. He was every cliché come true about what this kind of guy looks like. I will never forget his face.

No one knew then that Gravano was going to rat out Gotti and become this super-famous recognizable guy. At that time I thought, what if this guy moved next door to me and I knew who he was, but no one else knew. It was an interesting idea that I filed in back of my mind.

Been There; Done That

For the last ten years I've been living in Los Angeles, and working as a writer. A few years ago, I went back to New York for a visit, and when it was time to go home, Dave Martin, that same reporter-friend, drove me and my wife to Kennedy Airport. While we were in his car, the Gotti-Gravano courtroom experience popped into my mind and I blurted out, "I'm going to write that script."

My lawyer is a good friend whose father owns a condo in Palm Springs. I went out there, became a hermit, away from all telephone calls, and, as quickly as possible, wrote the screenplay for *The Whole Nine Yards.*

High Hopes

My agents were very happy with it and started sending it out to producers we have relationships with. Once you start sending out a script, if you have any kind of name in town, producers call the agent and say, "I want to see it, too."

The way it works is that each producer has a relationship with a specific studio. You have a first position producer–someone who tried to hire me, or someone I've already worked for. If that producer is excited about the script, he'll walk it into a specific studio. If they don't want it, then the second position producer will take it in.

The script was sent to maybe twenty or thirty producers and about half of them passed. The other half were excited about it, and they did bring it to the studios. My agents and I had a lot of high hopes. One by one, every studio passed. It was a complete shutout.

You Gotta Have Friends

After all of the studios turned it down, it looked like it was kind of dead. That's when A.K. (Allan Kaufman), a guy that I played golf with, asked, "Do you mind if I take a run at it?" A.K. was in the music business primarily, and only peripherally involved in the movie business. The way he got into the movie business, is that he had done some music supervision–recorded music for sound tracks. He had produced a little movie called *Free Enterprise,* and it was pretty good. I was happy that A.K. wanted to see what he could do with my script.

A.K. is also a percussionist, and quite often plays in Bruce Willis' band. He's known Bruce and Bruce's brother David for many years. Apparently, the Willis brothers, A.K. and the rest of the band were on a private jet, coming back from something like the opening of Planet Hollywood in Dubai. A.K. was reading my script and laughing. He has a very raucous, braying laugh. He laughed so much that the other people on the plane couldn't sleep. Finally, someone asked, "Okay, what the hell are you reading?" A.K. started passing the pages around.

I was told that by the end of the flight, Bruce Willis said, "Merry Christmas, boys. I'll do the movie."

'Twas Right Before Christmas

Once Bruce came onboard in the beginning of December, 1998, everything fell into place. My wife, Donna takes some credit for getting the director. She's an assistant art director and was supposed to be working on *Skin Tight,* the Carl Hiaasen book they were going to shoot, with Jonathan Lynn directing. Donna went to Miami to start the movie. Two days later she called to say that the movie was shut down. She knew that Jonathan Lynn was available and suggested we talk to him. We did and he came onboard. As a result of both Jonathan and Bruce being great magnets, the cast came together extraordinarily fast: A.K. went to Elie Samaha at Franchise Pictures, and with Bruce attached, Elie got European financing and Warner Bros. to distribute and BOOM!–six months later we were filming.

My favorite story with regard to the many rejections, is that when Warner Bros.–yes, our distributor–originally passed on the script, we heard that they said they didn't think they could cast it. It's funny, considering the cast we ended up with: Bruce, Matthew Perry, Oscar nominee Michael Clarke Duncan, Natasha Henstridge, Rosanna Arquette, Amanda Peet, and Kevin Pollak.

Jonathan Lynn was a successful writer as well as a director. He created the BBC series *Yes, Minister* and *Yes, Prime Minister* in England. Like so many directors do these days, he could easily have taken the script and said, "Thank you very much. I'll see you at the premiere." He didn't do that. He kept me involved throughout.

It went so amazingly well and was so much fun that I was pretty sure I was going to get hit by a bus the week before the opening.

My Kingdom for a Horse

The saying goes, "A camel is a horse designed by committee." This is a town that makes camels, and as a result, it's very rare when only one writer is on a film. *The Whole Nine Yards* is my only script that didn't go into studio development, and after everyone said *no* to it, not only did it become a movie, it became a *hit* movie.

Hoosiers

Written by Angelo Pizzo

In the Beginning . . .

For a long time, starting back in college, I had talked about the idea for *Hoosiers* with David Anspaugh, who was my college roommate as well as my best friend. I went to USC Graduate School and right after, got a job as assistant to Philip Mandelker, an executive producer of a television series. I learned a lot from him about making movies, breaking down and analyzing scripts. I had no intention of being a writer. Back then, I didn't really know what I wanted to be. I thought perhaps in development, a studio job, or producer. And that's what I did. For five years I held various development positions. I worked at Warner Bros. in the story department, and at a couple of other companies in development, and I ended up producing.

Like a lot of people in development, after meeting the writers, I entertained the notion that I knew exactly how to solve their story and script problems. I never disrespected writers, but when they came back and still didn't solve their problems, I had the inkling or the itch to try my hand at writing. I had a question about whether I could do it, or whether I really wanted to do it. The idea of going into a room all by myself for any length of time to just write, seemed both boring and terrifying to me because I really liked the social aspects of doing the jobs that I was doing. What you do as a development or studio person or producer is support the creative artists, without any of the pressure being on you. The true pressure is on the writers, directors, actors and cinematographers.

I was director of MOWs for Time Life Films. During that time, I submitted a treatment I had writ-ten of what was to be *Hoosiers* to the development department. They thought it was a great fabric, a great background and area—a really good story that should be put into development. To move the project along, I needed to have a script written. It wasn't something I thought I could or should do. I interviewed writers, but couldn't find the right one.

It was at that point, after Time Life Films had made eighteen MOWs and had five feature films completed, that there was the antitrust suit. In those days, multi-tiering was not allowed. Exhibitors could not also be producers, and HBO (an exhibitor) owned Time Life Films (a production company). I had just signed a contract for another year with Time Life Films as vice president of production for feature films, when they had to disband. HBO gave me a choice: a job in development, or they would pay out my contract in full. Since I didn't like the person I'd have to work with in development, I thought, if I ever had an opportunity to experiment, it would be to write, and that seemed like the perfect time for it. That's when I took the money and spent a year in Indiana to research and write *Hoosiers*. I did it because of a kind of reverse motivation.

Remember the film *Breaking Away?* I grew up in Bloomington, Indiana, where the *Breaking Away* bicycle race took place. I knew those people. I knew the differentiations between the *stonies* and the *cutters* and the *gowns*. I think *Breaking Away* is a terrific film. I have great admiration for Steve Tesich as a writer. But Steve didn't really know Bloomington. Anybody who grew up in Bloomington would not recognize it as their town. In the film it was a generic college town. It could have been Salem, Oregon. It wouldn't have mattered. The film still would have worked. The film had its own charm, but it was Bloomington, Indiana, as seen through the eyes of two outsiders. (Steve was a Chicago boy and director Peter Yates was from England.) That aspect of *Breaking Away* was ultimately instrumental in my writing *Hoosiers.* It was also the reason I couldn't find anybody to write the movie from my treatment. What I thought was really important for *Hoosiers,* as opposed to *Breaking Away,* was the place. I saw Indiana as a character in the movie and it had to be accurate. I wanted the writer to know how the people walk, how they talk, how they shuck and jive, how they breathe basketball. One of the factors that I think made *Hoosiers* a success is the accumulation of details. We worked so hard to get it right. The specificity of the *mise en scène* was all-important.

Meanwhile, Back Home Again in Indiana

It was really hard writing the script. Working as an editor, you work from one side of the brain. You have that logical, rational, linear, objective approach to breaking down the work. That's not a good place to work from. That's why I definitely do not believe in screenwriting classes. It took me about six weeks to write about twenty pages. I had that little critic on my shoulder, that little editor who kept saying, "Ridiculous. What is that for? Why are we doing that? What's that about?" over and over and over again. I finally had to destroy that critic or put him aside.

A terrific writer I worked with on my first job, John Sacret Young, taught me an important lesson which I have adhered to ever since, which is: Once you finish writing a page, turn it and never look back. Keep going. Go to the end, or you will end up second-guessing and rewriting yourself to death. All of those voices are voices of doubt.

John also told me that it is absolutely critical—more critical than writing the perfect outline—to find out who the characters are by giving them voice. You have to allow them to breathe. You can't force them into a rigid outline form until you know who they are. I knew the ending of the movie. I also knew that there were a lot of different characters and I wanted to tell their stories, so I just let myself go and I just told them all. That's why, when I came to the end of the script, it was 205 pages, and I didn't know what I had.

Everyone's a Critic

When I got back to L.A., I sat there with my script, terrified of giving it to anybody, even to my friend David, who I wanted to direct the film.

I finally decided to give the script to the person who hired me out of film school, who believed in me and was my mentor and taught me everything about filmmaking from the ground up—ten times more than I ever learned by going to film school. Nobody could break down, analyze and explain the strengths and weaknesses of a screenplay better than he.

With great trepidation I handed Philip the screenplay, shaking, shaking, shaking. He was going to Paris and planned on reading the script on the flight from L.A. to N.Y. He called me from JFK Airport, and told me that it was one of the worst scripts that he had ever read. There was not one redeeming factor; there was not one interesting character; it was a badly told story and that I wasted a year of my life and that I was great in development, excellent working with writers, but that I was not a writer. His exact words were, "Angelo, you simply are not a writer. Let it go!"

Devastating was not even the word for it. It was beyond devastation. It was humiliation. It was a shame. There was a guilt, a self-loathing, a feeling of waste. The sense of failure was so profound, I didn't get off my couch for five days. I had a girlfriend at the time and she insisted on reading the script—she was the only other person I would let read that script–she really liked it, but what did that mean? She was my girlfriend.

I didn't give the script to David. I told him it was terrible. I took the script and, literally, threw it in the back of my closet. After a couple of weeks, I called up people and said I needed work and that's when I got a job at Paramount.

A Pulitzer Prize-Winning Angel

Eight months after I had thrown the script in back of the closet, I was at a dinner party, seated next to a guy that I had heard about and had tremendous respect for, even though I hadn't read any of his work. His name is Scott Berg, a biographer. He had written a book about Maxwell Perkins and has subsequently written about Sam Goldwyn and last year he won the Pulitzer Prize for his biography on Lindbergh. Scott grew up in a show business family–brother, Jeff, has been Chairman/CEO of ICM for a long time–but he went to Princeton and is an intellectual of sorts.

Scott and I started talking and we talked and talked and talked. He asked me if I had ever written anything. He thought I had the sensibility of a writer. I laughed and told him the story about the script and how terrible it was. He asked me, "How many people read it?" I told him, "Two." I also told him what Philip said about it. He knew Philip and said, "That guy never saw a shade of grey in his life. Everything's black or white."

Scott asked if he could read the script. I said I would rather walk on hot coals than humiliate myself one more time. This guy worked on me for a couple of months until he wore me down. He was convinced that it couldn't possibly be as bad as Philip made it out to be. When I finally handed the script–all 205 pages– to him I said, "I know you're never going to speak to me again."

Scott called me up later that day and said, "There's a great movie in here and I have some ideas

for cuts." Thanks to those ideas, in the next couple of days, I cut the script down to size. It wasn't like I rewrote it. All the scenes in the movie were already in that script.

Show Me the Money

I gave the trimmed-down script to David and he flipped out. We were ready to make the film. At that point, I wasn't outside the castle gates. I didn't have to knock on doors to get an agent.

I had worked with every agent in town, and, in fact, I had an agent who negotiated contracts for me as a producer and development person. He was with Creative Artists, the most powerful agency at the time. He read the script and said, "No, we don't do this kind of movie. It's an independent regional film. Go raise the money for it in Indiana."

When I originally wrote the film, I didn't have a title for it. I didn't know what to call it. Once I knew that we'd be trying to get the financing, I called the film *Hoosiers*. I figured that it was a good title for inducing wealthy Indiana investors.

David and I went back to Indiana and we worked very hard, but all we could raise was about $700,000. To do the film, we felt we needed at least $4.5 million. We went through the process of knocking on doors back in Los Angeles. It wasn't hard to get people to read the script, and we had a couple of bites. One from a former Warner Bros. president who had an overall deal at that studio. He wanted to option the story, get rid of David as director, and pay me to update it. I didn't have to think twice about turning that offer down.

I got to the point where I thought that this was a movie I'd get to make after I made the big-money movie. I'd do a successful film and then be allowed to do this personal project that didn't have commerciality. There wasn't a tremendous amount of anxiety about it on my part, because I was working in development at Paramount. But I wasn't the only one involved. David, who was directing *Hill Street Blues,* was eager to direct his first feature film.

It's Not What You Know...

Years ago, David was a ski instructor at Aspen, and had taught Jack Nicholson and his daughter how to ski. When David then went to film school at USC, Jack Nicholson wrote a letter of recommendation for him, and David had maintained contact with him for the ten years since USC. David came up with the idea of letting Jack Nicholson read the script and help us raise the money, since Jack knew the independent film world and he loves basketball.

So we went to see Jack, and gave him a copy of the script. I was sure he would never read it. There was a pile of scripts as tall as I am, waiting to be read by him. We didn't hear from him for about six months. Then, one day, I got a call from David saying, "Jack said he'll do it. He'll play the coach." I could hardly believe what I was hearing. All of a sudden Creative Artists came swooping down. "We love this script. What do you mean we said we think it's a regional movie?"

We went through a song and dance with Jack's agent. It was a complicated story. Jack was involved in a lawsuit at the time with a movie that fell apart, and he was enjoying not working. Then he had *The Two Jakes* lined up. I don't know the exact reason he gave us, but Jack said something like, "I'd have to go to Indiana, and it has to be shot in the fall and I'm not going to be available for two falls, and in three years from now I could be dead." Nicholson also said, "Give it to Hackman or Duvall."

The script went to Gene Hackman who read it and liked it. Gene Hackman. You'd think the movie is made, right? No. For the next year we tried different configurations. We got close lots of times. That's when we learned that a lot of people who claim they have independent money, don't.

After hundreds of turn downs, we finally got somebody interested in doing it. When people read your script, they make a determination, "Oh I know who'll love this, so-and-so. So-and-so is from Indiana. So-and-so loves basketball." Well, all of those so-and-sos from Indiana and all of those so-and-sos who love basketball turned the script down. None of them liked it. In fact, we got comments like, "Oh this guy doesn't know Indiana." "This guy doesn't know basketball." All of the experts, the afficionados, were the first people who turned us down.

The person who said, "Yes," was from England. He barely had heard of the state of Indiana and he knew absolutely nothing about basketball. This Englishman, John Daley from Hemdale Pictures, who had put together a lot of money from European sources and made a bunch of movies, including *Platoon,* read the script and was moved by it. He cried. His father was an alcoholic who, a number of times, embarrassed his son by showing up drunk at his soccer game.

John Daley said, "I don't know how many people want to see this movie, but I do." The lesson here? You just have to find that one person who will shed a tear, and then write a check.

A Fight to the End

It was a most difficult and most rewarding film to make. We fought every step of the way.

When we went into production with Hemdale, their understanding and the distributors understanding was that we were going to change the title. At that point, I had grown rather fond of *Hoosiers* and so had the director. We said that it's what we want. They said that they weren't going to release it under this title. They started sending us lists of proposed titles. Then they came up with *The Last Shot.* We fought bitterly. The thing that saved the title more than anything else was our first test preview screening. The response was so enthusiastic that we gained a little momentary power. Of course there's no way of knowing how your film would have done had it had a different title. It's all alchemy. It's just one little portion of the potion that the alchemist mixes together. In foreign countries, because there's no translation for the word *Hoosiers,* the film is called *Best Shot.* And we all gave it ours!

The Tag

Director David Anspaugh ran into Jack Nicholson at an Oscar party, the night the film was nominated by the Academy. It was the first time David had seen Nicholson since the movie was made. Nicholson said, "Great job! Hackman was great. I loved the movie. You really did it!" David said, "I've always wondered what *Hoosiers* would have been like if you were in it." He slapped David on the back and with his Cheshire-cat grin on his face he said, "Megabucks, kid! Megabucks!"

What's So

I think for a movie like *Hoosiers,* there was a window of opportunity. Four years after I wrote the script, that window opened up and we happened to be there. This movie would never be made today. In screenplay form, it doesn't break down to a poster. If you reduce *Hoosiers* to a log line, it sounds banal, and marketing people will tell you that they can't sell it. The marketing departments run the creative departments much more than ever before. They would tell me: It can't be reduced to a log line that would be interesting. It's dusty. It's regional. It's rural. It doesn't translate to a global marketplace; there are no international possibilities of marketing. This would not be made now at a studio, although if Harvey Weinstein cried after reading the script . . .

CHAPTER 5

THE PITCH

Now that you have prepared your script and have compiled a wish list of players, it's time for the next step—honing your "pitching" skills. Any contact you make with anyone who is even remotely connected to the film industry—whether by phone, query letter, e-mail, or in-person meeting—should be considered pitch potential. For this reason, it is important to always be ready. You must know your story as if it were your own autobiography, and be able to pitch your script in whatever form is appropriate for the situation. This means you must prepare a logline and a paragraph or two. You must also prepare a one- or two-page written synopsis of your script, as well as a version that you can verbalize in a start-to-finish ten-to-twenty-minute pitch session. The information in this chapter shows you how. This chapter also describes the components of a good query letter, which you will be sending out to those players on your wish list.

When it comes to those all-important in-person pitch meetings, this chapter offers helpful guidelines, including plenty of tips from screenwriters, agents, directors, and other industry professionals. Beginning on page 187, you'll find a must-read Q & A session with development exec Andrea McCall, who offers lots of valuable information for any screenwriter. The chapter concludes with an often-overlooked essential staple: business cards—both having your own and collecting others.

Roll up your sleeves. You've got some work ahead of you. It

requires writing and rehearsing. Fortunately, you're a writer, so you're starting with a big advantage.

PREPARING FOR THE PITCH

You never know when you're going to come into contact with the right person. By *right* person, we mean someone who is in a position to help further your career. And it can be anyone—from a producer, development exec, or agent, to a producer's reader, a development exec's assistant, or the receptionist at an agency. It can even be the owner of your neighborhood deli. If you're saying to yourself, "That's ridiculous," remember that Steven Spielberg's mother may have handed you a menu at her kosher dairy restaurant.

When opportunities arise—and they will, because you are going to actively set the stage for them—you must be prepared. You can't afford to wing it. It's too important. So it's time to get to work, and figure out how best to describe your script's story.

Logline

A logline is the *TV Guide* version of your story. In a few words or sentences, it tells your story in the most appealing and intriguing way possible. Since you can't give many plot points in a sentence or two, your job when creating a logline is to have it convey the essence of your story. You'll want it to stimulate and titillate the imagination of the person to whom you're pitching, so that she will want to hear more—and, hopefully, ask to read your script or invite you in for a pitch meeting.

The higher the film's concept, the fewer words needed to describe the story. The classic high-concept film example is *Titanic*. That single word says it all. Here's a logline for the high-concept film *Liar Liar:*

> **"A lawyer has to tell the truth for 24 hours."**

After reading this logline, don't you immediately start imagining the implications, ramifications, repercussions, all the possibilities that make for an entertaining film? The logline makes you want to know more about the story.

Popular author and screenwriter William Katz wrote the novel *Surprise Party*. Here is his logline as a film pitch:

> **"*Surprise Party* is about a woman who discovers that her husband is a serial killer.**
>
> **This will do for marriage what *Jaws* did for beaches."**

It would be easy for any producer to picture the line: *This will do for marriage what Jaws did for beaches* on the movie poster, also known as the *one-sheet*. Producers and development people often think in terms of the one-sheet. At a pitch meeting, an executive may ask the writer, "What does the one-sheet look like?" For this reason, you might want to consider incorporating a line or two in your logline that might be catchy enough for a one-sheet.

Here are some one-sheet lines. They may help give you some ideas for creating your own script's logline and one-sheet:

Who could forget the impactful *Jaws* one-sheet?

> **"Just when you thought it was safe to go back in the water."**

Hollow Man has two one-sheets:

> **"Think you're alone? Think again."**

and

> **"What would you do if no one could see you?"**

This is *Bless the Child's* captivating one-sheet:

> **"Mankind's last hope just turned six."**

Here's the one-sheet for *Little Nicky:*

> **"If Your Father Was the Devil**
> **And Your Mother Was an Angel**
> **You'd Be Messed Up Too."**

And then there is this one-sheet:

> *—Enemy at the Gate—*
> *Saving Private Ryan* **meets** *High Noon*

If you can come up with a provocative one-sheet line that encapsulates your screenplay, great; but you will most likely need another line or two to tell what your story is *really* about. A logline doesn't necessarily have to have a line that is appropriate for a one-sheet to be impactful. Writer William Katz shared the logline he pitched for a project that led to an ABC-TV movie:

> **"A woman is walking through a mall.**
> **She's approached by a younger woman who says,**
> **'I'd like to introduce myself. I'm having an affair with**
> **your husband, and he's about to murder you.'"**

Don't these intriguing lines make you want to know more about the story?

Once you come up with a logline for your script, ask yourself: On the basis of this logline, will people want to know more? Will their interest be heightened? Your answer must be "yes." And if it isn't, keep working on your logline until you come up with one that you believe will make everyone who hears or reads it want to know more about the story. Then try it out in social situations. Whenever you tell people that you've written a screenplay, and they ask what it's about, give them the logline and watch their reactions. If they don't respond the way you had hoped, rework the logline, and then rework it again if necessary. In fact, keep reworking it until people respond to it positively. Then you'll be ready to use it in business situations.

Know that when you call a production office, an agency, a management company, a development person, or anyone to set up a meeting or to ask about their script-submitting policy, you may be asked about your screenplay. Always be prepared with the logline. If it's a real grabber, it just may be enough to illicit a request to see your script. A great logline can also be worked into that irresistible query letter you'll be sending out to the players on your wish list. (We'll be discussing query letters later in this chapter.)

A Paragraph . . . or Two

In addition to creating an attention-grabbing logline, it is also important to prepare a paragraph or two about your screenplay. This should include where and when the story takes place, the setup (the situation that needs resolving), and the circumstances that change the life of the main character or characters.

Since you're going to be using the paragraph as a selling tool, make it as appealing as possible. In it, you may want to compare your story to a similar box office hit, or write about it being a cross between two big hits. As long as you're being honest, write whatever will make the person you are talking with or writing to want to know more about the story, or, ideally, want to read the script.

Remember William Katz's logline for the ABC-TV movie on page 164? Well, here's the paragraph that he used to pique interest even further. Four short sentences that tell so much:

> "Two women who have every reason to detest and resent each other join forces. One wants to change her life . . . to stop being the conniving mistress. The other wants to save her life. They both love the same man, and they both set out to destroy him."

So few words that say so much. Anyone hearing or reading that paragraph can imagine the drama and emotion, the suspense and betrayal, the conflicts and ironic camaraderie. It's also clear that there are a couple of juicy roles for women.

Write your paragraph as a succinct and interest-piquing summarization of your story, and use it in networking and schmoozing situations. That same paragraph can also be used in the query letter that you'll be preparing and sending out to people on your wish list.

A Synopsis

In addition to preparing a logline and a paragraph that summarizes your work, you must also write a synopsis—a detailed summary of your story that is written in the present tense. It should be one to two double-spaced pages long; a 12-point standard font, such as Times or Times New Roman is appropriate.

There are two kinds of screenplay synopses. One type is the cut-and-dried story summary that is prepared by a studio or agency reader as part of a coverage report. The other type is the summarization of the story as told by its creator. There's a big difference between the two. As explained in Chapter 3, a studio reader doesn't have to sell the story; she must only summarize it. As a screenwriter, however, your synopsis must be entertaining and irresistible. You are the writer and storyteller, and you are pitching a story that you want to sell.

When preparing your synopsis, keep in mind that the summary of your story as well as your writing skills will be judged. Your goal should be to tell your story in the briefest yet most captivating way. You may want to begin the synopsis with your logline, or by asking a titillating question that gets answered as the plot is revealed. Or you may want to tell the story simply and concisely from beginning to end. Most important, you want your synopsis to generate interest.

Writing a synopsis is another way of organizing your story. In doing so, your familiarity with it will help you prepare for in-person pitching. And, at some point in your writing career, you will probably have to do in-person pitching—hopefully sooner than you think.

PROSE FROM A PRO

Hook the Reader
by Dov S-S Simens
Founder, Hollywood Film Institute

Even if someone says they don't read unsolicited manuscripts, it is only human nature to skim a look at page 1. If page 1 is great, they will invariably read ten pages. If the ten pages are great, they will sit down and read the entire script. Now here's how to make page 1 great:

First, you're not writing a novel, so limit the amount of exposition. When you write your slug line (EXT-BEACH-DAY) don't spend 5 to 10 lines describing the beach. Cut to the chase. Cut to the dialogue. Get to the story and make sure that line 6 or 7 is a grabber. TV viewers have attention spans of fifteen seconds, and then they hit the remote. Script readers know this. Consequently, fifteen seconds into your script you should have a grabber that really gets their attention and holds it.

Figuring that one page of a script, properly formatted, is one minute of running time, then fifteen seconds into the film is line 6 or 7 on page 1. Make this line a shocker.

Now go to the bottom of page 1. What is so great that happens on the last line that makes the reader want to turn the page? Make sure this line *makes* them turn the page.

Some producers and development people ask for a synopsis along with the script, while others may request it instead of a script. We hate when that happens, but we comply and hope that the synopsis makes the person want to read the script. Many writers send out their synopsis along with their query letter. We don't. Unless we are specifically asked for a synopsis, we prefer to *not* send one. Sending material that hasn't been requested seems to be viewed as the sign of an amateur.

THE QUERY LETTER

So why a query letter? A query letter serves as your introduction to the people on your wish list—to those who are in a position to represent you, to option or buy your screenplay, or to hire you as a writer. When you begin the submissions process (detailed in the next chapter), your query letter is key. The goal of this letter is to get the reader interested enough to request your script.

Unless you have received specific instructions to do so, generally, it is not recommended to send out copies of your script along with a query letter—it is an unnecessary expense and a waste of time and effort. Keep in mind the volume of submissions that inundate agencies and production companies each day. Sending a good query letter is all that is necessary in most cases. This is the general industry rule; however, as we expressed in this book's Introduction, there are differing opinions for every rule. For instance, NYU Film School professor and produced screenwriter Charlie Purpura, believes in bypassing query letters altogether, opting to send out only completed scripts instead. Although unconventional, and not what we recommend, in fairness to a differing opinion, we present his strategy, which is detailed in "Screenplay versus Query Letter" on pages 168 and 169.

What to Include in a Query Letter . . . or Not

Because your query letter can be your introduction to influential industry players, it should be packed with punch and designed to make anyone who reads it sit up and take notice of you. Take your time when writing your query, giving it just as much thought and attention as you gave your screenplay. Remember, getting people to respond favorably to this letter is necessary if you want them to ask for your script. If your letter is a turn-off, your script won't stand a chance of being read.

So what are the rules? Should a good query letter include specific information? Does it have to follow standard industry guidelines, as spec scripts do? Although there isn't a set-in-stone required format for query letters, there are a few formatting suggestions that should be followed to give your letter an attractive professional look:

- Use a professional business-letter format.

- Use 8.5-x-11-inch stationery in white, cream, very light gray, or pastel.

- Stationery letterhead should include your name, address, telephone and fax numbers, and e-mail address.

- The letter should be no more than one single-spaced typed page in length.

- An easily readable font, such as Times or Times New Roman, is recommended.

- Fold the letter in thirds and mail it in a standard #10 business envelope.

The actual content of the letter should contain a few basic components—a proper salutation and introduction, information about your project, details about you and your background, and an invitation for the addressee to read your work. Many writers create succinct paragraphs in which they include these basic elements, but it is not necessary to do so. As a writer, you may want to exercise your creativity, for instance, by letting the genre of your script dictate the style of your letter. No matter what type of approach you take, no matter how you style your letter, what's important is that you include these basic components. Let's take a closer look at them.

The Salutation and Introduction

Every letter, of course, should begin with a salutation, such as "Dear Mr. Adamo." Using the salutation Mr. or Ms. is a little formal, but it's more respectful to be formal than to be too familiar and use the person's first name only. Another option is using both first and last names, which is actually recommended if you're not sure of the per-

PROSE FROM A PRO

Screenplay versus Query Letter
by Charlie Purpura
Professor of Dramatic Writing at NYU Film School.
Screenwriter: *Heaven Help Us, Satisfaction.*
CBS Schoolbreak: *The Day the Senior Class Got Married*
(Emmy Award Winner and Humanitas Prize Recipient).

I never bothered wasting time sending a query letter and waiting for someone to say, "Don't send your screenplay." I tell my students, if you send your script to a production company, priority mail, a government agent in a government uniform will take that screenplay, drive it out to the airport, put it on a government plane, fly it out to L.A., where another government agent will take it past the guard at the studio gate and set the script down on the desk with all the other scripts belonging to hot writers.

When producers go through them and come to yours, they'll say, who is this guy? It's not from an agent. I never heard of this person. At that point, the producer or the producer's assistant has to say to himself, am I going to just toss it in the garbage, send it back unread, go to bed tonight and think I may have just dumped the next *Home Alone,* or should I hand it off to a reader and say, take a look and see if there's anything there? Chances are, that's what will happen. Someone will read it.

A lot of production companies have a standing policy of not accepting unsolicited scripts. But they have to open the envelope and take out the contents to know that it's an unsolicited script. Unless they don't mind being haunted by the thought of the treasure they may be letting slip through their fingers, how can they risk *not* glimpsing at the first few pages? (I did get scripts back unopened, but the majority of the scripts I sent out were opened, read and responded to.)

Also, if you tell them what it's about, give them a logline, they may not be turned on, but reading the script can make all the difference in the world.

I know a director who was pitched something. He didn't want to do it because he had just done something similar. He was on a plane, had nothing to do, the script was in his bag. He read it and loved it and decided to do it.

Although Charlie Purpura's strategy for sending out screenplays may be unconventional, and not what we recommend, we present it in fairness to a differing opinion.

PROSE FROM A PRO

You want these people to read your script. Talk to people at pro-duction companies and they'll say, "Send a query letter." They want short-cuts. They have a lot to do. The fact is, they only read fifteen to eighteen pages before they decide whether or not they're going to continue. If the assistant, secretary, or receptionist reads the first fifteen pages and says to the producer, "Hey, this is a great idea here," the producer will take it home and read it. It happens. I tell my students this now and the feedback from them is that they're getting their stuff read.

Some of the students are going by the book, sending the query let-ter. If they've got a dynamite logline and they say that they're students at NYU Film School, they stand a chance of being asked to send their script. But it would have to be a logline that's irresistible—a nine-year-old kid is left home alone and has to defend his house against Joe Pesci; or a guy falls in love with a mermaid—and you've written a smaller kind of char-acter-driven script with wonderful moments that a person can fall in love with, but it sounds like crap in a logline, you've got to get them to read the script, not a query letter.

I would send a brief cover letter with the script:

> *Dear Friends,*
>
> *Attached please find a copy of (title of the piece). I tell my students to say that they are students at the NYU Film School. (But I never said that.)*
>
> *I would appreciate any time and attention you can give to this screenplay.*
>
> *Thank you in advance.*
>
> *Sincerely,*

And I'm out of there. Some people are good at sending out clever letters. Not me. And I don't want to play with anybody's head. It's business.

They're looking to say no. Don't give them the rope they need to hang you with by offering a weak logline or synopsis. The minute I tell them what the script is about or give them a logline, they may not want to see it because they already have something similar in production, or they hate those kinds of movies. It's really about the screenplay, not a logline, not a synopsis . . . the screenplay!

son's gender—as in "Dear Jamie Koster." And be sure to spell the person's name correctly.

Never begin a query letter with "To Whom It May Concern," "Dear Producer," "Dear Development Executive," or any general form of address. Always use the appropriate person's name. This serves two purposes. First, it helps ensure that your letter is sent to the right person, and second, it demonstrates that you have done your homework.

After the salutation comes the introductory paragraph. What makes this paragraph so critical is that it has to make the reader want to continue reading the letter. Every writer has a different approach. We believe that if you have been recommended by someone, or there's a personal connection between you and the person to whom you're writing ("My wife coaches your daughter's soccer team," or "Our mutual friend, Larry Ashmead, thinks you will be interested in my script . . . and you know what great taste Larry Ashmead has."), you should mention it here. Of course, do this only if it is a good connection that will evoke a positive association.

When there is no connection to serve as an introduction, consider beginning your letter by hooking the reader with an attention-getting line or lines from the script. It's a perfect place for your captivating logline. Many writers find this a great way to begin their letters.

About the Screenplay

Be sure to include a paragraph that includes more detailed information about your script, including its genre and a catchy summary of the story. If you have done a good job earlier in preparing that paragraph for pitching purposes, you can use it here as well. The important thing is to present a few lines about your story that will make the reader want to hear more. Remember, you want them to request your script. By the way, *never* give away your story's ending.

This is also a good place to tailor or personalize your letter to the person on the receiving end. For example, if you are sending the letter to an actor or an actor's agent, be sure to emphasize the quality of the starring role. If the letter is addressed to a D-girl at a production company, you might briefly liken the script to similar films that have been very successful. Finally, if your script has won any type of award or has received recognition of any kind, be sure to mention it.

A Bit About You

In your query letter, include only personal accomplishments that help establish your credibility as a writer. If you have written other scripts, you may want to mention this, but don't list them—especially if there are six or seven. The person you query might wonder why your other work hasn't sold.

The goal of this paragraph is to tell the reader a little bit about yourself to help establish your credibility. If you have anything impressive about your background—the film school you've attended, awards or credits you've received, writing contests you've won, jobs you've held, or anything else that's industry-related—be sure to mention it.

But what if you don't have any screenwriting experience or didn't attend a film school? We suggest that, at the very least, you should mention your educational background, no matter what. If possible, share some interesting facet about yourself, particularly if it relates to your project. Perhaps you are a seasoned traveler, or have an interesting hobby, or had an unusual or life-altering experience that inspired you to write the screenplay. You never know what might entice the person who is reading your letter.

Remember that the purpose of this paragraph is to show your strongest credentials in terms of screenwriting. Do not include irrelevant accomplishments, however meaningful they may be to you. For instance, you may have been captain of your high school lacrosse team, but this isn't relevant as far as your capabilities as a screenwriter. (Of course, if your script is about a lacrosse player, then this glimpse into your background would be worthwhile mentioning.)

If you have written a number of scripts, you might want to mention this as well. However, don't list them, especially if there are more than six or seven. The person you query might wonder why none of your other work has been sold.

If you have already had work produced or published, this could be the best credential of all. Be sure to mention your writing credits. For example, "I wrote *Getting Off Lucky*, a seven-minute script for an AFI project that will be produced this summer." Or "My nonfiction book, *Live and Be Well*, made *The New York Times* bestseller list." Keep in mind, however, that while it is certainly a perk to have had something produced or published, it is not a prerequisite.

Invitation and Closing

The purpose of this concluding paragraph is to wrap up the letter. End with a "just say the word" line, offering to send them your script. Also mention that, for their convenience, you have enclosed a self-addressed stamped envelope (SASE) along with your letter. This will be used to mail back their response and, hopefully, a release form if they want to read your script.

Finally, add your complimentary close—"Yours truly," "Sincerely yours," and "Sincerely" are all appropriate. If you can think of something with more panache, fine, but keep it appropriate. Type your name with your handwritten signature placed above it.

We have presented these basic components of a query letter in a paragraph-by-paragraph setup. With these components in mind, remember that you are a writer and should be able to put your personality and creativity into the letter. Take a look at the query letter on page 176. Its unique approach caused most people who received it to request a copy of the script. It's a real education.

And Another Thing . . .

We'd like to share a few more words of advice—some do's and don'ts—regarding your query letter. If you want to be regarded as professional, adhere to the following pointers:

- Be sure your letter is free of typos, cross-outs, erasure marks, and coffee stains. Nothing should detract from the letter's content.

- Proof your letter carefully. You should know by now that you must never leave this job entirely up to your spell-checker. Having a qualified person double-check for errors is recommended.

- Do not handwrite your letter.

- Always address your query to a specific person (whose name you have gotten and verified through your research), and be sure to spell it correctly.

- Don't overcompliment the addressee. For instance, if you are sending the letter to a director or an actor, it is perfectly acceptable to make it clear that you appreciate and respect his work, but don't go overboard with the flattery. It's a turn-off.

- Unless it is requested (highly unlikely) don't include your resumé.

- Don't include a projected budget for your screenplay.

- Don't include pages with set or costume designs. If you have a professionally executed drawing that is absolutely intriguing and *helps sell your story*—an alien creature, a futuristic invention, an ancient magical relic—then send it. If the drawing is less than professional quality, it will come off as shoddy, and no matter how good your story is, it may not be given fair consideration because of that amateurish drawing.

■ Don't pitch more than one story per letter.

■ Above all, don't mention anyone else you have contacted about your project (it's foolish to advertise that a script has been shopped and rejected) unless you have a name attached. If the attached name is a bankable director or an actor with any kind of track record, mention this up front.

■ Unless you are certain that the addressee prefers fax or e-mail, send query letters via snail mail.

So now you have a realistic idea of what a good query letter should (and should not) include. In the following section, you will find an example of one screenwriter's approach to writing a query letter. It may serve to inspire you when writing yours.

Sample Query Letter

The query letter on page 176, was written by screenwriter, director, and documentarian Don Vasicek (*Warriors of Virtue, The Crown*) with input from Kerry Cox, former editor of the *Hollywood Scriptwriter*. Don sent his original letter to thirty agents, producers, and production companies. From this mailing, he received an astounding twenty-six requests for his script.

When the original query letter and its analysis first appeared online, it garnered accolades. It also generated heated debates within the industry over the pros and cons of what a query letter should contain. There are many approaches you can take when writing a query letter. Often, the genre of your script will dictate the best approach. We chose to include Don Vasicek's approach simply because it makes sense, and also, you can't argue with success—getting twenty-six responses out of thirty certainly spells success!

Don regards the query letter as a marketing tool that can get both your script read and you recognized in the highly competitive film industry. For starters, he feels that condensing your 100-plus page

Who Actually Reads My Query Letter?

Agents, managers, producers, development execs, directors, and actors are the people to whom you will be sending your query letters. Although your letter will be addressed to a specific agent or development executive, usually it is that person's assistant who reads it first. If the assistant thinks your project may be of interest to the company, she will pass your letter on to the person to whom it was addressed. Then the agent or executive will decide whether or not she would like to see a copy of your script or the synopsis of your story.

script down to a one-page letter exhibits your writing ability. He also believes that a dynamite query letter should achieve two goals. First, it should hook the reader and reel her in. Second, it should prompt the reader to contact you immediately.

Along with Don Vasicek's irresistible query letter is his invaluable analysis of it (starting on page 177). It should help serve as a guide when you write yours.

What to Expect from a Query Letter

Depending on your personal preferences, you will be addressing your queries to agents, managers, producers, development execs, directors, and/or actors. As mentioned earlier, in most cases your letters will be opened and read by their development people, secretaries, or assistants. If they determine that your project may be of interest to the company, they will pass your letter on to whom it was addressed. That person will make the next decision, and usually within a month, you can expect any one of the following responses:

- They will ask to see your script. In doing so, they will probably have you sign their release form. In Chapter 3, you learned that signing this form is standard procedure for those without an agent, manager, or lawyer.

- If you're in their area, they may set up a meet-and-greet or a pitch meeting.

- Most often, you can expect a polite, "Thank you, but no thank you" form letter, which, in essence, shuts the door.

- Occasionally, they will send a letter stating that they're not interested in the story that you pitched in your query letter, but welcome other ideas from you. This keeps the door open.

- Once in a blue moon, the person who reads your query letter will see something special in it, even if the project is not appropriate for the company; and she may recommend you to someone else like an agent or a production company that may consider your work. (Be sure to remember that person on an awards night when you're giving your acceptance speech.)

- The worst-case scenario is that your letter is thrown away and you never hear from them.

Don Vasicek's Sample Query Letter

(Date)

John Smith
Hollywood Fictitious Film Co.
12345 Wilshire Boulevard
Beverly Hills, CA 90210

Dear John Smith,

Last night, Generation Y's Jenny Black ate lasagna and a salad with her mom and little brother; she answered the doorbell; went outside and never came back.

Why?

It's a question that Lt. Icabod Poe has to answer fast. The chilling fact is, the more he learns, the more he realizes that she is living two lives . . . one as a normal daughter and sister, a high school honor student and budding artist; the other as a reclusive teenager who is depressed over her recently murdered dad . . . and she is terribly attracted to the moon.

And Jenny might be gone forever if Lt. Poe doesn't come up with the reason for her disappearance . . . and soon.

Dark Moon Jenny is a suspense thriller with a strong female protagonist, a deeply terrifying antagonist and a series of disturbing surprises that build to an ultimate shocker of an ending. It is also a story of love, trust, betrayal, courage and redemption and the fine line that separates the normal from the abnormal.

I'd like to submit *Dark Moon Jenny* for your consideration. I've been around the block twice with other screenplays. Two were made into movies, *Stupid and Stupider* and *The Girl Hunter*—okay, not Sundance or Nicholls' award winners. *Dark Moon Jenny* was a winner in the "Writer's Digest" Scripts Competition and a semi-finalist in Chesterfield Film Company's Writer's Film Project.

If you would like to read *Dark Moon Jenny,* you can reach me at 123–456–7890. I look forward to hearing further from you.

Thank you for your time and consideration.

Sincerely,

Don Vasicek

Query Letter Analysis

Here is Don's dissection of his query letter. It is a sentence-by-sentence analysis, which, as you will see, clearly defines his logical approach.

Last night, Generation Y's Jenny Black ate lasagna and a salad with her mom and little brother; she answered the doorbell; went outside and never came back.

Establishing a time in the mind of readers makes the story look more immediate and real. Introducing your main character immediately and telling readers something about them, hooks readers into your character, story and query letter, seducing them into wanting to read on. Evil is also implied here, which is a sure recipe for enticing readers to read on.

Why?

Asking the question, **Why?** here, and separating it from the first paragraph, makes it stand out and gives readers hope that they will find out more, compelling them to read on.

It's a question that Lt. Icabod Poe has to answer fast.

This sentence puts readers on edge with the word **fast.** It gives them a sense of urgency, particularly since you have already gotten them concerned about your main character and they can't wait to get to the next sentence.

The chilling fact is, the more he learns, the more he realizes that she is living two lives . . . one as a normal daughter and sister, a high school honor student and budding artist; the other as a reclusive teenager who is depressed over her recently murdered dad . . . and she is terribly attracted to the moon.

The word **chilling** in this sentence sets up the rest of the sentence. It hooks readers once again and reels them through the sentence. What they see is the heart of the story and character. Jenny Black, a high school junior, seemingly normal, misses her dad and adores the moon. Wouldn't you want to read on? I'm sure readers do because now they have a stake in Jenny. They know her, they like her, they see that she has possibly befallen some horrible experience and they want to help her.

The fourth sentence raises questions that they want answered. Why does she like the moon? How does her depression over losing her dad fit in here? Does it have anything to do with why she disappeared and why he was murdered? Is she a female werewolf? How does Poe know Jenny is lost and not dead? Why does he think she disappeared? Maybe she ran away. Maybe she was spirited away by the moon to communicate with her dad. How can Poe find the reason for her disappearance?

The more questions you raise in the mind of readers, the more they are going to want to read on. By now, readers are going to finish reading the query letter with interest, so you don't want to lose them.

And Jenny might be gone forever if Lt. Poe doesn't come up with the reason for her disappearance . . . and soon.

The words, **gone forever** and **soon** give an even greater urgency to Jenny's dilemma. This ups the stakes and tightens the tension. Readers will want to help Jenny and the only possibility of doing that is by continuing to read the letter.

Dark Moon Jenny is a suspense thriller with a strong female protagonist, a deeply terrifying antagonist and a series of disturbing surprises that build to an ultimate shocker of an ending.

Identifying the film genre and the gender of the protagonist and one other main character gives readers information they can use regarding the marketability of *Dark Moon Jenny*. It certainly dispels the question as to whether Jenny is a werewolf or not. If she were, the genre would be **horror** instead of a **thriller.** They know that this movie needs a 30's actor and a young actress and a thriller audience. The description of the villain gives them an idea that Lt. Poe isn't only dealing with someone who opposes him in finding Jenny, but also the potential exists that something very bad has happened to her. Utilizing the word **series,** creates the image that there is even more to the story. And to top things off, using words like **ultimate shocker** and **ending,** gives them a hint as to what they may expect, and is enough to tease them into reading the next sentence.

It is also a story of love, trust, betrayal, courage and redemption and the fine line that separates the normal from the abnormal.

This shows that the story is multi-dimensional, dichotomies with love, trust and betrayal, and the abnormal and normal. It also implies **evil** and whets readers' appetites for more.

I'd like to submit Dark Moon Jenny for your consideration.

This humble, but confident and professional offer to let them see the script increases interest for readers.

I've been around the block twice with other screenplays. Two were made into movies, Stupid and Stupider and The Girl Hunter—okay, not Sundance or Nicholls' award winners.

A light approach like this helps readers learn something more about you as a screenwriter and shows them that even though you're serious about your career, you do have the ability to laugh about it too. These sentences personalize you and help readers "bond" more with you.

Dark Moon Jenny was a winner in the "Writer's Digest" Scripts Competition and a semi-finalist in Chesterfield Film Company's Writer's Film Project.

This sentence identifies whatever awards and/or recognition the script has received. If your script hasn't won any professional recognition, but your aunt loved it, tell readers in a creative way that your aunt is as capable of rendering a learned opinion on your script as anyone else. After all, wasn't it screenwriter William Goldman who said, "Nobody knows anything in Hollywood?"

If you would like to read Dark Moon Jenny, you can reach me at 123–456–7890.

This sentence is utilized by sales persons to close a deal. It calls readers to action. This simple request of asking the reader to call you is to the point and gives readers the opportunity to read the script. The utilization of **you** personalizes the call to action and gives readers a good feeling that perhaps they are special and you haven't let anyone else in on your script as yet.

I look forward to hearing further from you.

The purpose of this sentence is to inform readers that you think highly of them and want to continue your communication with them.

Thank you for your time and consideration.

This sentence is a courtesy and it shows your appreciation. It gives readers a feeling of respect and professionalism.

We'd like to conclude this query letter analysis with some final words from Don Vasicek:

"Putting this form of query letter into service cannot guarantee that you will sell your script. It can, however, improve your chances that readers will request your script. And what more can you ask as you move forward in your screenwriting career? Since the film business is so subjective, it is possible readers may not like your script, but if they are impressed enough with the writing of your query letter and your script, they may ask to see other scripts you have and request to see the next script(s) you write, in addition to the possibility of being considered as a writer-for-hire and for a writing assignment. What more can you ask for in this business... unless you want to direct too."

Now you know how important the query letter is, how to structure one, and the hoped-for results. Okay, you send out your query letters and you dazzle a producer's development person. When she calls you, you mention that you're planning a trip to California. She sets up an in-person pitch meeting for you and her boss. Gulp! Read the next few pages and learn how to prepare for the meeting. Pay particular attention to the advice from successful screenwriters, and from development executive Andrea McCall in the Q & A session beginning on page 187.

IN-PERSON PITCH MEETING

If you are in California, New York, Florida, or wherever there's a producer, agent, manager, actor, or director—and that's just about everywhere—the opportunity may present itself for you to pitch your spec script and/or film ideas in person. That's a good thing. Most pitch meetings, at least in California and New York, come about after a development person, producer, agent, director, or actor has already read your script, but is not necessarily interested in it. However, this person may like your writing style or the way you think, and may want to hear about other scripts you have written or any ideas you may have for future works. And so, you'll be invited in for a pitch meeting.

The usual pitch meeting in Los Angeles is with a development exec at a production company, and is likely to take place in either the exec's office or the company conference room. Typically, there are one to four people present, at least one of whom is the exec's note-taking assistant. Others may include an assistant-in-training, a same-level exec as the one who set up the meeting, and maybe even the executive's boss. You will be introduced to everyone in the room. Pay attention.

This kind of pitch meeting can lead to any one of a number of good things. For instance, the company may want to option the story or the completed script that you have pitched, or they may ask you to further develop one of your ideas (with pay, of course). There is also a chance that they may want to set up another meeting at a studio or network and have you pitch your idea or script there, while attaching them as your producer. Or they may appreciate your writing talents and offer you an assignment—pay you to write a story that they want written.

Before the meeting, it's a good idea to find out who will be attending. Simply ask the person who makes the arrangements, "Who will I be pitching to?" Then tailor your pitch to those particular people. If, for example, you're pitching to an actor or the actor's development person or agent, be sure to talk about the lead character more than you would if you were pitching to an exec or a director. When you're pitching to an executive, let your pitch clearly-but-subtly identify the potential market for the movie. As a writer, what's most important when you pitch—regardless of who is in the room—is to tell your story or convey your ideas with passion and pleasure.

Whether you are pitching one script or ten, be sure to practice your pitch beforehand at home. Be prepared to pitch your logline, the paragraph or two, the synopsis, and a treatment for a ten to twenty-minute pitch. To some industry pro-

---

PROSE FROM A PRO

Pitch Meetings
by Screenwriter David Newman

Co-writer: Bonnie and Clyde; There Was a Crooked Man; Bad Company; Superman I, II, III.

Pitch meetings? Oh God, I just hate doing them. I go out to Los Angeles from New York about once every six or seven months and just gird my loins and do that week of pitch meetings. Hopefully, either the *pitch* will be *caught,* or somebody will say, "I'm so glad you came in because we were just thinking about you for something else."

Before the meetings, I sit down with my agents and they give me the battle plan: "Now here's who you're going to go to today: 'A,' 'B,' and 'C.'" They give me the driving instructions because my meetings are all over Los Angeles. Then they say, "'A' likes to hear a good, long pitch. He wants to hear all of the steps. 'B' just wants to hear the general concept. 'C' just wants to hear two lines."

Invariably, when you get to these producers' offices or production companies, they'll throw a curve at you. The last time I went out there, I had a particular pitch that I was pitching for a certain kind of film. There was one place my agent sent me and said, "Don't bother with the pitch there. They're not interested in developing pitches. They want to meet you and talk to you about a couple of things they have in-house." I thought, that's great. I don't have to do my dog-and-pony show. I got there and after we talked about what they wanted to talk about, the guy said, "So what are you doing out here? Are you pitching?" I said, "Yeah." The guy said, "Let me hear the pitch. I like listening to pitches." I felt like saying, "Screw you," but of course I didn't. Instead I did the pitch.

The main thing is that you show enthusiasm and try to knock 'em out of the park. Sometimes it works and sometimes it doesn't.

fessionals *synopsis* and *treatment* are interchangeable. As an unofficial rule, the synopsis is shorter and less detailed than a treatment. The average treatment, which is written as a narration in the present tense, is usually between three and ten double-spaced pages long. This kind of treatment will not only help you prepare your ten- to twenty-minute verbal pitch, it will *be* your verbal pitch.

There is also another kind of treatment. When a story idea goes into development and the writer gets a step deal, usually, the first step is a called a treatment. This kind of treatment is done in scene-by-scene detail and can run forty to sixty pages.

Whether you're pitching a script or an idea, we recommend beginning with the logline to pique interest. Then practice telling the paragraph version. Finally, tell the start-to-finish synopsis and/or treatment, which should take anywhere from ten to twenty minutes. The less time, the better.

While you're on the phone with the person who is setting up the meeting, you may want to ask what kind of pitch the person prefers—a logline, a paragraph, or the start-to-finish story in great detail—just so you know. Of course, it may not be the way you're told it's going to be, but if you're properly prepared, you'll be ready for anything that's asked of you.

A Pitching Experience

One of the most frightening pitch meetings we had was with a major player who was a partner in a prestigious and powerful production company. We were told that he *never* listens to pitches, but was making an exception. Even though both of us had been guests on national television shows many times and were never nervous, for this meeting, we were nervous wrecks. A friend of ours had gone out on a limb to set up this meeting and we wanted to make her proud. We rehearsed and rehearsed and were able to get our pitch down to about twelve minutes.

On the day of the meeting, we were greeted by the executive's development person, who led us to "Mr. Big's" office. While we were en route, she told us that he has a very short attention span, and if he reaches into his desk and takes out a nail clipper, it means that he has lost interest and we are history. We considered leaving right then and there, but of course, we didn't. As we were ushered into Mr. Big's office, one of us whispered to the other, "Showtime!" The troopers that we are, we knew exactly what we had to do.

The office door closed behind us. There we were, the two of us and Mr. Big. No development person. No secretary. No note-taker. We started the pitch with the setting of our story—a rundown bungalow colony in the Catskill Mountains during the early 1950s. Soon after, we discovered that the producer had been a waiter at one of the hotels in the Catskills during that same time period. An hour and a half later, as we continued telling our story, he was still sharing his Catskills' experiences with us. It was a great pitch meeting. Mr. Big wanted to put the film into development right then and there, but had to check it out with his partner first. They both had to agree on each project they bought. Unfortunately, the partner wasn't interested. She didn't even want to hear the pitch for our wonderful fish-out-of-water romantic Catskills comedy. The good news was that the next producer to whom we pitched this project, gave us a deal. The bad news was that by the time we finished writing the script, he was involved in a big budget production and let our script go into turnaround.

The point of our story is that you never know what is or isn't going to happen at a pitch meeting, or which idea will spark someone's interest. You must be prepared with all of your ideas, and then go with the flow. We recommend being fully prepared to pitch three stories. If the person to whom you're pitching isn't interested in any of them, don't drag out the laundry list and keep going. It is a good idea to ask for input, so that you can go home and regroup. There's nothing wrong with saying something like, "Is there any specific genre you have in mind, or any guidance you can give me so that I can come back and be more on target with what you're looking for?" You want to leave the door open. You also want to let it be known that you're available for an assignment. There's nothing wrong in saying that.

Probably the best advice on pitching comes from those who have had pitching experience, as well as those who are on the receiving end of all of those pitches. The following gives you that—great advice from both sides of the desk.

Advice From the "Pitchers"

Who best to advise you on pitching? The pitchers, of course, especially those who have been successful. This would include, among others, produced screenwriters. On the pages that follow, you will

New writers ask me about pitching all the time. I always tell them to remember that the mechanics of the story are obviously the most important thing, but it's the writer's passion for her material, for her characters, for the world she's creating that can bring a story to life for the exec she's pitching to. . . .

—Andrea McCall
Head of Story Department
DreamWorks SKG

find wonderful words of advice from experts on how best to prepare for those meetings and present those pitches. Learn from the best.

Fear-Conquering Exercise

Screenwriter Michael Colleary (co-writer *Face/Off*, *Things That Go Bump*) teaches at UCLA. He helps his film students conquer their fear of pitching with a simple exercise—he has them pitch their favorite movie. This helps them see what is important in terms of telling the story. Try it with your favorite movie. Then try to envision your story as if it were already a movie, and pitch it that way. This exercise should keep you from getting bogged down with unnecessary details.

Practice, Practice, Practice

Ron Bass (*How Stella Got Her Groove Back*, *My Best Friend's Wedding*, *Dangerous Minds*) would prepare for pitch meetings by rehearsing out loud, over and over and over again. He believes in practicing until you get to the point where you don't have to search for words, or go back and correct yourself, or figure out what to say next. Let the words roll off your tongue. He advises against memorizing the story because it becomes too mechanical.

Memorizing Is a No-No—Diligence Is a Yes-Yes

Always prepare well whenever you have the opportunity to pitch your story. You owe it to yourself and to the pitchees. Let's face it, you're asking these people to invest millions of dollars in your project. Although Deborah Dean Davis (*It Takes Two*) believes in being well-prepared, she doesn't believe in memorizing a pitch. She feels that it is better to play off the reaction of the person you're pitching to—and you can never second guess how that person is going to react.

To prepare, Deborah rehearses her story by telling it to anyone who will listen, including the lady at the Lancôme counter. Part of Deborah's preparation includes writing out a beat sheet—a list of plot points—which she brings with her to the meeting.

Like Talking to a Friend

Co-writers Lowell Ganz and Babaloo Mandel (*Father's Day*, *City Slickers*) are always pitching the scenes of their stories to each other as they work. They bring their conversational tone along with them to pitch meetings. Doing this makes them feel as if they are telling the story to a friend who they've just run into. It makes the pitch spontaneous and natural.

A Matter of Time

Michael Werb (co-writer *Face/Off*, *The Mask*) sold an idea at a pitch meeting by showing the execs a newspaper picture of a family. He pitched the story with an impactful "What if—" scenario that had to do with the family in the picture. It was a powerful pitch that took only three minutes. The execs bought it on the spot.

While the opportunity for this type of pitch doesn't happen often, the lesson to be learned here is that you don't need an hour to sell a story. Most industry professionals agree that your pitch shouldn't be longer than twenty minutes. Of course, it may turn out to be longer if the exec is interested and wants to hear more, or asks questions that lead to a discussion. But don't plan on more than a twenty-minute pitch. Less is even better. As the saying goes, "Leave 'em wanting more."

A Pitch Routine

Michael Colleary has a pitch routine. He starts with where and when the story takes place. He follows that with the setup of the story. Then he sketches the second act, and covers the resolution. He ends by talking about the characters a bit. Then he is prepared to answer any questions.

On Answering Questions

Steve Oedekerk (*Patch Adams*, *Ace Ventura: When Nature Calls*) advises that when executives start quizzing you on plot points, particularly if the pitch is for an as-yet-unwritten script (rather than your already-written spec script), don't expect to have all of the answers. Respond honestly. There's absolutely no shame in saying, "I don't know. I have to think about that. I'll have to work on it."

When Changes Are Suggested

The development exec may suggest changes . . . drastic changes. Lowell Ganz and Babaloo Mandel take into consideration the exec's participation in the project. If he's going to be the producer and take an active part as collaborator, it's wise to listen to and consider his input. Tactful lines like, "We need a little time to digest that" come in handy in these situations.

The exec who suggests you take your story in a different direction may be giving you valuable advice. Ron Bass' first major studio film deal happened after pitching a few ideas to the studio V.P. This smart exec explained to Ron how and why he should combine two of his ideas into one film. Ron agreed. The ironic part is that the studio didn't put it into development, but Ron liked the idea so much, he wrote it on spec, then sold it to the studio after the exec was no longer there.

You Go Girl—or Guy

Deborah Dean Davis suggests that you be emotional about your story. If this means making a fool of yourself, so be it. Become totally uninhibited. Bare your soul. If the story makes you want to cry, then cry. Show the passion that you have put on the page.

Take a Class

If you find that you have difficulty talking in front of people, Gigi Levangie (story by and screenplay co-writer of *Stepmom*) advises writers to take an acting class. She feels it is a good way to liberate yourself and prepare to perform at a pitch meeting.

Dudes with 'Tudes

Steve Oedekerk has a wonderful attitude when he goes to a pitch meeting. He feels that he's offering the executives a gift. Keep this in

---

PROSE FROM A PRO

Timing
by Charlie Purpura

Professor of Dramatic Writing at NYU Film School. Screenwriter: *Heaven Help Us, Satisfaction.* CBS Schoolbreak: *The Day the Senior Class Got Married* (Emmy Award Winner and Humanitas Prize Recipient).

Timing can play a big part in a script's saleability. In 1987, my brother, Pete Brown, wrote a screenplay about baseball. The script is set in 1912 and has some magic elements in it. Pete sent it around and was told across the board, "Nobody makes baseball movies. Plus it's a period piece. Plus it's got this quirky magic element to it."

Two years later *Field of Dreams, Eight Men Out, Angels in the Outfield,* and on and on and on. So he sent it out again, and they said, "Nah! Who wants another baseball film?" He came in too early and got back too late.

The hopeful thing about this business is that a good screenplay is never dead. Years go by, personnel keeps changing at studios and networks, sensibilities change, and suddenly, the timing may be right again for that screenplay.

I tell my students that by the time you write whatever you think they're looking for, they won't be looking for it anymore. Write what means something to you and float it out there and hope for the best. The hard truth is, all that we can control as writers is the quality of our work and the effort we make to get it out there. The rest is up to God, or whatever *magic elements* you believe in.

mind. If you really believe that you are pitching something wonderful, then you are truly entering that pitch meeting with a gift. If you exude this type of genuine confidence, the person to whom you are pitching will sit up and take notice. Also, if you maintain an attitude that suggests you don't need the deal—that you plan on giving another studio the opportunity to take on your script—they may not want to let it go. Be sure that your confidence is sincere, and all about your belief in the project.

Michael Colleary is another screenwriter who believes in the importance of a positive attitude. He thinks it will serve you well to bring good, happy energy into the room. Your positive presence will help lift everyone's spirit.

Take Comfort

If you feel that your pitch wasn't terrific, screenwriter Larry Gelbart (*Weapons of Mass Distraction, Mastergate, Bedazzled*) offers a comforting thought. He advises you to keep in mind that the person you pitch to today probably won't be there next year. This means that you will be able to go back and pitch your story to someone else at a later date.

Advice from a "Pitchee"— Insight from the Other Side of the Desk

Industry professionals who are on the receiving end of all of those pitches—the pitchees—can certainly be considered expert advisors on in-person meetings. You will find the interview beginning on page 187 with Andrea McCall—head of the story department at DreamWorks SKG—to be most insightful. In addition to providing valuable pointers on pitch meetings, she also offers encouragement and general words of advice for screenwriters who want to get a foothold in the industry.

As a seasoned professional to whom pitches are routinely made, Andrea answered our questions frankly and honestly. We believe this interview should be required reading at film schools and for all novice screenplay writers. Every talent agent and manager should hand out reprints of this interview to their writer-clients. The information is invaluable.

Agents and the Screenplay

I would not hitch my wagon to the idea that an agent will sell your work. By and large, agents don't want to have to sell your work, don't know how to sell your work, and they can't sell your work. Your work sells itself. For the bulk of my career, I had no agent at all. Before my career started, I met a couple of agents and I asked myself, how could these guys sell my work if a studio executive doesn't want to buy it? I didn't understand how anyone can sell a screenplay that isn't good. If the screenplay is good, all you have to do is get someone to read it. That's the most important thing.

—Dale Launer
Screenwriter

Interview with Andrea McCall

Currently the head of the story department at DreamWorks SKG, where she has worked since its initial startup in 1994, Andrea McCall started her career as an assistant to an agent at the William Morris Agency in 1985. She then went on to work in film packaging, film production, and as director of development for a production company. She knows the business, has a great passion for it, and works with writers.

Andrea, what does the industry look for in terms of new or unknown writers with spec scripts?

Talent. We want to find the next great writer; someone who has wonderful ideas and who is a terrific storyteller. It's what everyone is after. The trick is weeding out the good-but-average writers from the great new writers. Many studios receive anywhere from 80 to 150 pieces of material each week. These submissions can be in the form of scripts, videos (for remake), articles, plays, and treatments. That's a lot of material to sift through. Among these submissions are many fine, decent and well-written scripts, but few are unique enough or stylish enough or smart enough to be bought and turned into a movie. That's the hardest thing to explain to anyone who's trying to break into the industry as a writer. A new writer will have slaved over his or her script for ages, and is told by friends and family and agents that it's good and needs only to have an executive give it a brief skim. We're looking for an idea no one has seen.

If someone has a truly great script, will it eventually be found?

Yes. The job of an exec is to find that truly great script. A new writer's best introduction appears on the first page of the script. Understand that the exec really wants the script to be great—that's what the writer has going for her right off the bat.

A truly terrific script may be overlooked at a company or two, but if the writing is strong and the story is compelling, somebody somewhere at some point will read it and discover it.

Does the way a screenplay looks— three brads instead of two, an illustration on the cover, a cast list on page one—color your attitude toward that screenplay?

I'll still look at the screenplay, but anything other than a plain white script cover screams, "I'm an amateur. I don't know what I'm doing. I'm afraid my story may not be that good and isn't going to stand up on its own, so I'm going to impress you with a fancy cover, pictures, and articles to support it."

How many script pages do you read before you make a judgment?

I try and give it the first thirty pages. Usually I can tell before that, but sometimes something will kick in. I have been surprised. I recently read a script where the writer did an interesting thing. He made it seem like a predictable genre picture, but on page 30 it totally turned around and became a very original way of portraying an old familiar story.

Does the age of a new or unknown writer matter?

To me, no. Not at all. What matters is the writer's talent.

Does a writer have to live in Los Angeles to sell a spec script?

No, but it's helpful for the writer to live here. I've had meetings with both; I've worked with both. Sometimes it's refreshing to talk to out-of-town writers because they have a different perspective of the world. Other times, it's sort of like explaining physics to a cat. There's so much to know about this culture and about the process of script development. Some people instinctively pick it up as they go and they get it and flow with it. Others really don't understand the business of *the business*. It's hard to explain in one meeting with someone. It's just part of the culture of being in the industry. I am loathe to recommend moving to L.A., but often it's necessary.

What should writers know about pitch meetings?

There are two kinds of pitch meetings. The first is the type in which an agent calls and tells an exec that one of his writers has a great story and wants to come in to pitch it. The agent briefly describes it in very general terms—it's a sci-fi piece, or a western, or whatever. We'll take the meeting because we know and like the writer's work. We're secure that she can execute a script from a terrific idea. The writer comes in and pitches us that one story idea in some detail. She'll begin by giving us the story arena and describe the characters, and take fifteen to twenty minutes to lay out the story in a rough three-act structure.

Pitches should include key story beats, illustrating how the writer's going to handle important twists and turns. We want to wrap our heads around the idea quickly but also need enough information to see the story visually and know that it can play out on the screen. Of course, in the back of our minds, we're always looking for what the entertainment value of the movie will be.

And there's one more thing. New writers ask me about pitching all the time. I always tell them to remember that the mechanics of the story are obviously the most important thing, but it's the writer's passion for her material, for her characters, for the world she's creating that can bring a story to life for the exec she's pitching to. Then, if the studio or pro-

duction company likes the pitch, they buy it and hire the writer to write it.

The various levels of exec approvals that are needed to actually buy the pitch varies from company to company. Unless you're pitching to the head of the company, your pitch might go through one or two more execs before it is bought.

How many people sit in on a typical pitch meeting?

What's preferred is if the writer and maybe her producer attends and pitches to one or two execs. What often happens is that anyone that ever had anything to do with the pitch comes along with the writer because, if we should buy the idea, they want to be able to say they were in the room when it was pitched. The general feeling is that if you're in the room, then that automatically qualifies you as a producer. It's a ridiculous idea. Also, when you have eight people sitting in a room, it can get very distracting. The writer may not be getting his best shot if he comes in with a huge entourage. The writer needs to form a connection with the exec in order to sell his story. In a room full of people, that bond gets diffused.

Should a writer leave behind pages?

It's great if they do, even though execs generally take notes. Your agent may not wish you to do so, but it's very helpful and efficient for the exec.

What happens after the writer finishes the pitch?

Sometimes we give the writer feedback immediately, giving an indication of whether or not we liked the story. Usually, the writer leaves without knowing whether we want to buy it or not. At best, we will say we love the idea, it's great, and we want to do our best to bring it in. Other times we're noncommittal: "Thanks for coming in. You told a good story."

There are dozens of reasons why an exec won't want to commit to a "pass" or "consider" in the room. I know it's the worst thing for a writer to pitch his heart out and not get a response from an exec. Often, the exec simply wants time to process the idea alone or discuss it with colleagues. Or maybe the reason he needs to mull it over is simply inappropriate to discuss with the writer. And it could be many, many things. Perhaps there's a similar idea that came in through another exec who is waiting for his response. Or perhaps he may like a particular idea, but suspects his boss won't support that kind of movie; he's not sure and wants to check before saying anything to the writer. It could be anything and it often has a lot to do with the internal workings of the company. No exec wants to pretend that he's going to buy your pitch, only to tell the agent a few hours later or the next day that he's passing. That would be worse.

You said that there are two kinds of pitch meetings?

Right. The second is when an agent wants to introduce us to a new writer. Again, most execs won't take a meeting if they haven't read a writing sample. Execs need to be assured that the writer can structure a story, otherwise there's no sense in meeting him because you wouldn't be able to hire him. This is known as a "general writer meeting." It's a meet-and-greet to get to know one another. The writer will talk a bit about himself, where he's coming from, what he wants to do. He'll sketch out several ideas that he has, revealing the genre, the tone, and a brief paragraph of the story. This lets us know what kind of writer he is, and whether the material is more character driven or more plot driven; or whether the writer writes smaller, intimate films or has big action ideas. The stories are in the sketchiest form, but it gives us an idea of where the writer's head is. Execs want writers who have lots of ideas; those writers who are just brimming over with fresh, interesting, provocative stories. Bring in a ton. Some writers are unprepared.

If you want to write, you need to have more than a couple of movie ideas percolating. This is your opportunity to show how easily unique stories roll out of your brain and how good you are at setting them up plot-wise. You are also trying to gauge whether this exec is someone you click with and want to work with. By the end of the meeting, the exec also gets a sense of whether or not the writer is a match for his company.

Do you stop a writer if he pitches something that's inappropriate for the studio?

Yes. We'll say, "That's not for us. Tell us what else you've got." The writer shouldn't take this personally. Just be prepared with several ideas. Film executives are greedy for stories. Most writers have this idea that they shouldn't "give away" their ideas in a meeting. But it's important to find that common ground with an exec so that you can create a film together. The only way to do this is by talking about ideas 'til you find something you are both excited about. Executives will try and draw out as much as they can from a writer to see how prolific he is, how creative he is, and, as I said earlier, where his head is.

If you're interested in one of these sketchy ideas, what's the next step?

We talk a bit about it. If the writer is outlining the story, we'll say, "Let me know when you've got something; I'm really interested in it." Then we keep track of it until it's a script, either through the writer, if we have that kind of relationship with him, or through his agent. Or we will ask to work on it a bit with the writer, to further flesh out the story. If the idea shows increasing potential as a film, we may proceed to buy the idea, and have the writer write it.

What determines the kinds of material the studios look for at any given time?

What film execs look for has to do with second guessing the public. Like any other business, it's all about what the market will bear. You try and gauge what the public wants. That's the secret . . . what characters the audience wants to relate to, what they want to see or be emotionally moved by. Whoever knows this has the mastery of the marketplace.

What's the best and worst thing about working with a writer?

The best thing is sitting in a room and having the same vision, the same end goal as a writer, and working towards that goal to get the best possible screenplay that you can. That's the fun stuff. The worst thing about working with a writer is when they don't want to participate in the development process. Nothing gets accomplished.

What advice do you have for writers who want to break into the business?

Learn as much as you can about successful films. Figure out what makes a great film great. Understand the story-telling technique. Familiarize yourself with a variety of screenwriters' and filmmakers' bodies of work. Know film history. Expose yourself to great literature and the classics. That's what you're up against when you're dealing with a lot of studio execs who hear story ideas every day. This is all we

do. Good film execs will have a grounding in literature and the classics, and they will know their film history.

If you're just entering the business, you should know the basics of storytelling. You'll have appropriate frames of reference and be more conversant. It could only help you, your work, and your career. This knowledge gives us (writer/exec) a frame of reference, a point of connection, a shorthand to understanding each other. The exec can say, "Remember the moment in such and such a film, when the girl did this?" and the writer knows that exact moment and what you're both going for. The exec can say, "Okay, we're going for a moment like the final scene from *Casablanca*," and the writer immediately understands what is wanted. Also, I can't stress enough to remember that execs look at story ideas all day long. In order for your idea to stand out, it has to be unique, interesting, and not derivative of a movie we've already seen.

With all of the competition out there, what chance does a writer have of succeeding?

If you really understand story and are passionate about film; if you have talent and truly desire to be in this industry, you can do it. I've seen it happen many times. It takes an enormous amount of patience and perseverance, and you must be prepared to learn and work hard. Odds are, you can work as a writer. Just persevere!

Now that the mystique of the pitch meeting has been dispelled, we hope you look forward to your turn at bat. There's one more area to cover in terms of a professional approach, whether at a pitch meeting, schmoozing at a party, or while talking to an airplane seat mate. Business cards! Read on to raise your consciousness about these memorable little rectangles.

BUSINESS CARDS

When it comes to business cards, our advice is simple—Get them! Keep your business cards with you at all times. Hand them out whenever the opportunity presents itself. Create the opportunity to hand them out. There's nothing wrong with saying to someone in the business, "Let's exchange cards."

We have always had unusual business cards—the kind that people comment on; the kind that people keep. Our most recent card has our names and contact information set over a muted, artfully processed picture of the two of us. It's a little bold for writers, but whenever we hand our card to someone, we justify it by saying that it is for our on-camera work. The truth is, even if we didn't appear on television, we'd give out that card because it reminds people of who we are.

If you're at a meeting, conference, seminar, lecture, party, screening, class, or any other networking venue where you and a dozen other writers hand your cards to a producer, by the time the producer is at her desk the next morning, she's not going to be able to match any of the faces with the appropriate card. Nor will she want to, or have to. But if you have a card that stands out from all the rest, she'll notice. And when you call for an appointment, you can remind her, "We met at wherever, and I gave you my card. It's the one that says . . ." It may also be the one she will show to her colleagues, and the one she will keep in her card file.

Memorable Business Cards

Wouldn't you like to hand out a card that makes people smile and take notice? Here are examples of a few that may inspire you.

We know a screenwriter in Los Angeles whose day job is his small moving company—not moving pictures, moving furniture. His business card has all of his contact information on one side, and a drawing of a truck on the other side. On the truck it says:

> Man With a Van . . . And a Script

His card helps get the word out on both of his careers.

We went through our file and pulled out a few writers' cards. Even though these people are on our Rolodex, we keep their cards simply because they are unique—real keepers. These writers were kind enough to give us permission to show you their handouts, which are found below. (For obvious reasons their addresses and phone numbers have been omitted.)

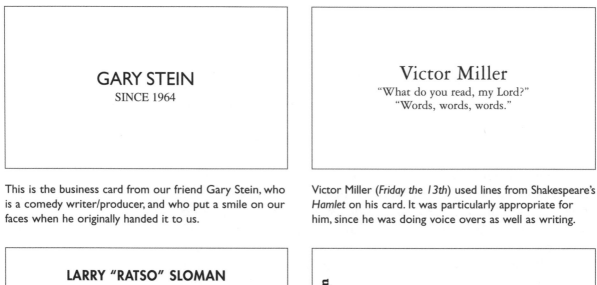

GARY STEIN
SINCE 1964

Victor Miller
"What do you read, my Lord?"
"Words, words, words."

This is the business card from our friend Gary Stein, who is a comedy writer/producer, and who put a smile on our faces when he originally handed it to us.

Victor Miller (*Friday the 13th*) used lines from Shakespeare's *Hamlet* on his card. It was particularly appropriate for him, since he was doing voice overs as well as writing.

LARRY "RATSO" SLOMAN
is allowed to walk on
the grounds unattended.

If found elsewhere contact:

Randee Mia Berman

Words.

Larry "Ratso" Sloman (co-writer *Private Parts*) stole the idea for this card from his friend, writer/musician Kinky Friedman.

Randee Mia Berman has a card that is dramatic and says it all.

You're a writer. You're clever and have a good imagination. Try to come up with something that will make your card a keeper. And shame-shame if you copy any of the cards above. Choose whatever style best suits you. If you prefer to keep it straightforward and simple, fine. In any case, just be sure that your card has the information needed to reach you.

As far as cost, you don't have to spend a lot for business cards. Depending on the card stock and design, cards from an office supply store like Staples or Quill can be reasonably priced. You can design your own cards on the computer and print them out yourself. You can also find good deals for business cards online.

Keep a Card File

It's important for you to keep a file of business cards. You may want to file them either by names or according to categories—producers, production companies, directors, agents, actors, writers, lawyers, copy shops, office supplies sources, etc. Any store that sells office supplies will have a selection of card files.

Make it a practice to ask people for their cards. Don't leave a meeting without getting cards from all of the people in the room. If possible, as soon as you leave the meeting, make notations on the cards to help you remember the face that goes with the card. A business card will tell you not only the person's name, but her title, too. You do not score points with executives when you spell their names incorrectly. Their cards will assure accuracy when typing labels, writing letters, or sending e-mails to these people. Business cards will also help you keep accurate records of your meetings.

Whenever you're networking, always ask for cards, especially from people who may be able to further your career in some way. If they have run out of cards, simply take out one of yours and have them write their information on the back.

Now that you know the importance of business cards, think of how you want to be represented on yours. Then do whatever it takes to get that vision in print at least a hundred times. With or without an attractive card case, carry your cards with you all the time, and hand them out at every appropriate opportunity. Also, get into the habit of asking for people's business cards. It will serve you well.

CONCLUSION

Once you've done your homework and have come up with a logline that's a grabber, an intriguing paragraph or two, and a synopsis of your script, you'll be empowered to come up with a knock-em-dead query letter that, hopefully, will result in requests for your script, or

Now that most people can be reached by telephone, fax, and e-mail, you may not want to have your home address on your business card. If you have an agent, you may want to include her name and contact info on the card in addition to or instead of your own.

invitations to a pitch meeting. Remember to order business cards. And don't leave home without them.

The next chapter presents a proven system of submitting your queries to the people on your wish list. This system will help minimize frustration, capitalize on organization, and maximize your chance of success.

Heaven Help Us

Written by Charlie Purpura

My First Screenplay

I wrote *Heaven Help Us* back in 1978, while I was a film school student at NYU. It's about kids in a Catholic school. I sent it around and it kept coming back with a positive response to the writing, but I kept being told that the script was uncastable. This was years before John Hughes and the coming-of-age pictures, so the timing was working against me. Also, no one seemed to want a film about Catholics.

I continued to send it around. I didn't have an agent. Now, as a professor, I tell my students, you don't really need an agent. You need a great screenplay. What you do, if you're smart, is to get a list of production companies and see what movies they've done. Start with companies that did the kinds of films you've written. Send out three or four copies of your screenplay at a time. If you've written a really good one, you'll get a response from somebody. They may ask you to come in and take a meeting and talk about the script. They may ask you to do some rewriting on spec. If they're legitimate producers who have relationships in the industry, or even a deal with some studio, you're going to do that rewrite on spec. That's what happened with me.

But Who Knows Where or When

One of the things I thought was so cool about being a writer is that you could live on the moon. I tell my students, you don't have to move out to L.A. You can be anywhere if you've got a great screenplay. So, although I was based in New York, I sent my scripts to producers in California as well as New York. If it's an exciting enough screenplay, they'll come here to meet with you. Most producers will not fly you out with their own money. They'll probably have to get the studio interested first. The action is mostly out there. There are east coast wings of California production companies, and there are some production companies based here in New York, but not that many viable ones. Even the New York offices of the major studios don't have much autonomy. Most of the decisions are made on the west coast.

In the process of just blasting the script out anywhere I could, I got a call from Dan Wigatow, who happened to be a New York producer, and he liked my script. He had a couple of films behind him and was the real deal. We had a meeting and he asked me to make some changes in the script. I did.

There I was, without an agent, making this deal with a producer, after doing the rewrite for no money. He explained to me—and it's true—producers, even the biggest producers, will rarely dip into their own pocket and pay you to make script changes that they think you need to make in order for them to set it up at a studio for development. They may have some discretionary money, but generally they use that to option books. In a rare case, a producer may put down some option money—maybe $2,500 to option a script for a year.

Anyway, I figured that this guy was on the inside; I was on the outside. He was going to put his time and energy into exploring his relationships for me, so I did the work without being paid. He said, when the time came, he would get me an agent, and he did. He introduced me to a young guy at a prominent agency who agreed to represent me for this one project.

It's really hard to get an agent without some activity going on with your script. But if you tell an agent that you have this producer who's done these films, and he's taking your script around, before you hang the phone up, the agent will be at your door. They smell the blood.

The producer started taking my script around and was getting the same response that I had gotten: Good writing; no market. Who's this movie for? Remember, this was before those coming-of-age movies kicked in. The producer kept at it for about a year. Aside from the fact that nothing was happening with my script, my life started falling apart.

Just When You Think It Can't Get Worse...

I had dropped out of school for financial reasons and was working a day job. Then everything happened at once. I suffered some personal disasters, lost my job, and had to file for bankruptcy. I applied for unemployment insurance but couldn't get it because when they asked me why I had a post office box, I told them, "I send out screenplays in the mail and they usually come back, so I need a big mail box." They said, "Oh, so you're a writer." I said, "Not really. I never made any money writing." They said, "It doesn't matter. You're writing on spec. You're employed!" I had a hearing and defended myself against three lawyers from the Department of Labor. The judge agreed with me, but I was still denied unemployment insurance. In the midst of my whole world collapsing, I decided to borrow some money and go to India to seek the counsel of a wise man that I knew. He had been telling me for the last ten years that this world is an illusion. That it's all plastic; none of it is real. At that point, I realized he wasn't kidding.

I went to the post office to get my passport. They wouldn't give it to me because my driver's license expired. I told them, "I'm not *driving* to India, I'm flying!" "It doesn't matter." I had my birth certificate and my baptism certificate. "Not good enough." Without an un-expired driver's license, I had to bring someone in who would testify that I was who I said I was.

Passage To and From India

Two or three weeks into my stay at a colony in the Punjab, I got a telegram from producer Dan Wigatow saying that he hooked up with Mark Carliner, a producer in L.A., who was interested in developing this project and was actually willing to put down $5,000 for an option. Dan also said to call him in New York right away. That was easy for *him* to say.

There were no telephones in this colony. I had to take a pony cart for three miles to the train station. Ponies in India are thin and small. People were walking past us as we slowly clumped along. Then I had to take a train for eight hours to Jullundur, the nearest town that had a post office with a telephone-satellite hookup. Once I got off the train, I had to take a rickshaw to the post office. There were buffalo in the street and it was like madness. So I'm at the post office and it takes about an hour to get this hookup. While I was standing there, surrounded by Indians who were offering to buy my clothes, I was thinking to myself, I waited my whole life for this phone call, and I have to have it here in Jullundur? By then it was about 4 AM in New York, but I didn't care. It was the only shot I had to call Dan. We talked and I said I'd be back in New York in three weeks.

This was in the fall of '82, when they were starting to cast young actors in those coming-of-age films. Young actors suddenly became box office. *Heaven Help Us* was the same screenplay that had been rejected over and over again, but the timing had changed. They looked at the script and said, coming-of-age with a Catholic twist. Let's do it!

California, Here I Come

As soon as I got off the plane, the money started falling through the ceiling.

In the winter of '82, I was flown to L.A. to meet producer Mark Carliner and to have a meeting at Fox, where the film was set up. I was told to go home to do a rewrite. A few months later, back to Fox, then back home for another rewrite.

Flashback: In the early days when I was sending the script around, I had submitted it to an agent at CAA. He turned it down, but another agent up there, Tina Nides, read it and liked it.

Flash-forward, after India, between rewrites for Fox: Tina recommended me to Linda Gottlieb at Highgate Productions in New York. She was doing a CBS Schoolbreak and needed a writer. Tina told Linda, "There's a writer running around New York. He's good. You should find him." Linda spent three months trying to find me. Meanwhile my agent was in the same building, two floors down from Highgate. I met with Linda and got an assignment. This event underlines another lesson I try to drive home to my students: even if you don't sell your screenplay, it's your calling card into the industry. So, A) it better be good; B) you better keep it out there.

While the producers were dicking around at Fox and not getting anywhere, Tina (who was still not my agent) slipped the script to someone at Silver Screen Partners, a company under the HBO/Time/Warner umbrella. They liked it and made an offer to green light the project. Fox was out; Silver Screen Partners was in.

In the fall of '83, I was flown out to L.A. to get everything in shape. They put me in a hotel by the beach. I was getting $100 a day per diem . . . in cash, plus an obscene amount of money for the rewrite. I spent three months working with the director on rewrites and waiting for the nod from Michael Fuchs, Chairman and CEO of HBO.

It came down to the wire. Fuchs finally gave it the green light and we were on the fast track. That's when I started to become the flavor of the week.

Take a Number

It amazed me to discover that having a *go* project on the west coast is such a rare thing. In Los Angeles, it is estimated that 97 percent of the activity happens around projects that never happen.

I was being treated like the Messiah. My phone was ringing off the hook. I had to hire somebody to take my calls. There wasn't anybody in town who didn't want to *do* lunch with me; who didn't want to be in business with me; who didn't want to know me . . . in the biblical way.

At that same time, my *prominent agency* went into panic mode. They didn't know, until then, that they represented me. So they flew a guy out to see if there was anything I wanted. You know, like, a better hotel room, a bigger car, more felt-tipped pens. I fired him and went with Tina Nides over at CAA. You remember Tina. She was the agent who got me to Highgate Productions, who in turn offered me the CBS Schoolbreak, that turned into a project that won me a couple of awards, including an Emmy.

I Came a Long Way, Baby

What a difference from kneeling in the sands of the Punjab, desperately trying to figure out what my life was about, to taking meetings poolside in the Hills of Beverly. Don't get me wrong, making money and being a hot shot in Hollywood, in the long run, is no more significant than sitting in the sands of the Punjab. The only real difference was that now I had the money to get my license renewed. When Mark Carliner drove me onto the lot at Fox, he stopped his car before a set replicating a New York street. From where we were, we could see the remarkably accurate facades of the buildings, but also the beams behind that were holding them up. "Take a good look, Charlie," he said to me, "this is as real as it gets out here."

Another producer once told me, "Nobody knows anything out here. What everybody does is try to hang out with the guy who's happening. They figure he must know what he's doing. Or maybe that his karma will rub off on them." That's what happened to me. I was getting assignments backed up for years. People were taking second and third positions to get me to write projects for them. The same people that turned down the screenplay were now falling all over themselves to get a piece of me.

I didn't get blown away by it, I think, because I had recently seen the other side of life—the down side—and this was the extreme flip side. It was amusing to me. In a way I was sort of detached from it all. That's not to say I didn't get corrupted by it somewhere down the line. But in the beginning, I was able to stay a little bit aloof from it all and not get swept away.

I think what is corrupting about the industry is that in the beginning, they tell you you're brilliant, you're a genius, you're good looking and you can't do anything wrong. I don't think you can sustain that kind of input before you start believing it. And then when you're not happening—and you WILL be not happening, sooner or later, here and there along the way—if you bought into it, you're in for a terrible crash. That's why all those child stars go bonkers by the time they're twenty-one.

Everyone's a Critic

Seven years after I wrote the first draft, *Heaven Help Us* opened to rave reviews around the country and throughout Europe. I did get slammed in one place. A Jesuit Priest, writing for a Catholic paper, said some very bad things about the movie, AND about me. He was mostly pissed about how I depicted the corporal punishment handed out by the Teaching Brothers. He denied that the Catholic School system ever engaged in that kind of brutal punishment. But here's what's interesting: this very same Priest was the model for one of the Teaching Brothers in the movie. In fact, HE was THE ANTAGONIST. You see, he used to teach at Brooklyn Prep, where he, himself, handed out most of the brutal, inventive punishments I depict in the film. How did I know this? When I was putting the story together, I collected some anecdotes from my brother-in-law, who went to Brooklyn Prep . . . this Priest was his teacher!

How Heaven Helps Us

Looking back at when and how my script was made

into a feature film, I start to think magically about how the Universe seems to work: The sages say, "You get what you want once you no longer want it." Of course I always wonder what good is having what you no longer want? But I guess it's about the law of *letting go*. That's the way it was for me when I went to India. Circumstances were such that the script wasn't really on my mind. I was concerned with survival at the time, not with being a screenwriter.

I don't advise people to send out their script, then get on the next plane, rickshaw, train and pony cart to the Punjab. Just don't send your heart out with your screenplay. Develop some kind of detachment and turn your back on the results and go on to something else—your next screenplay.

The Tag and Then Some

Fifteen years after my hearing for unemployment insurance, I got a letter saying that there was a class action suit brought against the Department of Labor and my ruling was overturned. I got a government check for $1,800. There's the Universe at work again: Once I no longer needed the money, I got it.

Wait! That's not all.

One reason I filed for bankruptcy and unemployment insurance was that I was fired from my job. I worked in an arm of the printing industry, doing color separations. The reason I was fired? The boss came up with some bogus one, but the real reason was that I was trying to organize the shop for the union, and he found out. You know, like Norma Rae.

Fifteen years later, yeah, around the time I got the unemployment check, I'm running a screenwriting class at Hofstra. Who's in my class? The boss who fired me. He too had gone bankrupt; his wife had thrown him out; he was recovering from a drug addiction, and living in a friend's apartment.

"Vengeance is mine, saith the Lord." I gave him a B— anyway.

Script to Screen? Well, almost...

Love 30 was optioned, but not produced. We didn't realize this until we had completed our interview with Susan Rice. By then, she had given us such good input based on her productive and successful years of experience, that we decided to make an exception and include this story anyway. Her credits include TV films *For Hope, A Match Made in Heaven, Something in Common, Tears and Laughter: The Joan and Melissa Rivers Story, Dangerous Affection, When Andrew Came Home,* and feature film *Animal Behavior.*

Love 30

Written by Susan Rice

Some twenty years ago, after writing movie criticism for several years, I had gone over to the then 20th Century Fox screening room, and saw *Blindman,* a spaghetti western. It was about a sharp-shooting blind cowboy and a boxcar full of naked ladies. As I was watching that movie, I said to myself, I could do something better than this. That's when I resolved to write a script.

Those Were the Days...

I saved up two or three thousand dollars to see me through, without working on anything else. That's what I invested as my own scholarship. It bought me three months on Martha's Vineyard, starting in April, before the tourists would come.

I didn't know what screenplays looked like. I had never seen one. So I got a copy of *Butch Cassidy and the Sundance Kid* written by William Goldman, which was in paperback. I looked at it and thought, Oh, I see how the action goes across the page . . . My approach was that primitive.

I wrote a script called *Love 30,* about a woman tennis player who was the best, but was now thirty years old and was wondering about some of the choices she had made in life. I finished it within that three-month period, and came back to New York.

I didn't have an agent, but I had a friend who had an agent. The friend read the script, loved it and gave it to the agent. The agent read it, loved it and got it to Jane Fonda's lawyer. The lawyer read it, loved it and gave it to Jane. I finished the script in June. In November, I was sitting in a hotel room with Jane Fonda, talking about the script.

It was a very different time then. I think the difference was that everything was much more direct. There weren't as many middle people around to say "no." It took some luck. It always takes some luck. But you could actually get something to somebody in three steps instead of forty-five. And you didn't have to attach a producer and go in and pitch.

Rice Paper

Jane Fonda's company optioned my script. They then had me do a rewrite, turning this simple and funny story of a woman coming to grips with the choices she had made, into a metaphor for the greediness of multinational corporations. I did this voluntarily—what did I know? After that, the script was dead in the water. It did, however, jumpstart my career.

On the basis of the *Love 30* option, I started getting assignments writing features. And I wrote them at a very high level. I worked with Sherry Lansing, Clint

Eastwood, Robert Redford–heavy hitters. Throughout those ten years of writing features, I never got a movie made.

Then a friend told me an idea that I thought was terrific. I wrote it as a television script–a MOW called *Something In Common*. It ended up getting made with Ellen Burstyn, Tuesday Weld, and Eli Wallach and directed by Glenn Jordan. I thought, this is great, it was made and I got to see it. I thought, this is easy. And then it got more difficult. I've been writing television movies now for what–twelve years, but I've seen maybe eight or nine of them get made. The point is to get movies made. I don't feel snobby about it. There is a certain formula to MOWs and a whole bunch of them are not of enormously high quality, but every once in awhile, you can slip through something really good. There are some bright and lovely people to work with. It's a neat way to make a living.

The Secret of Success

If I were starting out today, I'd probably do the same thing I did back then–go and write the script. I've taught screenwriting classes and most students want to know the secret of success. The *writing* is the secret. And it always will be. That doesn't mean that there aren't enormous numbers of talented people who are very frustrated and have a terribly difficult time of it. Ultimately, I think it's talent that wins. I'd like to think that every great script gets discovered, but there probably are some terrific scripts whose timing is wrong; scripts that should have been made when they were first written, but weren't, and later seem imitative or derivative when, in fact, they were the ground breakers. It has to do with luck and placement and the key, which is to find somebody who feels passionately about what you've written and will go to bat for you. That still happens. It's an uphill struggle because the studios are interested in reaching a much narrower market than they used to be. All of this so-called niche stuff doesn't seem to help.

Now, twenty-five years later, I just wrote another spec and, finally, I have a producer who optioned it for nothing, but nobody wanted to do it. I was told it was too edgy. I'm usually a *too soft* kind of person, but now I've moved into the *too edgy* category. When everything is said and done, it's just about taste. You'll have: "Too edgy." "Too edgy." "Too edgy." "Ooh. This is interesting." And that can change things around. Of course, it's so much easier for people to say "no" than to say "yes." Because so many more movies are failures than successes, people can sustain themselves by not making failures. They don't even have to make successes. Getting a "yes" is a very tough thing.

Writer as Director

As for the writer also directing . . . With a few notable exceptions, I feel that the job of writer and the job of director are separate for a reason. When a writer gets on the set and there's work to be done on the script, which is often the case, even just because of locations or technologies, I don't know how a person directs and addresses the script at the same time.

Coast to Coast

As a screenwriter, I think it's harder living in New York. If you're on people's minds, they think of you for something, and if you're not on their minds, they don't. It's as simple as that. If you're not in L.A., you need to have an active presence via your agent. I have wonderful representation at ICM in California. They have me in mind if nobody else does. Of late, I've come to realize that I have to go out there every few months and meet with people, just to say, "Hi," even if I don't have anything specific in mind. Then when something comes up, they think, "Oh that one was in the office last week." I think you have to do that. You have to make yourself present there. I've met people along the way whom I really like–producers and network people–so it's not an anathema to me at all.

What It's All About

I'd like television movies to pay better. Features are really the way to go in order to get a chunk of money. But you can make a decent living writing TV movies, if you're lucky. This sounds like a stupid thing, but it never has been about money for me. If it were about money, I would have moved to Los Angeles and written a series. Writing is about telling stories. I don't mean this in an arrogant way, but I've never written a script that I didn't believe in and many of those were assignments, but things I really loved. It's about sitting down every day with a set of characters and having them speak through you. It's a strange sort of exorcism, but it's neat. I've been a very lucky human being and have combined that with some very hard work. Talent has a good deal to do with it, but it's hard for me to say that. That's why I have an agent.

Drunks

Written by Gary Lennon

Writers often think that they're powerless and that they can't do anything without an agent. That's not true. You have to empower yourself and you have to get your material to everyone you can because you can make your work happen. It's as simple as that.

The Play's the Thing

I was an actor first, then I became a playwright, and I produced some of my plays. To support myself through all of this, I worked as a waiter.

In 1991, I joined forces with my friend, Kelly Kane, who ran the non-profit Second Generation Theatre Company. We raised $13,000 to produce *Blackout*, my play about people in recovery from substance abuse and alcoholism. We put the play on as a showcase at the Harold Clurman Theatre on 42nd Street in New York City, for a limited run, and then we extended it. We faxed everyone we could—anybody who had a contact with an agent, production company, or any-

one in the business. We had all of our friends come see it and lend their support. Out of that experience, a lot of people became aware of me as a writer.

I had a meeting with PBS about turning *Blackout* into a movie. A producer at HBO came to see it and was interested in turning it into a film. Paris Barclay who has now gone on to win Emmys directing *ER* and *City of Angels,* came to see it and was interested. Nothing happened. All of that interest fizzled out.

The play sat for about another year until Seraphim, a small theater company, approached me and said they wanted to do a production of *Blackout*. The company had my blessings. They did a good job mounting the play and it was well received. People responded to it very strongly.

There was an actress in it, Alicia Hoge, whose mother is Alice Arlen, co-writer of the film *Silkwood.* Alicia had also been in another play I had written called *Rated X,* so her mother was familiar with my work. When Alice saw *Blackout,* she said, "People have to see this play. You're a really good writer. You should be working." I was working . . . waiting tables.

The Power of Networking

Alice Arlen brought ICM's head honcho, Sam Cohn, to see the play, and he liked it. He then came back with his son, Peter, who was a writer and wanted to become a director.

The next day, I got a phone call from Peter Cohn, asking me if I would like to sell the play as a film. I was ecstatic. Peter and I met and we made a deal. He optioned the play and paid me as a writer-for-hire to adapt it to the screen.

I went to Key West and wrote the first draft of *Drunks* (the film version of the play *Blackout*), opening it up by taking it out of that one Alcoholics Anonymous meeting room. I came back to New York and gave it to producer/director Peter Cohn. I got notes from him and worked on the script for a while. It was innovative in a sense because it was the first time anyone was doing a movie about the inside rooms of Alcoholics Anonymous.

Peter started showing the script to financiers. Luckily, because of the subject matter—sobriety—it interested a lot of actors. I was co-producer and I sat in on the casting of it. It was so exciting to see different actors read my lines and bring different things to it. We gathered a strong cast including Richard Lewis, Parker Posey, Amanda Plummer, Dianne Wiest, Faye Dunaway, and Calista Flockhart, and got the money together and shot the movie. *Drunks* was released in 1997, the same year the play *Blackout* was published by Samuel French.

Pain Pays Off

Blackout was written as a way of making sense of my own life—of the years that I had spent drinking. I was a great student, but I was a teenage-blackout drinker. I'm sixteen years sober now. The play was cathartic

and therapeutic. Then to see it on screen and hear a lot of the stories which were based on my own experiences in life, was incredibly fulfilling. It was a testament to writing what you know, or writing of your experience.

It was also a lesson about this business. You've got to use all of your connections and relationships to get your play seen or your script read and keep trying to get recommendations. Everything in this business is by referral. If it weren't for Alice Arlen who wrote *Silkwood* with Nora Ephron, I would not have had a big agent come and see my play. I never forget that and I thank her. That was an incredibly generous thing for one writer to do for another.

A Writer's Impact

An old teacher of mine called me about a year and a half ago and said "I wanted to talk to you because I've just become sober. When I saw your movie, it made me realize that I had to get help." When he can't go to an AA meeting, he'll rent my movie and watch it. That's one person who was helped by seeing my film. It makes me wonder, how many others has it helped?

On a Roll

Another play I had written called *Dates and Nuts,* a romantic comedy about a nymphomaniac, had been optioned by a number of people, but nothing happened with it . . . that is, until I started writing *Drunks*. Producer Ed Pressman bought the film rights and engaged me as a writer-for-hire to adapt my play for the screen. As soon as I finished the screenplay for *Drunks,* I started on the screenplay for *Dates and Nuts*. I also became a proud member of the Writers Guild. Oh yeah, and I quit my job waiting tables.

Ed Pressman didn't make *Dates and Nuts*. I got the rights back last year; I'm trying to set up the movie now . . . and I have the feeling that I will.

I believe that we have no idea what's in store for us. We just have to keep showing up.

CHAPTER 6

---

*U*SING THE
SQUARE ONE SYSTEM

If you want to be in "show business," it's time to get down to *business* and *show* what you've got. Talent is a major factor, but not the only one. It also helps to be organized, diligent, and persistent. Using the eight-step Square One System will get you organized. As for diligence and persistence, well that's up to you and how determined you are to succeed. The Square One System will be a constant reminder, and, hopefully, a motivating factor on your road to success as it supports your script-selling efforts.

In this chapter, we will take you through our systematic program step by step, guiding you in sending out your query letters to a select group of prospects. If you are like most writers, you will want to mail a letter to everyone in Hollywood immediately. We suggest that you start the submissions process by sending query letters to the top five names on the wish list you developed in Chapter 4. Five is a manageable number. It's realistic and do-able. It will get you in the submission-swing of things, and give you a good feeling of accomplishment and expectancy.

There are several reasons why a mass mailing may not be the best course of action. As you learned in Chapter 4, there is research involved on each wish list name. The task of gathering data on several dozen companies or people at one time can be overwhelming even to the most motivated writers. Also, if your first batch of query letters is not eliciting any positive responses, you may want to rethink your approach and rewrite the letter before sending it to the next group of prospects. Of course, there's always the chance that you will get a positive response from one or more of your letters. If an agent asks to read your script, and then wants to represent you, you may not have to send out any more queries.

Okay, so now you know not to buy out the first-class stamps at your post office. If you followed the guidelines that were offered in Chapter 5, you should have the all-important query letter, including a super logline and paragraph about your script, ready to tempt the reader to request that script. You should also have the refined wish list that you created in Chapter 4. With these two components—query letter and wish list—you're ready to set up and use the Square One System—all eight steps—for initiating and tracking contacts. What are you waiting for? It's time to go steppin'!

AN EIGHT-STEP PLAN

If you're an organized person, you're going to love this Square One System. If you are in the majority and are not as organized as you know you should be, you, too, are going to love this Square One System. Each simple step will help you maximize your chance of selling your spec script. You'll start by refining your wish list further, prioritizing and filling in the details on each name. Next you will tailor each query letter accordingly, and then you will set up the Square One System of record keeping. Once that's in place, you will be ready to mail out the first five query letters. Then comes the next (and maybe the most difficult) step—you've got to be patient as you wait for replies. Of course, there are productive things to do during that waiting period. We'll get to that later. One step at a time.

Step One: Prioritize the Names on Your Wish List

The first step in the Square One System involves taking the names on the refined wish list that you created in Chapter 4 (the ones on the index cards), and prioritizing them. Start with the names of personal referrals, if any. It's much easier to reach a person when you can say, "So-and-so suggested I call or write to you." If you don't know anyone who knows anyone, and you're literally starting from "square one," consider things that you may have learned while initially researching the names on your list. If you've found any agents who are willing to consider new writers, or producers who are partial to producing films in the same genre as your script, then put the cards with their names first. After you've decided on the hottest prospects, your major consideration when further prioritizing depends on your personal desires. Are you most interested in a manager who may help you get an agent and a producer? Do you want to concentrate on getting an agent? Do you want to attach a director or an actor to your script? Do your instincts tell you to go after producers first? Do you want to start by querying one of each? Your answer to these questions will reflect the order in which you place the names.

Your prioritized list will have all of the names on your revised wish list, only this time in order of preference, with the most desirable names at the top. In the next step, you will be verifying all of the information of the top five names, which will make up the group for your first mailing.

Step Two: Verify Contact Information

When you researched the names on your refined wish list back in Chapter 4, you jotted down the basic contact information on each index card, including the phone number and street address. Even though you may feel that this early research provided all of the information you need, you *must* double-check it with a phone call. Why? Because you want your letter to go to the most appropriate person at the right company name and at the correct address. Things are constantly changing, especially in this industry. People are hired, fired, downsized, upgraded, and moved around; companies update their telephone systems, get new Internet carriers, and sometimes they move. There you are, ready to send out your query letter, and everyone's changed places . . . or not. That's for you to find out.

When making the calls, always use a friendly and professional voice. If you smile when you talk on the phone, it will make you sound happy and may encourage conversation. Keep in mind that the person who answers the phone may be in the middle of taking an urgent message or juggling three tasks at once. Instead of charging ahead with your questions, be considerate and ask, "Do you have a minute to verify some information?" Be patient if you're put on hold, and make it clear that you're willing to wait for as long as it takes. You understand how busy he must be.

As soon as you have that person's attention, treat him as your

Industry Humor...

INTERVIEWER

How many development execs does it take to change a light bulb?

DEVELOPMENT EXEC

Well, does it really have to be a <u>light bulb</u>?

confidante while maintaining a professional attitude at all times. Let's say, for example, that you are verifying the contact information of a development person at a production company. Explain, "I have a spec script that seems right for (give the name of the production company) and I want to send a query letter." If you have the name of a development person, verify that he is the most appropriate person to receive your letter. If you don't have a specific name when you call, find out the name of the person who should receive your query. Then ask if that person prefers to receive queries by snail mail, fax, or e-mail. *Always* verify the spelling of that person's name, title, address, room number, fax, e-mail address, and any other relevant information.

If your conversation seems to be going well, and you feel as though you're making a friend, consider asking how long it usually takes to get a response, or if there's anything else you should know when sending your query letter. The person on the other end of the phone may be the lowest paid person on the company's payroll today, but tomorrow is another day. It can be extremely helpful to befriend these people and have them as your allies. The person who answers the phone may also be the one who sorts the mail and can see that your query letter gets on top of the to-be-read stack. Or he could be the development person who's relieving the receptionist for five minutes—you just never know. What you *should* know is always to be prepared to pitch your logline and paragraph.

Years ago, we wanted to deliver a query letter to Anne Bancroft. We had the address and phone number of her New York apartment, but we didn't know if she was in town. So we had a plan. Lydia was going to call her home number. If Ms. Bancroft answered, she planned to use an English accent and say, "I must have the wrong number. Sorry." Then she'd hang up and we would know that Ms. Bancroft was home. Before calling, we prepared for a few different scenarios, rehearsing what to say to discover if Ms. Bancroft was home in case someone else—her maid or secretary—answered the phone. When Lydia called, much to her surprise, Mel Brooks answered the phone. *Mel Brooks!* We hadn't thought of that possibility. Lydia froze for a second, and then all she could think of doing was to talk like a little girl. Mel Brooks thought it was adorable and did everything he could to keep her from hanging up. She finally said, "I gotta go to the baffroom," and hung up.

Once we stopped laughing, we realized that we missed what

might have been a good opportunity to pitch our script to a person who could have helped us. We learned a major lesson that day—always be prepared to pitch your story. You never know who's going to pick up the phone. It could even be Mel Brooks.

Step Three: Customize Your Query Letters

Once you have verified all of the contact information for the top five names on your list, it's time to turn your attention to that wonderful query letter you have written. Although it is finished, we recommend that you customize each letter to the person or company who will be receiving it. Why? Because you don't want your queries to look like form letters that have been cranked out and are part of a mass mailing.

If you have any connection to the player or company that will be receiving your letter, say so up front. For example: "Dear (Agent's Name), You represent Arlen Kane, my former college roommate. Since we do not write the same kind of scripts, she suggested that I get in touch with you." Or: "Dear (Actor's Name), Your devotion to saving the endangered West Indian manatee leads me to believe that you will want to read my script." Or: "Dear (Name of Independent Production Company's Development Person), I saw and loved (title of the company's last film). The only story that's more horrifying than that is the one in my script, *Nails on a Blackboard*." And remember—there are any number of good reasons that these people or companies are right for your spec script. That's why they've made it on your wish list to begin with. It may be smart for you to mention those reasons, but only if you mean them.

PROSE FROM A PRO

Getting an Actor Attached
by Phillip M. Goldfarb

Unit Production Manager, Associate Producer, Line Producer, Co-Producer, and Executive Producer.

Film credits: *All The Right Moves, Taps, Taxi Driver.*
Episodic TV credits: *L.A. Law, Doogie Howser, NYPD Blue, Casey's Shadow.*

There are two versions of a script: one is the selling script, and the other is the shooting script. The selling script should have more embellishment and greater description appropriate for the actor reading it. For example, if the script were going to Dustin Hoffman, the leading character should not be described as 6 feet 4 inches and muscular. That may sound facetious, but when an actor reads the script, what the actor is looking for are points of identification. Can they fit into this? Can they wear this? To extend that metaphor a bit further, is this an item of clothing they will be comfortable in?

The more you can give an actor within the body of the material, with which to identify from a character standpoint, and obviously in addition to the dialogue and the story, the better chance you'll have of attracting and attaching the actor to the project. Once it's sold, the script takes on a different life and it's about the practical nature of what has to be done to make it work.

PROSE FROM A PRO

Screenplay Writing and the Movie Business
by Screenwriter Dale Launer
My Cousin Vinny, Ruthless People, Dirty Rotten Scoundrels, Blind Date, Love Potion No. 9.

The easiest thing . . . the best thing that you can do to sell a script is to write a good one. I know that sounds a little odd, but there is something that you should take into regard before you attempt to write a screenplay—write a screenplay that is more likely to be sold. To do that, you have to make sure you have a concept that is interesting. It doesn't have to be a high concept, it just has to be what I would call a "juicy concept," one that you could tell somebody on the street and they will smile, or they'll be intrigued. It should be a concept that even the most uncreative person can be creative with. Make sure the characters are all strong. Make sure that the lead character is going to be someone that a star is going to read and like.

I should stop at this point and say, this business is, unfortunately, not story driven. I'll be honest with you, it is story driven, but the movie business doesn't know that. A star will read a good script and then they'll want to be in the movie, but the rest of the business just wants the star. For them, the star is the vehicle that gets the movie made. The script is the bait to get the star. Whereas in reality, it is not the bait, it really is the movie, but they're so hungry, so desperate for stars. They're such shameless star-fuckers. What's funny is that every producer I know will absolutely deny that.

That's just how the business works. And to some degree, producers chase directors, and to a lesser degree, they chase writers. Writers are certainly needed and desired in the motion picture business. Yet, if you're in a room and there's a director in the room, you'll see that the energy goes to the director. It's very strange. I've had a lot of success and there will be a minor director who hasn't had a third of the success that I've had, and the energy in the room goes to the director. What's funny about it is, the director has respect for me. People will look at the director; the director will look at the writer.

Gentle reminder: You're a writer. Your query letter is your first audition. Be sure to make it entertaining, brief, and irresistible—make the reader want to know the person who wrote the letter.

Step Four: Set Up Your Record-Keeping System

Whatever you do to further your career in the film industry from here on in should be noted in a loose-leaf notebook that has been set up specifically for this purpose. (We mentioned this notebook in Chapter 4.) If you prefer to keep everything on your computer, fine . . . but also (and always) keep track of things on paper that won't crash, freeze, or refuse to boot up when you need it most.

You will be keeping track of every contact and business call you make and receive, every letter, e-mail, and fax you send and receive, every script that you submit, every meeting that you take, and every idea that you pitch. It's important that you do this for oh so many reasons including:

■ Maintaining efficient follow-up.

■ Avoiding the embarrassment of duplicating efforts.

■ Having a record of the history of a script. (Producers and agents always ask, "Where has it been shopped? Who has seen it?")

■ Having a record of your history with a company.

■ Substantiating business expenses for tax purposes.

■ Creating a paper trail. (You may need it as proof of script ownership for a credit arbitration, or any other potential situation for writer abuse.)

■ Having an accurate diary for when you're ready to write your autobiography, and/or we do the sequel to this book and want to interview you for our *From Script to Screen* feature.

The best, most efficient method of staying organized and keeping accurate records can be done with the following basic supplies. You can pick up these items in any stationery store.

• Standard size, 3-ring loose-leaf notebook

• A packet of page dividers with A-to-Z tabs

• A packet of page dividers with blank tabs

• Lined loose-leaf paper

On one of our trips to California, we had a pitch meeting with a development executive at the Walt Disney Company. Our driver dropped us off at the gate where the guard then gave us directions, "Walk straight down Dopey Drive, then make a right on Snow White Way." We could hardly believe our Pinocchio ears.

Right after the meeting, we flew back to New York, and had to send a script to the person with whom we met. The Disney office in New York has a pouch that goes out daily to the California offices. We

Look Who Turned Down What

There are many reasons—both professional and personal—for actors turning down roles. It may have absolutely nothing to do with the quality of the script or the appeal of the part, and everything to do with other commitments. If your script is turned down by an actor, take heart and take a look at the following list of actors and the roles that they have turned down.

★ Leonardo DiCaprio turned down a role in *Star Wars: Episode 1—The Phantom Menace.*

★ Gene Hackman turned down the role of Quint in *Jaws.* The film has grossed something like $470 million worldwide. He also turned down the lead in *Close Encounters of the Third Kind.*

★ Gene Hackman and James Caan both turned down the lead role in *One Flew Over the Cuckoo's Nest,* for which Jack Nicholson won an Oscar.

★ James Caan turned down the lead in *Kramer vs. Kramer.* Dustin Hoffman got to make that Academy Award acceptance speech.

★ Robin Wright Penn bowed out of playing opposite Tom Cruise in *The Firm.* She also turned down roles in *Batman Forever, Jurassic Park, Born on the Fourth of July,* and *Beautiful Girls.*

★ Remember Richard Gere in *An Officer and a Gentleman?* John Travolta was offered the part first, but turned it down. Mr. Travolta also turned down roles in *As Good as It Gets, Jackie Brown,* and *Good Will Hunting.*

★ Johnny Depp and Halle Berry were both offered the lead parts in *Speed.*

★ Burt Reynolds turned down the part of the aging astronaut in *Terms of Endearment.* Jack Nicholson got an Oscar for it.

prepared our script and walked it over to the Disney building. While one of us took it to the mailroom, the other talked to the receptionist and asked if she had a directory of Disney personnel. We wanted to check the titles of some of the people we had met at the pitch meeting. The receptionist, thinking we were important, gave us an official *Disney Directory* in an attractive Disney loose-leaf. From that day on, we've used what we refer to as the "Mickey Mouse book" for our record keeping.

This is our long-winded way of saying that you may want to get yourself a special loose-leaf notebook for this special information. Just be sure that the one you choose is a standard size for which refills are available.

To make your record-keeping as easy and as efficient as possible, first divide your notebook into two sections. One section will contain the Tracking Charts for each of your projects; the second section will house the Contact Reports.

Tracking Charts

The front half of your notebook is for the Tracking Charts for each of your projects. Every company you contact will have its own chart for an at-a-glance assessment of any communication you have with that company. These charts will help you maintain an ongoing status report for each project.

At this point, it's safe to assume that you have *at least* one project—one spec script. Write the title of this script on the blank tab of a page divider and place it in the front section of your notebook. Behind this divider, you will be placing all of the Tracking Charts for any players or companies you contact for this project. Each chart will contain all communication, including letters, phone calls, pitch meetings, whatever. . . . If you follow our system's guidelines and initially send out five query letters for your spec script, you will begin by filling out five separate Tracking Charts—one for each person or company.

If you have a second spec script (now or in the future), write its name on the tab of a second page divider. Behind it, place the Tracking Charts of any players or companies you contact in an effort to sell this project. Down the road, when you are at the point of having pitch meetings, each idea you pitch will have its own tabbed divider page, whether it is a completed script, a treatment, or just a few sketchy notes.

To prepare a Tracking Chart form, which will serve as a prototype, follow the sample that is provided on pages 212 and 213. You will be making copies of this form. If you are preparing the chart by hand or typing it out (still have a typewriter?), use a blank sheet of 8.5 x 11-inch paper turned sideways. This will allow for the various columns and maximize writing space. If you create this chart on a computer, use the landscape format. Whether you make copies of it from a computer printer or use a duplicating machine, each page must be 3-hole punched to fit in the loose leaf.

TRACKING CHART FOR "DRESS-DOWN FRIDAY"

Primary Player Name, Title, Company, Contact Info	Action Taken / Date
Maddie Henri—Development Executive Gross Profits Productions 310–555–0022 Assistant: Stacy	**4-2** • Initiated contact. • Called to verify info for M. Henri. Spoke to Stacy. • Sent query letter.
	4-12 • FedExed the signed release form and script.
	5-29 Scheduled meeting with MH on 6-6 at 10 AM (her office).

On these charts, you will be recording relevant "at-a-glance" information for the people you contact for each of your projects. (More detailed info will go on the Contact Reports, which we'll discuss next.) At the top of each Tracking Chart, place the name or title of the project, whether it is a spec script, pitched idea, treatment, or synopsis. In the sample chart, the project is a spec script titled "Dress-Down Friday." Below the title, divide the paper into four columns. The first column is for the name of the person you intend to read this spec script. This person's title, company or agency name, and contact information such as telephone number or e-mail address is also included in this first column. In the example, this person is Maddie Henri, a development exec at Gross Profits Productions. The name of Maddie's assistant—the person who answers her phone calls—is Stacy, and her name is placed here as well.

Follow-Up Plan / Date	Response To Action Taken / Date
*If there is no response by 4-16, Call Stacy to follow up on query letter.	**4-12** • MH called. • Interested in script. Asked for copy. • Faxed me release form. • Will get back within the month.
Wait until 5-12 to hear from MH. If haven't, call on 5-14 to follow up on script.	**5-14** • Made follow-up call. Spoke to Stacy. Told me script not yet read. • Said to call back at end of May.
Wait until 5-29 to hear from MH, then call to follow up on script per Stacy's instructs.	**5-29** • Left message on Stacy's voicemail—returned call immediately. Told me MH felt script not right for GPProds at this time, but wants to meet for possible writing assignment!
On 6-5, call to confirm meeting for following day.	**6-6** • Met with MH. • Given assignment.

*Crossed out this planned Follow-up because the Response on 4-12 made it unnecessary.

The second column is for recording any major actions taken to get the person in the first column interested in your project. Be sure to accompany all actions with dates—*always* mark down dates. As you can see by looking at the second column in the sample chart, a call was made to verify the contact information for Maddie, whose assistant, Stacy, took the call. A query letter was sent that same day.

Any intended follow-up plans and the dates on which they are to be made belong in the third column. In the sample chart, you can see that the first plan is to make a follow-up phone call two weeks after the query letter was sent. You'll also notice that this plan has been crossed out. Why? If you look at the entry in the fourth column—the place to record any responses to the actions taken in the second column—a timely call from Maddie, requesting the script for "Dress-Down Friday," made this follow-up plan unnecessary.

By reading the rest of the entries on this chart, you can easily track the communication made with Gross Profits Productions. After the script was FedExed along with a standard signed release form, a follow-up call was planned a month later. When the call was made, Stacy reported that the script hadn't been read yet, and gave instructions to check back in a month. Four weeks later, another follow-up call was made, but the message was left on Stacy's voicemail. When Stacy returned the call that same day, she had both good news and bad. The bad news was that Maddie had read the script, but didn't feel it was right for Gross Profits Productions at that time. The good news was that Maddie liked the writing and wanted to meet with the writer for a possible assignment. A meeting was scheduled for the following week, and the writer did, in fact, receive an assignment.

Once again, the purpose of each Tracking Chart is to provide at-a-glance progress on the communication with your contacts. Detailed information is recorded on the Contact Reports.

Contact Reports

For more detail than what is provided on the Tracking Charts, you will be filling out Contact Reports. Each production company, agency, director, manager, or actor that you contact will have its own page, and these pages will be filed alphabetically behind the appropriate A-to-Z divider tabs.

Type or write out a Contact Report prototype form on loose-leaf paper that you can run off at your local copy shop, or create the page on a computer and print copies as you need them. Use one page for each company or person you contact. See the sample Contact Report on page 215. It records the progress of "Dress-Down Friday," the same example used in the sample Tracking Chart. If you'd rather not stick with our format, that's fine, just be sure your page allows for the following (mostly self-explanatory) basic information:

- **Company.** Include the full, proper name of the company, correctly spelled.

- **Type of business.** Is it a TV and/or film production company? A talent agency? A management firm?

- **Street address.** Include building or bungalow number, and floor, suite, or room number when applicable.

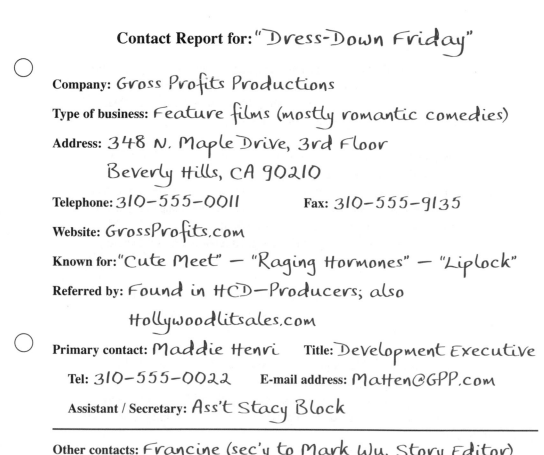

Contact Report for: "Dress-Down Friday"

Company: Gross Profits Productions

Type of business: Feature films (mostly romantic comedies)

Address: 348 N. Maple Drive, 3rd Floor
Beverly Hills, CA 90210

Telephone: 310-555-0011 **Fax:** 310-555-9135

Website: GrossProfits.com

Known for: "Cute Meet" — "Raging Hormones" — "Liplock"

Referred by: Found in HCD—Producers; also
Hollywoodlitsales.com

Primary contact: Maddie Henri **Title:** Development Executive

Tel: 310-555-0022 **E-mail address:** MHen@GPP.com

Assistant / Secretary: Ass't Stacy Block

Other contacts: Francine (sec'y to Mark Wu, Story Editor)

Special notes: Maddie is a vegetarian.

Other projects sent to this company:

Status:

4-2: Called to verify info. Talked to Francine, sec'y to story editor Mark Wu. She transferred me to Maddie Henri's ass't, Stacy, who confided in me that they're looking for something for Meg Ryan. I told her "DDF" is perfect, and asked if I should send the script. She said to send a query letter about the script, but not to mention Meg Ryan. She wasn't supposed to tell me that.

Changed query letter, describing Meg Ryan-type actress as the lead (without mentioning her name), and mailed it today.

4-12: Maddie Henri called. She's a no-nonsense person. She asked who I see starring in DDF. I told her Meg Ryan and Tom Cruise. She asked if it has to take place in NY. I said it could take place in any city where you could hail a cab on the street. When she learned I didn't have an agent, she faxed me a release form. She also gave me the company's FedEx account #1Z-2374822-407 and told me to send the script and the signed release. She said she'd get back to me within a month.

4-12: FedExed DDF along with the signed release form. Also sent brief cover letter reminding her that NY could be changed to Boston, Chicago, Milwaukee, even Toronto.

5-14: Made a follow-up call and spoke to Stacy, explaining that Maddie had said she'd get back to me within a month regarding DDF. Asked if it was a good sign that I haven't heard from her. Stacy checked Maddie's log and said that the script hasn't been read yet. She suggested that I call back at the end of the month.

5-29: In keeping with Stacy's suggestion, I called to see if Maddie read DDF. I left word on Stacy's voicemail. Stacy called back five minutes later, and said that MH passed on the script—felt it wasn't right for GPProductions (considering the other projects in development)—but she wants to meet me and talk about a possible writing assignment. We scheduled a meeting on 6-6 at 10 am. I asked if I should be prepared to pitch some of my ideas. Stacy said to have an idea or two ready, but Maddie seems to have something specific in mind.

■ **E-mail and Website addresses** (if available).

■ **Telephone and fax numbers.** Include party extensions, if applicable.

■ **Known for.** Add whatever information you can get. If it's a production company, list the films it has produced; if it's an agency or management company, list some of its clients; if it's a director or actor, list bodies of work.

■ **Referred by.** Name the person who suggested or recommended that you get in touch with this company. Don't trust your memory; write down the person's name. Months or even years from now, you may want to contact this company again, and that referral may come in handy. Also, once you get a deal with the company, this will remind you of the person to thank. If there is no personal referral, but you heard about this company at a writing seminar or a social gethering, or you read about it in a trade magazine, or it caught your eye on an online screenwriters' site, add this information here.

■ **Primary contact.** This entry is for the person at the company most appropriate for you to reach—the one you want to read your query letter or spec script. Also include this person's contact information, including a phone number (if different from main number), e-mail address, and name of assistant. *Always* get the name of the assistant, who can be your greatest ally (and the future president of the company!).

■ **Other contacts.** Add the names of anyone you speak to when trying to reach the person on your list. Be sure to include who they are—assistant, receptionist, etc.

■ **Special notes.** Jot down any information about this company (or the producer or agent) that prompted you to make it a prospect for your script. Add any other miscellaneous bits of info that you know or learn about the company or its staff members—even if they seem insignificant at the time. The smallest thing can prove to be valuable at some point.

■ **Other projects sent to this company.** Include the name of each project you bring to this person or company. We suggest using a separate Contact Report for each project.

I love being a writer.
What I can't stand is
the paperwork.

—Peter De Vries
Writer

■ **Status.** On the rest of this page and on any pages that may follow, keep a running log of any and all communication you have with the company. Get into the habit of starting each entry with the day's date. Include the gist of phone conversations, memos, letters, e-mails, faxes—everything. When you send out a script, be sure to write down the method of shipment used along with tracking numbers. If you keep hard copies of the correspondence that you send, you may want to keep each copy with its appropriate company page.

Each time there is activity on a project—you send a query letter to an agent; you submit your script to a production company; a director's agent returns your call—make note of it in two places. First, document it on the appropriate Tracking Chart—under the specific project; and then write out a more detailed note on the A-to-Z Contact Report—under the name of the company or individual with whom contact was made.

As you make more and more contacts and submissions, and have all kinds of activity going on with more than one project, your career will benefit greatly by efficient record keeping, tracking, and follow-up.

Step Five: Mail the First Five Query Letters

It's now time to send out your query letters to the five people at the top of your list. First, finalize the five letters (which you have already customized in Step Two) by adding the date, and then checking the names one final time for correct spellings.

Even though this is a fairly informal industry, the salutation should read "Dear Ms. Hope," or "Dear Marlene Hope," not "Dear Marlene," unless you know her, or have spoken with her and she has asked you to call her by her first name. Do not use the title "Mrs." unless you know that the woman is married and prefers "Mrs." to "Ms, " and never use the title "Miss"! Don't forget to sign each letter with your full name.

Along with keeping these letters on your computer's hard drive or on a disk, we recommend printing out copies to keep in your notebook behind the appropriate Contact Reports. This makes them easily accessible and able to serve as quick references. As for mailing, always use standard #10 business envelopes for your letters. Incidentally, we strongly advise against faxing queries, unless requested. If you think that faxing will be faster, you're right; but there's no controlling the quality of a facsimile transmission. Don't risk a distracting black line down the middle of your letter, or blurry type, or an obliterated patch. Mail your query letters first class, literally and figuratively, and only after you can honestly answer "yes" to the following questions:

- Is your loose-leaf set up with the proper Tracking Charts and Contact Reports?

- Have you logged in the calls that you made to confirm information, including addresses and correct spellings, for the letters that you're sending?

- Have you recorded the letters you're sending and the date?

Proofread your customized query letters one last time. Be sure each letter goes into the right envelope, add the proper postage, and then mail that first batch. *Expect a miracle.* Really! Enjoy that glorious feeling of expectancy. It will help you through the next steps.

Step Six: Be Patient, Be Productive

Your query letters are out there and you're now waiting for a response or two or five. Instead of letting this waiting time immobilize you, be productive. Prepare the next five query letters. This means calling to verify information, customizing the letters, filling out Contact Reports, and making notes on the appropriate Tracking Charts. All of this is in addition to the daily time allotted for working on your newest script. Also, always keep your eyes and ears open for new wish list contacts. This means keeping up with industry happenings—read trade magazines and newspapers, and watch entertainment-type television programs. You never know what you might see or hear that can help further your career.

Step Seven: Follow-Up

Since there's no hard-and-fast rule about when to make that follow-up call, we think that if you haven't had a response to your query letter within two weeks after sending it, chances are, you're not going to be getting one. At that point, you have nothing to lose by calling and telling the person who answers the phone (the one with whom you may have had a friendly conversation—check the Contact Report for his name) that you never heard back from So-and-so. You may ask to speak to So-and-so's secretary to find out whether or not So-and-so received your letter. You may be asked to mail or fax a copy of it again. Or you may be told that if you haven't heard from So-and-so, it means he's not interested.

If you've gotten a promising response to one or more of your first five query letters—an agent asked to read your script; a producer's development person wants a synopsis—always ask when you can expect to hear back from these people. You may not want to send out any more query letters until you get an answer from the agent or the development person. These are people who were at the top of your list, and if they say "yes," you may not need to continue your mailings.

Step Eight: Continue Your Mailings

If nothing seems to be happening as a result of the first five letters, send out the second batch of five about two or three weeks after the first batch.

Keep adding to and revising your wish list. Keep personalizing your query letters. If you've gotten any feedback on your letters, you may want to incorporate that feedback into a revised letter for future mailings. Or you may want to focus your creative energy and try a different approach in your query letters. Don't be afraid to experiment, just be sure that your letter is tasteful, well written, and that it gives enough information about your script to make people want to read it.

Remember to keep logging in your calls, letters, and responses on the Tracking Chart and Contact Reports. Keep working on your next script, and keep expecting a miracle. Miracles happen daily and seem to be attracted to people who are most focused and work diligently to reach their goals. If you're not buying into this, just read the "miraculous" *From Script to Screen* stories at the end of each chapter. They are written by screenwriters who were once where you are now.

Writers Writing About Writers

Writers are always told to write about what they know. Screenwriters know about screenwriters, so lots of theatrical and television films are about the entertainment industry, and many with the screenwriter playing a prominent part.

Robert Pardi, *TV Guide Online* film reviewer, helped us compile a list of films that depict the life of a screenwriter in some way or other. Check TV listings, the library, and your local video rental store for these films. They may give you insight as to how business is done and ideas for getting in the door. More important, in order to avoid some of the pitfalls, many of the films show you what *not* to do.

The Bad and the Beautiful (1952) *screenplay by Charles Schnee; story by George Bradshaw.*
Impactful story of a Hollywood producer's rise to the top, and the people he trampled along the way, including his screenwriter.

Barton Fink (1991) *written by Ethan Coen & Joel Coen.*
Playwright Barton Fink goes to Hollywood in 1941 to write for the movies, and comes down with a severe case of writer's block. Don't ask!

Best Friends (1982) *written by Valerie Curtin & Barry Levinson.*
A romantic comedy about two successful screenwriters and the effect marriage to one another has on their collaboration.

The Big Picture (1989) *screenplay by Michael Varhol & Christopher Guest & Michael McKean; story by Michael Varhol & Christopher Guest.*
A promising young writer-director finds himself completely corrupted by the temptations of Hollywood.

Bowfinger (1999) *written by Steve Martin.*
A desperate schlocky producer finds a unique way to turn a script into a movie.

Cabin by the Lake (2000) *written by C. David Stephens.*
This TV movie, billed as a comedy thriller, is about a screenwriter who kidnaps and drowns young women in the name of script research.

Ed Wood (1994) *written by Scott Alexander & Larry Karaszewski.*
Somewhat true story of a writer-director of terrible movies.

The Elevator (1996) *written by Gabriel Bologna.*
Big-time Hollywood producer gets stuck in an elevator with small-time screenwriter.

Fellow Traveler (1989) *teleplay by Michael Easton.*
British TV film about a screenwriter who hides in England rather than testify before the House Un-American Activities Committee.

French Exit (1996) *written by Michael A. Lerner & Daphna Kastner.*
This romantic comedy is about the love/hate relationship between two screenwriters who vie for the same job.

The Front (1976) *written by Walter Bernstein.*
This entertaining film is also a history lesson about the shameful blacklisting period in America in the 1950s. It focuses on blacklisted writers who find a man to *front* for them by submitting their scripts with his name on them. Incidentally, in real life, Walter Bernstein was one of the blacklisted writers.

The Harvest (1993) *written by David Marconi.*
A screenwriter is sent to Mexico to develop a story for a movie. Oy, what happens to his kidney.

Hijacking Hollywood (1997) *written by Jim Rossow & Neil Mandt.*
This charming low-budget film is about a filmmaker who kidnaps and ransoms a reel of film.

In a Lonely Place (1950) *written by Edmund H. North and Andrew Solt; from a book by Dorothy Hughes.*
A psychological thriller about an on-the-edge screenwriter whose bad temper makes him a murder suspect.

Irreconcilable Differences (1984) *written by Nancy Meyers & Charles Shyer.*
It's "family versus career" when a young daughter wants to divorce her parents. Dad is a teacher who becomes a successful screenwriter-director.

Living in Oblivion (1995) *written by Tom DiCillo.*
The writer-director's horrendous happenings during the making of a no-budget film.

The Lonely Lady (1983) *screenplay by John Kershaw and Shawn Randall; adaptation by Ellen Shepard; based on the novel by Harold Robbins.*
An aspiring screenwriter is used and abused by every man she meets.

Mistress (1992) *screenplay by Barry Primus & J.F. Lawton; story by Barry Primus.*
A dark comedy about a writer's attempt to get his script financed while preserving his artistic integrity.

Movers and Shakers (1985) *written by Charles Grodin.*
A Hollywood producer hires a writer to write a screenplay to fit the title *Love in Sex.*

The Muse (1999) *written by Albert Brooks & Monica Johnson.*
When the studio tells a screenwriter that he's lost his edge, another screenwriter puts him on to "the muse" to help inspire him.

Never Give a Sucker an Even Break (1941) *written by Prescott Chaplin, W.D. Fields, and John T. Neville.*
A funny thing happened on the way to selling a film story to Esoteric Studios.

Paris When It Sizzles (1964) *screenplay by George Axelrod; story by Julien Duvivier and Henri Jeanson.*
High-living screenwriter has two days in which to meet his deadline.

The Player (1992) *written by Michael Tolkin; based on his novel.*
This dark comedy about the movie industry focuses on a fatal relationship between a studio executive and a screenwriter.

Ratchet (1996) *written by John Johnson.*
Blocked screenwriter plagiarizes a script.

RKO 281 (1999) *HBO original movie by John Logan, Richard Ben Cramer, and Thomas Lennon.*
The story of Orson Welles' battle over the preparing and releasing of *Citizen Kane.*

State and Main (2000) *written by David Mamet.*
A film crew, including the screenwriter, takes over a small town. The residents will never be the same.

Sullivan's Travels (1941) *written by Preston Sturges.*
This classic is about a writer-director who becomes a hobo to learn more about life.

Sunset Boulevard (1950) *written by D.M. Marshman, Jr., Charles Brackett, and Billy Wilder.*
This masterpiece is about an out-of-work screenwriter who gloms onto a has-been movie star who's getting ready for her comeback close-up.

Swimming With Sharks (1994) *screenplay by George Huang.*
An assistant to a powerful Hollywood producer gets revenge on his boss for all the abuse he's had to endure. The assistant's screenwriter-girlfriend also gets in on the action.

Twisted Obsession (1990) *written by Manolo Matji, Menno Meyjes, and Fernando Trueba.*
This mystery thriller is about an American screenwriter in Paris who's hired to write a script that may change his life—not necessarily for the better.

IF THERE IS INTEREST IN YOUR SCRIPT

After sending out lots of query letters—perhaps a couple dozen—it's time to evaluate the results. If you have gotten several requests for your script, that's extraordinary. If one of those requesters subsequently wants to represent you, or to option or buy your script, there's your miracle. You've broken through and you're on your way. If your query letters garner requests for the script, but it is read and rejected, there may be a problem with the script itself. If this is your situation, turn to Chapter 8, "If It Doesn't Happen." There, you will find help in figuring out why there are no takers for your script. For now, let's discuss a more positive scenario—there's interest in your script. How should you proceed? What can you expect? First, be sure you can answer "yes" to the following questions:

- Have you registered and/or copyrighted your script?

- Is your script properly formatted, covered, and bound? And do you have clean copies of it?

- Do you have a one- or two-page synopsis of your script that you are prepared to mail, fax, or e-mail if it is requested?

If you're still nodding "yes," then you're ready to deal with the submission nitty-gritty—the release form, the cover letter, and mailing the package. Are you getting the feeling that writing the script is the easy part?

Submission Agreements or Release Forms

When a producer is willing to read your screenplay, and you don't have an agent, manager, or lawyer to submit it for you, you will probably be asked to sign a submission agreement or submission release form. Whatever it's called, it is a little frightening to read, as you can see from the sample release form beginning on page 224. It contains a lot of legalese, but basically, this form absolves the production company from a lawsuit if it produces a film similar to yours after reading your script. If you don't sign the form, the producer will not read your unsolicited script.

Copyright your script with the Library of Congress and/or register it at the Writers Guild, and you should feel better about signing the release form. (Details on protecting your work are found in Chapter 2.) The only way to guarantee that no one will steal your script or its concept is to never tell anyone about it, and never give it to anyone to read. Just because you may be a little paranoid, doesn't mean your paranoia is unfounded. You can't copyright an idea, and writers' ideas have been stolen, but this happens very rarely. Write a great script and producers will want to buy it, not steal it.

You have to get your script out there for it to be read and bought. A producer once told us, "You can't hit a home run if you don't get up at bat." Go to reputable producers and know that you're going to have to sign their release form in order to "Play ball!"

Sample Submission Release Form

Although submission release forms may vary in format and wording from one production company to another, the form below is a fairly typical one.

(Date)

Production Company's Name
Company Address
Somewhere In, CA 91210

Gentlemen:

I (Screenwriter's Name) desire to submit to you material (herein called 'submitted material') owned and/or controlled by me as so as to offer you the opportunity to decide whether you want to enter into negotiations with me with respect to your possible use of the submitted material in the motion picture, television and entertainment fields. The submitted material is described as follows:

I shall not receive any compensation for submitting the submitted material to you, and understand that you may submit such material to other parties. I recognize the possibility that the submitted material may be identical with or similar to material which has or may come to you from other sources. Such identity or similarity in the past has given rise to litigation so that unless you can obtain adequate protection in advance, you will refuse to consider or read the submitted material. The protection for you must be sufficiently broad to protect you, all related parties including, but not limited to, your and their officers, directors, share-holders, employees, agents, representatives, licensees, assigns, and all parties to whom you or they submit material or have been or may be involved in developing, financing, or exploiting materials and properties generally. Therefore, all references to 'you' shall include each and all of the foregoing related parties.

Accordingly, as an inducement to you to examine the submitted material, I represent, warrant and agree, as follows:

1.   I acknowledge that the submitted material is submitted voluntarily and not in confidence or in trust, and that no confidential or fiduciary relationship is intended or created between you and me by reason of such submission or otherwise. Nothing in this agreement, nor the submission of the submitted material, shall be deemed to place you in any different position from any other member of the public with respect to the submitted material. Accordingly, any part of such material, which could be freely used by any member of the public, may be used by you without liability to me or any other party claiming from or through me.

I understand and agree that your use of material similar to or identical with the submitted material or containing features or elements similar to or identical with those contained in the submitted material shall not obligate you to negotiate with me nor entitle me to any compensation or other entitlement if you determine that you have an independent legal right to use such other material (either because, e.g., such features or elements were not new or novel, or were not originated by me, or were or may hereafter be independently created by or submitted to you); provided your determination with respect to such independent legal right shall be subject to the provisions of Paragraph 4 below.

2.   I represent and warrant that I wrote the submitted material. I further represent and warrant that I own the submitted material, free of any lien or encumbrance; that it is original with me and not based on any other material or source; that the use and exploitation thereof will not violate or infringe any third party rights; and that I have the right to submit and to offer such material to you without obligation to any third party.

3.   I agree that no obligation of any kind is assumed by or may be implied against you by reason of your receipt or potential or actual review of the submitted material or any discussions or negotiations I may have, except pursuant to an express written agreement which may hereafter be executed by you, on the one hand, and me, on the other hand, which agreement, by its terms, will be the only contract among the parties.

4.   If there is any dispute arising out of this agreement, including the substance, validity, operation, or breach hereof (including, but not limited to: if you should determine that you have the independent legal right to use material which, in whole or part, is similar to or identical with the submitted material without entering into a written agreement for compensation to me, and if you proceed to use the same and if I disagree with your determination), the dispute between us shall be determined solely by submitting such to arbitration in Los Angeles, California, before an arbiter mutually selected by the parties who is experienced in the field with respect to the use of material similar to the submitted material; or, if we cannot mutually agree, then such arbiter shall be selected in accordance with the Commercial Arbitration rules of the American Arbitration Association. The arbitration shall be controlled by the terms of this agreement, and any award favorable to me shall be limited to the fixing of compensation for your use of the submitted material, which shall bear a reasonable relation to compensation normally paid by you for similar material taking into account the relative stature of

the owner or author of similar materials. Such award will provide for each party, respectively, to bear its own costs of arbitration and attorney's fees. The pendency of the arbitration, the proceedings, any evidence or other material, and the award shall be maintained and remain confidential, except that an award may be confirmed by a court of competent jurisdiction provided no award which has been fully satisfied within 14 days of its issuance may be so confirmed.

5. I assume full responsibility for any loss of the submitted material for any reason including, but not limited to, whether it is lost, stolen or destroyed in transit, or while in your possession or otherwise. You shall have no obligation to read or consider the submitted material nor to return the submitted material to me.

6. Except as otherwise provided in this agreement, I hereby release you of and from any and all claims, costs, demands and liabilities of every kind whatsoever, known or unknown, that may arise in relation to the submitted material or by reason of any claim now or hereafter made by or through me or on my behalf (even though I realize that such might be based on facts or circumstances not now known or suspected by me to exist, which if known or suspected, would have materially affected my decision to enter into this agreement) that you have used or appropriated the submitted material, except for fraud or willful and intentional injury on your part. I waive all rights of injunctive or other equitable relief (including rescission) against you, in connection with this agreement and exploitation of the submitted material and in connection with any other material, whether or not in whole or part identical with or similar to the submitted material.

7. I shall not have the right to use (nor authorize the use of) your name, in any manner or means whatsoever.

8. Should any provision of this agreement be void or unenforceable, such provision shall be deemed omitted, and this agreement with such provision omitted shall remain in full force and effect.

9. This agreement is entire and shall be binding on the parties respective successors, assigns, licensees and all affiliated and related parties. No statements or representations have been made except those expressly stated in this agreement. This agreement may be modified only by subsequent written agreement. 'I,' 'me' and 'my' refers to the party or parties submitting the material to you.

10. You may freely assign, in whole or in part, your rights hereunder.

11. This agreement will be interpreted in accordance with the laws of the State of California applicable to agreements entered into and fully performed therein.

Very truly yours,

_____
Screenwriter's Name (Signature)

AGREED TO AND ACCEPTED:

_____
Screenwriter's Name (Printed)

By: _____
(Production Company Executive)

Prepare a Cover Letter

Along with a copy of your script and the signed release form, you must also prepare a cover letter to accompany this package. It should be printed on letterhead that includes all of your contact information. There is no need to do a selling job on your script with a clever, snappy, or lengthy cover letter. Let your script (which has already been requested) speak for itself. Model your letter after the one below.

Sample Cover Letter

Jessica Noelle

(Date)

Jay James
Tri-Film Co.
12345 Beverly Boulevard
Beverly Hills, CA 90210

Dear Jay James,

In keeping with your request, enclosed is a copy of my spec script, "Ask an Angel to Dance." You will also find my signed release form. Thank you for your consideration.

Sincerely,

Jessica Noelle

Jessica Noelle

321 JUMP STREET • NEW YORK, NY 10000 • 212–555–9000 • JNOELLE@ABC.COM

The cover letter that accompanies your requested spec script should be brief and to the point, as shown in the sample at left.

Mailing the Package

It usually takes some doing to get to the point where you are asked to submit your script. Be proud of yourself for getting to this point. You don't want to mess up now. So, along with all of your hopes and dreams, don't forget to include a cover letter, a synopsis (only if requested), the signed release form (if requested), and of course, your wonderful script, properly formatted and bound.

Priority Mail is the most economical first-class way to send anything weighing more than 13 ounces (and your spec script will fall into this category). The post office provides free, sturdy, script-size Priority envelopes that are red, white, and blue. Of course, you can send your script fourth-class mail and save some money, but it usually takes a week or two longer for delivery, and you can't use the sturdy Priority mailer. There's no telling how your script will arrive if you send it in a plain manila envelope, and a good padded envelope will eat into your postage savings, so you may as well spend the extra money and send your script Priority Mail.

If you think by shelling out big bucks for Federal Express overnight delivery that you're going to impress the agent, development person, or producer to whom you're sending your script, think again. Chances are, that person's assistant will take the script out of its envelope and place it on his boss' "to read" stack. Forget trying to make an impression this way, and save your money.

Here's another money-saving tip—*do not* send a self-addressed stamped envelope (SASE) with your script. Federal law requires that mail weighing more than a pound must be brought to the post office, even if it includes the correct postage. That being the case, don't waste your money including a stamped return envelope with your script. No one who receives your script is going to take it to the post office if-and-when it is read and rejected. Another thing—according to federal law, "postage-metered" mail weighing more than a pound does not have to be taken to the post office. This does not mean you should send a return envelope that has been stamped with metered postage. By the time the script is read, the date on the metered postage is likely to have passed and will no longer be valid. Besides, it is unprofessional to attach a return envelope to a script. SASE? A thing of the past. Forget it, unless the person to whom you are sending the script requests one.

Sometimes a production company will swing for the postage and return the script with a rejection letter. Our feeling has always been that the turned-down script has negative karma attached to it, and we wouldn't want to send out that copy of the script again. Also, if the script was read, it will probably look it. Psychologically, we don't think it's a good idea to send someone a script that looks as though it's been read and, obviously, rejected.

You may choose to include an SASP—self-addressed, stamped postcard—with the package. It will be returned to you, verifying that your script has reached its destination. Make the message simple. The sample postcard below is appropriate. Be sure to write in the title of your work and your name. Before enclosing the postcard with the package, double-check that you have put your name and address on the front. And, of course, be sure that it has the appropriate postage.

Sample Self-Addressed Stamped Postcard (SASP)

Once the package is on the way to its destination, make the proper entries on the Tracking Chart and Contact Report. Don't forget to include how the package was sent (FedEx Overnight, UPS Ground, U.S. Priority Mail), and remember to record the tracking number on the Contact Report.

Yes, we received _____ "Ask an Angel to Dance" _____

by _____ Jessica Noelle _____ on _____.
                                              (Date)

_____
            (Name of Person Returning Card)

at _____.
                (Name of Company)

Postcard to accompany submitted spec script.

CONCLUSION

There are three kinds of people in this world: those who make things happen, those who watch things happen, and those who wonder what happened.

It's within your power to be a person who makes things happen, and now you know how. Prioritize your wish list, organize your loose-leaf, customize your query letters, and get them in the mail.

Loving Jezebel
Written and Directed by Kwyn Bader

Clowning Around

I grew up in Rockville, Maryland, loving movies, and I was always writing stories. It never really dawned on me that people made a living doing that—writing movies. As soon as I knew that there were screenwriters, there was absolutely nothing else I wanted to do. When I was a teenager, getting ready to go to college, if I had told my parents, who are scientists, that I wanted to be a screenwriter, it would have been like saying I wanted to be a circus clown.

Listen Up

In 1987 I came to New York to go to Columbia. After graduating, my first job was for a production company that did documentaries. I was working with a small team led by Horace Ove and Madison Davis Lacy who had won an Emmy for one of his *Eyes on the Prize* documentaries. That was a great opportunity because it allowed me into the lives of intriguing people. For instance, we were working on a project about Richard Wright, author of *Native Son* and *Black Boy,* and who had lived in Paris for thirteen years. Because I was the junior member of the team, I was always the one sent first to try to get somebody to agree to an interview. In that year, I got to travel around and talk to great artists who had spent decades in Europe. People tend to point out now that I get nuances to characters in my writing and I think it came out of that experience. Also, it made me pay attention . . . quickly.

Time Outs

As happens with documentaries, we would work for a while and then would have to go separate ways because of fund raising. During that separate-ways time, I was hopping on any New York film set I could, in whatever capacity they would have me. I worked as a PA (production assistant) and even as a talent coordinator.

I had a girlfriend in L.A., so during another break between documentaries, I made a foray out west and stayed for five months. I was so naive then. The only thing I had going for me was knowing people through family and friends. I wasn't focused on getting something. It was more about meeting people and learning what I should do. What I did learn was that I wasn't ready for that town yet. I knew I wouldn't be going back until I had something that was needed there, or that I was close to breaking down a door.

Thanks! I Needed That

In the fall of '95, I was working with a producer named Art Cromwell, writing a documentary on jazz that was funded by PBS. While I was doing that job, I also wrote my first screenplay in a three-month period of time. It was a love story set in Paris in the '40s, and traversed different time periods, like New York in the 1930s. It came out of people I had been around. It was a totally unrealistic film for me to do as my first one, but a great experience of having nobody telling me what to do, and finding my way through this script.

Through friends, the script was forwarded to Lynn Auerbach at the Sundance Lab, and, even though it wasn't a Sundance type script, she called me and said, "We think you're a talented writer and we want to encourage you to keep going." One of my friends who was already a Hollywood screenwriter was also very supportive. The good words from those two different sources kind of kicked me into another level. It made me more determined than ever to write something that I knew I could do.

This was about 1995. It was at the same time my friend Seth Rosenfeld, who wrote and was directing his first film, *A Brother's Kiss,* said that I could work as his assistant. The night before the first day of production, the line producer called and told me that the budget didn't allot for a director's assistant. I showed up the next day anyway and told Seth, "I don't care. I'm going to be here every day anyway." And I was. Eventually, they found some nickels and dimes for me, but the money was not the important thing. What was important was that it was a very inspiring experience for me. I wanted to write and direct my own movie.

Write On

After coming off that experience, I did what I call the smartest/stupidest thing I had ever done. I had no money; I had no job and I decided that I was going to take the time to write *Loving Jezebel,* which was something that had been incubating in my head for months.

It started when somebody who was married, basically put it out there, saying to me, "My marriage is just not working, and I really adore you." I knew this was not good. Rather than get myself into a bad situation, I started thinking out this script. I wanted to tell the story about a lovable ne'er-do-well, who spends his whole life falling in love with other guy's girlfriends, starting from the time he's a little boy. I knew I wanted to take some funny and oftentimes painful experiences and infuse them with the spirit of a Chaplin movie.

I spent one day working as a PA on a booty video and all I remember is that I had to wear overalls and hold a chicken. That earned me my food money for a month and a half while I cranked out this first draft

and had a great time doing it. That was in October 1995.

As soon as I completed *Loving Jezebel,* I went on a camping trip with a crew of my friends, including Seth Rosenfeld. He told me to bring my script. There we were, sitting in the woods reading it and playing all the parts. When we finished he said, "I think you got the one you need."

On-the-Job Training

After dealing with the immediacy of paying rent (I worked as a waiter), I realized that if I wanted to do my movie my way, I'd have to learn how to get money. I got a job on the business side of the industry, working for the WKRP of independent film distributors. It was nuts! They had very limited resources and I got dropped in the fire.

At first I was the foreign delivery guy who had to deal with making sure that prints and slides and everything else got to where they needed to go. The only problem was, the company never paid vendors, so this was a big headache job. The perk was, for a year, I was sent around the world to every foreign film and TV market. It was not like I was in the big Disney booth at these trade shows; I was basically in with what was like the used-car salesmen of the world. I saw how cruelly films are treated in that environment. It wasn't about anything that had to do with: Is the movie good? Is there an artistic quality? It was about: Well, it's got Pat Morita for ten minutes in the movie, so I'm sure you can put that on your twelve o'clock slot on television in Germany–$20,000. People bought films without even seeing them. It really taught me what you have to do to protect yourself, and I also learned the considerations that validate a certain budget. When I look back at that year, I don't know when I slept. When I wasn't on the road, I was in the office, hustling *Loving Jezebel.* That was another perk, access to a phone for long distance calls.

Making Progress

A Tony award-winning actor read my script, loved it, and attached his name to it. This created a buzz. For the first time, I wasn't chasing after agents. I had three at one time interested in me. There was one indie producer who liked the script and was talking to agent Matt Leipzig at Original Artists. Matt and Jordan Baer started the agency and it wasn't quite a year old. These two guys had impressive backgrounds. Matt had run Roger Corman's company and Jerry Weintraub's company. He and Jordan met while working for Frank Price. With great taste and a sense of chance, they had this idea that instead of servicing talent that was already in Hollywood, they were going to break in new people. Yes, they would have the guy who wrote a hit film, but they were also interested in a guy like me who hadn't done anything yet, but who had his own voice.

I met Matt when he came to New York for a weekend, and I loved him. Someone at one of the big three agencies called and said, "Please don't make a decision for a week." Then they called and said that again. I realized that I wanted an agent that I could be a priority for, rather than just be another part of the machinery. I decided to go with Original Artists and I've been really happy with that choice. They knew they weren't going to make any money for a while and they were into helping me get the movie made.

One Lesson After Another

In early '97, I went to L.A. for three weeks. The agency used my script to get me introduced, and they set up about thirty meetings for me, three or four a day. That's when I met David Lancaster. He started as a play producer in New York (*Night Mother, American Buffalo*) and had originally gone to L.A. to produce the film version of *Night Mother*. He stayed in California and had become mostly an HBO cable movie producer, with a great record of getting movies made, coming in under budget and having them all make money. David liked the idea of getting involved with a feature again and he and I agreed that we were going to take my film out.

I thought, I'll be up and in production in no time. Also, I figured, I have an agent; I've got it made now. I can quit my job and I'll just go pitch and before long I'll have a writing assignment and I'll be rich. I was still naive, and obviously, I had some more lessons to learn. I hadn't learned yet that no matter how good the producer is, you have to push him to actually take the movie to the studios and to his money people. Also, everyone is going to want you to keep tinkering with the script until they feel it's perfect.

The hardest lesson to learn, especially knowing that I was broke again, was that I was pitching projects, but I had no political leverage at all. I would give a really good pitch, but I was always coming in as the number two person. If you were HBO at that time, you wouldn't give Kwyn Bader the job when someone like Matty Rich was there because his was more of a name cachet.

In Living Black and White

At a certain point during all of this, there was an offer from a fairly prominent director to buy the script. I knew how he wanted to change it. The nature of my movie is a story of character. I wrote it, using the world of people I had always been in and navigated. It happens to be a very multi-racial film, but it doesn't take that issue on at all. It takes it for granted. It's here in New York. The main character is of mixed race and the women in his life are all different and so are the people around him. It's the New York that I know. Now it has started getting praise for that. At the time, it was becoming something that was stopping our progress. I was getting black executives saying, "This isn't really a black movie. I don't know how we're going to market this. What's your market?" I had it planned out. I would say, "I think it could be these things," and I said all the things that now are those markets for the film. They all said "No. No." Then we had distributors that rely on foreign money saying, "This is a black movie and black movies don't sell overseas. I don't see this working." At a certain point, we got so many of those objections, I felt myself coming to the end of my rope. What got me through that period was just pure faith.

I did think of it as a character-driven movie and it just as easily could be a John Cusack type of movie. But then, NO, I knew I had to stick with what I wrote the way I wrote it. David agreed and stuck it out with me.

Fulfilling an Obligation

Before we started getting bites, I had to write a documentary about the Tuskegee Airmen, the first black fighter pilots in American history. It was a project I had been attached to for about five years, since I started working on documentaries. Every year I would get this call, "Kwyn, it's not dead." I'd say, "Okay. Call me next year." Next year finally came and I had to take time out to do it. It was a challenge to write because it wasn't as though I could guide them in their interviews as to what they should ask, based on what I wanted to write. It was the other way around. The interviews were already done, so I created a collage for the whole piece and then I wrote within that. Ossie Davis did the narration. It was great to have him read my words, and it kept me up and going.

All It Takes Is One...or Two...

My script for *Loving Jezebel* got accepted by IFFCON (International Film Financing Conference) that happens every year in San Francisco. It's where they select what they consider the fifty most viable independent, unproduced scripts. The purpose is to link producers directly with foreign buyers and to get foreign money into these projects. We made contacts, but were getting a lot of the same old thing of not knowing how they can market this movie.

Then one of the executives from Encore, a big cable company, said, "We love this script." While they didn't bite right away, they expressed a very firm interest. When more than one company does that, you really start to get somewhere. Around the same time, APIX, which was mostly a video company, got interested and wanted to make it for a low amount of money. Believe me, I wasn't looking for a lot. I, ultimately, did the movie for $1.2 million.

The Kwyntessential Audition

Even though it would be a practically risk-free movie for APIX because it was going to be made for so little money, they wanted to see that I had some directing talent. They wanted me to shoot a scene on video and were going to give me $500 to do it. I'm not really a video guy, so I said, "Give me the $500 and I'll do something." I was going to do what I called "a postcard" for the movie. A friend hooked me up with a guy who had shot his Academy Award-winning short, and we went out for a day with a Bolex. I had done a little storyboard, and with no sync sound, we did this little short. I played the lead. That way I was sure the actor would be there on time and would listen to the director. This postcard was my ode to Chaplin. Encore saw the short, too, and then stepped to the plate and said, "We want to buy the script and for you to direct it." Within a month and a half, I was in preproduction. That was in the summer of 1998.

HILLarious

I was happy. Money was being spent. The crew was being hired. Little did I know that the travails weren't over, but I soon found out when I got a call in the middle of the night that dropped my stomach into my ankles. Remember that Tony Award-winning actor whose name was attached to my movie? He had signed on to some other project months before for one of his best friends, and had taken money for it. It was something that hung together with foreign pre-sales and it had to shoot that month or they would lose their insurance.

I immediately went into war mode and devised a plan for each of the following days in the production office: if this, then this; if this, then this.

Thankfully, the Encore guys had already booked their flights and were coming to town. At least it prevented them from pulling the plug from far away. I wanted them to know that I could pull this movie off. I had them come in as I was auditioning people so they could see, even under this pressure, I wasn't losing it. I got all of the actors who I thought were viable and would legitimize my budget on the phone all in one day. Within no time, I hired Hill Harper, an actor I really wanted, and whose work I admired. As the leading man, Hill brought a lot of humor to the part. The movie moves to a more serious inner place as it goes along, and it was good that Hill understood that and knew to get us laughing earlier than I had intended.

The shoot was five weeks. We finished on time and on budget. Postproduction was completed in June 1999. We didn't have theatrical distribution. That was a whole other thing, going to some festivals and having screenings until we got picked up. *Loving Jezebel* opened in October 2000, exactly five years after finishing the first draft.

From a Director's POV

I think that directing has made me a thousand times better writer because I'm ruthless now with material. I'm so fearful that I'm going to have a bunch of stuff that I shot but can't use, or that I'm going to get in that editing room and feel that the architecture of the story is not well-built. Those are panic issues that come from battling to hold together my first movie, and I'm extra-sensitive to them now.

I've seen movies directed by first-time directors who were also the writers, and some tend to be a little literal, and you could tell that they were very protective of their material. Not that that's always bad. The good thing about a writer directing is that you know the story is going to get told.

As a director, I like to see somebody not always hitting those same notes, but putting harmony on it, or even sometimes fighting what the words are saying, just to make it interesting and to bring out the levels that are going on in a movie. I love putting on the director's hat and picking up my own script saying, "Who the f___ wrote this? Where's the damn writer?" and telling the actor, "Say what you said. It's better than what the writer wrote." I learned quickly that it was necessary to stop being precious about my words.

CHAPTER 7

$\mathcal{T}$HE DEAL

There's interest in your spec script. Exciting? Yes! . . . Are you vulnerable? Maybe. . . . Knowledge is power, and if you know what to expect, if you know what your rights are, and if you take an active part in making informed decisions, you have a good chance of safeguarding your work and enjoying a productive and prosperous career in the industry. Chances are, when there's interest in your screenplay, you will have an agent, business manager, or entertainment lawyer negotiate a deal for you. In fact, if you haven't been able to get an agent, the magic words, "There's interest in my script," make it a lot easier to get one. So although you may not have needed an agent to get you that first sale, you may want one now to negotiate, and then to continue representing you.

Deals are complicated for many reasons including the use of legalese in contracts, and the fact that scripts have merchandising and afterlife potential (prequels, sequels, spin-offs, syndication, interactive rights, videos, DVDs, novelizations, stage plays, and more). There are countless ways in which writers and their work need to be protected.

This chapter is about familiarizing you with the Writers Guild's basic terms, provisions, rates of pay, and types of deals for the professional writer—which could be you with your first spec sale. It also includes valid recommendations and cautions for non-Writers Guild members when dealing with non-signatory producers. And, if you have a writing partner, before you two write another word together, be sure to check out "Collaborators, Listen Up!" beginning on page 247.

WRITERS GUILD'S
MINIMUM BASIC AGREEMENT (MBA)

The Writers Guild of America Theatrical and Television Basic Agreement is the formal name of the Minimum Basic Agreement, or MBA. It is a collective bargaining agreement that the Writers Guild renegotiates approximately every three to four years with the Alliance of Motion Picture and Television Producers (AMPTP) and the television networks. More specifically, it is the contract between the Writers Guild and Management that governs the conditions, the compensation, and the rights and responsibilities under which members of the Guild work.

The MBA is a complex document, hundreds of single-spaced pages long. We have extracted and summarized the topics that are most relevant to writers with spec scripts, and then translated them to what we hope is plain-talking English.

Signatories

As mentioned above, the MBA is the bargaining agreement between the WGA and Management. The term Management refers to the employers—production companies, studios, TV networks, and independent producers—who negotiate with the Guild every three years or so, and who sign the MBA. These employers are considered Guild *signatories*. If a signatory options or buys your spec script, or hires you as a writer, you become eligible to join the Guild.

For theatrical motion pictures, the Guild offers an incentive to signatories to make deals with writers who are not Guild members. A production company will get a 25-percent discount off the MBA writer's *scale*, which is another term for minimum payment. If the movie is produced and the writer receives a writing credit, compensation must be adjusted to 100 percent of scale.

Not all companies producing theatrical or television films have signed the Guild agreement. This means they're not signatories. Once you're a member of the Guild, it is a violation of Guild Working Rules for you to sell or option literary material to a non-signatory. If a non-signatory producer wants to buy a Guild member's script, that producer must sign the MBA and become a signatory.

If you have any question about whether or not a producer or a production company is a WGA signatory, call the Writers Guild East or West and they will gladly check any company's signatory status. If you sign a contract with a signatory, a copy of that contract goes to the Guild and is reviewed to make sure that it complies with the MBA.

Options

If a producer wants to *option* your spec script, it means he wants you to give it to him exclusively for a specified amount of time—generally for at least six months to a year—in exchange for an agreed-upon amount of money and terms.

The Writers Guild MBA regulates options. A signatory may not take the property of a writer who has professional writer status, test the waters with it, and have the right to set it up without paying the writer the MBA option minimum. There's one exception: an if-come deal in television, which we will explain after defining professional writer.

Professional Writer Status

A brief but you'll-get-the-point definition of a *professional writer* according to the WGA, is one who has a theatrical motion picture or television credit, or has had at least thirteen weeks of prior WGA-covered employment. Professional writer status is also given to authors who have had a novel published, and to playwrights for a produced play.

"If I get my hands on first-time writers who are in the process of selling their original screenplays to Guild signatories," advises Alexis DiVincenti, Contracts Administrator of the WGAE, "I tell them to get the company to deem them a professional writer." If you don't fulfill the requirements of a professional writer at this point in your career, have whomever is negotiating for you ask the production company that's buying your script to include the following sentence in the contract: "For purposes of this deal or agreement, this writer is deemed professional writer." According to Alexis, "If the company agrees to that in writing, and most do, it could help to avoid problems down the road in terms of you doing the first rewrite, or in re-acquiring the property if the company doesn't produce your script."

PROSE FROM A PRO

Negotiating
by Screenwriter Dale Launer

My Cousin Vinny, Ruthless People, Dirty Rotten Scoundrels,
Blind Date, Love Potion No. 9.

What happens is a studio VP wants to do my project. He goes into a room. Not only does he have to talk the next guy up into it, he has to talk the whole room into it. Generally, if the whole room wants to do it, then the next guy up, the chairman, has to approve it. Then they give it to the business affairs guy to do the deal.

I used to let my lawyer negotiate. I hired my lawyer, who I'm still with, largely because I thought he was an honest man. An honest man may not always be the best one to have as your point man in negotiating. This lawyer of mine is such a nice, decent guy, he's like a Rabbi.

I used to be in sales—I was a very serious salesman at one time—and, for me, the idea of selling and negotiating is actually kind of fun. So I started to not let my lawyer negotiate. I would get on the phone with business affairs execs and I would do the negotiating, tête-à-tête with them.

All the business affairs guy can do is run interference. All he can do is try to talk you out of stuff. He can't up the price. He can't really negotiate. He's more of an official legal messenger boy. But you let them pretend that they've got some sort of leeway, some sort of power to negotiate.

What they do is make you an offer to which you say, "That's beyond insulting." Then you make a counter offer and they come back and say, "That's beyond outrageous." And then you come to somewhere in the middle.

They give you reasons why they can't give you this deal or that deal, and you can find reasons why they can do it. There are ways to use creativity in negotiating. For instance, somebody wanted me to do a rewrite, so I said I wanted $125,000 a week. They said, "That's beyond outrageous. That's more than anybody has ever gotten. We cannot break that precedent." I said, "What would you pay me to do a rewrite on the script? Would you pay $350,000?" And they said, "We could probably do that." I said, "I'll tell you what. Pay me $250,000 and I'll have it for you in two weeks." They said, "Okay." They look good and I break a precedent.

If-Come Deals

If-come deals apply only to television movies, and are the exception to the MBA payment requirement for an option. A production company that enters into an if-come deal with a writer does not have to pay the writer option money for his script while actively trying to get financing for it, or generate network interest in it. As part of the if-come situation, the writer's deal must be fully negotiated, so that in the event the company's efforts are successful (the *if* part), the writer will have her deal already in place (the *come* part) and attached to the project.

Spec Sale Compensation

You send out your query letter to a Guild signatory production company that asks to read your script. You send them your script with a signed release form, and a month later, the producer's assistant calls to tell you that they want to buy your script. As we already mentioned, at this point you will want an agent or lawyer to negotiate the deal for you. Even so, it is still important for you to know what you can expect from this, your first deal with a Writers Guild signatory.

"How much you get paid for your work," according to WGAE Assistant Executive Director, James H. Kaye, Esq., "is the core of any union contract." Mr. Kaye, who has worked with the WGA Minimum Basic Agreement for over twenty years, recommends that writers contemplating the sale of literary material or who anticipate being employed to furnish writing services consult the WGA Schedule of Minimums. This "Ratebook" indicates WGA scale for motion pictures and numerous genres of television writing.

The rates change every May, according to the last negotiated MBA contract. There are two sets of Guild minimums for the sale of theatrical motion pictures by professional writers—high budget and low budget. The *high-budget rates* apply to motion pictures that cost $5 million or more to produce; *low-budget rates* apply to motion pictures costing less than $5 million.

As a rule, signatories pay first-time writers minimum plus 10 percent, which covers the agents' fees. Check the trade papers and the online databases that report spec script sales figures, and you'll see that there are exceptions to the rule. We've all heard about those million-dollar deals for first-time writers. They really are the exception.

To give you an idea of the Guild's payment rates for screenplays, based on the WGA's Schedule of Minimums (as of this writing), see the fee schedule on page 241. It presents the high- and low-budget ranges for original and non-original screenplays for theatrical motion pictures. To better understand this payment schedule, we have provided basic definitions for the following terms:

- **Treatment.** An adaptation of a story, book, play, or other literary, dramatic or dramatico-musical material for motion picture purposes in a form suitable for use as the basis of a screenplay.

- **Original treatment.** An original story written for motion picture purposes in a form suitable for use as the basis of a screenplay.

- **Original screenplay.** The final script with individual scenes, full dialogue, and camera setups.

- **Non-original screenplay.** The final script adapted from a story, book, play, or other literary, dramatic, or dramatico-musical material, with individual scenes, full dialogue, and camera setups.

- **First-draft screenplay.** A first complete draft of any script in continuity form, including full dialogue.

- **Original story.** Literary or dramatic material, indicating the characterization of the principal characters and containing sequences and action suitable for use in, or representing a substantial contribution to, a final script.

- **Non-original story.** Literary or dramatic material based on a story, book, play, or other literary, dramatic, or dramatico-musical material, indicating the characterization of the principal characters and containing sequences and action suitable for use in, or representing a substantial contribution to, a final script.

- **Rewrite.** The writing of significant changes in plot, story line, or interrelationship of characters in a screenplay.

- **Polish.** The writing of changes in dialogue, narration, or action, but not including a rewrite.

It's good to sell your spec script. It's great to sell it to a Guild signatory. It is also great to have one of your ideas put into development. Read on and learn what you may expect when that glorious thing happens.

Development Deal or Step Deal

A production company reads your script and doesn't want to produce it, but thinks you have big talent and wants to hear your other ideas. An in-person or telephone pitch meeting is set up. You pitch a

The fee schedule below is based on the Writers Guild's Schedule of Minimums. It presents the high- and low-budget ranges, as of this writing, for original and non-original screenplays for theatrical motion pictures. The terms used in this agreement are defined on page 240.

WGA Theatrical and Television Basic Agreement

Theatrical Compensation

WRITING ASSIGNMENTS	PAYMENT RANGES:	LOW	HIGH
■ Original Screenplay, Including Treatment		48,731	91,408
Installments: Delivery of Original Treatment		22,082	36,566
Delivery of First Draft Screenplay		19,192	36,566
Delivery of Final Draft Screenplay		7,457	18,276
■ Non-Original Screenplay, Including Treatment		42,647	79,308
Installments: Delivery of Treatment		15,991	24,379
Delivery of First Draft Screenplay		19,192	36,566
Delivery of Final Draft Screenplay		7,464	18,363
■ Original Screenplay, Excluding Treatment or Sale of Original Screenplay		32,747	67,029
Installments: Delivery of First Draft Screenplay		25,290	48,753
Delivery of Final Draft Screenplay		7,457	18,276
■ Non-Original Screenplay, Excluding Treatment or Sale of Non-Original Screenplay		26,649	54,842
Installments: Delivery of First Draft Screenplay		19,192	36,566
Delivery of Final Draft Screenplay		7,457	18,276
■ Additional Compensation for Story included in Screenplay		6,098	12,187
■ Story or Treatment		15,991	24,379
■ Original Story or Treatment		22,082	36,566
■ First Draft Screenplay, with or without option for Final Draft Screenplay (non-original)			
First Draft Screenplay		19,192	36,566
Final Draft Screenplay		12,791	24,379
■ Rewrite of Screenplay		15,991	24,379
■ Polish of Screenplay		8,000	12,187

Step Deal Steps

by Screenwriter David Newman

Co-writer: *Bonnie and Clyde; There Was a Crooked Man; Bad Company; Superman I, II,* and *III.*

Every deal is a step deal. The steps are usually laid out according to a formula, which is first draft, second draft—no, it's not called that anymore. It's first draft and a set of revisions and a second set of revisions and a polish. Something like that. And it's all euphemistic because what they call a set of revisions is very often a complete second draft. Inevitably, once you've gone through those three or four stages, it really isn't ready yet anyway, and then they ask you to do another one. Sometimes, when you see it coming, you can negotiate that, and say, "I'm out of contract. You've got to pay for it." Sometimes, when you're working for a production company and there's a studio involved, they say to you, "Before we turn this into the studio, we all want to believe it's the best it could be because then it'll have the most chance of being made, so would you mind just giving this one more pass. It'll only take you three weeks." And you've got to say "yes." You just don't say "no," not if you want to get your movie made.

feature film idea to the producer. She loves it. She takes you to a studio to do the same pitch. The development execs at the studio also love it and want to put your idea into development. Congratulations! You have a producer and a studio that's going to give you a *development deal*—also called a *step deal*. This means that the studio will pay you a specified amount of money as an advance, and some additional money with each script-development step you take, provided the studio wants you to continue stepping. If they decide not to go to the next step, that's the end of that deal.

In today's market, the average development deal for the new writer is between $50,000 and $100,000. Typically, you may get 20 percent of that as an advance, then another 20 percent for the first step, which usually involves writing a scene-by-scene *treatment*. If the execs like the treatment, you then advance to the second step, writing the *first draft*, for which you will get paid another 20 percent. The third step may be a *rewrite* for which you'll get another 20 percent. If they're happy with the rewrite, you'll get the last 20 percent. If they feel the script needs another rewrite, or just a *polish*, then you'll move up to the fourth step and get the last 20 percent. If and when your script is produced, and no other writers have worked on it, you may expect another $50,000 to $100,000 production bonus.

Assignments

There's the chance of another scenario as a result of your spec script. The production company that reads it doesn't want to produce it, but recognizes your writing talent, and may want to give you an assignment. The company may own a property—a novel, short story, article, play—that it wants you to adapt for the screen. Assignments are usually step deals, as described above.

Your Credit

You will be notified of the screen or television credit you are to receive after the completion of *principal photography*—the main photography, which includes the performers, not the filming of scenery and background work. Credit notification can come any time after principal photography, but before the film is released in theaters or televised. If you think you have not been fairly credited, or if you feel that others receiving writing credits are not entitled to them, then you have the right to a WGA arbitration, providing, of course, the production company is a Guild signatory. The Writers Guild has the final credits determination for the theatrical and television films of signatories.

When you're involved in arbitration with others who are claiming credit, each of you must present your case in a separate letter to the Arbitration Committee. The arbitrators—three for each arbitration—are writers who are members of the Guild. Every word, every fact, every detail is read and taken into consideration. The better your records, the better your case. In addition to the letters from each of the people seeking credit, the arbitrators are given every draft of the script along with the final shooting script.

With any luck, you won't have to test the importance of well-kept records because of a credit dispute, but make sure you have them anyway. You'll find that good records will come in handy for many reasons. Don't get lazy. There are no shortcuts. *Keep accurate records!* "Protect Your Credit" on page 244 further reinforces the need to keep good records and create a paper trail.

PROSE FROM A PRO

Rewriting

by Screenwriters Josann McGibbon & Sara Parriott

Exactly 3:30, Runaway Bride, The Favor.

You can't be resentful of rewriting. It's part of your job. You can turn in a great draft and they can love it, but they're going to come to you to rewrite and tailor it. You serve a lot of masters.

We often get work because we're considered easy to work with. We don't get mad when they want changes. Often, writers get resentful and all artistic and huffy. You can't afford to do that. It's a collaborative medium where you have to accommodate people.

Pick your battles. Don't fight the small stuff. If you feel strongly about something, save up your fit for the big thing. Of course, you'll get fired and they'll bring in someone who didn't think the big thing mattered.

WORKING FOR NON-SIGNATORIES

Most first-time writers get deals with independent producers, many of whom are not Writers Guild signatories. Writers who work with non-signatories are not eligible to join the Guild and don't have the Guild and its MBA to protect them. There are two major problem areas writers may run into with non-signatory producers—screen credit and payment.

Protect Your Credit

The Other Writer

The *other writer* has become so ubiquitous in this profession, unfortunately, that you almost know going in, there's a good chance that it's going to happen—they're going to call in another writer. It didn't happen nearly as often in the past as it does now. All you can do is guard against it, and then trust that when it comes down to what gets on film and the inevitable WGA credit arbitration, that you are going to win and see your name on screen.

—David Newman
Screenwriter

The Writers Guild has the final say with regard to theatrical and television film credits produced by signatories. With independent non-signatories, there is no guarantee of credit. Some will say something like, "We can't promise you a credit because the Guild determines credits, and, if we promise you a credit, then a Writer's Guild signatory (studio or network) wouldn't want to buy the script, because we promised you a credit, and they know that the Guild determines credit." That's double talk to set you up in case they decide not to give you a writing credit.

WGAE's Contracts Administrator Alexis DiVincenti advises you to have an agent or entertainment lawyer work to get you the best deal possible, whether it is with a Guild signatory or not. In deals with non-signatories, there should be the guarantee of a writing credit and an additional sentence saying, "The parties understand, that should this project become covered by the WGA, that the Guild determines credits." This way, the production company can't accuse you of holding back a sale to any studio or network over an agreement to give you credit. With that added sentence, you will have a credit guarantee whether or not a Guild signatory gets involved.

So now you know how to assure yourself of a writing credit in your contract, whether or not the production company is a Guild signatory. Hold that thought while picturing this: You sold an original screenplay. The producer had you make all kinds of changes. The director came on board and had input. In fact, he and his assistant rewrote several scenes. Then the star was hired, but not until her dialogue changes were woven into the script. Okay, the film is in the can. You find out that the producer has a writing credit, the director has a writing credit, the star was willing to forego an "additional dialogue by" credit, and your credit, because the producer is feeling generous, is "Based on a Story by." It can happen.

To prevent such a scenario, you should proactively do whatever it takes to make sure that it doesn't happen. Keep every draft of the script that you write. Keep every note and memo from all of the parties involved (producer, director, star) regarding script changes. Document every telephone call and every meeting; make a habit of writing memos, summing up exactly what was discussed. Print them out and also save every e-mail in an online file. Send a copy to whomever you talked to or met with about the script. Give copies to others who are involved. And be sure to keep copies for yourself. Everyone wants to have creative input, and their creativity pervading your original material can get messy. If someone makes a suggestion and you incorporate it into your script, you're still the writer. Even if another writer is called in and changes are made, chances are that enough of your original story and script will survive for you to get the writing credit you deserve.

Ms. DiVincenti says she gets calls constantly from non-Guild members who have deals with independent non-signatory producers. A typical call goes something like this:

> I registered my script with the Guild. I got a deal with Joe Schmo, independent (non-signatory) producer. After I've rewritten my script, let's see, this is the fifty-third draft, Joe Schmo says that he's going to put his name on it and his brother-in-law's name on it because, in the five years I've been rewriting it, they sat down with me for an hour and talked about it. It's not a Guild-covered project, but I did register the script with the Guild. What can I do?

By the time Alexis gets one of those calls, unfortunately, the best advice she can usually give is, "Don't make the same mistake again!"

Alexis has seen enough to know that writers want to please. They also feel that if they cooperate on this, their first project, then the producer will want to continue working with them. That may be true. Why wouldn't they want to continue working with you if you'll do rewrite after rewrite without being paid adequately, if at all, and are willing to share or give up your credit?

What can a writer do about that kind of abuse? Alexis says that

You sell a screenplay like you sell a car. If somebody drives it off a cliff, that's it.

—Rita Mae Brown
Screenwriter

there are a couple of options, but unfortunately, neither is good. First, you can sue the producer or production company. This means taking them to court. Most companies have E & O (errors and omissions) insurance, so if a writer accuses them of stealing material, they'll tell the writer to go ahead and sue them. They know that their insurance company will handle it, while the average writer can't begin to afford the legal fees involved in bringing this kind of case to court.

Second, the writer can go into mediation or arbitration with the producer through an independent mediator or arbitrator. Both are less expensive processes than going to court. However, this type of action is possible only if there is a negotiated clause in the contract that allows the writer to do this. It's not likely that a producer will agree to putting such a clause in the contract.

When your credit appears on screen, it tells the world that a professional writer is responsible for what is about to be seen. It tells people in the industry that your work was good enough to be bought, produced, and aired. That credit can get you your next sale or assignment, and it is important to get every credit you deserve. If you're dealing with a Guild signatory, you are eligible to join the WGA, which means you will have built-in credit protection. If you're a non-Guild member and are dealing with a non-Guild signatory producer, you must take every precaution to ensure that you receive proper screen credit.

When dealing with non-signatories, proper payment is another crucial area for a writer. The following section will tell you how to keep your guard up when an indie wants your spec script.

Payment and the Bottom Line

There are many honest, talented, and terrific non-signatory producers who buy scripts and hire writers, giving them major opportunities and fair and decent deals. There are others who are abusive to writers.

When a writer is hungry, maybe even desperate, and some sleazy, non-signatory producer offers her a deal, it's tempting to accept. But is it worth it? Alexis has heard horror stories about writers who do dozens of rewrites, get paid really poorly (if they get paid at all), and then have their credits taken away—*if* the films are ever made. The same thing can happen to Guild members who work for signatories, but at least Guild members get decent money, even if they're just getting scale. And if they deserve screen credit, the Guild sees to it that they get it.

If a non-signatory wants your script, be sure to get an agent or entertainment lawyer to negotiate the contract. If a non-signatory wants your script and gives you a non-negotiable contract, saying, "Yeah, kid, it's my standard contract. This is the chance of a lifetime. Take it or leave it," invest in an entertainment lawyer to look at the contract before you take it. If you have confidence in yourself and your work, you may want to leave it. After all, if this hotshot with his standard contract wants your script, maybe a Guild signatory or one of the honest independent non-signatory producers will want it too.

"Forewarned is forearmed" as the saying goes. Now that you've been forewarned, it's up to you to assure yourself of a happy experience with a non-signatory producer. Take care of business up front. If the producer is totally uncooperative and disagreeable in terms of your credit and payment, be willing to walk away, and consider yourself lucky that you've been spared all kinds of future abuse. Then find an ethical producer to buy your script.

All this talk about dealing with producers is important, but if you're working with a collaborator, there's some additional forewarning that needs to be addressed before you go any further.

COLLABORATORS, LISTEN UP!

Two friends go to the movies. They leave the theater, sorry that they wasted their time and money. Both agree that they can write a better film than the one they just saw. By the time they chug down a couple of beers, the two friends are making notes on their napkins for an opening scene. Does this scenario sound familiar? Are you writing with a friend? Want to stay friends? Then you'll do well to heed the following advice:

"Never collaborate on a spec script, or any other writing, without putting together a legal agreement between you and your writing partner(s)." These words of wisdom are from Alexis DiVincenti. As the Writers Guild person who fields phone calls from hysterical non-members as well as members of the WGA, Alexis has heard it all—every way in which a writer can be used and abused, ripped off, jerked around, worked over, and left for dead. So when she advises

> Never collaborate on a spec script, or any other writing, without putting together a legal agreement between you and your writing partner(s).
>
> —Alexis DiVincenti
> *Contracts Administrator,*
> WGAE

you to draw up an agreement with your writing partners, no matter how well you know and trust them, you'd be smart to take her advice.

Almost always, the people who enter into a collaboration have a close relationship—a best friend from the old neighborhood, a lover, a former lover, a fraternity brother, a cousin, a colleague at a day job—and no one ever thinks it could turn ugly. Chances are it won't turn ugly if you make it legal. No matter how close or how friendly you are with your collaborator, and no matter how good a time you're having collaborating, you've got to remember that it is a business. Instead of pulling people apart, a legal agreement keeps them together by protecting their productive, ongoing relationship.

Generally, problems start to develop when there's interest in the project. That's when writers start thinking: I wrote more. It was my idea. I came up with all of the characters. I spent more hours at the computer. Alexis gets phone calls asking, "How many words do I have to have written in order for it to be my screenplay and not my partner's?"

Once you're writing with a partner, there's no such thing as *separable material*. In other words, you can't separate the material into your contribution and your partner's contribution. If, however, you're

---

Writing Credits—Take Notice

When you see writing credits and there's more than one writer, their names are separated either by the word *and,* or by an ampersand (&). When the word *and* separates the names, it means that the writers did not work together. The producer may not have been completely satisfied with the script and called in another writer, or the director may have changed the script enough to warrant a credit. An ampersand

STORY BY
Steve Franks

SCREENPLAY BY
Steve Franks
and
Tim Herlihy
& Adam Sandler

separating names indicates a writing team.

The credits to the left are for the film *Big Daddy*. They tell us Steve Franks wrote the original screenplay. Once the writing team of Herlihy & Sandler entered the picture, they made enough changes in the script to warrant a shared "Screenplay by" credit with Steve Franks, and since it all started with Franks' original idea, Franks got a "Story by" credit.

writing something based on a pre-existing piece of material—for instance, you and your partner have an agreement that both of you are going to write a screenplay based on your story—then that story is considered separable material. A producer could then read the screenplay and say, "I don't want this script, but I'm interested in the story." That story can be separated out. The producer can buy your story and not the screenplay that was written in collaboration. If the two of you write something together that is *not* based on anyone's story, that material cannot be separated.

Alexis tells people, "I don't care if you're sitting on a barstool or eating a hot dog in the park, if you decide to write with someone else, get a couple of paper napkins from the bartender or hot dog vendor and write out and sign two of the same original agreements." Each agreement should include:

- Both of your names and the date that you write the agreement.

- The project you're going to work on together and your intention. Is it a Story? Screenplay? Teleplay? Identify the project in some way, and cover all possibilities, so that if you write it as a theatrical motion picture, and it sells as a television film, the agreement is still valid.

- Your working arrangement. Determine where and when you work, and how much time each one of you plans to put in on the project on a daily or weekly basis. Be as specific as possible.

- Division of money. If it's not a 50–50 split, then come up with a formula and reason for the formula. If the work is based on one writer's story, or one writer will work on it full time while the other will be more of an editor or sounding board, then you may agree to a 60–40 split. Decide all of this up front and spell it out clearly in the agreement.

- Whose name comes first in the credits.

- A "what-if"clause. This is very important. "What if" one of you doesn't live up to this agreement. "What if" one of you wants out after having tremendous creative input? Think it through and come to terms before you start working together. If you can't agree on an agreement, chances are, you'll have problems with your working relationship. Find out now.

Sample Agreement Between Two Collaborators

A sample agreement between two writers who are collaborating on a spec script is found below. It includes all of the relevant information.

Components

Names and Date ▶

Project Name ▶

Project Intention (story, screenplay, teleplay, etc.) ▶

Working Arrangement (where and when the work will be done) ▶

Division of Money ▶

First Name in the Credits ▶

"What If" Clause ▶

Signatures and Dates ▶

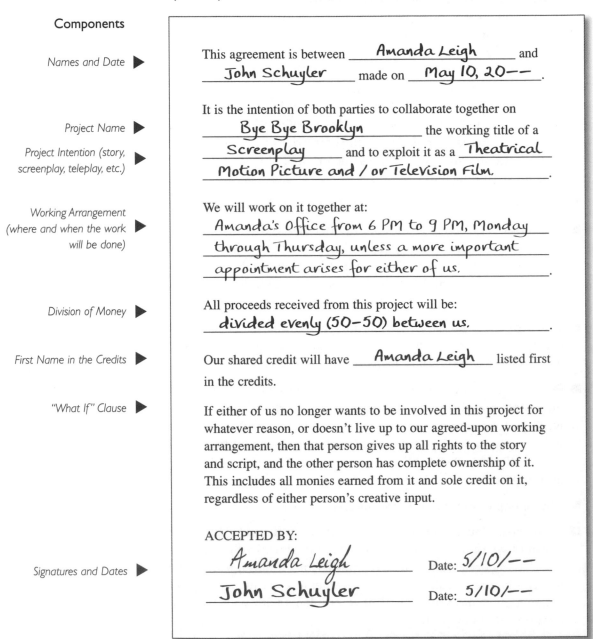

This agreement is between ___Amanda Leigh___ and ___John Schuyler___ made on ___May 10, 20––___.

It is the intention of both parties to collaborate together on ___Bye Bye Brooklyn___ the working title of a ___Screenplay___ and to exploit it as a ___Theatrical Motion Picture and / or Television Film.___

We will work on it together at: ___Amanda's Office from 6 PM to 9 PM, Monday through Thursday, unless a more important appointment arises for either of us.___

All proceeds received from this project will be: ___divided evenly (50–50) between us.___

Our shared credit will have ___Amanda Leigh___ listed first in the credits.

If either of us no longer wants to be involved in this project for whatever reason, or doesn't live up to our agreed-upon working arrangement, then that person gives up all rights to the story and script, and the other person has complete ownership of it. This includes all monies earned from it and sole credit on it, regardless of either person's creative input.

ACCEPTED BY:

___Amanda Leigh___   Date: ___5/10/––___
___John Schuyler___   Date: ___5/10/––___

After both of you have signed and dated both copies of the agreement, put your copy in your legal agreements file folder for safe-keeping. Hopefully, you will never need it; but just in case you do, you'll have it.

Although a simple agreement will serve almost every collaboration, you may want to chip in with your collaborator for a more formal agreement. Once your legal underpinnings are in place, there will be no misunderstandings anywhere down the road. All that's left is enjoying the collaboration and reaping the rewards.

CONCLUSION

Now you have a basic understanding of the kinds of deals that are out there waiting for you. Getting a deal with a Writers Guild signatory, making you eligible to become a member of the Guild, is a good thing. If you have interest from an independent non-signatory (or even a signatory), it's up to you to protect your script, your credit, and yourself from abuse. Also, if you're part of a writing team, safeguard your collaborative relationship by having an agreement in writing that leaves no room for disagreement.

Detroit Rock City

Written by Carl V. Dupré

We'll Give It Two Years

I went out to California in 1992, but was jaded by the whole Hollywood scene before I even got there. Several people back home in Providence, Rhode Island, warned me that chances were slim-to-none that anything was going to happen in terms of a career as a screenwriter. Those people spoke from experience. They had gone to the west coast and, sure enough, nothing happened, and they moved back east.

I told my wife that if I stick it out for two years and nothing happens, we'll move back home and at least I won't be kicking myself for not trying.

While most people are waiting for their big break, they're waiting tables or working for a messenger service. To have any kind of a career in the business is a blessing. By '94, I was able to get work on a regular basis as an assistant film editor. I thought, okay, I'm doing better now than when I moved out, we'll give it another two years.

For Pete's Sake

As assistant editor, I was working on a rock-and-roll type movie that was stimulating my creative juices. It kept bringing me back to my early teens when I found shelter in rock-and-roll, and was able to come to grips with adolescence by listening to the music. Kiss was the first band I was into. A lot of their songs took me through some hard times. Peter Schink, the editor with whom I was working on this rock-and-roll movie, is my age, and we would trade stories about going to concerts. He even had a Kiss pinball machine.

One of my favorite movies of all time, *I Wanna*

Hold Your Hand, an early Bob Zemeckis & Bob Gale movie, is about a bunch of girls going to see the Beatles when they appeared on the Ed Sullivan Show. The movie took place in 1964. I told Peter, "Somebody should do a movie like *I Wanna Hold Your Hand,* but with the band Kiss as the Holy Grail." Peter said, "You've got to write that script!"

I wrote about thirty pages of what promised to be a really awful script. In those days, my M.O. (method of operating) was to write the first two or ten or thirty pages of a script and, if I didn't like it, I'd abandon it instead of trying to fix it and make it better. Fortunately for me, I've shed that old skin and now I'm a finisher. But then—at the end of '94—I had thirty pages that I wasn't happy with, and I said to myself, forget about it . . . it's not going to work.

Lunch, Lies, and a Feature Filmscript

A few months went by and Peter Schink, the editor, took me to lunch with James Melkonian, the director of the movie that we had all been working on. While we were sitting and eating, Peter said to the director, "Carl's working on a script now that takes place in the '70s. It's about a bunch of kids that go to see a Kiss concert." I never told Peter that as far as I was concerned, this project was history. Meanwhile, Peter was talking about it to the director like it was alive and well. The director then asked me, "How far along are you?" Before I could say anything, Peter chimed in, "Oh, he's been working on it for the last six months." The director said, "You should be finished with it sometime soon." I said, "Yeah. Yeah. A couple more months." The director figured, "This is February. A couple more months? March, April. You should have a completed script in April, right?" "Yeah, right, April." I kind of got railroaded into having to write the script.

I had written about three or four scripts before that. I paid a lot of attention to structure; where act breaks should be, and counting the page numbers. With *Detroit Rock City,* I thought I'll just write something that has a beginning, middle and end, and not worry about it structurally. It was instinctual rather than clinical. I just let things happen the way I felt they should happen.

By April of '95, the script was written and I gave it to the director. He thought it was good and said, "Now all you have to do is get it to Kiss . . ." "Yes, so how do I do that?" The director said, "I don't know." I thought to myself, I just made the biggest mistake of my life. I wrote a script with a known entity in it that I have no connection to at all.

Whoever read the script had the same reaction: "It's a decent script. Are you going to get it to Kiss?" I would if I could, but I couldn't. The script sat on my shelf for about a year.

How's This for Synchronicity!

I was working as an assistant editor on another movie that had a revolving door of assistant editors. Each would stay for a couple of days or a couple of weeks, then be replaced. I struck up a conversation with one of these temps and he told me he wanted to make some short films. I said that I'm working on some feature-length screenplays, and I told him about *Detroit Rock City.* He said, "One of my best friends is a huge Kiss fan. He's also an actor. He should read your script. I gave the script to the assistant editor and he gave it to his actor-friend, Kevin Corrigan, who absolutely loved it.

Meanwhile, a big reunion was set for August of '96, with the original Kiss lineup in full makeup, the way they were in the '70s. That generated lots of interest in my script. Suddenly, people were really eager to read it.

At that point in time, it was as though the planets were coming into alignment for the script. To use another analogy, it was like I had a lottery ticket and was watching the numbers come up. "Oh, that's my number. Hey, that's my number too."

Kevin, the actor, brought it to his manager, Molly McCarthy. Molly brought it to her associate who brought it to another person and another person and finally it wound up with a casting director who wanted to be a producer. On the day the casting director got the script, she was meeting with a man named Barry Levine who used to photograph Kiss back in the late '70s. He also wanted to become a film producer.

When the casting director met with Barry Levine, she slid the script across his desk and said, "This is really funny. I'm meeting with you, the man who used to photograph Kiss, and here's this Kiss script that I received today." Barry said, "Great. I'll read it on the plane later today." He then explained that he had just gotten a call to fly to London to photograph Kiss for their big reunion concert.

Sealed with a Kiss

As promised, Barry Levine read it on his way to London. When he got off the plane, he handed it to Kiss' manager. It was on a Friday of one week that I received the phone call from Kevin, the actor, who said he was going to give it to his manager. By Friday of the next week, Gene Simmons had read the script. Word came back from Kiss that if we could get the film going, we could use their stuff—their name, their logo, some of their songs. So Kiss was tentatively attached to the project.

That's Show Biz

By then it was 1996. I was working on a Saturday morning TV show and while I wasn't able to write full time, I felt the door was open and it was just a matter of time before I'd be able to get in. My wife and I agreed, we'll give it another two years.

Barry Levine and his company were taking the script from place to place. It had been at several studios. Either the right people were passing on it, or the wrong people liked it and wanted to do a bunch of silly things to it.

For a while it was at Fox when they had a movie-of-the-week division. That was in the beginning of 1998. It was also when I met Gene Simmons at a meeting at Fox. It looked like it was going to happen, but then the movie-of-the-week division suddenly got shut down. The script was back in limbo again.

Timing Is Everything

Soon after the Fox letdown, the script got to Kathleen Haase who was working at a low-budget production company. She read the script and said, "It's great. My boyfriend is a director and loves Kiss. I have to get it to him." She brought it to her boyfriend, director Adam Rifkin. Adam had just had the hit film *Mouse Hunt* and was looking for a new project—someone's script to direct. My script was given to him at the perfect time. Adam read it and said he wanted to do it. Coincidentally, the editor Adam works with on his films is his good friend, Peter Schink, the same editor who originally pushed me to write the script.

So, not only did we have Kiss, we also had a director attached. That was a big selling point.

Barry Levine went with the package to New Line Cinema because he had heard that they were itching to do a Kiss movie. When the script got there, they said that they've been working for the past two years on trying to get a Kiss movie going. They had several Kiss-oriented projects in development, but when the New Line people read *Detroit Rock City,* they said, "This is it! It's about the fans. This is the movie we want to make."

A Once in a Lifetime Experience

It took twenty-one days–an absurd and ridiculously short amount of time for a script to get the green light. The development process usually takes more like two years. Obviously, they just wanted to get this movie made right away. It was faster than the fast track; it was the *bullet train* track. Very little of the script got changed. They didn't have enough time to make many changes. I can't imagine it ever happening like that again.

It Was Just Meant to Be

Detroit Rock City was my first spec sale. It was the Big Kahuna for me. When it happened in '98, I said to my wife, "Okay, we're here for good."

It's a major thing to sell something that you wrote on your own, without having any reputation or track record. I know writers out here who have been working for years and years, making a decent living, but they've yet to have their name on a produced work.

I've often wondered what would have happened if I had had an agent handling the script for me.

It was almost mystical the way my screenplay got into the right people's hands. A producer-friend summed it up perfectly in one word: *Kiss*met.

In Case You're Wondering...

Kevin Corrigan, the actor and huge Kiss fan who brought the script to his manager, is one of the supporting characters in the movie. Peter Schink, who kicked me in the butt to do the script, was the film editor.

Men of Honor

Written by Scott Marshall Smith

A Writer's Nightmare

In 1994, I was working a day job, had a wife, two kids, a third on the way and was writing screenplays at night in an unheated garage in Hermosa Beach, California. I had just finished writing a wonderful screenplay about arson and the twisted psychology behind it. It was called *The Fire Song*. As a reward for completing the script, I decided to treat myself to a movie.

I settled into my seat (always in the front row) and watched as the screen flickered to life. The first shot was of a magnificent fireball. Truly glorious. My heart dropped through the floor and landed somewhere in the basement. Even before I knew that I was watching the trailer to Ron Howard's *Backdraft,* I was sure of one thing . . . my script—my baby born out of a year's worth of sleep deprivation—was never going to sell.

In the words of Jake Gittes, "When I'm right, I'm right." And I was right. The script went out and laid there like a boat anchor. Of course, every executive in town said exactly what I'd seen so clearly in my head that night in the theater—"Well, they just made *Backdraft*. . . ." Only that's not all they said. Some of them were impressed. They liked the writing. I got meetings. A lot of them. One in particular changed my life.

Diving In

One person who had liked my writing was Jeri Roberts. At the time she was the Director of Development at Paramount in Los Angeles. We met in some small nook of an office on a hot spring day. She said, "I think you're really good and you should do some-

thing with us over here." Nice words and oft' spoken in Hollywood. I left figuring that was it.

A month later, the phone rang. It was Jeri. She said, "I want you to come in and listen to this story about the first black Navy diver." I heard "come in" and was elated. They wanted me back. But those last words, "first black" something . . . That sounded alarm bells in my head. I didn't care whether the story was about a Navy diver, sous chef, whatever. And I wasn't alarmed that the subject matter would invariably involve racism. My concern was simple—surviving in Hollywood means writing scripts that get made into movies. "First black" bio stories were and still remain the fodder of movies of the week. The chances of *Navy Diver* ever seeing the light of your local multiplex screen were slim to none. Then another thought crept in—Jeri was actually trying to get me hired. She believed in me. Doubts or no doubts, I had to do it.

Meeting #2

Jeri dumped what seemed like a six-foot-high manuscript on my lap. It turned out to be a number of exhaustive and tremendously dry official accountings of the service record of Navy Master Diver Carl Brashear. I took the research home and began sifting through it. As I went, I read with mounting fascination. This truly was an interesting story. Then came startling news—this guy, this Navy diver, had lost his leg trying to recover a nuclear bomb for his country.

I stopped. Put the book down. Thunderstruck. Knowing one thing—characters who lose limbs while battling insurmountable odds win Academy Awards.

Born on the Fourth of July came to mind as well as dozens of other films about that kind of struggle. Okay, the Academy Award thing was a fantasy, yes, but the deeper realization was very real. Carl Brashear's life was full of moving and captivating achievements. His indomitable spirit pushed its way out of even the driest Navy prose. There was a great human drama to be told here. I was hooked. Now all I had to do was figure out how to make it a movie.

Backstory to the Future

According to Carl Brashear, producers had been pursuing his life story as a potential movie for twenty years. The last option currently belonged to Bill Cosby and his producing partner Stan Robertson. Stan had spotted a news article about Carl and was fascinated. At the time he and Cosby had a development deal with Paramount. So Jeri set up a meeting on the lot.

I found Stan in his office in Paramount's venerable Dressing Room building. Stan was big–6'3" maybe taller–genial but wily and tough. He'd had to be to make it as one of the first black executives in the entertainment business. He watched me come in the door. He was nice. Polite. But I knew he was thinking: "How is this white kid ever going to nail this story? How could he, culturally, even begin to wrap himself around what this Carl went through?"

My dad had briefly flirted with a jazz singing career and Stan loved the music too. We spent most of the hour talking about horn players and vocalists, and discovered that we actually had a lot in common. At the end of the meeting Stan said, "So, are you going to come back and pitch me this story?" I said, "Yes, definitely." He said, "I've got to tell you, I've heard twenty-seven pitches on this story. I've heard musicals, gangster movies, everything, but I've never heard the right pitch."

That was encouraging. I went home. The pressure was on.

It Takes a Villain...

In the end, what we are as artists relies upon one thing–that tiny tuning fork recessed deep in our brains that only rings true when you have hit upon something honest and real. Mine hit a clear C-note a few nights later when I had a breakthrough. Carl's story had everything–great hero, fascinating world, stirring theme, action to boot–but one thing was glaringly missing...a villain. Someone Carl could have steady conflict with. Someone formidable. And tough. Someone who believed in suppressing Carl just as much as Carl believed in elevating himself. In fact, during his long career, Carl had struggled with a number of people. Many were racists. Others opposed Carl's bid to come back to active duty after losing his leg. But there was no overriding villain that would be a sounding board for Carl's travails.

So I looked deeper into the material. Combed its cobwebby corners and discovered that at crucial junctures in Carl's career, there were some Navy men who would secretly come to him, urging him to tough it out and beat the odds. I took those men and combined them into a single character. *Billy Sunday* swaggered right out of a 50's era Technicolor military epic. He was bantamweight in size, but something in him inspired terror in even the biggest of men. Embittered by the spiral of his once-promising Navy career, Sunday was hell on wheels–sadistic, racist, hard drinking and harder fighting. Oh, and there was one thing more about him–way deep inside his tiny black heart there burned the flame of honor. All I had to do was find a way to fan it.

Once I had those two characters, Carl Brashear and Billy Sunday, I knew I had the makings of a drama that might, just might, exceed the movie-of-the-week genre and become a studio film. Now I was excited about this project. I began to take Carl's real experiences and embellish them, invent around them, do whatever I had to do to raise them to a higher dramatic plane. I did all of this in my garage at home at night.

The Pitch

I finished the story and it was time to go in and pitch Paramount. Jeri arranged for me to meet with her boss, Michelle Manning, who was Vice President of Production.

I probably did it exactly the wrong way. I have a history of pitching long. I get so into it, I can go on and on. (I'm told I may hold the pitch record with Harvey Weinstein of one hour straight. Whether I did it right or wrong, I can't say, but I did get a three-picture deal at Miramax.) So I pitched my story to Michelle. I told her it wasn't a *race* film. *Race* was just an obstacle. It was a film about overcoming anything.

Michelle was very nice. A quiet, clearly very intelligent person who listened patiently, nodding at all the right places along the way. When I was done, she looked down for a second and shook her head. I was sure that that headshake meant, I'm sorry but I don't think there's a movie here. I don't think we should do this. Instead, she looked up at me and said, "You got it. We'll call you."

You Do What You Have to Do

When I began *Navy Diver,* I was still working at my day job for the motion picture camera company Panavision. My job was Director of Marketing at the Panavision/Hollywood office in L.A. It wasn't working the ER at Bellevue on a hot night in August, but my division was growing fast and it was a hectic, often high-pressured gig. It also provided the income that my young family relied upon. Quitting my job was out of the question. But I had a movie assignment and I had to interview Carl Brashear. So I did what any decent writer would do—I made up a story. I told my boss that a relative had gotten sick and I boarded a plane and flew to Virginia where I spent a solid week with Carl.

The more I interviewed Carl, the more any lin-

gering doubts I may have been harboring were banished—Carl's spirit was simply that infectious. Only a man like Carl could have gotten through that particular era. As tough as he was, there was nothing offensive about him. He loved people. He would level those deep brown eyes at me and say, "I didn't let that man get away with that," and I knew that he didn't. He had that way of both embracing people, but knowing how to show them that he wasn't going to bow. It was this amazing personal style that saw him through his incredible Navy career.

To this day, even among the Hollywood glitterati that I've seen him mingle with, Carl still operates this same way. Needless to say, I was very taken with the Master Chief. When we'd go to a restaurant, he'd park in a regular parking spot rather than the handicap parking places, and we'd walk. He wears a prosthesis but you'd never know—his gait is that smooth. I remember thinking, I'm into something magical here.

Where There's a Will There's a Way

Our interviews ended. I went home and the proverbial boom fell. It was time to write. I stared at my blank computer screen terrified all over again. But there wasn't a whole lot of time to fret—the first draft was due in twelve weeks. I got busy.

Money

Money is important. So important, it comes up twice in these pages. For one, money (or a *writer's quote*) is among the primary yardsticks by which a writer's status in Hollywood is measured. I had no status. So they paid me Writers Guild minimum plus ten percent. And that was generous. After taxes and fees, there was hardly anything left. But I wasn't doing this for money. I kept writing.

Schedule

The weeks passed. My day job roared along. Panavision/Hollywood was booming. It's a great organization that we had built from eighteen people to sixty-something at the time. I had to keep this job alive and keep my whole life going. So here was my schedule: Come home at seven o'clock. Play with the kids. Give them baths. Spend five minutes with my wife. Go out to the garage, which was freezing 'cause it was cold in L.A. that year, turn on the computer and write until 2 in the morning. Six hours later I'd get up and do it all over again. I wasn't tired, I was courting a trip to intensive care.

Oddly, one of the things that kept me going was Carl's example. If he could endure all that he had, I could lose a few hours of sleep. So I worked, determined to make this more than just another studio assignment. I was deep into the screenplay now. In the middle of the night I'd find myself getting choked up for my hero. I became obsessed with him. I agonized for his setbacks, reveled in his triumphs. Watched, too, as Sunday's character slowly but steadily ennobled himself over the course of events. After awhile, these characters and their conflicts were completely real to me. For me, full immersion into the world of the drama you are creating is what writing is all about.

I finished the script on time and got it to Stan Robertson. He called me the next day and said, "Wow, this is really good." We submitted it to the studio. The very next Monday, Jeri Roberts called and said, "Scott, this is good."

I didn't know what their expectations were, but I heard in their voices that they were kind of amazed. In retrospect, I understand why. They had a problem on their hands. The script came out better than they ever thought it would, and it clearly pointed toward a movie and, just as clearly, it was the kind of movie that the studio didn't want to make at that time.

Within a few weeks, the news was official. The script wasn't going into turnaround, but they weren't going to go forward with it either. I was incredibly disappointed. I slept. A lot. Mulled for weeks. Grew briefly depressed. And recovered. And moved on. Meanwhile, *Navy Diver,* as it was then called, went into a little Paramount script jacket and was placed on a high, dusty shelf and promptly forgotten.

New Hope, By George

Navy Diver was a popular read on the executive circuit around town and helped push my career up a notch. Within months of its completion, I was able to leave Panavision. I began working as a full-time writer in the business. Years passed. My agents and I would occasionally have this standard-operating conversation: "Where's *Navy Diver?* What's going on with *Navy Diver?*" We knew that De Niro had once circled it. It was originally offered to him by Paramount, but came freighted with a bunch of other things he didn't want to do. He passed.

More time passed. By 1998 my agents, Alan Gasmer and Rob Carlson, had acquired another client–a young director named George Tillman, Jr. George had just finished his first small studio feature, *Soul Food.* He and his producing partner Bob Teitel had made the movie for $6 million. It went on to gross something like $45 million domestically. Needless to say, George was a real star on the way up. He and Bob went into a deal with Fox 2000. One weekend, George read the first draft of *Navy Diver* and asked to meet me.

It was one of those nights in L.A. when the clouds just open up. As the torrential downpour thrummed without let up, I parked my car in the lot at Fox, got out and headed toward the distant lights of a ramshackle office complex. By the time I got to George and Bob's offices, I looked like a wet sewer rat. I remember going into the men's room and taking paper towels to try to dry myself off. It was like something out of a Woody Allen movie.

Still sopping wet, I wove through a warren of grungy little cubicles and found George and Bob. They were young, bright guys, interested in getting their next movie off the ground. George had read a lot and passed on a lot. We talked nicely for a moment and then fell on the subject of the script. And George said something I'll never forget, "You know, Scott, I don't think this is a race movie; it's about overcoming obstacles." We were on the same page. The meeting ended with George saying, "I think we ought to do this."

Scott Free

At the time, Laura Ziskin was running Fox 2000 and she said to George, "We'll get the movie out of turnaround." She also said the words every writer in Hollywood dreads: "And we'll get you anyone you want to rewrite it." To his credit, George said, "No. I really like this guy, Scott, and I think he can do it." To Laura's credit, she let me go to work and never again mentioned replacing me. In the end, I enjoyed a rare privilege–I was the only writer on *Navy Diver*.

When Laura gets going, she's a freight train. With the dogged help of Gasmer, Carlson and Bill Cosby, she was able to get the script from Paramount. Immediately, she started pushing hard, and I started rewriting. I lost count of the number of drafts I wrote. I wasn't paid all that much for the work that I did. I also worked on the film the entire time on the set and wasn't paid for that either. But it was never about money; it was about making this movie.

A lot of writers early in their career get hung up on the money. You have to be smart about what's worth putting sweat equity into. In the case of *Navy Diver,* I knew it was a movie and I had a lot of passion in my heart to see it finished. Often, my passion probably worked against me. People could simply smell that I was going to do the work whether I got paid for it or not. And I did it. Invariably, each draft made it better.

Like every true Virgo, I will slavishly save every draft. I save and carefully catalogue them because I think in the back of my mind, I'm probably going to go back and use that earlier material. To date, I've never ever retreated to an earlier draft. I always seem to go forward.

It's Called the "Delete" Key

In the spring of '99, we finished the draft that Laura Ziskin felt she could back, and she began to push heavily. As soon as Bill Mechanic, President of Fox 2000 at that time, said he was going to make the movie, the wheels began to grind. By then, my family and I had left Los Angeles and moved back to New York. So I packed up and went to L.A. to work on rewrites.

While I was sitting in George's office, a call came in from Laura. She said, "Bill Mechanic feels there are too many scenes that take place in Kentucky, too much childhood, too much rural stuff." George and Bob pressed Laura, "Was Bill getting cold feet?" Thank God Laura was straight with us and said, "Yes."

We hung up the phone and sat there in stunned silence. It was the first time we felt that the movie was in real jeopardy of stopping. To his great credit, Bill was in a tight spot. This was an iffy movie for him to make because it certainly was not a sure thing, down-the-middle hit, especially since half of it was a race movie. Bill's backing of us and the film was pure heart and instinct on his part. And if he was wavering, we were in trouble.

We had worked hard on the Kentucky section of *Navy Diver.* There was wonderful, poignant stuff in it and the sobering reality was it had to go. We made ourselves comfortable, ordered Chinese food, and I wrote as George and Bob sat there with me. By the end of that one long night, we had cut twenty pages of the Kentucky stuff, and turned the script around. Bill read it that weekend and called the producer on Sunday and said, "You're on."

Full Speed Ahead

We went courting for cast. To his credit, Robert De Niro came on for a lot less than he usually makes and agreed to play Billy Sunday. True to legend, De Niro was meticulous in his approach to his character. He was also a friend to the production, always a gentlemen and wise counsel in the ways of the movie business. He has been a potent backer of my career ever since.

Cuba Gooding, Jr. was less sure about coming on. I first met him in New York. Like Carl Brashear himself, Cuba is a room lighter. One of those guys that comes in and just takes over. He was instantly friendly and enthusiastic. And totally perfect for the part. (He even looked like Carl.) His misgivings were understandable. But the more he said "no," the more we wanted him. In the end, he joined the cast and brought a whole new level to the Carl I had written. During the course of filming, Cuba was tireless.

We were ecstatic. We had a helluva cast and knew it. Production began in the summer of '99.

When the film was completed and screened, it tested extremely well with women audience members. However, the studio felt the title *Navy Diver* turned women off. With that title, people thought it was going to be a big Navy action movie. The title was changed from *Navy Diver* to *Men of Honor*.

Who Knew?

If I've bored you to tears, I'm sorry. But the lesson is glaringly apparent, isn't it? A writing career is all about sheer grit. You just have to believe in yourself and your project long past the point where even your closest friends and relatives have given up. I've never gotten anything out of luck. I've always made my own luck. If I'd been lucky enough to sell my two specs for a ton of money, I might not have the respect for hard work that I have now. Yes, it was tough. But in the long run, it made me a better writer.

That Burt Reynolds' line sometimes haunts me, "Nobody calls to tell you when your career is over." There's the inverse of it, "Nobody calls to tell you when you're career has taken off." You just kind of realize it one day by the deals that you have and the volume of stuff that's coming through, and you see that everything has changed for the better. But fame is a lover who's bound to leave you for someone else. The trick is to enjoy the affair while you can and try not to miss it too much when it's gone.

The Moral of the Story

One day in the mid-nineties, this kid from New York called me, asking for advice. I was five years into pursuing my career and still at my day job in L.A. I said, "If you can, you should move out to L.A. and put yourself in the heart of the business. And by the way, don't expect much from the spec market. Take it from a guy who's been there–its very volatile."

Six months later, the kid called me back. He'd ignored my advice, hadn't moved to Los Angeles yet. But he had done one thing–sold his script. For a million dollars.

Keep writing. There's hope for us all.

CHAPTER 8

$\mathcal{I}$F IT DOESN'T HAPPEN

The aim of this book is to help you increase your odds of selling your spec script and/or break into films or television as a writer. That *will* happen for many of you. For most, it may not happen as quickly as you would like, but it will happen if you have staying power. For others, it may seem as though it's *never* going to happen. If you've done your homework and diligently followed the steps of the process and have given it more than enough time to get some kind of positive result, but haven't, then you must pinpoint the problem and make appropriate changes.

In a famous scene from *The Godfather*, Michael Corleone and his brother Sonny discuss a brutal action that had to be taken. "It's not personal, Sonny," Michael reminds his brother. "It's strictly business." Ideally, this is the way rejections should be viewed. The agent, producer, development exec, director, actor... none of them are passing judgment on you as a person, and may not even be passing judgment on you as a writer. A rejection letter may simply mean that at this time, the production company is not interested in a film on your subject, or the agent, in all fairness to his other clients, isn't taking on any more action-adventure screenwriters. Then again, if in response to the many query letters you've sent out, there was no response at all, or you received some polite form letters, but no one has asked to read your script, it's hard not to take it personally... and even harder not to feel bad about it. Obviously, the query letter may need work. If, however, your query has people asking to see the script, but the responses to it are polite form rejections, then the script may need work.

First, try to get over feeling bad. Re-reading the *From Script to Screen* stories found at the end of each chapter can help. Several of the produced screenwriters have shared stories of how their scripts had been turned down by countless producers before finally getting made. Jeff Arch's story about *Sleepless in Seattle* (page 29), for example, will help you realize how vital it is to keep faith in yourself and in your work. Scott Marshall Smith tells how he kept rewriting *Men of Honor*, mostly for no pay, because he *knew* that his script should be a film (page 255). Once again, read about Angelo Pizzo and all that he went through to get his award-winning film, *Hoosiers*, on the screen (page 156). Also, think about the roller coaster ride Josann McGibbon and Sara Parriott endured for the ten years that it took for *Runaway Bride* to be produced (page 121).

Screenwriter and director James Toback (*The Gambler, Bugsy, Two Girls and a Guy*) feels that confidence is the most important thing, and without it, you're lost, no matter how talented you are. That confidence lets you feel that you know what you're doing, and that you have some significant claim on people's attention.

If you're reading this, you know what you're doing. You're looking for help. And you've come to the right place.

IDENTIFYING THE PROBLEM

There are a few basic reasons why query letters and scripts don't illicit a good response—the genre and concept of the script, its timing and marketability, the approach used in your query letter or the way in which it was written, the budget needed to film your script, the people you chose to send your letters, or any combination of these reasons. Let's start with the query letter. Analyzing it may help give you insight into its possible weakness. Then we'll take a look at the script.

Pinpointing and Correcting Any Query Letter Problems

There may be one or more components of your query letter that are stopping you from getting requests to read your script. Have your query letter in hand as you go down the following list to help you determine your letter's problem or problems. Once you've pinpointed any weak areas, rework them until you reach your goal, which is a strong, compelling letter that will be a standout and get you positive responses.

Script Description—Genre, Logline, and Paragraph

When first assessing your query letter for possible weaknesses, pretend that you don't know the entire story, with all of its intriguing plot points, scintillating surprises, crisp dialogue, and satisfying ending. Read the description of your script as you have presented it in the query letter, and, as objectively as possible, put yourself in a producer's mindset. Does it sound like a script that has audience appeal? That may win awards? That you can be proud to attach your name to? If you cannot honestly answer "yes," then rework your logline and paragraph until it represents your script in the best, most appealing way. Make it one that generates enough interest to make the reader want to know more. (Review the suggestions for writing a winning query in Chapter 5.)

Be sure the description of your story is in keeping with the genre of your film. If the genre is comedy, the description should be light and funny, or it should clearly spell out the opportunities for hilarious situations. If it's a thriller or a horror film, the description should send chills up the reader's spine. If the genre is action-adventure, let the reader visualize the excitement on screen, just from your descriptive paragraph.

Marketability

Nowadays, the marketing departments of studios and television networks have a big say in what's bought. Is there an audience for your film? The question asked in the industry is: Will one million people pay to see it? If the market and marketability of your script isn't obvi-

---

PROSE FROM A PRO

What Hollywood Buys
by Charlie Purpura

Professor of Dramatic Writing at NYU Film School.
Screenwriter: *Heaven Help Us, Satisfaction.*
CBS Schoolbreak: *The Day the Senior Class Got Married.*
(Emmy Award Winner and Humanitas Prize Recipient.)

If you want to sell a screenplay, the first thing you should do is write a great screenplay. What I mean is, a screenplay that houses a great idea. My experience is that Hollywood doesn't buy screenplays, they buy ideas incorporated into screenplays. They're really not that concerned with the execution as much as they are with the idea. They can always get you to rewrite it, or somebody else to polish it. To me, it all comes down to that. There are other ways to get scripts made—timing and luck . . . the whimsy—but if you have a strong kick-ass idea, you're probably going to be in business.

PROSE FROM A PRO

Putting the Odds in Your Favor
by Richard Styles

Writer-producer-director: *Cease Fire, Shallow Grave, Sorceress II, Escape, Picture Perfect Murders.*

First, you have to understand what a good screenplay is, and then you have to know how to write a good screenplay. Nowadays, writers have tools that we never had before. You can go online and pull up almost any screenplay. You can read classic screenplays and analyze their technical structure. You can also rent videos and break down a movie scene by scene, beat by beat, line by line, transition by transition, see the character arcs, the setups, and the payoffs. There are two renowned screenwriting teachers, Robert McKee and John Truby. Both have video and audiocassettes and books.

Second, if you're going to sell a screenplay, you have to know who buys them. If you're trying for studio level, pay attention to the movies that are coming out and to which ones make money. If you want to put the odds in your favor, you have to understand what is selling and gear yourself towards writing those kinds of movies.

ous, you have to find a way to point out who the audience is for your film. One good way to do that is to compare it to a similar film that was successful, which means it made money. You can also emphasize the genre, that is, if it's a money-making genre, like a summer horror film for teenagers, or a family holiday film.

Just as you put yourself in a producer's mindset earlier, now put yourself in the mindset of the marketing manager and figure out how to turn your script into a marketable film. You may get an idea for a line or two that will add more appeal to your query letter.

Production Cost

The producer's development person has your extremely well-written query letter in hand. Right from the first paragraph, she knows you can write. You have style and a way with words. She's sure she would enjoy reading your script. The story sounds exciting and, whoa—"Back in time to a gala at the Palace of Versailles." The budget just quadrupled and the query letter went in the basket. Next!

If your script hints of special effects, computer animation, period costumes and sets, many exotic and exterior locations, a cast of thousands, or anything else that skyrockets a budget, then you'd better send your query letter only to the limited number of producers who do big-budget films, or to one of a handful of superstars who may be able to get a deal with his name attached.

Timing

Your script's genre and concept may be popular, and because of its popularity, the market may be saturated with your kind of film. The studios and networks may want to stay away from the flavor of the week . . . the week that you sent out your query letters. Check the recently released films and the soon-to-be released films. You can do this by going to the movies and paying attention to the coming attractions. A month or two before summer and Christmas, your local newspaper usually devotes the entertainment section to the upcoming season's films. Also, keep up on industry happenings, including upcoming movies, through trade magazines and newspapers (check the Resource List for suggestions). Don't forget those online sources, such as the Internet Movie Database (www.IMDb.com), which offers an extensive list of movies that are "coming soon."

If you discover that there are a number of movies coming out that are similar in genre and concept to yours, this might be the very reason you haven't gotten any requests for your script. If you feel that this may be your case, set aside the script for a season or two, and then resubmit it. In the meantime, focus on sending query letters for one of your other spec scripts. If you haven't written any others, this may be a good time to start.

Your Approach

You are a writer. The way in which you have written your query letter—your approach—can be the very thing that turns your readers on or turns them off. Being as objective as you possibly can be, does your query letter seem as though it were written by a winner? Someone with real potential? Is it clear? Upbeat? Assertive without being pushy? Well written? Creative in some way? If you didn't know you, after reading your letter, would you want to meet you?

If you think you zoomed in on the problem, rewrite the letter. In fact, rewrite it several different ways. (Once again, the pointers for writing winning query letters in Chapter 5 may be helpful.) Then select the two best versions and show them, along with the original query, to people whose taste and opinion you trust and value. See what they say. If all agree on one particular letter as the best, then send it out to the next five or six people on your wish list.

If you can't figure out what the problem is (and even if you can), there's nothing wrong with asking for help, particularly from people on the inside, who may be able to shed some light on the matter. Who are these people? Check your Square One System Contact Reports to

While you're waiting for something or other—for responses to your query letters or spec script, for the timing to be right to submit (or re-submit) your script, for contest results to be announced—you should be writing your next screenplay.

remind you of anyone who was friendly when you made your initial calls to verify the mailing information. Or get the names of those who signed any rejection notes you may have received. Contact these people. Once you get them on the phone, always begin by asking if they can spare a few minutes to talk. If they're on two other phones, volunteer to call back at a more opportune time. If they say, "What is this about?" in as few words as possible, be prepared to say exactly what you want. "I need your professional input. I really want to work as a writer, and I seem to be doing something wrong. I sent you a query letter and didn't get a response." (Or "I got a form rejection.") Continue by asking, "Would you be willing to tell me what it was in my approach that stopped you from asking to read my screenplay?" If the response is positive, offer to read, fax, or e-mail your letter to the person.

This sort of approach is a real long shot, but it may be worth a try if you have the kind of telephone personality that can pull it off gracefully. Make this sort of call *only* if you're comfortable with it. To avoid tripping over your words requesting help, prepare your little speech and read it (without sounding like you're reading it, of course).

If you've gone this far and the person is willing to give you input, while you're at it, ask if you can run your rewritten query letter by that person. People love to be looked upon as authorities. People love to give advice. It makes them feel smart and important. It's also a wonderful way to make a friend. Who knows, this "friend" may ask to read your script.

If There's a Problem with Your Script

If your query letter gets people to respond by asking for the script, that's wonderful. No problem there. It means that the requesters are interested in the genre and the concept. Terrific. But, if after sending the script you keep getting impersonal letters of rejection—Houston you've got a problem. Okay, so you haven't found the person who loves your script enough to devote a couple of years of his life to it and spend millions of dollars on it. That does not happen often. But every once in a while, someone in the industry who reads your script, whether it's a producer or the producer's assistant, someone should be offering words of encouragement, or telling you that they like the writing and want to see more of your work. If that's not happening, then your script may need a rewrite.

We're thinking that you wrote the script the way you thought was best. If, in fact, it does need a rewrite, we're also thinking you need guidance of some kind in order to do that rewrite. Consider the following ways of getting that guidance.

Learn From Your Rejections

If your script was rejected, think of how helpful it would be to discover the reason or reasons why. To get such feedback, contact each person who initially requested your script. When doing this, always be respectful of that person's time. If you're in the same city (most likely, Los Angeles), offer to take him to lunch. Offer to bring lunch in. Do not, however, overstep your bounds. A picnic in the park over the weekend is not appropriate. You have to use your discretion and sensitivity when approaching a person for help. Without being apologetic, use an understanding phrase like, "I can imagine how busy you must be . . ." This gives the person an out if he doesn't want to help you, and if he does, you'll know soon enough.

What you want from this person who read and rejected your script is to know why the script didn't work for him. It would be ideal if he would give you a copy of the coverage, but it's not right to ask for it. Let him volunteer it,

> ### PROSE FROM A PRO
>
> ## The Key to Writing a Standout Script
> **by Screenwriter Gary Lennon**
> Film credit: *Drunks.*
>
> Write from the heart. Make your spec script original, unique; make it that you're the only person in the whole world who could have written it. If you write something and your heart isn't in it, it's going to show on the page. Write what you are passionate about and that, too, will show on the page and will separate you from whatever anybody else is trying to do.
>
> I pitched a script idea to my agent and he said, "I don't think it's a spec," meaning that it's not highly commercial, not your one-liner. I then pitched the same idea to a producer and she said, "I love that story. It's a difficult sell, but write it!" I'm writing it.
>
> You have to think about what is unique about you and use it in your writing. That's what's going to separate you from the pack.

which he probably won't do unless you become good friends. You want suggestions for a rewrite. Hopefully, he will take an interest in your progress, and will want to see your revision. No need to ask, "May I show you the rewritten script?" Instead, once you have done a rewrite and have confidence that it is much better than the original, thanks to this person's input, call and thank him. *Then* ask if he would be willing to read it.

Enroll in a Screenwriting Class

Screenwriting classes at a college or film school can be ideal arenas for both analyzing your existing work and further developing your screenwriting skills. A film teacher can be your script's most constructive critic, especially if he is aware that you have been trying to sell it. Furthermore, fellow film students can be good sounding boards. A give-and-take spec script exchange with classmates can provide valuable criticism for your work, while sharpening your skills in analyzing the work of others. And, of course, you may be able to take what you learn in the class about script structure, character development, and dialogue, and apply it to a rewrite, as well as to your next script.

Read Books

There are many wonderful books that may help you focus on how to rewrite your script and get that sale. Your script may need anything from minor tweaking to major restructuring. For that you may find Syd Field's *Screenplay: The Foundations of Screenwriting* helpful. *You Can Write a Movie* by Pamela Wallace, *Making a Good Script Great* by Linda Seger, and Lew Hunter's *Screenwriting 434* are other good choices. Jennifer Lerch may give you helpful hints in *500 Ways to Beat the Hollywood Script Reader*. Additional worthwhile titles are presented in the "Recommended Reading" section of the Resource List.

Turn Your Script Into a Novel

Sometimes, it's easier to get a novel in print, than it is to get a script on film. The classic example is *Love Story* by Erich Segal. It was first written as a screenplay, made the rounds, and was rejected by everyone. Erich Segal turned it into a book and got a publishing deal. It became a runaway bestseller, and Paramount bought the film rights after rejecting the original script.

Having a book in hand may give you credibility when trying to sell your story to a production company or talent agency. Some agents and producers are more inclined to give a book coverage sooner than a screenplay. If you turn your screenplay into a book, but can't find a mainstream publisher who is interested in it, consider contacting an Internet e-publisher who offers a service called print-on-demand

If you are like most starting-out screenwriters, who are either working on or trying to sell a screenplay, you'll probably have to get a "day job" to pay the rent while you're waiting for your break. Screenwriter James Orr believes taking a job that you really don't like will fuel your ambition to make it as a writer; whereas taking a job that you really do like may distract you and ultimately cause you to put your screenwriting dreams aside. He feels that you should do something to earn a living, but nothing that will draw you away from what you truly want.

Turnaround Turning Out Triumphant

If you've had the good fortune to sell a script, but the film isn't made and the script goes into turn-around, you're in great company. Here's a list of films that were taken out of turnaround and turned into major successes:

★ The English Patient   ★ The Matrix   ★ Shakespeare in Love
★ E.T.:The Extra-Terrestrial ★ One Flew Over the   ★ There's Something
★ Forrest Gump   Cuckoo's Nest   About Mary
★ Good Will Hunting   ★ Pulp Fiction   ★ Speed
★ Home Alone   ★ Runaway Bride   ★ Star Wars

(POD). POD publishers can produce one bound book at a time and fill orders as they come in.

Writing a novel, however, is no simple task. You have to have a feel for the form, and your script has to lend itself to it. In the time it may take you to turn your work into a novel (and do it properly), you might be able to write another screenplay or two. Taking this "novel" approach is only a suggestion and may not be the most practical one for you. For the writer who is the exception, this may be something to consider. You'll find e-publishers who offer POD services in the Resource List.

Use the Services of a Script Consultant or Analyst

When a writer writes a script, he pictures the movie in his mind's eye. Sometimes, the script loses something in the translation from that mind-movie to the page, but the writer may not realize it when he reads his script. It's hard for a writer to be objective about his work because of his more complete vision of the story. Family and friends who are chosen by the writer to read the script can't always be trusted as the best judges. It's not their fault; their subconscious desire to want to like the work may make them too partial to be constructively critical. And so, a strictly objective script consultant may be the best choice to help pinpoint the problem (or problems) that are stopping the writer from getting encouraging responses from his script submissions.

People are always telling writers, "Write what you know." Screenwriter Daniel Waters doesn't necessarily agree. If that were always the case, Waters says that he would write only movies about grouchy screenwriters with rapidly developing potbellies. Instead, he believes you should use writing as an excuse to seek out and conquer themes that have always fascinated you.

If you are interested in the services of a script consultant, it's important to select one whose input you trust. The following list includes a number of pertinent questions to ask before handing over your work. The consultant's answers should help you decide whether or not he is right for you and your script.

■ What are your credentials? How long have you worked in the industry? In what capacity? (It is best to choose a person who has had experience in development or some other job that involves working with writers.)

■ Have you worked on feature films? Television movies? (Ask about whatever type of work applies to your project.)

■ Do you have any experience working on action films? Dramas? Thrillers? Documentaries? (Ask about whatever genre applies to your project.)

■ How do you consult with a writer? How specific do you get? What form or forms of analysis do you use? A coverage report? Scene-by-scene notes? In-depth telephone conversations?

■ May I see a sample of your work? (Script analysis, coverage, notes—depending on the consultant's answer to the previous question.)

■ Can you tell me any success stories of scripts that sold after you worked with the writers?

■ After I rewrite my script according to your input, will you read it and offer comments?

■ How much do you charge for your service? Fees range from $200 to $2,000, depending on the service or services provided—from oral critiques to comprehensive written analyses. (Remember that consultant's fees are not etched in stone. If you are quoted a price that will be difficult to pay, explain your situation and ask if there's some way to work out a more feasible deal.)

If you are interested in hiring a script consultant to read your work to analyze its strengths and weaknesses, you'll find a list of contacts in the Resource List, beginning on page 294.

OTHER VENUES FOR YOUR SCRIPT

If you can't get beyond the query letter, which means your script is *not* being read, or if your script *is* being read but you're not getting positive responses, there are other venues for your script—contests and fellowships. For you to consider entering contests and applying for fellowships, you need to have confidence in your script. Do you know that it is a fine piece of writing that will make an excellent film? Don't waste your time and money—yes, it costs money to enter most contests—unless you're really confident about the quality of your project. If you feel sure that your script is something special, and think it can compete with the hundreds of other entrants, good for you. Get busy exploring screenwriting contests and fellowships.

Enter Contests

A screenwriter's career can be launched through a screenplay contest. The best part is that a writer doesn't necessarily have to win first prize for this to happen. There are many studios, production companies, and agents who are in touch with contest coordinators, and ask to read the leading contenders, as well as the winning scripts. Also, many of the contest judges are industry professionals whose hidden agendas are to discover scripts and/or writers that they can work with.

So, if you're great at writing scripts, but not so great at query letters, or if you want to increase your chances of getting your script into the right hands, scriptwriting contests may be perfect for you. You can enter these contests at the same time that you're going down your wish list, and sending out query letters. If you win or even place in a contest, that credit will be an impressive addition to your query.

PROSE FROM A PRO

If It Doesn't Work, at Least It Makes for a Good Story
by David Mack

Co-writer: *Star Trek* and *Deep Space 9* episodes.

My partner, John Ordover, had come up with the notion of selling our screenplay through an online auction service. It cost about $25, and we figured, if nothing happened, at least we would get some press out of it.

We checked around and, to the best of our knowledge, no one had attempted to sell a screenplay in this manner before. So we took a shot at it on eBay and sent out a press release to all of the major industry trade publications and news portal services. Only *Star Trek Today* picked up the story and that was because we're known for the *Star Trek* episodes we've written.

What happened was, the same week we tried to do this innovative thing, there was some big ruckus about a guy who tried to sell a kidney on eBay. All the news services picked up on the story about the kidney and the black market for organs.

Weeks later we realized, what we should have done is put an ad that said, "For sale: Screenplay—Minimum bid: $250,000—With every sale, we'll throw in a free kidney."

It's fairly easy to enter a screenwriting competition. The hard part is making sure that the contest you enter is legitimate, what with the dozens of contests that seem to spring up daily. Anyone can sponsor a screenplay contest, charge an entry fee, and declare his brother-in-law the winner, or not have a winner, or not actually have a contest. There are a few ways to help you guard against entering a phony competition:

- Make sure the contest has a track record. Consider a first-time contest only if it has gotten good publicity and has reputable names attached, like Project Greenlight sponsored by Miramax in association with Matt Damon, Ben Affleck, and Chris Moore.

- If you are instructed to mail your application, script, and entry fee to a post office box, don't do so until you have done some more checking. Start by calling to ask where a list of last year's winners was published. What? No telephone number? Forget them and look for competitions that have phone numbers and who invite you to ask questions.

- Visit a contest's website to see if the names of last year's winners are posted. Verify that the contest awards the prizes it promises, which may include one or more of the following: money, a staged reading, publicity, an option, a production deal, meetings with industry professionals, and possible travel and hotel expenses when attending those meetings or when accepting your award at a ceremony or film festival.

- Most contest entry fees range from $20 to $50. Be suspicious of any contest that asks for higher fees.

- When investigating contests, visit websites that list screenwriting competitions, and click on any links to writers' chat rooms and message boards. When a contest isn't legitimate, word gets out after awhile.

Most contests supply applicants with guidelines (also called submission rules and regulations), an entry form, and a release form or agreement. Begin by reading the guidelines carefully to determine if you qualify to enter the contest. For instance, one contest may require script entries to have a female protagonist, while another may call for two-thirds of each script to have Boston exteriors. If your script complies with the qualifications, then continue. If a requirement eliminates your script, don't waste your time. Go to the next contest.

Contest guidelines also include information such as the entry deadline, the date that the results will be announced, the script parameters (number of pages, length of synopsis), entry fee instructions, and mailing directions. Some contests request that you also send a self-addressed stamped postcard so they can acknowledge receipt of your submission.

The entry or application forms are easy to fill out. They ask for the writer's contact information. In addition, some ask for the genre, and a logline and/or a synopsis of the script. Some applications ask questions about the writer's background and professional status. Don't be surprised to see a release agreement as part of the application, or as a separate page. The release has the writer attest to the fact that the material being submitted is the original work of that writer. If it isn't, the release basically relieves the contest holder of any and all liabilities, claims, demands, losses, costs, damages, judgments, and expenses with regard to the submitted script. The release may also recap the terms of the contest, having the writer sign off on them. For example: the contest holder may not be obligated to return the script to the writer.

If you are interested in entering your script in a contest, be sure to turn to page 290 of the Resource List for a substantial selection of legitimate competitions. The contests that we list are recognized in the industry. The winners and the semi-finalists get more attention than those of lesser-known contests that are not industry-affiliated. You can also find contests listed in screenwriters' magazines, trade papers, and on many websites. Go to any good

---

PROSE FROM A PRO

Passion Pays Off
by Phillip M. Goldfarb

Unit Production Manager, Associate Producer, Line Producer, Co-Producer, and Executive Producer. Film credits: *All The Right Moves, Taps, Taxi Driver.* Episodic TV credits: *L.A. Law, Doogie Howser, NYPD Blue, Casey's Shadow.*

Producers can make calculated guesses as to what might work and what might not work. It's not that we have a lock on it. As Steven Bochco always points out, "If research really worked, we'd make only hits." Obviously, research works up to a point, but, as William Goldman said, "Nobody knows anything," and given the fact that they know they don't know anything, the writers who come in firmly believing in what they've written, stand a much better chance of getting heard and getting sold because production execs want to believe. A writer's absolute belief in his own work allows execs to go along because they can say that he sounded like he knew what he was talking about. Production executives may read fifty scripts, maybe more, over a month's time, and they're looking for something to believe in. They're looking for something that they can adopt, something that they can embrace. If the passion is there, it gives them a greater opportunity to find that passion and make it their own.

search engine, such as yahoo.com, dogpile.com, altavista.com, or google.com and type in "screenwriting contests" for a sizeable listing of contest sites. Also, contact your state film commissioner and chamber of commerce to see if they offer contests or other opportunities for screenwriters (you'll find their phone numbers listed under "State Offices" of your telephone book).You can feel confident about the legitimacy of these competitions.

Keep in mind that the most desirable contests to enter and win are those that have an affiliation or sponsorship with industry-recognized companies or organizations. They are also the most popular, which means they have the most entrants. If you have confidence in your script, go for it! Here's hoping there's a prize with your name on it.

Apply for Fellowships

People often shudder at the thought of applying for a fellowship. You hear phrases such as, "It's such a tedious process." "There's so much work involved." Well, not so in show business. The entry process for screenwriting fellowships is basically the same as for screenwriting contests. Contests and fellowships are so much alike, in fact, that they are usually listed together.

Fellowships are prestigious competitions for writers to win. They receive lots of industry attention and their financial rewards are superior to those given in most contests. Furthermore, a fellowship usually involves the nurturing of a screenwriter's career, along with a commitment on the writer's part to write another script. The popularity of screenwriting fellowships is reflected in the tremendous numbers of entrants.

After a year of work, Mike Rich, at age forty-one, completed his first screenplay and entered it in the notable Nicholl Fellowship. Among the 4,500 entries, Mike's script was selected as one of the five final fellows, with a prize of $25,000. Meanwhile, a friend of Mike's had given his script to her agent-husband who sold it a week before the final Nicholl Fellowship awards were announced. The good news was that the sale of Mike's script made him a professional writer; the bad news was that his professional-writer status disqualified him from receiving the fellowship. The best news is that the script Mike wrote was *Finding Forrester,* and we don't have to worry about his not receiving that $25,000 fellowship. Mike Rich felt that the attention his script had received as a Nicholl Fellowship contender helped get his script read and ultimately sold.

The point of this story is to show the impact a screenwriting fellowship can have on a writer's work. This story also gives you a dose of reality . . . only five finalists were chosen out of 4,500 entrants. Mike Rich made it, so why not you? If you're interested in applying for a fellowship, check out the listing beginning on page 293 of the Resource List.

THE BOTTOM LINE

Believe in yourself. Believe in your work. If what you're doing isn't getting results, reinvent your approach. Be creative, not only in your writing, but in your ongoing sales effort.

Patience and perseverance are a winning combination. For every spec script that sells soon after it was written, there are hundreds of scripts that have taken years to get a deal. *Back to the Future*, written by Bob Gale & Robert Zemeckis, took four years to get made after being turned down by practically everyone. The first draft of *Trespass* by the same writing team was written in 1977 and was made fourteen years later. This is just one example of oh-so-many. The *From Script to Screen* stories found at the end of each chapter have given you insight as to how deals happen and how long it can take. Even when you get a deal, it doesn't necessarily mean your film is going to be in theaters any time soon. Screenwriter Mitchell Kapner (*The Whole Nine Yards*) has a script that has been in active development for so long that the major studio's creative exec who bought it—the first property he ever bought—is now president of that studio. Incidentally, at the time of this writing, there's a movie star attached to the script and the green light is imminent.

You've got to work at making it happen, and be willing to hang in until it does. To paraphrase television writer and novelist Dennis Foley, "Show Business is the only business where you cannot fail. You can only quit trying."

This piece is a little different from the others in the book. Oh sure, Jim tells how *White Water Rebels* eventually made it to the small screen as a television movie, but mostly, he shares his insights, observations, and industry advice for writers. Considering that his credits as a screenwriter include *Rush Hour, Stakeout, Another Stakeout, Gang Related, Operation Dumbo Drop, Disorganized Crime, Class, Secret Admirer, American Dreamer, Up the Creek, The Hidden,* and *Miracles,* his words are worthwhile reading.

White Water Rebels

Written by Jim Kouf

For Starters...

For a writer to get started, he or she has to write as good a script as possible. There's not a lot of great writing going on out there.

There's no great trick to it, you just have to write well. The story's got to be good. There's got to be good twists. The dialogue has to be sharp. The characters have to be great. You have to start out trying to write an Academy Award-winning script. If you write well, you'll get hired and you'll make a living at it.

That spec script is your best calling card. It's better than whatever school you went to; it's better than your resume. What really counts is what you can put on that page. You've got to sweat blood to get the first script done right. The problem with a lot of young writers, I find, is they tell you how good their script is, and usually, it's not the case. So you should have other people read your script—professionals more than just the neighbor because the neighbor doesn't know what makes a good script. It's a hard thing to describe. I think it's a kind of a gut instinct. You either know how to do it or you don't. I'm not sure this kind of thing can be taught and learned. A person is either witty and funny or not. I don't know how you teach someone to be funny. You must have a feeling for it. Get that script into the best shape possible and people will either produce it or hire you to tell the next story you want to do, or have you fix a story that they've got.

You have no control over whether or not that spec script gets made, but if the writing is good enough, you will get your foot in the door to start making a living as a writer. That's the way I've seen it work for a lot of people. That's the way it's worked for me.

Filling in the Details

I was an English major, history minor and wrote only plays in college. When I graduated, I really didn't know what a screenplay was. I had to get a copy of a screenplay in order to become familiar with the form. I didn't go to film school. It wasn't a requirement when I started. I think it helps now, especially if you want to be a director.

When I started, it was a much smaller business. There were only about five studios and then there were the foreign groups that paid next-to-nothing but kept you employed. I wrote this script called *White Water Rebels*. It was probably the sixth script I had written. My agent at the time was working in the mail room at ICM. It was Dan Petrie Jr., who went on to became a successful writer and the president of the WGAw.

Dan and I go way back. He optioned my script to his mother for $500. What I learned from Dorothea Petrie, a very well-known television producer, is the importance of rewriting. She made me rewrite again and again and again. I didn't understand that, having not gone to film school. I just thought you wrote the script and that was it and they made it. I didn't realize that you have to just beat it to death or beat yourself to death to get it right. That was a great lesson I learned from her. With all the rewriting, she ultimately could not get the movie made.

Under Jack Gilardi's letterhead—he was a *real* agent at ICM—Dan Jr. took the script and sent it out to foreign guys, and other low-budget groups. They loved the writing, and while they didn't want to make the movie, they hired me to fix their scripts. I was able to earn a living as a writer, fixing other people's scripts. I had a bit of a knack for it and they gave me the opportunity. It was learn and earn by doing. I worked on a lot of low-budget films. That allowed me the freedom to come up with my own ideas.

Meanwhile, *White Water Rebels* kept making the rounds. Somebody would like it here, but they didn't want to make it; somebody would like it there, but they didn't want to make it either, but it got me going as a writer. It opened all the doors for me. I got to the point where I didn't care if it didn't get made.

At least five years after I had written *White Water Rebels,* I gave it to a friend of mine who was trying to get stuff going in television and she's the one who got it made at CBS.

Back to the Early Days

Writer David Greenwalt and I were Dan Jr.'s only clients when he started out at the agency. One day, Dan came up with a writing job. Instead of one of Dan's clients having a job and the other one not having a job, we thought we'd do the job together. So Dan sold us as a writing team, although we had never written anything as a team. David and I went on to work together for about ten years. We wrote *Class, American Dreamer,* and *Secret Admirer.*

It Can Happen

With *Stakeout,* I was at Disney then. They were much smaller at the time. Katzenberg, Eisner and Hoberman had just taken over the studio. I was at Paramount with Katzenberg before that and I followed him to Disney. So it was just going up to him and saying, "This is the story I'd like to do." I remember pitching *Stakeout* to David Hoberman and he said, "Yeah, do it!" I went away and wrote it. I think they pretty much made the first draft. And the movie came out pretty close to the script. That was one of those too easy experiences. I pitched it, wrote it and we were in production within a year. There was very little pain and suffering on that movie. That's not usually the case.

Be Where the Action Is

Television is even harder to break into than features. It's a real closed shop. Unless you know somebody to get your script read in the television world, I don't know how you break in. It used to be, when I started, you could write a great script and someone would read it somewhere and you could get going. But now, there's such a flood because there are so many film schools, and every university has a film department. You have all of these people writing screenplays and trying to get them read.

I get a lot of these query letters and I don't think they work. I don't read them. I don't know who actually does. The best way to get into the business is to get a job in the business. Don't try to write from Chicago or somewhere in South Dakota. Move to Los Angeles or New York. Get a job whether it's as a production assistant or a reader. Whatever it is, get a job working in the industry, even if they pay you $2 an hour. When you're working in the industry, you'll meet the director, you'll meet the star, you'll meet somebody somewhere who will read your script and can do something about it.

Last year, an assistant on *Buffy the Vampire Slayer* and on *Angel* consistently came up with good ideas for the writers. David Greenwalt, the executive producer of the two shows, made this former assistant a staff writer on *Angel* this season.

If you come up with good ideas and you're on the inside, people will listen to you. If you're on the outside submitting stuff, it's been my experience that people just don't have enough time to read it because there's so much material generated by the writers who are already in the business.

To try to do it at arm's length is extremely difficult. If you want to be in Hollywood, and you want to be in show business, then be in it. Come out here and jump into the pool. There's no reason why you shouldn't start as a production assistant or a reader or just be out here. You've got to live, eat and breathe it for a period of time. I think that's the only way, unless you're coming in with a track record as a playwright or novelist, or you were born into the business.

Married to the Mob

Written by Barry Strugatz & Mark R. Burns
This story by Barry Strugatz.

I attended NYU undergraduate film school, then worked as a production assistant and location scout for many years on features in New York City. I was able to work for and observe such great directors as Milos Forman, Woody Allen, and Peter Bogdanovich.

All the while, I wrote scripts that were constantly rejected (although there were a couple of pathetic options along the way). When I got out of school, I teamed up with my classmate Mark Burns and we wrote a spec script that didn't sell. Then a number of years later, we teamed up again and wrote another script that we couldn't sell, but it got us an agent, Annette Van Duren, who was a friend of a friend.

Mark and I came up with several ideas we thought were commercial, that the studios would like. Our agent brought us out to Los Angeles for an intense week of pitching. We struck out, but decided to give it another shot and write something that we

wanted to, and not try to second guess what "they" were looking for. We sat down and wrote *Married to the Mob* in ten weeks. Our agent got it to two new producers Bill Todman and Joel Simon. They in turn got it to Jon Sheinberg who was then a VP at Orion Pictures. Sheinberg gave it to Jonathan Demme. He liked it. We had a deal within a few short weeks of finishing the script.

"We were very lucky. The making of *Mob* was a great experience. The way it should always be, but rarely is. I learned so much throughout the process. Orion was an ideal studio to work with. Their philosophy was to get the writer together with the director and leave them alone. Demme and his producer Ed Saxon made us welcome throughout. They made working on the rewrites an exciting, fun challenge. Michelle Pfeiffer was brilliant in the lead role and a delight to work with—and she didn't change one word!

CONCLUSION

"A professional writer is an amateur who didn't quit."
—Richard Bach

If you've reached this page in the book, you will know exactly what you have to do to sell your spec script, and you probably have the determination to do it—unless you've looked for shortcuts and you've skipped chapters. If that's the case, go back and read it all until you learn your way here. There's a good chance that your career will profit by it.

For those of you who go by the book . . . this book . . . and sell your spec script, it will probably happen in an outrageous way that no one, especially you, could anticipate or predict. If you will then step back and view the big picture, you will most likely see that your golden opportunity came to you as a result of doing everything you did—initiating contacts, sending query letters, submitting scripts, making follow-up calls—exactly the way you did it. Those will have been the steps needed to be taken to get you down the path that ultimately resulted in a deal.

Until you get that deal, all you have is the process and the dream. Make the process of selling your script a wonderful adventure, and enjoy every aspect of the journey. Make the dream of selling your script the motivation that keeps you going.

Close your eyes—*Not now! After you've read this*—and imagine the thrill of sitting in a dark movie theater with a few hundred other people, watching the credits. You see the Stars' names . . . And . . . With . . . Introducing . . . Casting by, Costume Designer—*getting close*—Music Supervisor, Music Composed by, Production Designer—*getting closer*—Editor, Director of Photography, Executive Producer, Co-Producer, Produced by—*finally*—Written by . . . and there it is—your name. Feel that feeling of sheer joy. Imprint that feeling in your mind. Recreate that feeling as you write, as you send out query letters and scripts, as you network, as you rewrite, when you take a meeting, or get someone on the horn, or pitch an idea, or do lunch, or schmooze with people in the industry. If you truly love being a writer, and you can keep deriving joy from the process, consider yourself successful. If you sell your script, consider yourself successful and richer. If your script is produced, consider yourself successful, richer, and lucky.

The following screenwriter acknowledgment is from David Brown, producer of many successful films including *Jaws, The Player, A Few Good Men,* and *Chocolat.* Let his words empower and inspire you.

Nothing moves without the script. It is the acorn from which the oak of a movie grows. A screenplay starts the process of budgeting, casting, hiring of key personnel. Offices are redecorated, monster Winnebagos are leased, trucks loaded with equipment roll to locations, artists feverishly create scene sketches. Following the shoot, the post-production crew, the music and sound technicians and the marketing mavens come aboard. A hundred million dollars may well be spent based on 120 pages or so of a screenplay by someone who might not even be invited to the set, the dub, the mix or the scoring session, although the hundreds of men and women, including the director and stars who have worked on the picture, owe their jobs to the culmination of the writer's work.

And finally, there are the words of Steven Spielberg: "It all begins on the page." May your pages be the ones that get produced.

We invite you to share your good news with us. If you find the time and a few well-chosen words, e-mail us at Scriptalking@aol.com or snail-mail us:

> Wilen Sisters
> PO Box 230416
> Ansonia Station
> New York, NY 10023–0416

Every good wish,
Lydia Wilen & Joan Wilen

RESOURCE LIST

The resources on the following pages were selected with great care, hoping to help screenwriters save time in locating the best of everything a writer may want or need. We checked and rechecked each company, organization and publication, each phone number, street and e-mail address, and website. Even so, information of this sort changes often. Be sure to confirm the accuracy of the listing by visiting the website and/or calling before you drop in, subscribe to, send a check to, or participate in any way with any of the resources.

RECOMMENDED READING

We know you're busy sending out query letters and scripts, working on your next script, schmoozing, taking meetings, doing lunch, signing contracts, getting ready for awards dinners—so we've kept our recommendations to a select and varied few. Between pitch sessions and acceptance speeches, check out these books that can help round out a writer's education.

Adventures in the Screen Trade: A Personal View
of Hollywood and Screenwriting
by William Goldman. New York: Warner Books, 1983.
Mr. Goldman, a super-successful screenwriter, author, and two-time Academy Award winner, presents a personal view of Hollywood and

screenwriting in this must-read industry classic. An author who doesn't censor himself, Goldman tells it like it is with attitude, anecdotes, and advice.

All You Need to Know About the Movie and TV Business
by Gail Resnik and Scott Trost. New York: Simon & Schuster, 1996.

Written by two prominent entertainment attorneys, this book gives the reader insight into the nature of jobs in the business, and the machinations behind movie and TV deals. It is a helpful guide to the ins and outs of the deal-making process.

The Film Encyclopedia: The Most Comprehensive Encyclopedia of World Cinema in a Single Volume, Fourth Edition
by Ephraim Katz. Revised by Fred Klein and Ronald Dean Nolen. New York: Harper Resource, 2001.

This tome contains over 1,500 pages of biographies and filmographies of actors, directors, and producers, as well as screenwriters, editors, musical directors, cinematographers, and production designers. It also includes technical movie-making data. Not only is this a great reference guide, it's also a great read, thanks to the talented film historian Ephraim Katz, who set the tone and writing standard in the original edition.

The First Time I Got Paid for It: And Other Tales from the Hollywood Trenches
by Laura Shapiro and Peter Lefcourt. New York: Public Affairs, 2000.

This collection of essays by over fifty leading film and television writers is as much fun and enlightening as the "From Script to Screen" stories in this Wilen sisters' book, *How to Sell Your Screenplay.*

How to Write a Movie in 21 Days
by Viki King. New York: HarperPerennial, 1988.

The author, a script consultant and lecturer, devised the Inner Movie Method. It's a specific step-by-step process designed to get the story that is in the writer's heart onto the page . . . in three weeks.

Making a Good Script Great: A Guide for Writing and Rewriting, Second Edition
by Linda Seger. New York: Samuel French, 1994.

Author, international lecturer, and script consultant, Dr. Linda Seger emphasizes how to rewrite your script to get it on track, while preserving its original creativity.

Screenplay: The Foundations of Screenwriting
by Syd Field. New York: Dell Publishing, 1984.

Author Syd Field pinpoints the structural and stylistic elements essential to every good screenplay. He presents a step-by-step, comprehensive technique for writing the script that will succeed.

The Screenwriter Within: How to Turn the Movie in Your Head into a Salable Screenplay
by D.B. Gilles. New York: Random House/Three Rivers Press, 2000.

This screenwriting book is a little different from the others on the market because of the writing style of D.B. Gilles. He presents all of the basics —writing technique, dialogue, and character development—in a way that is like a friend visiting with you at home.

The Screenwriter's Bible: A Complete Guide to Writing, Formatting, and Selling Your Script
by David Trottier. Los Angeles: Silman-James Press, 1998.

This well-indexed handy reference book is filled with information that you can trust on every phase of writing and selling screenplays.

Story: Style, Structure, Substance, and the Principles of Screenwriting
by Robert McKee. New York: Regan Books, 1997.

Based on McKee's acclaimed screenwriting seminar, this is a comprehensive guide to the essentials of screenwriting and storytelling.

Which Lie Did I Tell? More Adventures in the Screen Trade
by William Goldman. New York: Pantheon Books, 2000.

On the back cover of the book, writer John Gregory Dunne says, "If you are thinking of going to film school, don't. Read *Which Lie Did I Tell?* instead. It will save you a great deal of money and tell you more about the realities of the picture business than any academic course of study." We agree.

The Whole Picture: Strategies for Screen-writing Success in the New Hollywood
by Richard Walter. New York: Dutton Plume, 1997.

The author, who is a lecturer and chairman of the screenwriting department at UCLA, lets the reader in on the many aspects of the writer's relationship with the art of filmmaking and the world of Hollywood.

The Writer Got Screwed (but didn't have to)
by Brooke A. Wharton. New York: HarperPerennial, 1997.

This is a helpful guide to the legal and business practices of writing for the entertainment industry.

Writing Screenplays That Sell
by Michael Hauge. New York: HarperPerennial, 1991.

Hauge is a screenwriter, independent producer, screenplay consultant, and he was a teacher for more than eleven years. He has presented his two-day intensive screenwriting seminar to over 7,000 writers and producers throughout the U.S., Canada, and England. This book evolved as a result of his outstanding experience.

Writing the Script: A Practical Guide for Films and Television
by Wells Roots. New York: Henry Holt Trade Paperback, 1979.

In the words of screenwriter Barry Strugatz, "I know there are tons of how-to screenwriting books out there by legions of cutting-edge gurus who advertise the salaries of former students. But this one book that I like is by an old-time Hollywood screenwriter, Wells Root. He clearly and concisely explains dramatic conflict and classic movie structure." Although currently out-of-print, this book is available online through amazon.com and barnesandnoble.com.

You Can Write a Movie
by Pamela Wallace. Cincinnati, OH: Writers Digest Books, 2000.

Academy Award-winning co-writer of *Witness*, Wallace provides screenwriting instructions along with savvy advice.

TRADE PUBLICATIONS

As a screenwriter, keeping your finger on the pulse of the entertainment industry is critical. The following newspapers and magazines are filled with industry news, trends, tips, interviews, who's where and buying what, and all kinds of show business scoops. They may give you a lead, or spark an idea that can pay off.

Creative Screenwriting

6404 Hollywood Boulevard, Suite 415
Los Angeles, CA 90028
Phone: 323–957–1405 / 800–SCRN–WRT
Fax: 323–957–1406
Website: www.creativescreenwriting.com

Each issue of this bimonthly magazine includes a listing of spec-script and pitch sales, along with loglines; it also includes the agents, agencies, managers, producers, and studios involved in these deals. The magazine also lists upcoming script competitions with contact and application information; presents feature articles and interviews on the business of screenwriting; and has informational columns that assist screenwriters in marketing their finished scripts. Available by subscription, *Creative Screenwriting* is also found at many large newsstands and major bookstore chains, such as Barnes and Noble.

The Hollywood Reporter

5055 Wilshire Boulevard
Los Angeles, CA 90036
Phone: 323–525–2000
Website: www.hollywoodreporter.com

Reading this daily trade publication is a great way to keep up on the latest industry happenings. Each year, *The Hollywood Reporter* publishes a special issue covering the American Film Market, and lists participating production company members. It's a good list of active indies. Available by subscription, *The Hollywood Reporter* is also found at many large newsstands and major bookstore chains, such as Barnes and Noble.

New York Screenwriter

655 Fulton Street, Suite 276
Brooklyn, NY 11217
Phone: 718–398–7197
Website: www.nyscreenwriter.com

This monthly publication bills itself as "Gotham City's Guide to Making It!" We think it has more national interest than that. Its informative editorials on getting read, represented, and produced, along with in-depth interviews with successful screenwriters, agents, producers and studio executives, provide industry insight, no matter which coast you're on (or anywhere in between). Its annual *Screenwriters Guide,* which includes how-to feature articles, lists of industry professionals, services, schools, competitions, fellowships, guilds and unions, and more, is free with a paid subscription, or you can order it without being a subscriber. Call, write, or visit the website for publication information, including subscriber rates.

Scenario

116 East 27th Street, 6th floor
New York, NY 10016
Subscription info: 800–222–2654
E-mail: info@scenariomag.com
Website: www.scenariomag.com

Each issue of *Scenario* features three complete, feature-length screenplays. What's outstanding is that they are the writers' preferred drafts—most likely the versions that first attracted the studio, producer, director, and stars. For an incredible education, read the screenplay and then watch the movie. It will give you great insight as to how a story on paper translates to the screen. To round out this educational experience, each script is accompanied by an in-depth interview with the writer, explaining the evolution of the script. *Scenario* also offers screenwriting articles and short pieces by or about writers. Leave room on your bookshelf. This is a magazine you will want to keep as a reference. Available by subscription, *Scenario* is also found at many large newsstands and major bookstore chains, such as Barnes and Noble.

Scr(i)pt Magazine

5638 Sweet Air Road
Baldwin, MD 21013
Phone: 410–592–3466
Subscriber info: 888–287–0932
Fax: 410–592–8062
E-mail: editors@scriptmag.com
Website: www.scriptmag.com

This bimonthly publication is dedicated to the art, craft, and business of writing for film. In addition to each issue's news, contest listings, market-trend analyses and interviews, there are articles and tips from some of the industry's most successfully produced writers. *Scr(i)pt* serves as both a resource for the craft of screenwriting and source of inspiration from professionals in the field. Available by subscription, *Scr(i)pt* is also found at many large newsstands and major bookstore chains, such as Barnes and Noble.

Variety

5700 Wilshire Boulevard, Suite 120
Los Angeles, CA 90036
Phone: 323–857–6600

245 West 17th Street
New York, NY 10011
Phone: 212–337–7001
Website: www.variety.com

With a daily Los Angeles edition, a daily New York edition, and a weekly bi-coastal edition, *Variety* is considered the quintessential source for current entertainment industry news. Each year at the end of June, this legendary trade publication puts out an issue that includes "Facts on Pacts," a compilation of producers (including some stars) who have on-the-lot production deals at major studios. All *Variety* editions are available by subscription. They are also found at many large newsstands in select cities, and at major bookstore chains. Visit the website for daily headlines and articles.

Written By

Writers Guild of America, West
7000 W. Third Street
Los Angeles, CA 90048
Subscriber Hotline: 888–WRITNBY
Website: www.wga.org

This excellent monthly magazine is for and by film and television writers. Each issue contains interviews with writers, and in-depth articles about the craft and business of writing. This journal is sent to every WGAw member. Non-members can call the toll-free number for a paid subscription. *Written By* is also for sale at some major bookstore chains, such as Barnes and Noble, and at large newsstands in Los Angeles.

DIRECTORIES

Industry directories are great sources for wish list contact information. They are also good places for finding new names of industry players to add to that list.

Directors Guild of America (DGA) Directory of Members

This sourcebook contains listings of DGA members, along with their contact information—an office number, the name and number of their agent or business manager—and their credits. It also includes a geographical listing of DGA members, as well as listings of ethnic minority members, women members, and agencies that are WGA signatories. The Directory is published every January or February, and can be purchased through the DGA offices. Contact information is found under "Guilds and Organizations."

Hollywood Creative Directories (HCD)

IFILM Publishing
3000 Olympic Boulevard, Suite 2525
Santa Monica, CA 90404
Phone: 310–315–4815 / 800–815–0503
Website: www.hcdonline.com

IFILM Publishing is responsible for a comprehensive series of Hollywood Creative Directories (HCD). Each directory provides valuable contact information of industry players, including agents and managers, producers, distributors, film buyers, film writers, and below-the-line talent. The directories are available in print form, as well as online. Call IFILM or visit the website for additional information.

The two most helpful directories in this series for screenwriters are *Agents & Managers* and *Producers. HCD Agents & Managers* lists over 1,500 agencies and management companies throughout the country, and over 4,700 agents, personal managers, and casting directors, including their titles, addresses, telephone and fax numbers, e-mail addresses, and websites if available. Each listing specifies the type of agency or management company, and the kinds of talent it represents. Updated versions are published twice a year.

HCD Producers is a wonderfully cross-referenced directory that lists over 1,700 production companies. It includes the names of over 8,100 producers, development executives, and other company principals, along with their titles, addresses, telephone and fax numbers, e-mail addresses, and websites if available. This directory, which is published three times a year, also lists studio and network executives, companies with studio deals, and TV shows and their staffs.

Hollywood Literary Sales

www.hollywoodlitsales.com

This site has an extraordinary online Spec Screen-play Directory—a database of screenplay sales from 1990 to the present. It lets you know who's buying and selling your type of material. Each listing is alphabetized by title and provides some or all of the following script information—a brief logline, the screenwriter, genre, agent, agency, buyer, company contact, lawyer, purchase price, and date of sale. The listings are cross-referenced by agent, agency, buyer, screenwriter, first-time sale by screenwriter, genre, lawyer, keyword, and more. The site is updated daily.

In addition to this sales directory (and a free online demo), the website offers interviews with industry players, informative articles, script coach consulting services, a forum to ask Hollywood professionals questions, and a screenplay contest database.

Writers Guild of America— Member Directory

This *Directory,* which is published every two years, contains listings of WGA members and their coast affiliation (East or West). The entries also include members' contact information—agents, managers, and office numbers—and their credits. You can purchase the *Directory* by visiting or calling the WGA office on either coast. Contact information is found under "Guilds and Organizations."

GUILDS AND ORGANIZATIONS

Academy of Motion Picture Arts and Sciences (AMPAS)

8949 Wilshire Boulevard
Beverly Hills, CA 90211–1972
Phone: 310–247–3000
Fax: 310–859–9351
Website: www.oscars.org

With over 5,000 active members who represent various aspects of filmmaking, this organization is devoted to supporting technical research and education in moviemaking. Its members nominate and vote for the Academy Awards. Membership is by invitation only.

Academy of Television Arts and Sciences (ATAS)

5220 Lankershim Boulevard
North Hollywood, CA 91601–3109
Phone: 818–754–2800
Fax: 818–761–2827
Website: www.emmys.org

The Academy is most known for its presentation of the annual Primetime Emmy Awards for national nighttime programming. The Daytime Emmy Awards are under the jurisdiction of the National Academy of Television Arts & Sciences in New York, and are administered in cooperation with the Academy.

Actors Equity Association (AEA)

5757 Wilshire Boulevard, Suite 1
Los Angeles, CA 90036
Phone: 323–634–1750
Fax: 323–634–1777

165 West 46th Street
New York, NY 10036
Phone: 212–869–8530
Fax: 212–719–9815
Website: www.actorsequity.org

This labor union represents over 40,000 American actors and stage managers who work in the professional theater. It negotiates wages and working conditions for its members, administers contracts, and enforces the provisions of various agreements with theatrical employers across the country.

Alliance of Motion Picture & Television Producers (AMPTP)

15503 Ventura Boulevard
Encino, CA 91436
Phone: 818–995–3600
Fax: 818–382–1793
Website: www.amptp.org

Film industry organization that negotiates with unions and guilds on behalf of its members. It also advises members on compliance with labor laws, and monitors governmental activities affecting the industry on local, state, and federal levels.

American Association of Producers (AAP)

15030 Venutra Boulevard, PMB 675
Sherman Oaks, CA 91403
Phone: 818–503–6102
Website: www.tvproducers.org

Formed in 1983, this association represents the needs and concerns of over 500 members from many different categories of television, feature film, and new media production personnel.

American Federation of Television and Radio Artists (AFTRA)

5757 Wilshire Boulevard, Suite 900
Los Angeles, CA 90036–3689
Phone: 323–634–8100
Fax: 323–634–8194

260 Madison Avenue, 7th Floor
New York, NY 10016–2402
Phone: 212–532–0800
Fax: 212–532–2242
Website: www.aftra.com

This is the craft union for actors and broadcasters who work on television, videotape, and radio.

American Film Marketing Association (AFMA)

10850 Wilshire Boulevard, 9th Floor
Los Angeles, CA 90024–4321
Phone: 310–446–1000
Fax: 310–446–1600
E-mail: info@afma.com
Website: www.afma.com

The trade association for the independent film and television industry. AFMA's global membership distributes and often produces the films and programs made outside the major U.S. studios.

American Film Institute (AFI)

2021 N. Western Avenue
Los Angeles, CA 90027
Phone: 323–856–7600
Fax: 323–467–4578
Website: www.afionline.org

This non-profit organization is dedicated to advancing and preserving the art of the moving image. The AFI has headquarters in Beverly Hills, California, and Washington DC. It offers classes, workshops, and seminars, and provides grants and industry internships.

Directors Guild of America (DGA)

7920 Sunset Boulevard
Los Angeles, CA 90046–3347
Phone: 310–289–2000
Agency Listing: 323–851–3671
Fax: 310–289–2029

110 West 57th Street
New York, NY 10019–3385
Phone: 212–581–0370
Fax: 212–581–1441
Website: www.dga.org

This is the trade union for film, television, and radio that represents directors, assistant directors, unit production managers, production associates, and stage managers.

Filmmakers Alliance

4420 Sunset Boulevard, Suite 716
Los Angeles, CA 90027
Phone: 323–876–0241
Fax: 323–876–0939
Website: www.filmmakersalliance.com

This largest collective of filmmakers in the world is a production-intensive organization created and managed by and for filmmakers. Its unique mutual support structure has guided the production of hundreds of shorts, features, documentaries, commercials, music videos, and more. The goal is to establish itself as a major filmmaking force, an alternative talent pool, and a model of creative self-empowerment.

Motion Picture Association of America (MPAA)

15503 Ventura Boulevard
Encino, CA 91436
Phone: 818–995–6600
Fax: 818–382–1799
Website: www.mpaa.org

One of the primary functions of this organization for movie distributors is to determine ratings for films that are released in the United States.

National Conference of Personal Managers (NCOPM)

46–12 220th Place
Bayside, NY 11361
Phone: 718–224–3616
E-mail: purcell@aol.com
Website: www.ncopm.com

Established in 1942, NCOPM is an association committed to the advancement of personal managers and their clients. Its members include personal managers who exhibit professional experience, conduct, and ethics, and have expertise in concerts, motion pictures, publishing, radio, recordings, television, and theater.

Organization of Black Screenwriters, Inc.

PO Box 70160
Los Angeles, CA 90070–0160
Phone: 323–882–4166
Website: www.obswriter.com

This international non-profit organization began in 1988 to address the lack of Black writers represented within the entertainment industry. Its goal is to assist Black screenwriters in the creation of works for film and television, and to help them present their work.

Producers Guild of America (PGA)

6363 Sunset Boulevard, 9th Floor
Los Angeles, CA 90028
Phone: 323–960–2590
Fax: 323–960–2591
Website: www.producersguildonline.com

In existence since 1950, this non-profit organization represents the interests of individual producers as career professionals in the motion picture and television industries. Its membership and affiliated membership includes over 1,500 working motion picture and television producers worldwide.

Screen Actors Guild (SAG)

5757 Wilshire Boulevard
Los Angeles, CA 90036–3600
Phone: 323–954–1600
Actors to Locate: 323–954–1600
Fax: 323–549–6603

1515 Broadway, 44th Floor
New York, NY 10036–8996
Phone: 212–944–1030
Talent Agency Dept: 212–944–6797
Fax: 212–944–6774
Website: www.sag.com

This is the craft union governing actors who work on film for television as well as for theatrical release.

Talent Managers Association (TMA)

12358 Ventura Boulevard, #611
Studio City, CA 91604
Phone: 310–205–8495
Website: www.talentmanagers.org

Founded in 1954, the Talent Managers Association is a non-profit mutual-benefit corporation. Its members include professional talent managers who have shown themselves to be ethical, knowledgeable, and skilled.

Writers Guild of America, East (WGAE)

555 West 57th Street, Suite 1230
New York, NY 10019–2967
Phone: 212–767–7800
Fax: 212–582–1909
Website: www.wgaeast.org

Writers Guild of America, West (WGAw)

7000 West 3rd Street
Los Angeles, CA 90048–4329
Phone: 323–951–4000
Agency Listing: 323–782–4502
Fax: 323–782–4800
Website: www.wga.org

The WGA is a labor union representing writers in all areas of the entertainment industry—motion picture, television, and radio. The Guild has over 12,000 members and offices on both the East and West Coasts. Although the Writers Guild East and the Writers Guild West are affiliates, each has its own officers, which form the Guild's National Council. Membership is open to anyone who is employed by a Guild signatory.

SCREENWRITING CONTESTS

In an effort to protect our readers from scam artists, we consulted an industry authority—a writer/managing editor for a screenwriting magazine who reports on contests, and whose knowledge, standards, and integrity are outstanding. The contests listed here have been deemed *legitimate* by our expert, who based her recommendations on the fact that these contests have track records—they publish the names of winners, award the guaranteed prizes, and follow through on any promises, such as introducing the winners to industry professionals.

Deadlines, entry fees, prizes, and rules change from year to year, so we have listed only the contact information for each contest. Be sure to check websites, call, or write for up-to-date entry fees and other requirements. Where applicable, we have also provided specific screenplay qualifications to help you zoom in on competitions that may be particularly appropriate for you. *Please note that just because a contest is not on our list, doesn't mean it isn't legitimate.*

American Cinema Foundation (ACF)
9911 W. Pico Boulevard, Suite 510
Los Angeles, CA 90035–2715
Phone: 310–286–9420
Fax: 310–286–7914
Website: www.cinemafoundation.com

Austin Heart of Film Screenplay Competition
1604 Nueces
Austin, TX 78701
Phone: 512–478–4795
Fax: 512–478–6205
Website: www.austinfilmfestival.org

Carl Sautter Memorial
The Scriptwriters Network
11684 Ventura Boulevard, #508
Studio City, CA 91604
Phone: 323–848–9477
Website: www.scriptwritersnetwork.com/
    compete.html

To enter the Feature/MOW, Half-Hour TV, or One-Hour TV competitions, you must be a member of the Scriptwriters Network. If you are not already a member, this means tacking on a one-time application fee and one-year membership dues to the competition entry fee.

CineStory Screenwriting Awards
University of Chicago
Gleacher Center, Suite 36
450 N. Cityfront Plaza Drive
Chicago, IL 60611
Phone: 312–464–8725 / 800–6STORY6
Website: www.cinestory.com/awards.htm

This contest consists of feature-length screenplays and short forms (35 pages or less).

The Cynosure Screenwriting Awards
3699 Wilshire Boulevard, Suite 850
Los Angeles, CA 90010
Phone: 310–855–8730
E-mail: cynosure@broadmindent.com
Website: www.broadmindent.com

This competition promotes women and minorities.

Empire Screenplay Contest
12358 Ventura Boulevard, #602
Studio City, CA 91604–2508
Phone: 661–420–9919
Website: www.geocities.com/Empirecontact/

"Film in Arizona" Screenwriting Competition
Arizona Film Commission
3800 N. Central Avenue, Building D
Phoenix, AZ 85012
Phone: 602–280–1380
Website: www.azcommerce.com
Screenplays must embrace an Arizona theme and locations.

Final Draft Screenwriting Competition
16000 Ventura Boulevard, Suite 800
Encino, CA 91436
Phone: 818–955–8995
Fax: 818–955–4422
E-mail: info@finaldraft.com
Website: www.finaldraft.com

Klasky Csupo Scriptwriting Competition
6353 Sunset Boulevard
Los Angeles, CA 90028
Phone: 323–468–3030
E-mail: writerscompetition@kaskycsupo.com
Website: www.klaskycsupo.com
This competition is for kid-appropriate seven-minute animation teleplay episodes for a series. The Klasky Csupo Production Company has done the animation for *Rugrats, Duckman,* and *The Simpsons.*

Massachusetts Film Office Screenwriters' Competition
10 Park Plaza, Suite 2310
Boston, MA 02116

Phone: 617–973–8800
Website: www.state.ma.us/film
Authentic Massachusetts locations must be included in 85 percent of each screenplay.

Maui Writers Conference
Screenwriting Competition
4821 Lankershim Boulevard, Suite F–241
North Hollywood, CA 91601
E-mail: mauiscript@aol.com
Website: www.mauiwriters.com

Monterey County Film Commission
Screenwriting Competition
PO Box 111
Monterey, CA 93942
Phone: 831–646–0910
E-mail: Filmmonterey@redshift.com
Website: www.filmmonterey.org

Nantucket Film Festival
Screenplay Competition
PO Box 688
Prince Street Station
New York, NY 10012
Phone: 212–642–6339
E-mail: info@ackfest.org
Website: www.nantucketfilmfestival.org

Nashville Screenwriters Competition
c/o Tennessee Screenwriting Association
PO Box 40194
Nashville, TN 37204–0194
Phone: 615–316–9448
Website: www.tennscreen.com

Nebraska Screenwriting Contest
Nebraska Film Office
PO Box 98907
Lincoln, NE 68509–8907

Phone: 402–471–3680 / 800–228–4307
Fax: 402–476–4356
E-mail: Laurier@filmnebraska.org
Website: www.filmnebraska.org

Nevada Film Office Annual Screenplay Competition

555 E. Washington Avenue, Suite 5400
Las Vegas, NV 89101
Phone: 720–486–2711 / 877–NEV–FILM
Fax: 720–486–2712
Website: www.nevadafilm.com

Authentic Nevada locations must be included in 75 percent of each screenplay.

New Century Writer Awards

32 Alfred Street, Suite B
New Haven, CT 06512–3927
Phone: 203–469–8824
Fax: 203–468–0333
E-mail: newcenturywriter@yahoo.com
Website: www.newcenturywriter.org

This contest includes screenplays, stage plays, short stories, and novel excerpts.

The New York International Latino Film Festival

250 West 26th Street, 4th Floor
New York, NY 10001
Phone: 212–726–2358
Website: www.nylatinofilm.com

This competition, presented by MTV FILMS, is open only to Latino writers with scripts of any genre.

Organization of Black Screenwriters (OBS)

PO Box 70160
Los Angeles, CA 90070–0160
Hotline: 323–882–4166

E-mail: obswriter@compuserve.com
Website: www.obswriter.com

Categories of this competition include feature-length screenplays, spec scripts for current hour-long and half-hour television shows, and original television pilot scripts. Open to Black writers only.

Project Greenlight

LivePlanet, Inc.
7610 Beverly Boulevard
PO Box 48649
Los Angeles, CA 90048
Website: www.projectgreenlight.com

The online Project Greenlight contest is sponsored by LivePlanet, in conjunction with Miramax Film Corp. and Home Box Office (HBO).

Rhode Island International Film Festival

Brooks Pharmacy Screenplay Competition
c/o RIFF
PO Box 162
Newport, RI 02840
Phone: 401–861–4445
Fax: 401–847–7590
E-mail: flicksart@aol.com
Website: www.film-festival.org

Santa Clarita International Film Festival

Screenplay Competition
PO Box 801507
Santa Clarita, CA 91380–1507
Phone: 805–257–3131
Fax: 805–250–0167
Website: www.sciff.org

This competition is for socially responsible films and screenplays that are suitable for a general audience, and express a fundamental respect for the positive values of life. The acceptable genres include drama, comedy, animation, and sci-fi/adventure.

**Santa Monica Film Festival's
MOXIE! Awards**
MOXIE!/SMFF
3000 W. Olympic Boulevard
Santa Monica, CA 90404
Phone: 310–264–4274
Fax: 310–388–1538
Website: www.smff.com
Acceptable screenplay genres for this competition include drama and comedy.

The Slamdance Screenplay Competition
5526 Hollywood Boulevard, #520
Los Angeles, CA 90028
Phone: 323–466–1786
Fax: 323–466–1784
E-mail: mail@slamdance.com
Website: www.slamdance.com
This competition accepts feature screenplays that are 70 to 140 pages in length.

Sundance Institute
Film Feature Program
8857 W. Olympic Boulevard
Beverly Hills, CA 90211
Phone: 310–360–1981
Fax: 310–360–1969
E-mail: featurefilmprogram@sundance.org
Website: www.sundance.org

FELLOWSHIPS

The entry process for screenwriting fellowships is basically the same as it is for screenwriting contests. Be sure to check websites, call, or write for up-to-date details on deadlines, entry fees, prizes, and rules.

Chesterfield Film Co.
Writer's Film Project
1158 26th Street, Box 544
Santa Monica, CA 90403
Phone: 213–683–3977
E-mail: info@chesterfield-co.com
Website: www.chesterfield-co.com/html/wfp.html

New York Foundation for the Arts
Artists' Fellowship
155 Avenue of the Americas, 14th Floor
New York, NY 10013
Phone: 212–366–6900 ext. 217
Fax: 212–366–1778
E-mail: nyfaafp@nyfa.org
Website: www.nyfa.org

Nicholl Fellowships in Screenwriting
Academy of Motion Picture Arts and Science
8949 Wilshire Boulevard
Beverly Hills, CA 90211–1972
Phone: 310–247–3000
E-mail: nicholl@oscars.org
Website: www.oscars.org/nicholl/index.html

**Nickelodeon Productions Fellowship
Program**
2600 Colorado Avenue, 2nd Floor
Los Angeles, CA 90404
Phone: 310–752–8880
Website: www.fellowshipprogram.nick.com

**Walt Disney Studios/ABC Writers
Fellowship**
Fellowship Program Administrator
500 South Buena Vista Street
Burbank, CA 91521
Phone: 818 –560–6894
Website: www.members.tripod.com/~disfel/
  index.html

SCRIPT REGISTRATION AND COPYRIGHT

Registering and/or copyrighting your material is never having to say, "Oops! I really should have . . ." Call, write, or check online for current registration procedures and fees.

It is not necessary for you to be a member of the Writers Guild of America, East or West, to be able to take advantage of its script registering service.

Writers Guild of America, East (WGAE)

555 West 57th Street, Suite 1230
New York, NY 10019–2967
Phone: 212–767–7800
Fax: 212–582–1909
Website: www.wgaeast.org

Writers Guild of America, West (WGAw)

7000 West 3rd Street
Los Angeles, CA 90048–4329
Phone: 323–951–4000
Registration: 323–782–4500
Fax: 323–782–4803
Website: www.wga.org

U.S. Copyright Office

Library of Congress
101 Independence Avenue, SE
Washington, DC 20559–6000
Phone: 202–707–3000 (to speak to a staff
             member for information)
        202–707–9100 (to leave a message
             requesting an application form)
Website: www.loc.gov/copyright

SCRIPT CONSULTANTS

If your spec script is getting read but not optioned or bought, and the feedback has not been encouraging, you may want to have it professionally analyzed by a script consultant before reworking it. With countless consultants across the country, it can be difficult zeroing in on one. Start by asking anyone you know in the business for personal recommendations, or investigate any of the names we have recommended in the following list. Before you plunk down your money for this service, review the guidelines for analyzing script consultants on page 270. Be sure to determine whether or not the consultant's method of working is in keeping with your needs and expectations.

Marilyn Horowitz

Script Doctor, Script Consultant, Script Coach
New York, NY
Phone: 212–496–9631
Fax: 212–877–3069
E-mail: MIHorowitz@aol.com
Price Range: $250 – $500

Melody Jackson

Smart Girl Productions, Inc.
15030 Ventura Boulevard, #914
Sherman Oaks, CA 91403
Phone: 818–907–6511
Fax: 818–990–5293
E-mail: smartgirls@smartgirlsprod.com
Website: www.smartgirlsprod.com
Price Range: $295 – $1,295

Dara Marks

Script Consultant
513 Pleasant Avenue
Ojai, CA 93023

Phone: 805–640–1307
Fax: 805–640–1239
E-mail: dara@ojai.net
Website: www.daramarks.com
Price Range: $1,000 – $1,500

Howard Meibach
The Script Coach
Phone: 310–828–4946 (9AM – 5PM PST)
Website: Hollywoodlitsales.com
Price Range: $200 – $300

Peter Mellenkamp
Script Consultation/Story Analysis
3668 Motor Avenue, #312
Los Angeles, CA 90034
Phone: 310–204–4561
Fax: 310–253–5005
Website: www.members.aol.com/Petemellen/
    indexhome.htm
Price Range: $195 – $500

Jeff Newman
StoryNotes
15721 Brighton Avenue, #D
Gardena, CA 90247
Phone/Fax: 310–715–6455
Website: www.storynotes.com
Price Range: $300 – $1,000

ScriptSharks
1024 North Orange Drive
Hollywood, CA 90038
E-mail: ScriptSharks@ifilm.com
Website: www.scriptsharks.com

ScriptSharks' staff of industry professionals will read, analyze, and fill out a coverage report on your script, and then give it a RECOMMEND, CONSIDER, or PASS rating. Scripts that receive a CONSIDER or RECOMMEND are placed on the IFILMpro SpecMarket (www.ifilmpro.com), which has over 20,000 industry subscribers, including agents, managers, development/studio executives, and talent. If your script receives a RECOMMEND, ScripSharks will proactively try to set you up with a Hollywood agent. For an additional fee, writers whose work get a PASS, may be interested in getting Story Notes—five to eight pages of studio-style notes, addressing the main elements of the work. Also for a fee, you can get a Treatment Analysis—a two- to four-page report on your story, its market feasibility, and next-step suggestions.

SCHOOLS

With countless writing seminars and schools across the country, in addition to colleges offering screenwriting courses, it can be difficult zeroing in on the best one for you. Start by asking anyone you know in the business for personal recommendations, or by investigating the two popular and diverse schools listed below. Before signing up for any seminar, workshop, class, or course, ask questions to determine whether or not the method of teaching, curriculum, and price are in keeping with your needs and expectations.

Gotham Writers' Workshop
1841 Broadway, Suite 809
New York, NY 10023
Phone: 212–WRITERS / 877–WRITERS
Fax: 212–307–6325
Website: www.writingclasses.com

Gotham Writers' Workshop (GWW) is the country's largest private creative writing school and offers ten-week screenwriting, television writing, and playwriting classes. It also offers a ten-week workshop called "Film Analysis From the Screenwriter's Point of View." Call for a brochure, or check out the website to learn more about its classes, as well as its interactive, comprehensive, and easy-to-use online workshops. GWW also offers one-day workshops, private instruction, and a program for young writers.

Hollywood Film Institute (HFI)

PO Box 481252
Los Angeles, CA 90048
Phone: 800–366–3456
Website: www.webfilmschool.com

Hollywood Film Institute is the number-one independent film school of its kind in North America. According to founder Dov S-S Simens, HFI's weekend crash courses in screenwriting, producing, and directing are for adults who want the most information in the shortest time.

WEBSITES

Our select collection of websites has just about everything a screenwriter needs . . . yes, even job opportunities. The following list is organized alphabetically, according to the website's most useful or outstanding feature. We suggest that you read through each listing because some websites have many useful features. Better yet, see for yourself by visiting each site. You'll find it worth your time.

America's Greatest Movies

www.afionline.org/century/

This site has the American Film Institute's list of America's 100 greatest movies, selected by 1,500 leaders of the American movie community.

Essays and Advice

www.wordplayer.com

This site has dozens of extremely well-written essays covering all facets of screenwriting, writ-

ten by working screenwriters and other Hollywood industry professionals, including directors, producers, development executives, and agents. The home page refers to the material as, "Collectively, a full course in writing screenplays from an insider's perspective."

Film Festivals

www.filmfestivals.com

This site lists film festivals around the world, and the films that have made it into the festivals.

Internet Movie Database

www.IMDb.com

This priceless source lists over 260,000 film and television productions made since 1892, about a half-million actors, and over 50,000 directors, and hundreds of thousands producers and writers. We suggest you take the website's "Guided Tour" to learn all it has to offer.

Job Board

www.hcdonline.com

In addition to learning about the Hollywood Creative Directories that are published by IFILM Publishing, this site has job listings for a variety of industry positions and opportunities.

Links

www.timelapse.com

American Time-Lapse is a company specializing in time-lapse special effects and stock footage. Click on "TVLink" for an awesome assortment of well-organized links to everything pertaining to film and television.

www.scriptsales.com

In addition to the extraordinary "Done Deal Links," this website has agency and manager lists, all kinds of resources, writing reference books, book reviews, industry news, interviews, articles, and more.

Print on Demand Publishers

www.xlibris.com

www.iUniverse.com

www.stbarthelemypress.com

In Chapter 8, we talked about possibly turning your script into a novel. These online publishers provide print-on-demand service (POD), and will print books one at a time.

Screenplays

www.ZZippeddskripptzz.com

This is a database with hundreds of downloadable produced screenplays.

Screenplays, Job Listings, Contests, Development Hell, Dialogue, Plot/Structure, Supplies, Television Writing

www.screenwriting.about.com

About.com bills itself as the Human Internet, where real people help you get whatever you want from the Web. They've proven themselves with regard to screenwriters.

Contests, Job Listings, and More

www.moviebytes.com

This website is known for its directory of screenwriting contests and updated contest news. It also has a list of agents and managers, job listings for writers, a free newsletter, and industry news.

Software, Books, Seminars on Tape, Training Cassette Sets

www.writersstore.com

In addition to essentials for writers, the Writers Store, which is an actual store located in Los Angeles, offers helpful information about writing seminars and workshops.

www.masterfreelancer.com

This site has a large selection of screenwriting and marketing magazines, plus free downloads, writers' web events, and a freelance job market. It also offers a weekly edition of *Freelancing for Money* for which you have to subscribe. Each issue contains between twenty to thirty-plus freelance writing opportunities. As an extra bonus, each issue features about ten to fifteen detailed listings of cash-giving contests, grants, and fellowships.

www.write-brain.com

This site offers product recommendations, a book section that lists selected writing resources, and a research section that provides expert information on various writing topics. It also features extensive links that connect to areas of interest to writers, including guilds, organizations, classes, and much more.

Spec Script Sales

www.hollywoodlitsales.com

In addition to Hollywood Literary Sales' online spec-script sales directory, this site is one of the best sources for breaking entertainment news, interviews, and articles. It also provides a screenplay contest database, a resource links database, and lists of thoughtfully chosen production companies, agencies, management companies, and law firms. The site also lists producers seeking material, and provides a forum to ask Hollywood professionals questions. Finally, Hollywood Literary Sales offers a free newsletter.

Writers' Groups

www.asascreenwriters.com

The American Screenwriters Association was organized for educational purposes, including the promotion and encouragement of the public's participation and knowledge of screenwriting as a literary art form. This site has plenty of worthwhile information, including a list of agents, links, and information on how to start a writers' group.

SOFTWARE PROGRAMS

There is a big selection of screenwriting software on the market. We've listed what we perceive to be the two most popular scriptwriting programs in the industry. Both programs excel at professionally formatting scripts according to industry standards, and are available at most large computer stores. Check out both websites for the latest versions and features offered for each program, and for free demos.

Movie Magic Screenwriter 2000
Screenplay Systems, Inc.
150 E. Olive Avenue, Suite 203
Burbank, CA 91502–1849
Phone: 800–84–STORY
Website: www.screenplay.com

Final Draft
Final Draft, Inc.
16000 Ventura Boulevard, Suite 800
Encino, CA 91436
Phone: 800–231–4055
Website: www.finaldraft.com

CAREER ENHANCERS

Spec Script Marketplace
PO Box 1365
Santa Monica, CA 90406
Phone: 310–396–1662
Fax: 310–399–6196
E-mail: scriptmarketplace@compuserve.com
Website: www.scriptmarketplace.com

This company offers two valuable marketing services for screenwriters. It lists scripts that are for sale in a bimonthly print publication, which is sent to over 1,300 script buyers, including producers, and development and studio executives. The scripts are arranged by genre, and each has a synopsis of fifty words or less. In addition, Spec Script Marketplace offers writers the opportunity to pitch their scripts—four per year—in five-minute one-on-one private appointments with development executives from production companies, major studios, and independent producers, as well as network and cable television producers. Call or visit the website for information regarding rates, publishing deadlines, and upcoming pitch dates.

Career Counselor
Donie A. Nelson
Career Strategies for Writers
10736 Jefferson Boulevard, #508
Culver City, CA 90230–4969
Phone: 310–204–6808
Fax: 310–839–3985
E-mail: wrtrconsult@earthlink.net

Donie Nelson is an industry professional with twenty years of impressive and diverse experience. Her broad-based background in feature films, prime-time network, first-run syndication, and cable television has prepared her to offer a unique mentoring service for writers. Donie assists clients in setting career and marketing goals, and formulating strategies for reaching them. She will review query letters, read scripts, and then give you the kind of help you need, whether it be a list of producers to target, or referrals to agents, script consultants, classes, online service, or books. Depending on the service provided, Donie's rates range from $75 to $100 per hour.

About the Authors

Lydia Wilen and Joan Wilen have written and sold feature film scripts and a TV movie. The Wilen sisters have also written a number of best-selling books, including *Chicken Soup & Other Folk Remedies*, the sequel, *More Chicken Soup & Other Folk Remedies*, and *Shoes in the Freezer, Beer in the Flower Bed*. As journalists, Lydia and Joan have written articles for a wide variety of magazines and newspapers, including *Parade* and the *New York Daily News*. The Wilens are currently writing a new screenplay.

$\mathcal{I}$NDEX

A Soldier's Story, making of, 123–124

Actors, as film industry players, 118–119, 126

Actors Equity Association (AEA), 148–149

AEA. *See* Actors Equity Association (AEA).

Agents/Agencies, 95–98, 103, 125–126, 135

Above-the-line budget, 9

Academy of Motion Picture Arts and Sciences (AMPAS), 9

Act breaks, 9, 13

Action (genre), 43

Action points. *See* Plot points.

Action-Adventure (genre). *See* Action; Adventure.

Action-Suspense (genre). *See* Action; Suspense.

Adaptation of written work, 9

Adventure (genre), 43

"Advice to the Writer Who Just Finished a First Spec Script" (McGibbon & Parriott), 10

AFI. *See* American Film Institute.

AFM. *See* American Film Market.

AFMA. *See* American Film Marketing Association.

AFTRA. *See* American Federation of Television and Radio Arts.

Agency meeting, 9

A-List, 9

Alliance of Motion Picture and Television Producers (AMPTP), 10, 236

American Federation of Television and Radio Artists (AFTRA), 10, 118–119, 149

American Film Institute (AFI), 10

American Film Market (AFM), 132

American Film Marketing Association (AFMA), 10, 92

AMPAS. *See* Academy of Motion Picture Arts and Sciences.

Ampersand, use in credits, 10, 54, 248

AMPTP. *See* Alliance of Motion Picture and Television Producers.

Analyst. *See* Script consultant.

Anderson, Jane, 8
Anguish, making of, 82–84
Animation (genre), 43
Anime movies, 10
Annotated script, 10
Anspaugh, David, 14
Antagonist, 10–11
Anticlimax, 11
Antihero, 11
Arbitration, Credit. *See* Credit
　　Arbitration.
Arc, 11. *See also* Character arc.
Arch, Jeff, 29
Archetype, 11
Arena, 11
Aristotle, 228
Assignments, writing, 242–243
At the end of the day, 11
Attachments to projects, 11
Auction sale of property, 11. *See
　　also* Bidding war.

Bach, Richard, 279
Backdoor pilot, 11
Backend, 11. *See also* Deferred
　　payment; Points.
Backstory, character's, 11
Bader, Kwyn, 230
Baggage attached to projects, 11
Bankable attachment to
　　projects, 11
Baseline, Inc., 143–146
Bass, Ron, 183, 185
Beat, 11–12
Beat sheet, 12
Below-the-line budget, 12
Berlin, Michael, 82
Between brads, 12. *See also*
　　Brads.
Biblical Epic (genre), 43

Bidding war, 12. *See also*
　　Auction sale of property.
Big Heist/Caper (genre), 43
Biograph Film Company, 89
Biography (genre), 43
Bit, 12
Blockbuster film, 12
Blue pages, 12
Box office, 12
Brads, 12
Brass, film industry, 12
Breaking the fourth wall, 12
Brown, David, 280
Brown, Rita Mae, 245
'bu, 12
Buck, 12
Buddy (genre), 43
Budget, 12
Burns, Mark R., 278
Business cards, 191–193
　　samples of, 192
Button, end-of-scene, 12
Buzz, 12

California Labor Commission,
　　96, 97
Cameo role, 12
Can, in the, 18
Cannes Film Festival, 13. *See
　　also* Film festival.
Caper (genre). *See* Big
　　Heist/Caper.
Caught, making of, 33
Certificate of authorship, 13
Certificate of registration, 81
Character arc, 13
Chayefsky, Paddy, 69
Class, enrolling in. *See* Writing
　　class, enrolling in.
Cliffhanger, 13
Climax, 11, 13, 14

Collaborators, 10, 13
　　considerations for, 247–249,
　　　251
　　sample agreement between,
　　　250
Colleary, Michael, 183, 184, 186
Comedy (genre), 43
　　Dark/Black, 43
　　Romantic, 43
　　Screwball, 43
　　Slapstick, 43
Coming-of-Age (genre), 44
Concept, film, 13
Conflict, 13, 14
Contact Reports, 214–218
Contacts
　　making, 125–126
　　sources of, 129–134. *See also*
　　　Directories.
　　verifying information on,
　　　205–207
　　See also Contact Reports;
　　　Wish list.
Contests, entering, 271–274
Contingent compensation, 13
Co-producer, 13, 111. *See also*
　　Producer.
Copyright, 78
　　length of, 80
　　notice of, 81
　　registration mark on script,
　　　54
　　registration procedure, 80–81
　　what is and isn't protected
　　　by, 78–80
Courtesy read, 13
Courtroom Drama (genre), 44
Coverage, 13, 39, 113–115
　　sample form, 114–115
　　See also Story analyst.
Cover letter, 227

Cox, Kerry, 174

Creative meeting, 13

Creative Screenwriting, 132–133

Credit, screen, 14, 243
    collaborators and, 248
    protecting, 244–246

Credit arbitration, 13, 243

Credits. *See* Credit, screen.

Crime (genre), 44

Crisis, 14

Criticism, constructive, 40

Cross between, 14. *See also* Meets.

Crossover film, 14

Dailies. *See* Rushes.

Daily Variety, 130–132

Daily Variety Gotham Edition. See Daily Variety.

Danson, Ted, 79

Date (genre), 44

Davis, Deborah Dean, 183, 185

De Vries, Peter, 218

Deal memo, 14

Deferred payment, 14

Demographics, 14

Denouement, 14

Detective/Mystery (genre), 44

Detroit Rock City, making of, 252–254

Deus ex machina, 14

Development, 14, 91, 112

Development deal, 14, 240, 242

Development executives, 112–113. *See also* Development girl (or guy).

Development girl (or guy), 14. *See also* Development executives.

Development hell, 14

DGA. *See* Directors Guild of America.

D-girl (or guy). *See* Development girl (or guy).

"Differences Between Motion Pictures and Television Films" (Goldfarb), 130–131

Directories, 134–142

Directors, as film industry players, 116, 118, 126

Directors Guild of America (DGA), 14, 118, 149
    Directory of Members, 140–141

Directrex Database, 145

Direct-to-video (DTV) films, 14

Disaster (genre), 44

Distributors, film, 14

DiVincenti, Alexis, 237, 244, 245, 247

"Do Everything" (Rossio), 103

"Do What It Takes" (Newman), 148

Documentary (genre), 44

Dovetailing of scenes, 14

Downer film, 14

Drama (genre), 44

Dramatic rights, 14

Drunks, making of, 201–202

DTV. *See* Direct-to-video (DTV) films.

Dupré, Carl V., 252

E & O insurance, 246

Eastman Kodak, 90

Edison Film Company, 89, 90

Eight-step plan. *See* Square One System Eight-Step Plan.

Eisner, Philip, 85

El Paso, 15

Entertainment lawyers, 108–110, 126

Entertainment Weekly, 95

Ephron, Delia, 70

Ephron, Nora, 29, 70

Epic, Historical (genre), 44–45

Episodic TV, 15

Erotic Drama (genre), 45

Event Horizon, making of, 85–87

Event, more, 17

Exclusivity, as contract stipulation, 15

Executive producer, 15, 111. *See also* Producer.

Exhibitors, 15

Exploitation films, 15

Exposition in dialogue, 15

Family (genre), 45

Fantasy (genre), 45

Fantasy Musical (genre), 45

Farce (genre), 45

Fast track, 15–16

Fauci, Dan, 79, 80

Feature film. *See* Motion picture.

Fee schedule, agent's, 97

Feedback, 38–41

Feel Good (genre), 45

Fellowships, applying for, 274–275

Field, Syd, 268

Film festival, 16

Film industry
    changing face of, 91–92
    facts about, 4–5
    news, keeping up with, 127
    overview of, 89–94
    terminology, 9–28

Film noir (genre), 16, 45

Film pitch. *See* Pitch, the.

Films, list of, depicting screenwriter's life, 221–222

First run, 16

First-draft screenplay, 16
First-look deal, 16
Fish-Out-of-Water (genre), 45
500 Ways to Beat the Hollywood Script Reader (Lerch), 268
Fix it in the pinks, 16. *See also* Blue pages.
Fluff, 16
Foley, Dennis, 275
Foreshadowing technique, 16–17
Fourth wall. *See* Breaking the fourth wall.
Franchise, 17. *See also* Tentpole movie.
Free option, 93–94
Free TV, 9, 16
Friday the 13th, making of, 152–154
Fuller, Charles, 123
Futuristic film, 17

Gale, Bob, 275
Gangster (genre), 45
Ganz, Lowell, 183, 184
Gelbart, Larry, 186
General Film Company, 89
Genre, 17, 42, 263
    identifying, 43–47
    making it work, 48
    plus opportunity, 49–50
Get inside the script, 17
"Getting an Actor Attached" (Goldfarb), 207
Give me more event, 17
Goals and expectations, determining your, 5–7
Gofer, 17
Golden retrievers, 17
Goldfarb, Phillip M., 6, 130, 144, 207, 273

Green light, 17
Gross player, 17
Gross points. *See* Points.
Guilds. *See* Organizations, unions, and guilds.

Hackman, Gene, 14
Hamill, Pete, 5
Hang a lantern on it, 17
Hay, Louise L., 133
HCD. *See Hollywood Creative Directory (HCD)* series.
Heat, as term describing industry player, 17
Heaven Help Us, making of, 195–198
Heavy, as term describing industry player, 17
Helm a film, 17
High concept, 17
High-budget rates, 239, 241
Hip-pocketing, 17
Holocaust (genre), 45
Hollywood Creative Directory— Agents & Managers, 103, 134–137
Hollywood Creative Directory— Producers, 112, 119, 137–140
Hollywood Creative Directory (HCD) series, 134–140. *See also Hollywood Creative Directory—Agents & Managers; Hollywood Creative Directory— Producers.*
Hollywood Literary Sales, 112, 146–148
Hollywood Reporter, The, 132
Hollywood Reporter East, The, (THR East), 132
Holzer, Erika, 49, 50
Hook, 17–18

"Hook the Reader" (Simens), 166
Hoosiers
    deferred payment and, 14
    making of, 156–160
Horowitz, Marilyn, 51
Hostage, holding a script, 18
Housekeeping deal, 18
"How to Get an Agent" (Simens), 96
Hunter, Lew, 268
Hyphenate, 18

Idiot page. *See* Synopsis.
"If It Doesn't Work, at Least It Makes for a Good Story" (Mack), 271
If-come deals, 238–239
IFILM Publishing, 134
"Importance of the Genre, The," (Goldfarb), 144
In the can, 18
Inciting scene, 18
Independent film companies, compared with major studios, 91–94
Independent movies, 4
Independent producer/ production company, 18, 126
Indies, 18, 91
    novice screen writer and, 92–94. *See also* Non-signatories.
Industry humor, 7, 205
Industry terminology. *See* Film industry, terminology.
In-house producer, 18
Ink a contract, 18
Intellectual Property Registry. *See* Writers Guild of America, Registration Service.

Internal story, 18

Internet Movie Database, 48, 118, 143

Iowa, as term describing script, 18

"It May Cost, But It May Pay" (Launer), 117

Jungle (genre), 45

Junior. *See* Lightweight.

Kapner, Mitchell, 154

Katz, William, 163, 164, 165

Kaye, James H., 239

"Key to Writing a Standout Script, The" (Lennon), 267

Knowers telling knowers, 18

Kouf, Jim, 276

Launer, Dale, 117, 186, 208, 238

Lawyers. *See* Entertainment lawyers.

"Learn to Take Criticism" (Strugatz), 40

Leave-behind, 18–19

Legs, as term describing property, 19

Lennon, Gary, 201, 267

Lerch, Jennifer, 268

Lerner, Alan Jay, 68

Levangie, Gigi, 185

Levy, Michael, 49–50

Library of Congress Copyright Office, 77, 78. *See also* Copyright.

Library shot. *See* Stock shot.

Life rights, 19

Lightweight, as term describing industry player, 19

Line producer, 19, 111. *See also* Producer.

Literary agents. *See* Agents/Agencies.

Live action, 19

Logline, 19, 162–165, 263

Long-form TV, 19

Los Angeles Daily Variety. See Daily Variety.

Love 30, making of, 199–201

Loving Jezebel, making of, 230–234

Low-budget rates, 239, 241

Mack, David, 271

Majors, 19, 91
    novice screenwriter and, 92–94
    See also Signatories.

"Make It Easy on the Eye" (Strugatz), 52

Make it muscular, 19

Making a Good Script Great (Seger), 268

Managers/Management companies, 103–105, 108, 126

Mandel, Babaloo, 183, 184

Mangan, Mona, 237

Marketability, 263–264

Married to the Mob, making of, 278

Martial Arts (genre), 45

Master script, 19

MBA. *See* Minimum Basic Agreement.

McCall, Andrea, 182
    interview with, 187–190

McGibbon, Josann, 10, 121, 243

Meet-and-greet meeting, 19

Meets, as term describing film, 19. *See also* Cross between.

Melodrama (genre). *See* Woman's Film.

Men of Honor, making of, 255–260

Military (genre), 45

Miller, Victor, 152

Minimum Basic Agreement (MBA), 19, 28, 93, 236–243

Mise en scène, 19

Mission, protagonist's, 19

Motion picture, 19

Motion Picture Association of America (MPAA), 19–20, 92

Motion Picture Patents Company (MPPC), 89, 90

Motivation, character, 20

Movie of the week (MOW), 20

Movie studio, 20

MOW. *See* Movie of the week (MOW).

MPAA. *See* Motion Picture Association of America.

MPPC. *See* Motion Picture Patents Company.

Muscular, make it, 19

Musical (genre), 46

Musical Biography (genre), 46

Mystery (genre). *See* Detective/Mystery.

Myth (genre), 46

National Conference of Personal Managers (NCOPM), 104–105, 149

"Nature of the Business, The," (Goldfarb), 6

NCOPM. *See* National Conference of Personal Managers (NCOPM).

Negative cost, 20

"Negotiating" (Launer), 238

Net points. *See* Points.

Network
    description from, 69

famous window scene from, 73–74

Network, television. *See* Television network.

New York Screenwriter, 133

Newman, David, 148, 180, 242, 244

Niad, Wendi, questions and answers with, 106–108

Nicholl Fellowship, 274

Non-signatories
    Guild members and, 236–237
    working for, 244–247

Nontheatrical distribution, 20

Notice of Copyright, 81

Numbers, box office, 20

Oedekerk, Steve, 184, 185

On a Clear Day You Can See Forever, character description from, 68

On the nose, 20

One-sheet, 20, 163, 164

Online databases, 142–148

Open market, 20

Open up a plot, 20

Option agreement, 94

Option(s), 20, 91, 94, 237–239

Organizations, unions, and guilds, 148–150

Original screenplay, 20

Orr, James, 8, 268

Out on submission, 20

Outline, screenplay, 20

Over the top, as term describing story line, 20

Over the transom, 20–21

PA application form, 80

Packaging a project, 21

Page-oner, as term describing script, 21

Palmer, Linda, 21

Pardi, Robert, 43

Parriott, Sara, 10, 121, 243

Pasadena, 21

Pass on a project, 21

"Passion Pays Off" (Goldfarb), 273

Pay or play, as contract clause, 21

Payoff, 21

Per diem, 21

Period piece, 21

Perry, Frank, 48

Pickups, film, 21

Pipeline, 21

Pitch, the, 21, 161–162
    preparing for, 162–167
    See also Pitch Meeting.

Pitch meeting, 21
    advice on, 182–186. *See also* McCall, Andrea, interview with.
    authors' experience at, 181–182
    in-person, 179–181
    See also Pitch, the.

"Pitch Meetings" (Newman), 180

Pitch session. *See* Pitch meeting.

Pizzo, Angelo, 14, 156

Planting. *See* Foreshadowing.

Players, industry, 21, 94–95
    actors, 118–119
    agents, 95–96
    development executives, 112–113
    directors, 116, 118
    entertainment lawyers, 108–110

    managers, 103–105
    producers, 110–112
    readers, 113, 115–116
    writers, 119

"Plenty of White Space" (Simens), 64

Plot points, 21

Plotline, 21

Points, 21

Polish, 22, 240, 242

Pomerantz, Edward, 33

Post. *See* Postproduction.

Postproduction, 22

Preemptive bid, 22

Premise, film. *See* Concept, film.

Premium run. *See* First run.

Preproduction, 22

Prequel, 22

Premiere magazine, 95

Principal photography, 22, 243

Print-on-demand (POD) publishers, 268–269

Priority Mail, 228

Prison (genre), 46

Producer(s)/Production companies, 22, 110–112, 126

Producer's notes, 22

Product placement, 22

Production, 22

Production bonus, 22

Production company, 22

Production cost, 264

Professional writer status, 237

Proofreading, 77

Property, 22

Protagonist, 22. *See also* Antagonist; Antihero.

Public domain, 22–23

Punch up a script, 23

Purpura, Charlie, 167, 169, 185, 195, 263

"Putting the Odds in Your Favor" (Styles), 264

Query letter, 23, 167
  analysis of sample, 177–178
  approach, problems with, 265–266
  correcting problems of, 262–263
  customizing, 207–208
  evaluating results of, 223
  follow-up call to, 219–220
  formatting suggestions, 168
  mailing of, 218–219, 220
  sample of, 174–175, 177
  waiting for response to, 219
  what to and what not to include, 167–168, 171–174
  what to expect from, 175
Quote, 23

Ramp it up, 23
Raucher, Herman, 87
Reader. *See* Story analyst.
Record-keeping system, 208–218
Registration of work, 77–81
Rejections, 261–262
  identifying reasons for, 262–270
  learning from, 267
Release form. *See* Submission agreement.
Residuals, 23
Resolution, 23
Re-up, 23
Reveal, 23
Rewrite, 23, 240, 242
"Rewriting" (McGibbon & Parriott), 243
Rhyme, 23

Rice, Susan, 199
Rich, Mike, 274–275
Road (genre), 46
Roles turned down by actors, 210
Romance (genre), 46
Romance, nervous (or neurotic) (genre), 46
Rossio, Terry, 103
Runaway Bride, making of, 121–123
Running gag, 23
Rushes, 23

SAG. *See* Screen Actors Guild.
Sales, effect of genre upon, 49–50. *See also* Spec sale compensation.
Sardi, Jan, 65
SASP. *See* Self-addressed stamped postcard.
Satire (genre), 46
Scale, pay, 23
Scene, 23–24
Scene cards, 24
Schmooze, 24
Schtick. *See* Bit.
Science Fiction (Sci-Fi) (genre), 46
Screen Actors Guild (SAG), 24, 118, 149
Screenplay, 24
  before trying to sell, 37–41
  first-draft, 240, 242
  getting feedback on, 38–40
  non-original, 240
  original, 240
  protecting your, 77–81
  standard format of, 50–77
  warning about sharing, 41
  See also Spec script.

Screenplay: The Foundation of Screenwriting (Field), 268
"Screenplay versus Query Letter" (Purpura), 169–170
"Screenplay Writing and the Movie Business" (Launer), 208
Screenwriter, having what it takes to be, 5–7
Screenwriters Guide, 133
"Screenwriting at Its Best and Worst" (Strugatz), 25
Screenwriting class. *See* Writing class, enrolling in.
Screenwriting 434 (Hunter), 268
Scr(i)pt, 133
Script assignment, 24
Script consultant, 269–270
Script doctor, 24
Script notes, 24
Second-act curtain, 24
Secondary action line. *See* Subplot.
Segal, Eric, 268
Seger, Linda, 268
Self-addressed stamped envelope postcard (SASP), 229
Self-promoting, 24
Senior Citizen (genre), 46
Separable material, 248
Sequel, 24
Sequence, 24
Setup, 24
Seven-act structure, 24
Sexploitation films. *See* Exploitation films.
Shapiro, Marty, questions and answers with, 99–100
Shelved, 24. *See also* Direct-to-video (DTV) film.
Sherman Antitrust Act, 90

Shoot, movie, 24
Shooting script, 24
Shop a property, 24
"Show Gratitude" (Strugatz), 41
Signatory, 24, 28, 91, 93, 236–237
Simens, Dov S-S, 64, 96, 166
Sleeper, 25
Sleepless in Seattle, making of, 29–32
Smith, Scott Marshall, 255
"So Many Changes; So Many Reasons" (Styles), 16
Soft, as term describing script, 25
"Somewhere Between Drafts . . ." (Styles), 38
Spec sale compensation, 239–240
Spec script, 3, 25
    actions and sounds in, 66–67
    basic rules for, 51–52
    binding of, 76
    character names and cues in, 67–69
    cutaway. *See* Spec script, insert in.
    descriptive text in, 63–65
    dialogue in, 74
    ellipses, dashes, and parentheticals in, 74–75
    formatting rules for, other, 76
    insert in, 71–72
    length of, 52–53
    mailing, in response to query letter, 228–229
    margins in, 58
    marketability of, 263–264
    montage in, 65–66
    novelization of, 268–269
    numbers in, 74
    off screen in, 72–73
    page endings in, 76
    page numbers in, 58
    paper and covers for, 53
    point of view in, 73–74
    problems with, 266–267
    sample pages of, 56–58
    scene slugs in, 60–63
    spacing in, 59
    special effects in, 65
    tabs in, 58–59
    telephone conversations in, 69–70
    terms of, 53
    text on a computer screen in, 70–71
    title page of, 54, 55
    typeface in, 53
    venues for, other, 271–275
    voice over in, 72
    See also Screenplay.
Speculation script. *See* Spec script.
Spielberg, Steven, 280
Spine, screenplay, 25
Spoof (genre), 47
Sports (genre), 47
Spy/Espionage (genre), 47
Square One System Eight-Step Plan, 204–220
Stakes, 25
Standards and Practices, 25
Start date, 25
Step deal, 25–26, 240, 242
"Step Deal Steps" (Newman), 242
Stock footage. *See* Stock shot.
Stock shot, 26
Story, 26
    non-original, 240
    original, 240
Story analyst, 26, 39, 113. *See also* Coverage.
Story editors. *See* Development executives.
Storyboard, 26
Structure, script, 26
Strugatz, Barry, 25, 40, 41, 52, 109, 111, 278
Studio system, 90–91
Studio, movie. *See* Movie studio.
Styles, Richard, 16, 38, 264
Submission agreement, 26
Submission Release Form, 109, 223–224
    sample, 224–226
Subplot of story, 26
Subtext within script, 26
Suggested by, as credit line, 26
Suit. *See* Brass, film industry.
Summary paragraph(s), 165, 263
Summer of '42, making of, 87
Sundance Film Festival, 26. *See also* Film festival.
Supernatural (genre), 47
Suspense/Thriller (genre), 47
Swashbuckler (genre), 47
Synopsis, 26, 166–167, 181

T & A, 26
Take, 26
Talent Managers Association, Inc. (TMA), 104, 105, 149–150
Teleplay, 26
Television network, 26–27
Tentpole movie, 27. *See also* First run.
Terminology, film industry. *See* Film industry, terminology.
Thalberg, Irving, 119

Theatrical agents. *See* Agents/Agencies.

Theatrical distribution, 4

Theatrical film. *See* Motion picture.

Theme, 27

Thin, as term describing script, 27

THR East. See Hollywood Reporter East, The, (THR East).

Three-act structure, 27

Thriller (genre). *See* Suspense/Thriller.

Through line. *See* Spine.

Tie-in, 27

Timing, 264–265

"Timing" (Purpura), 185

TMA. *See* Talent Managers Association, Inc.

Toback, James, 262

Top brass. *See* Brass, film industry.

Toronto International Film Festival, 27. *See also* Film festival.

Track record, 27

Trackers, 27

Tracking charts, 211–214

Trade magazines and newspapers, 129–134

Trade papers, 27

Trades. *See* Trade papers.

Transition points. *See* Plot points.

Treatment, 27, 39, 181, 240, 242

Turnaround, 27, 269

Tweaking, 27

Twist, in script, 27

Unions. *See* Organizations, unions, and guilds.

Unsolicited script, 28, 95. *See also* Submission agreement.

Vanity deal, 28

Vasicek, Don, 174, 176, 177

Vehicle, as term describing script, 28

Vigilante (genre), 47

Visco, Frank L., 75

Vitagraph Film Company, 89

Wallace, Pamela, 268

War/Anti-War (genre), 47

Ward, David S., 29

Waters, Daniel, 42, 270

Weiss, Steve, questions and answers with, 100–102

Werb, Michael, 184

Western (genre), 47

WGA. *See* Writers Guild of America.

WGA Theatrical and Television Basic Agreement, 241

"What Hollywood Buys" (Purpura), 263

"What It's Like to Be a Screenwriter" (Anderson), 8

"When Asking a Favor" (Strugatz), 111

White Water Rebels, making of, 276–278

Whole Nine Yards, The, making of, 154–155

Wide distribution, 28

Wish list
considerations, 127–128
creating, 127–129

prioritizing names on, 204–205

refining, 128–129

workbook, 127

Woman, Gutsy (genre), 47

Woman's Film, 47

Work for hire, 28

Writers, as film industry players, 119

Writers Guild of America, East, 28

Writers Guild of America, West, 28, 133

Writers Guild of America (WGA), 5, 28, 150
Member Directory, 141–142
Minimum Basic Agreement, 19, 28, 93, 236–243
registration mark on script, 54
Registration Service, 77–78, 81
Schedule of Minimums, 241

Writers Guild of America Theatrical and Television Basic Agreement. *See* Writers Guild of America (WGA), Minimum Basic Agreement.

Writing class, enrolling in, 39, 40, 268
warning about, 41

Written by, as credit line, 28

Written By, 28, 133–134

You Can Write a Movie (Wallace), 268

You've Got Mail, computer text format in, 71

Zemeckis, Robert, 275

All writers dream of seeing their books in print. While some succeed, the fact is that most don't. Why? Most writers simply don't know what publishers are looking for. Or they didn't—until now. Written by a publisher with over twenty-five years of experience, this book helps you avoid the common pitfalls that foil most writers, and maximize your chance of getting your nonfiction book into publication.

This book begins by helping you define your book's category, audience, and marketplace so that you know exactly where your book "fits in." Following this, you will be guided in choosing the best publishing companies for your book, and crafting a winning submissions package. Then the Square One System will tell you exactly how to submit your package so that you optimize success, while minimizing time, cost, and effort. A special section on contracts will turn legal mumbo-jumbo into plain English, allowing you to be a savvy player in the contract game. Most important, this book will help you avoid the errors that so often prevent writers from reaching their goal.

$16.95 • 252 pages • 7.5 x 9-inch quality paperback • 2-color • Reference/Writing • ISBN 0-7570-0000-2

Perhaps you began writing poetry as a means of private expression. Or maybe your verse was meant to share your feelings with that special someone. But now those goals have changed, and you want to get your poetry into print.

Written for the poet who wishes to enjoy greater success in the world of publishing, this book is a complete guide to breaking into the world of print poetry. The book begins by providing a window to the publishing world so that you can see the kinds of publications you should target. You will learn about great market resources for locating appropriate publishers, and you will learn the importance of defining your audience. Following this, the author helps you write a persuasive submissions package, and presents a proven step-by-step system for sending your package out—a system designed to maximize results. When the acceptance letters start rolling in, the author helps you select the publications that will help you meet your personal goals. You will even learn of the resources that can help you further develop your special gift.

$14.95 • 192 pages • 7.5 x 9-inch quality paperback • 2-color • Reference/Writing • ISBN 0-7570-0001-0

How do you get your story idea looked at, let alone accepted? Should the article be written first, or only after getting an editor's go-ahead? Where do you start? Freelance article writer Shirley Kawa-Jump has written a book designed to answer all the novice writer's common questions about getting articles published by magazines, journals, newspapers, and online publications.

While some writers write for pleasure, others may want to start a career. And for some, frequent publication is simply a requirement of their chosen profession. Part One examines each of these possibilities, and then goes on to explore the available writers' markets and explain how they work. Part Two provides a complete system of article submission geared to maximize the writer's odds of getting an acceptance, while avoiding those errors that can turn off an editor. Part Three reviews the nuts and bolts of the profession—from idea development to contract negotiation.

$17.95 • 352 pages • 7.5 x 9-inch quality paperback • 2-color • Reference/Writing • ISBN 0-7570-0016-9

For more information about our books, visit our website at www.squareonepublishers.com.